LIVING LANGUAGE®

GERMAN
DICTIONARY

GERMAN-ENGLISH
ENGLISH-GERMAN

REVISED & UPDATED

THE LIVING LANGUAGE® SERIES

Living Language Basic Courses,
Revised & Updated

Spanish*   *Japanese**
French*   *Russian*
German*   *Italian**
Portuguese (Brazilian)
Portuguese (Continental)
Inglés/English for Spanish Speakers

Living Language Intermediate
Courses

Spanish 2   *French 2*
German 2   *Italian 2*

Living Language Advanced Courses,
Revised & Updated

Spanish 3   *French 3*

Living Language Ultimate™
(formerly **All the Way™**)

Spanish*   *Spanish 2**
French*   *French 2**
German*   *German 2**
Italian*   *Italian 2**
Russian*   *Russian 2**
Japanese*   *Japanese 2**
Inglés/English for Spanish Speakers*
Inglés/English for Spanish Speakers 2*
Chinese (1999)

Living Language® Essential Language
Guides

Essential Spanish for Healthcare
Essential Spanish for Social Services
Essential Spanish for Law Enforcement
Essential Language Guide for Hotel &
Restaurant Employees

Living Language Children's Courses

Spanish   *French*

Living Language Conversational
English

for Chinese Speakers
for Japanese Speakers
for Korean Speakers
for Spanish Speakers
for Russian Speakers

Living Language Fast & Easy™

Spanish   *Italian*   *Portuguese*
French   *Russian* *Czech*
German   *Polish*   *Hungarian*
Japanese *Korean* *Mandarin*
Arabic   *Hebrew*   *(Chinese)*
Inglés/English for Spanish Speakers

Living Language All Audio™

Spanish *French* *Italian* *German*

Living Language Speak Up!®
Accent Elimination Courses

Spanish   *American Regional*
Asian, Indian and Middle Eastern

Fodor's Languages for Travelers

Spanish *French* *Italian* *German*

Living Language® Parent/Child
Activity Kits

Learn French in the Kitchen
Learn Italian in the Kitchen
Learn Spanish in the Kitchen
Learn French in the Car
Learn Italian in the Car
Learn Spanish in the Car

*Available on Cassette and Compact Disc

GERMAN
DICTIONARY

GERMAN–ENGLISH
ENGLISH–GERMAN

REVISED & UPDATED

REVISED BY WALTER KLEINMANN

Coordinator of Language Programs

Sewanhaka Central High School District

◆

Based on the original

by Genevieve A. Martin

and Theodor Bertram

LIVING LANGUAGE®
A Random House Company 🏠

This work was previously published under the title *Living Language™ Common Usage Dictionary—German* by Genevieve A. Martin and Theodor Bertram, based on the dictionary developed by Ralph Weiman.

Published by Living Language, A Random House Company, 201 East 50th Street, New York, New York 10022.

Random House, Inc. New York, Toronto, London, Sydney, Auckland

www.livinglanguage.com

Printed in the United States of America

Library of Congress Catalog Card Number: 56-9318

ISBN 0-609-80301-8

10   9   8   7   6   5   4   3   2

CONTENTS

Contents

INTRODUCTION

The *Living Language® German Dictionary* lists more than 15,000 of the most frequently used German words, gives their most important meanings, and illustrates their use. This revised edition contains updated phrases and expressions as well as many new entries related to business, technology, and the media.

1. More than 1,000 of the most essential words are capitalized to make them easy to find.

2. Numerous definitions are illustrated with phrases, sentences, and idiomatic expressions. If there is no close English equivalent for a German word, or if the English equivalent has several meanings, the context of the illustrative sentences helps to clarify the meanings.

3. Because of these useful phrases, the *Living Language® German Dictionary* also serves as a phrase book and conversation guide. The dictionary is helpful both to beginners who are building their vocabulary and to advanced students who want to perfect their command of colloquial German.

4. The German expressions (particularly the idiomatic and colloquial ones) have been translated into their English equivalents. However, literal translations have

been added to help the beginner. For example, under the entry *Kuh*, cow, you will find: *Er ist bekannt wie eine bunte Kuh.* He is well-known everywhere. ("He's a colorful cow.") This dual feature also makes the dictionary useful for translation work.

EXPLANATORY NOTES

Literal translations are in parentheses. Colloquial is abbreviated to *coll.*

Gender is indicated by *m.* for masculine, *f.* for feminine, and *n.* for neuter.

Case is indicated by *nom.* for nominative, *gen.* for genitive, *dat.* for dative, *acc.* for accusative.

Possessive is abbreviated to *poss.*, pronoun to *pron.*, adjective to *adj.*, preposition to *prep.*

THE NEW GERMAN
SPELLING REFORM

The educational ministries of all German states have agreed upon a spelling reform, which is supposed to make German spelling a little easier on students and natives alike. The spelling reform will become mandatory in 2000. The following are the most important new rules.

- After short vowels *ß* becomes *ss*. *ß* remains *ß* after long vowels, if the stem of the word shows no more consonants: *Fass* (keg) but *Straße* (street).

- Double consonants after a stressed short vowel: *nummerieren* (to number), *Ass* (ace), *Tipp* (tip).

- Always write as two separate words: verb combinations with *sein* such as *pleite sein* (to be destitute), combinations of two verbs such as *kennen lernen* (to get to know), combinations of verb and participle such as *gesagt haben* (to have said), combinations of verb plus noun such as *Rad fahren* (to ride a bicycle), combinations of verb and adverb such as *beiseite legen* (to set aside), combinations of verb plus adjective such as *gut lesen* (to read well), and verb + *-ig, -isch, -lich,* such as *lästig fallen* (to be a burden).

- Capitalize all nouns and derivatives of nouns: *Trimm-dich-Pfad* (fitness trail), *Leid tun* (to be sorry), *das Dutzend* (the dozen), *im Deutschen* (in German), *Schweizer Käse* (Swiss cheese).

- Write out all letters that meet: *Schiff=Fahrt=Schifffahrt* (boat ride).

- In letters, *du* (you), *dir* (to you), *dein* (your), *eure* (your [pl.]), etc., are written in lowercase.

- Many foreign words receive a "Germanized" spelling: *Fotograf* (photographer).

- Words separate after spoken syllables: *Fens-ter* (window), *Bä-der* (bathroom), *A-bend* (evening).

- Commas are no longer necessary before *und* or *oder.*

German-English

A

AB 1. *adv. off, down, away from, from.*
ab heute   *from today.*
ab und ab   *now and then.*
ab und zu   *to and fro, now and then.*
von hier ab   *from here.*
von nun ab   *henceforth.*
2. *separable prefix (implies a movement down or away, imitation, appropriation, deterioration, destruction).*
Das Flugzeug stürzte ins Meer ab.   *The plane fell down into the sea.*
Einige alte Häuser werden abgebaut.   *Some old houses will be demolished.*
Er hat ihm tausend Mark abgeschmeichelt.   *He got a thousand marks from him by flattery.*
Ich schreibe meine Aufgabe ab.   *I copy my homework.*

Abart *f. variety; variation of species*

abbeissen *to bite off*
sich die Nägel abbeissen   *to bite one's nails.*

abbezahlen *to pay off.*

abbiegen *to turn off*

Abbild *n. copy, image.*

abbinden *to unbind*

Abbitte *f. apology; forgiveness*

abbrechen *to break up, interrupt, deduct, gather*
Blumen abbrechen   *to gather flowers.*
die Arbeit abbrechen   *to cease work.*

abdanken *to dismiss, abdicate.*
Der Fürst hat abgedankt.   *The prince has abdicated.*

abdrehen *to turn off, switch off.*
Drehen sie das Radio ab!   *Turn off the radio!*

abdrucken *to print*

ABEND *m. evening.*
diesen Abend   *this evening.*
Es wird Abend.   *It is getting dark.*
heute Abend.   *tonight*

Abenteuer *n. adventure.*
auf Abenteuer ausgehen   *to look for adventure.*

abenteuerlich *adventurous.*

Abenteurer *m. adventurer*

ABER *but, however, anyway.*
Ich wollte ausgehen aber das Wetter war zu schlecht.   *I wanted to go out but the weather was too bad.*
Das Kind wollte spielen, die Mutter aber wollte nicht.   *The child wanted to play but the mother did not want to.*

Der König aber . . .   *The King, however, ...*
Nein aber!   *I say!*
Nun aber!   *But now!*
tausend und aber tausend   *thousands and thousands*

abermals *again, once more.*

abfahren *to set off, depart.*
Der Zug fährt um drei Uhr ab.   *The train leaves at three.*
Sie fuhr übel ab.   *She got the worst of it.*

Abfahrtsort *m. place of departure.*

abfinden *to settle, come to an agreement.*

abführen *to lead away, carry away.*

Abführung *f. removal*

Abgabe *f. tax, tribute, delivery.*
abgabenfrei   *tax free.*
abgabenpflichtig   *taxable; accessible.*

Abgang *m. departure, exit*

ABGEBEN *to give, supply, deliver, pay taxes.*
sich mit etwas abgeben   *to occupy oneself with a matter.*
Wir können die Waren zu diesem Preis nicht abgeben.   *We cannot supply the merchandise on these terms.*

abgehen *to depart, go off.*
Er lässt sich nichts abgehen.   *He denies himself nothing.*
von seinem Vorhaben nicht abgehen   *to persist in one's plans.*

abgemacht *agreed.*

abgewinnen *to win from.*

abgewöhnen *to disaccustom, give up.*
Ich habe mir das Rauchen abgewöhnt.   *I have given up smoking.*

Abgrund *m. abyss, precipice.*

abhalten *to hold off, restrain.*
Lassen Sie sich nicht abhalten!   *Don't let me stop you!*

abhängen *to unhang, hang up (phone). disconnect.*

abhängig *sloping, dependent on.*

abheben *to lift off, uncover, become detached.*
Die helle Gestalt hebt sich auf dem dunklen Hintergrunde vorteilhaft ab.   *The light figure is brought into relief against the dark background.*

Abhilfe *f. relief*

abholen *to get, collect.*
Das Taxi wird mich abholen.   *The taxi will pick me up.*

Abkunft *f. descent, origin.*

ablenken *to divert, distract.*

ablesen *to pick up, read off.*

abliefern *to deliver.*

ABMACHEN *to remove, loosen, agree, settle.*

Abgemacht! *Agreed!*

abnehmen *to take off, gather, pick up
(phone), to lose weight.*

Er nimmt seinen Hut ab. *He takes off his
hat.*

er hat zehn Pfund abgenommen. *He lost ten
pounds.*

Abneigung *f. dislike, antipathy.*

Abort *m. lavatory; W.C.*

abräumen *to take away, remove*

ABREISE *f. departure*

eine unvorhergesehene Abreise *an
unexpected departure*

Absage *f. refusal*

absagen *to refuse, to cancel, call off.*

eine Gesellschaft absagen lassen *to call
off a party. ,*

Falls Sie mir nicht absagen, komme
ich. *Unless you call it off, I'll come.*

Abscheu *m. aversion, horror.*

abscheulich *horrible, abominable, nasty.*

Das war abscheulich von ihm. *It was very
nasty of him.*

ABSCHIED *m. departure*

Abschied nehmen *to take leave.*

Ich werde Abschied von Ihnen nehmen
I am going to leave you.

den Abschied bekommen *to be dismissed.*

Der Offizier hat seinen Abschied
genommen. *The officer has been
placed on the retired list.*

abschreiben *to copy, to deduct.*

abseits *prep. (gen) aside, apart, away from.*

ABSICHT *f. intention, purpose, view.*

in der Absicht *with the intention.*

Er tat es in böser Absicht. *He did it with
a malicious intention.*

absichtlich *on purpose.*

(sich) abspielen *to occur, to take place*

Abstand *m. distance, interval.*

Er nahm Abstand von seiner
Erbschaft. *He gave up his
inheritance.*

Er nahm Abstand von dem schnell vorbei
fahrenden Zug. *He stood back from
the fast passing train.*

Absturz *m. fall, crash*

Er wurde bei einem Flugzeugabsturz
getötet. *He was killed in a plane
crash.*

ABTEIL *n. compartment, division, section*

Abteil erster Klasse *n. first-class
compartment*

Nichtraucherabteil *non-smoking
compartment.*

Abteilung *f. department (in a store).*

Schuhabteilung *f. shoe department.*

abtrocknen *to dry off, wipe*

das Geschirr abtrocknen *to dry the dishes.*

abwärts *downward.*

abwechseln *to vary, change, alternate.*

abwesend *absent.*

Abwesenheit *f. absence.*

abzahlen *to pay off.*

abziehen *to retain, take off, subtract*

Der Arbeitgeber zieht die Steuer vom
Einkommen ab. *The employer
retains taxes from the salary.*

Abzugskanal *m. sewer*

ach! *Ah! Oh!*

ACHT *eight*

heute in acht Tagen *A week from today.*

achtmal *eight times.*

ACHTEL *eighth.*

achten *to esteem, regard, respect.*

ACHTUNG *f. esteem.*

Achtung! *Beware! Attention!*

achtungsvoll *respectful.*

ACHTZEHN *eighteen.*

ACHTZEHNTE *eighteenth.*

ACHTZIG *eighty.*

ACHTZIGSTE *eightieth.*

ACKER *m. field, soil.*

Ackerbau *m. agriculture.*

ackern *to plough.*

Ackersmann *m. ploughman*

addieren *to add up.*

Adel *m. nobility, aristocracy.*

Ader *f. vein.*

Adjektiv *n. adjective.*

adelig *noble.*

ADRESSE *f. address*

Hier ist meine Adresse. *Here is my
address.*

adressieren *to address.*

Adverb *n. adverb.*

Affe *m. monkey.*

Affekt *m. excitement.*

affektiert *affected.*

Agent *m. agent.*

ahnen *to have a premonition.*

Es ahnt mir Unglück. *I have a
premonition of evil.*

Ich habe keine Ahnung. *I don't have the
slightest idea.*

ähnlich *similar, like.*

ähnlich sehen *to look alike.*

Ähnlichkeit *f. similarity, resemblance.*

Akademie *f. academy, university.*

Akten *pl. deeds, documents.*

Aktie *f. share, stock.*

aktiv *active.*

Akzent *m. accent, stress.*

Alarm *m. alarm.*

Alkohol *m. alcohol, liquor.*

ALL (aller, alle, alles) *entire, whole, every,
each, any*

all die Leute *everybody.*

4

all und jeder   *each and every.*

alle Tage   *every day.*

auf alle Fälle   *in any case.*

ohne allen Grund   *for no reason at all.*

ALLEIN *alone, single, solitary, apart, lonesome.*

Ich bin allein.   *I am alone.*

Sie lebt allein.   *She lives alone.*

allerart *diverse.*

allgemein *universal.*

Alphabet *n. alphabet*

ALS *when, than, as, like.*

Als Bismarck starb, gab es noch keine Flugzuege.   *When Bismarck died, they still didn't have any airplanes.*

Sie ist Grösser als ihr Bruder.   *She is taller than her brother.*

als ob   *as if, as though.*

Er tut, also ob er die Antwort kenne.   *He acts as if he knew the answer.*

so bald als   *as soon as*

ALSO *so, thus, in this way.*

"Also sprach Zarathustra . . ."   *"Thus spoke Zarathustra . . ."*

ALT *old, aged, ancient.*

alte Sprachen   *ancient languages (classics)*

altehrwürdig   *venerable.*

altgläubig   *orthodox.*

altmodisch   *old-fashioned*

eine alte Jungfer   *an old maid.*

ALTER *n. age, old age, antiquity.*

Mittelalter   *n. Middle Ages.*

älter *older, elder, senior.*

Altertum *n. antiquity.*

Altertumshändler   *m. antique dealer.*

älteste *oldest*

am (an dem) *on, at.*

Amerikaner *m.* **-in** *f. American.*

amerikanisch *American.*

AMT *n. office, charge, board. In compound words, the suffix amt designates a government office:*

das Auswärtige Amt   *the Foreign Office.*

Polizeiamt   *n. police station.*

Zollamt   *n. customs.*

in Amt und Würden stehen   *to be a person of position.*

amüsant *amusing.*

AMÜSIEREN *to amuse.*

sich amüsieren   *to enjoy oneself.*

ich habe mich bei der Gesellschaft sehr amüsiert.   *I enjoyed myself at the party.*

AN 1. *prep. (dat. when answering question. Wo?; acc. when answering question. Wohin?, and depending on the idiom).*

an die Arbeit gehen   *to go to work.*

an der Arbeit sein   *to be at work.*

an der Donau   *on the Danube.*

an und für sich   *in itself.*

Er starb an seinen Wunden.   *He died of his wounds.*

Es ist an mir. Ich bin dran.   *It is my turn.*

Ich gehe an die Tür.   *I go to the door.*

Ich weiss, was an der Geschichte dran ist.   *I know what the story is.*

soviel an mir liegt   *as far as I am concerned.*

2. *separable prefix. (implies movement closer to the speaker, proximity, contact, attraction, climbing, beginning).*

Der Hund ist angebunden.   *The dog is tied.*

Der Tag bricht an.   *The day begins.*

Er behielt seine Schuhe an.   *He kept his shoes on.*

Er zieht seine Jacke an.   *He puts his coat on.*

Ich steige langsam den Berg hinan.   *I climb the mountain slowly.*

anbehalten *to keep on.*

Ich will meinen Mantel anbehalten.   *I want to keep my coat on.*

anbieten *to offer, volunteer.*

Anblick *m. sight, view.*

Andenken *n. memory, souvenir.*

zum Andenken an meine Eltern.   *In memory of my parents.*

ANDER *other, another, different, next.*

am anderen Morgen   *the next morning.*

anderer Meinung sein   *to be of a different opinion.*

ein andermal   *another time.*

einen Tag um den andern   *every other day.*

etwas anderes   *another thing, something else, something different.*

nichts anderes als   *nothing but.*

unter anderem   *among other things.*

anderenfalls *otherwise.*

anderseits *on the other side.*

andeuten *to indicate.*

Anerbieten *n. offer, proposal.*

Anfall *m. attack, fit.*

Herzanfall   *m. heart attack.*

Anfang *m. beginning, start.*

anfangen *(to) begin, start.*

von Anfang bis Ende   *from beginning to end.*

Anfrage *f. inquiry.*

anfragen *to inquire.*

anfreunden (sich) *to become friends.*

angemessen *suitable, accurate.*

Angesicht *n. face, countenance.*

von Angesicht zu Angesicht   *face to face.*

angesichts *considering, in view of.*

Angewohnheit f. habit, custom.

angrenzen to border.

Angriff m. attack.

    in Angriff nehmen   to set about.

Angst f. anxiety.

ängstigen to frighten.

    sich ängstigen vor   to be afraid of.

    sich ängstigen um   to feel anxious about.

anhaben to wear, have on.

    Er hat einen neuen Anzug an.   He's wearing a new suit.

anhalten to stop, pull up.

anhören to listen to.

Anker m. anchor.

anklagen to accuse.

ankleiden to dress.

anklopfen to knock at.

ANKOMMEN to arrive, approach, reach.

    Es kommt darauf an, ob Sie Zeit haben.   It depends on whether you have time.

    Der Zug ist um 15.00 Uhr ankommen.   The train arrived at 3:00 P.M.

ANKUNFT f. arrival.

anmelden to announce, notify, report.

Anmut f. grace, charm.

anmutig graceful, charming.

Annahme f. acceptance, assumption.

annehem to accept, receive, assume, take care of.

anpassen to fit, suit, adapt.

anprobieren to try on.

anrechnen to charge.

    zu viel anrechnen   to overcharge.

    Ich rechne Ihnen Ihre Hilfe hoch an.   I appreciate your help very much.

Anrede f. address.

anreden to address, accost.

    Der Schutzmann redete mich an.   The policeman spoke to me.

anregen to incite, stimulate, excite.

Ansage f. announcement, notification.

ansagen to announce, notify.

anschauen to look at, contemplate.

anschaulich evident, clear.

Anschrift f. address (letter).

anschuldigen to accuse.

ANSEHEN to look at, consider, regard.

    dem Ansehen nach   to all appearances.

    im Ansehen stehen   to be esteemed.

    vom Ansehen kennen   to know by sight.

Ansicht f. view, sight, opinion.

    nach meiner Ansicht   according to my opinion.

Ansichtskarte f. picture postcard.

Ansprache f. speech, address.

Anspruch m. claim, pretension.

    Anspruch haben auf   to be entitled to.

Anstand m. manners, decency, etiquette.

    ohne Anstand   without hesitation.

anständig decent, respectable

ANSTATT (statt) 1. prep. (gen.) instead of; also conj.

    Anstatt eines Regenschirms nahm er einen Hut.   Instead of an umbrella, he took a hat.

anstrengen (sich) to strain, exert.

anstrengend tiring, trying, exacting.

ANTWORT f. answer.

ANTWORTEN to answer.

anvertrauen to entrust, confide.

Anwalt m. lawyer, attorney.

anwesend present.

Anwesenheit f. presence.

Anzahl f. quantity, amount.

anzahlen to pay on account.

Anzeige f. notice, advertisement.

anzeigen to notify, report, announce

    Ich halte es für angezeigt.   I consider it advisable.

(sich) anziehen to put on (clothes); to dress oneself.

ANZUG m. suit, dress.

Anzüglichkeit f. suggestive remark.

anzünden to light the fire, set fire to.

APFEL m. apple

    in den sauren Apfel beissen   to swallow a bitter pill.

APFELSINE f. orange

Apotheke f. pharmacy.

Apotheker m. pharmacist.

Apparat m. apparatus, appliance, telephone.

    Bleiben Sie am Apparat!   Hold the wire!

Appetit m. appetite.

applaudieren to applaud.

APRIL m. April

Äquator m. equator.

ARBEIT f. work, job.

ARBEITEN to work, manufacture.

    arbeitsfähig   able-bodied.

    arbeitsunfähig   unfit for work.

Arbeiter m. (-in, f.) worker, laborer.

    Arbeiterstand   m. working class.

Arbeitgeber m. employer.

Arbeitnehmer m. employee.

arbeitsam industrious, diligent.

Architekt m. architect.

Architektur f. architecture.

arg bad, mischievous.

    Sie dachte an nichts Arges.   She meant no harm.

Ärger m. annoyance, anger, worry.

ärgerlich annoying, angry.

ärgern to annoy, irritate, bother.

    sich ärgern   to be angry.

Argument n. argument.

Aristokrat m. aristocrat.

Aristokratie *f. aristocracy.*

aristokratisch *aristocratic.*

ARM *m. arm.*

ARM *poor*

Armband *n. bracelet.*

Armbanduhr *f. wrist watch.*

Ärmel *m. sleeve*

Armlehne *f. arm of chair*

Armut *f. poverty.*

Arrest *m. arrest.*

ART *f. kind, manner, way, type.*

artig *good, well-behaved.*

Artikel *m. article.*

Arznei *f. medicine (drug).*

Arzneikunde *f. pharmacy (profession of).*

Ast *m. branch (tree).*

Atem *m. breath, suspense.*

> Dieser Kriminalroman hält uns in
> Atem. *This detective story keeps us
> in suspense.*

atemlos *breathless.*

atemraubend *breath-taking.*

> Der Film war atemraubend. *The movie
> was breath-taking.*

Athlet *m. athlete.*

atmen *to breathe.*

AUCH *also, too, even.*

> was auch   *whatever.*
> wer auch   *whoever.*
> wo auch   *wherever.*
> Was auch geschieht, Sie sind
>   verantwortlich. *Whatever happens,
>   you are responsible.*
> Wer auch kommen mag, ich bin nicht zu
>   Hause. *Whoever comes, I am not
>   home.*
> Wo auch immer er auftauchen mag, man
>   wird ihn erkennen. *Wherever he
>   appears, he will be recognized.*

AUF 1. *prep. (dat. when answering
question, Wo?; acc. when answering
question, Wohin?, and depending on
the idion) on, upon, at, in, to, for,
during.*

> Er kommt auf die Strasse hinab. *He
>   comes down to the street.*
> Ich kaufe Gemüse auf dem Markt. *I buy
>   vegetables at the market.*
> Ich traf sie auf dem Ball. *I met her at the
>   ball.*
> Ich fahre auf das Land. *I drive to the
>   country.*
> Sie wohnen auf/in diesem Schloss. *They
>   live in that castle.*
> Die Jäger gehen auf die Jagd. *The
>   hunters go hunting.*
> Der Tag folgt auf die Nacht. *The day
>   follows the night.*
> alle bis auf einen *all except one.*

> auf der Rückfahrt von Wien *during the
>   return from Vienna.*
> auf deutsch *in German.*
> auf einmal *suddenly.*
> auf keinen Fall *in no case.*
> auf Wiedersehen! *Good-bye!*
> Liebe auf den ersten Blick *love at first
>   sight.*

2. *adv. up, upwards.*

> auf und ab *up and down.*

3. *Separable prefix (implies motion
upward or outward, opening,
completion).*

> Ich setze meinen Hut auf. *I put my hat
>   on.*
> Die Sonne geht auf. *The sun is rising.*
> Bitte, machen Sie das Fenster auf. *Please
>   open the window.*

aufbewahren *to keep, preserve, stock.*

Aufbewahrung *f. preservation, storage.*

aufbrauchen *to use up.*

aufeinander *one on top of the other.*

Aufenthalt *m. stay, residence.*

aufessen *to eat up.*

Auffassung *f. conception, interpretation.*

Aufgabe *f. task, duty, problem.*

aufgeben *to commission, order, lose, give up,
resign, check, send.*

> die Hoffnung aufgeben *to lose hope.*
> ein Telegramm aufgeben *to send a
>   telegram.*

aufhängen *to hang up.*

aufheben *to pick up, rise, abolish.*

aufheitern *to cheer up.*

aufklären *to clear, explain.*

Aufklärung *f. explanation.*

aufmachen *to open, unlock, undo.*

aufmerken *to pay attention, attend.*

aufmerksam *attentive.*

Aufmerksamkeit *f. attention.*

Aufnahme *f. taking up, admission,
enrollment, snapshot.*

aufnahmefähig *receptive.*

Aufnahmeprüfung *f. entrance examination.*

aufnehmen *to lift, take up, admit,
photograph, record (a voice).*

aufpassen *to adapt, fix, pay attention.*

> Aufgepasst! *Attention!*

Aufpasser *m. watcher, spy.*

aufräumen *to arrange, put in order, clean.*

aufrecht *upright, straight.*

aufregen *to stir up, excite.*

aufregend *exciting, seditious.*

Aufregung *f. excitement, agitation.*

Aufsatz *m. main piece, top, ornament, article
(newspaper); composition.*

aufschliessen *to unlock.*

Aufschluss *m. opening up, explanation,
information.*

Aufschluss über eine Sache geben *to give some information about something.*

aufschreiben *to write down.*

Aufsehen *n. sensation, attention.*

Er erregt Aufsehen. *He attracts attention.*

Aufstand *m. tumult, revolt.*

AUFSTEHEN *stand up, rise, get up.*

aufstehen gegen *to rebel against.*

Stehen sie auf! *Get up!*

aufstellen *to set up, erect, draw up, nominate.*

Eine Behauptung aufstellen *to make a statement.*

Auftrag *m. commission, instruction.*

im Auftrage von *by order of.*

einen Auftrag ausführen *to execute an order.*

auftragen *to carry up, serve up, draw, charge.*

Er hat mir viele Grüsse an Sie aufgetragen. *He sends you his regards ("He charged me with many greetings for you.")*

aufwachen *to awaken.*

aufwachsen *to grow up.*

Aufwand *m. expenditure, expense.*

aufwärts *upwards.*

Er schwimmt een Fluss aufwärts. *He swims upstream.*

aufwecken *to wake someone up.*

aufziehen *to bring up, raise, wind a watch, pull up, tease.*

Aufzug *m. procession, parade, attire, outfit, act (play), elevator.*

AUGE *n. eye.*

Er versuchte mir Sand in die Augen zu streuen. *He tried to deceive me ("throw dust into my eyes").*

gute Augen haben *to have good eyesight.*

grosse Augen machen *to look very surprised.*

Ich habe kein Auge zugemacht. *I did not sleep a wink.*

unter vier Augen *privately ("among four eyes").*

Wir haben ihn aus den Augen verloren. *We lost sight of him.*

Augenarzt *m. oculist, eye doctor.*

Augenblick *m. moment.*

im Augenblick *for the moment.*

augenblicklich *immediately.*

Augenbraue *f. eyebrow.*

Augenlid *n. eyelid.*

Augenwimper *f. eyelash.*

AUGUST *m. August.*

Auktion *f. auction, sale.*

AUS 1. *prep. (dat.) out, out of, for, from, in, upon.*

Aus den Augen, aus dem Sinn. *Out of sight, out of mind.*

Er kommt aus dem Theater. *He comes out of the theater.*

Er hat es aus Liebe getan. *He did it for love.*

Meine Uhr ist aus Gold. *My watch is made of gold.*

Sie stammt aus Paris. *She is a native of Paris.*

2. *adv. out, over, up.*

von hier aus *from here.*

von mir aus *for my part.*

3. *separable prefix. Implies the idea of motion out (in this case also combines with him or her), achievement.*

Die Vorstellung ist aus. *The performance is over.*

Ich gehe aus dem Speisezimmer hinaus. *I go out of the dining room.*

ausbilden *to form, develop, cultivate, educate, train.*

ausbleiben *to stay away, fail to appear, escape.*

Ihre Strafe wird nicht ausbleiben. *You will not escape punishment.*

Ausblick *m. outlook, prospect.*

ausbrechen *to break out, vomit.*

in Tränen ausbrechen *to burst into tears.*

Ausbruch *m. outbreak, eruption, escape.*

Ausdauer *f. perseverance, assiduity.*

ausdauern *to hold out, outlast, endure.*

ausdehnen *to expand, prolong.*

ausdenken *to invent, conceive, imagine.*

Ausdruck *m. expression, phrase.*

ausdrücken *to squeeze, express.*

sich kurz und klar ausdrücken *to express oneself briefly and to the point.*

auseinander *apart, separately.*

ausführen *to take out, export, realize.*

ausführlich *adj. detailed, full; in detail, fully.*

Erzählen Sie mir alles ausführlich. *Tell me everything in detail.*

ausfüllen *to fill out, stuff.*

Ausgabe *f. delivery, edition, issue, publication.*

Ausgang *m. way out, exit, end.*

ausgeben *to give out, deliver, issue, deal (cards).*

ausgehen *to go out, come out, run out, proceed, start from, end.*

frei ausgehen *to go free.*

ihm geht die Geduld aus. *He is losing his patience.*

Wie wird diese Sache ausgehen? *How will this matter end?*

AUSGEZEICHNET *excellent, distinguished.*

ausgleichen *to make even, equalize, settle, arrange, compensate.*

aushalten *to bear, suffer, support, hold out, last.*

Aushang *m. notice (posted); poster.*

aushängen *to hang out, post a notice.*

Aushilfe *f. aid (temporary); assistant.*

auskleiden *to undress.*

auskommen *to manage, get along.*

  Es ist schwer mit ihm auszukommen. *It is difficult to get along with him.*

  Ich komme nicht mit dem Papier aus. *I can't manage with the paper. (I don't have enough of it.)*

Auskunft *f. information*

Auskunftei *f. information bureau.*

auslassen *to leave out, omit, let out.*

Auslese *f. choice, selection.*

auslesen *to select, choose, read through.*

ausmachen *to put out, constitute, come to, settle, amount.*

  Das macht nichts aus. *It does not matter.*

Ausmass *n. measurement, scale, proportion.*

  mit solchem Ausmass *to such an extent.*

ausmessen *to measure, survey.*

Ausnahme *f. exception.*

  ohne Ausnahme *without exception.*

auspacken *to unpack.*

Ausrede *f. excuse, pretense.*

ausreden *to finish speaking, excuse.*

  einem etwas ausreden *to dissuade somebody from something.*

ausrichten *to execute, deliver, obtain.*

  Haben Sie es ihm ausgerichtet? *Did you give him the message?*

Ausruf *m. cry, exclamation.*

ausrufen *to cry out, admonish, proclaim.*

ausruhen *to rest*

  sich ausruhen *to rest oneself.*

Aussage *f. statement, assertion, declaration, evidence.*

aussagen *to affirm, declare, give evidence.*

ausschalten *to cry out, switch off.*

  Schalten Sie den Motor aus! *Switch off the motor!*

ausscheiden *to separate, withdraw.*

ausschiffen *to disembark, land.*

ausschliessen *to exclude.*

ausschliesslich *exclusive (of).*

ausschmücken *to decorate, adorn.*

ausschneiden *to cut out, snipe.*

AUSSEHEN *to look out, appear.*

Aussehen *n. look, air.*

aussen *on the outside, abroad, without.*

  von aussen *from the outside.*

aussenden *to send out.*

AUSSER 1. *prep. (dat.) out of, out, besides.*

  ausser der Jahreszeit *out of season.*

  ausser sich *beside oneself.*

  2. *conj. except, unless, but.*

  Ausser Sonntags, gehe ich jeden Tag in die Schule. *I go to school every day except Sunday.*

ausserdem *besides, moreover.*

äusserlich *external; on the outside.*

äussern *to express.*

äusserst *utmost.*

aussetzen *to set out, put out, offer, bequeath.*

  auszusetzen haben *to find fault with.*

Aussicht *f. view, prospect.*

aussöhnen *to reconcile.*

aussondern *to separate, select.*

Aussprache *f. pronunciation, accent.*

aussprechen *to pronounce, express.*

aussuchen *to seek out, search.*

Austausch *m. exchange.*

austauschen *to exchange*

Auster *f. oyster.*

austragen *to deliver, distribute.*

austreten *to treat under, trample, retire.*

Ausverkauf *m. clearance sale.*

ausverkaufen *to sell out, clear off (a shop).*

Auswahl *f. choice, assortment, selection.*

auswählen *to choose, select.*

Auswanderer *m. emigrant.*

auswandern *to emigrate.*

Auswanderung *f. emigration.*

auswärtig *foreign, abroad.*

Ausweg *m. way out.*

ausweichen *to avoid, evade, shun.*

Ausweis *m. certificate, document, identity card.*

ausziehen *to undress, pull out, extract, move, remove.*

Auszug *m. departure, extract, removal.*

Auto *n. automobile, car.*

Autobahn *n. parkway.*

Autobus *m. bus.*

Axt *f. axe.*

B

Bach *m. brook.*

BACKEN *to bake, fry.*

Bäcker *m. baker.*

Backobst *n. dried fruit.*

Backofen *m. oven.*

Backpulver *n. baking powder.*

BAD *n. bath, spa.*

Badeanstalt *f. baths, swimming pool.*

Badeanzug *m. bathing suit.*

Badehose *f. swim trunks.*

Bademantel *m. bathrobe.*

Badeort *m. spa.*

Badetuch *n. bath towel.*

Badewanne *f. bathtub*

Badezimmer *n. bathroom*

BAHN *f. track, road, way, railway.*

Bahnarbeiter *m. railway worker.*

Bahnbeamte m. railroad official.

Bahngleis n. track.

BAHNHOF m. train station.

Bahnsteig m. platform.

Bahnübergang m. railroad crossing.

Balance f. balance, equilibrium.

balancieren to balance.

BALD soon, shortly.

    bald ..., bald ... sometimes ...,
    sometimes ...

    bald darauf soon after.

Balkon m. balcony.

Ball m. ball, dance.

Ballett n. ballet.

Ballon m. balloon.

Band n. ribbon.

Bande f. band, gang.

bändigen to tame, to break.

Bandmass n. tape measure.

BANK f. 1. bench, seat.

    auf die lange Bank schieben to postpone,
    delay.

    2. bank.

    Geld auf der Bank haben to have money
    in the bank.

Bankanweisung f. check.

Bankbeamte m. bank clerk.

BAR bare, naked, devoid of, pure.

    barfuss barefoot.

    die bare Wahrheit the bare truth.

    bar bezahlen to pay in cash.

Bär m. bear.

Bargeld n. cash.

    bar zahlen to pay cash.

barmherzig merciful.

Barmherzigkeit f. mercy.

Baron m. (-in, f.) Baron (ess).

Bart m. beard, whiskers.

BAU m. building, construction, edifice,
    frame.

Bauch m. belly, stomach.

BAUEN to build, construct, cultivate.

    Luftschlösser bauen to build castles in the
    air.

Bauer m. peasant.

Bauernhof m. farm.

Bauernvolk n. countryfolk.

baufällig dilapidated.

BAUM m. tree, pole.

Baumschule f. nursery (trees).

Baumwolle f. cotton.

Baustein m. brick.

beabsichtigen to intend.

beachten to observe, notice.

Beachtung f. consideration, attention.

beachtenswert noteworthy.

Beamte m. official, civil servant.

    Zollbeamte m. customs officer.

beängstigen to alarm.

beanspruchen to claim, demand.

beantworten to answer, reply.

beaufsichtigen to supervise.

beben to tremble.

    vor Angst beben to tremble with fear.

Becher m. cup, goblet, dice box.

bedacht thoughtful, considerate.

bedanken to thank.

Bedarf m. need, requirement.

bedauerlich deplorable, regrettable.

bedecken to cover.

    Der Himmel ist bedeckt. The sky is
    overcast.

bedenken to think, think over, reflect, ponder.

    sich eines andern bedenken to change
    one's mind.

bedenklich doubtful.

Bedenkzeit f. time for reflection.

(sich) bedienen to help oneself.

Bedienung f. service.

    einschliesslich der Bedienung service
    included.

bedürfen to need, require.

Bedürfnis n. need, want, necessity.

(sich) beeilen to hurry oneself.

beeindrucken to impress.

beerdigen to bury.

Beerdigung f. funeral.

befassen to touch.

    sich befassen mit to concern oneself with,
    to deal with.

    Er befässt sich mit Politik. He is
    concerned with politics.

Befehl m. order, command.

befehlen to order, command.

befestigen to fasten, fortify.

befolgen to obey (someone).

befreien to free, liberate.

Befreier m. liberator.

Befreiung f. liberation.

befreunden to befriend.

    sich befreunden mit to become friends
    with.

befriedigen to satisfy, content.

befriedigend satisfying.

Befriedigung f. satisfaction, gratification.

befürchten to fear.

Befürchtung f. fear, apprehension.

befürworten to recommend.

begabt gifted.

begeben (sich) to set about.

begegnen to meet, encounter.

begeistern to inspire, fill with enthusiasm.

begeistert inspired, enthusiastic.

Begeisterung f. inspiration, enthusiasm.

Beginn m. beginning.

BEGINNEN to begin, start.

beglaubigen to attest, certify, to authenticate.

begleiten to accompany.

    nach Hause begleiten   *to see (someone) home.*

begründen *to found, to prove.*

Behaglichkeit *f. comfort.*

behalten *to keep, retain, remember.*

    Behalten Sie das Kleingeld!   *Keep the change!*

behandeln *to handle, deal with.*

behaupten *to maintain, assert, affirm.*

Behelf *m. help, expedient.*

behelfen *(sich) to manage, do without.*

BEI 1. *prep. (dat.) at, by, near, with, because of, in case of.*

    bei der Hand   *by hand.*

    Bei Feuer müssen wir die Feuerwehr rufen.   *In case of a fire, we must call the fire department.*

    Bei ihrem Charakter wird sie unglücklich werden.   *With (because of) her character, she will be unhappy.*

    bei Tage   *by day.*

    bei weitem   *by far.*

    beim Arzt   *at the doctor's.*

    Er arbeitet bei Licht.   *He works by light.*

    Hast du Geld bei dir (*or* dabei)?   *Do you have any money on you?*

    Ich kaufe meine Kleider bei Engels.   *I buy my clothes at Engels.*

    Meine Schwester wohnt bei mir.   *My sister lives with me.*

Beichte *f. confession.*

beichten *to confess.*

BEIDE *both.*

    wir beide   *both of us.*

    einer von beiden   *one of the two.*

    keiner von beiden   *neither of them.*

    beiderseits   *on both sides, mutually.*

BEIFALL *m. approval, approbation, applause.*

beifolgend *herewith, enclosed.*

beiläufig *accidental, casual; incidentally.*

beilegen *to add, enclose.*

Beileid *n. sympathy.*

    Beileid bezeigen   *to console somebody.*

beim (*bei dem*) *at, by.*

BEIN *n. leg, bone.*

    sich kein Bein ausreissen   *to take it easy.*

    Er ist immer auf den Beinen.   *He's always on his feet.*

beinahe *nearly, almost.*

beisammen *together.*

beiseite *aside, apart.*

BEISPIEL *n. example.*

    zum Beispiel   *for example.*

    Das ist ein schlechtes Beispiel.   *This is a bad example.*

beispiellos *unheard of, without example.*

beissen *to bite.*

    Der Hund beisst nicht.   *The dog does not bite.*

beistehen *to help, stand by.*

beistimmen *to agree with.*

Beitrag *m. contribution, subscription.*

bejahen *to answer in the affirmative, assent, accept.*

bejammern *to lament.*

bejammernswert *deplorable, lamentable.*

bekämpfen *to combat, fight, struggle.*

BEKANNT *well-known, acquainted.*

    bekannt machen mit   *to introduce to.*

Bekannte *m./f. acquaintance, friend.*

Bekanntmachung *f. publication, announcement, notice.*

bekennen *to confess, admit, profess.*

    sich schuldig bekennen   *to plead guilty.*

beklagen *to complain, lament.*

BEKOMMEN *to get, receive, catch, agree with.*

    Das ist nicht mehr zu bekommen.   *You can't get that any more.*

    Es bekommt mir nicht.   *It does not agree with me.*

bekräftigen *to confirm, corroborate.*

belächeln *to smile at.*

belachen *to laugh at.*

belästigen *to molest, trouble.*

beleben *to animate, revive.*

Beleg *m. proof, evidence, illustration.*

BELEGEN *to cover, reserve.*

    Ich möchte einen Platz belegen.   *I want to reserve a seat.*

    belegte Brötchen   *sandwiches.*

    eine Vorlesung belegen   *to enroll for a course.*

belehren *to enlighten, instruct.*

    eines Besseren belehren   *to correct.*

beleidigen *to offend, insult.*

beliefern *to supply.*

belohnen *to reward.*

Belohnung *f. reward.*

belügen *to lie (falsify).*

belustigen *to amuse, entertain.*

Belustigung *f. amusement.*

bemerkbar *noticeable, perceptible.*

bemerken *to notice, observe, remark.*

bemerkenswert *noticeable, noteworthy.*

Bemerkung *f. remark, observation.*

bemitleiden *to pity, be sorry for.*

bemitleidenswert *deplorable.*

benachrichtigen *to inform, advise.*

Benachrichtigung *f. information, advice.*

benachteiligen *to prejudice.*

Benachteiligung *f. prejudice, injury.*

(sich) benehmen *to behave oneself.*

    Benimm dich nicht wie ein kleines Kind!   *Don't behave like a child!*

beneiden *to envy.*

benötigen *to require.*

benutzen *to use, employ, utilize.*

beobachten *to observe, watch.*
  heimlich beobachten *to shadow.*
BEQUEM *comfortable, convenient, lazy.*
  Sei nicht so bequem! *Don't be so lazy!*
  Wir sitzen bequem. *We are seated comfortably.*
bequemen *to condescend, comply, submit.*
Bequemlichkeit *f. convenience.*
beraten *to advise.*
Berater *m. adviser.*
beratschlagen *to deliberate.*
berechnen *to calculate, estimate.*
bereden *to talk over, persuade.*
Beredsamkeit *f. eloquence.*
Bereich *m. & n. reach, range, area, zone, domain.*
BEREIT *ready, prepared.*
  bereit halten *to keep ready.*
  bereitwillig *willing, ready.*
Bereitwilligkeit *f. willingness.*
bereuen *to repent, regret.*
BERG *m. mountain, hill.*
  über alle Berge sein *to be out of the woods.*
  Mir standen die Haare zu Berge. *My hair stood on end.*
Bergmann *m. miner.*
berichten *to report.*
berichtigen *to correct, amend, settle (a bill).*
Berichtigung *f. correction, amendment.*
berücksichtigen *to consider.*
Berücksichtigung *f. consideration, regard.*
BERUF *m. profession, occupation.*
beruflich *professional.*
berufstätig *working, employed.*
beruhigen *to quiet, calm*
Beruhigung *f. reassurance, comfort.*
BERÜHMT *famous, celebrated.*
Berühmtheit *f. fame, celebrity.*
besänftigen *to soften, appease, soothe.*
beschädigen *to damage, injure, harm.*
beschäftigen *to occupy, engage, employ.*
  sich beschäftigen *to occupy oneself.*
Beschäftigung *f. occupation.*
beschäftigungslos *unemployed, out of work.*
Bescheid *m. answer, information.*
  Bescheid geben *to inform.*
  Ich habe ihm gehörig Bescheid gesagt. *I told him off.*
bescheiden *modest, moderate.*
Bescheidenheit *f. modesty.*
bescheinen *to shine upon.*
bescheinigen *to certify, attest.*
Bescheinigung *f. certificate, receipt.*
beschleunigen *to hasten, accelerate.*
beschränken *to limit, confine, restrict.*
Beschränkung *f. limitation, restriction.*
beschreiben *to write upon, describe.*
Beschreibung *f. description.*

beschuldigen *to accuse.*
Beschuldigung *f. accusation.*
Beschwerde *f. complaint, hardship, trouble.*
(sich) beschweren *to complain.*
  Beschwerdebrüro *n. complaint department.*
Besen *m. broom.*
besetzen *to occupy, trim, set.*
  Es ist alles besetzt! *All seats are occupied.*
  Besetzt! *Occupied! Busy!*
Besetzung *f. occupation, cast.*
  Die Besetzung ist aussergewöhnlich gut. *The cast is outstanding.*
besichtigen *to view, inspect, visit.*
Besichtigung *f. view, inspection.*
besiegen *to conquer, beat, defeat.*
besinnen *to consider, reflect.*
  sich besinnen *to remember.*
  sich eines Besseren besinnen *to think better of.*
besinnlich *contemplative, thoughtful.*
Besitz *m. possession, property, estate.*
besorgen *to take care of, fetch, procure, provide.*
Besorgnis *f. fear, alarm.*
Besorgung *f. care, management.*
  Besorgungen machen *to go shopping.*
besprechen *to discuss, talk over, criticize, review.*
BESSER *better.*
  umso besser *so much the better.*
bessern *to improve, recover.*
  sich bessern *to improve oneself.*
Besserung *f. recovery, improvement.*
  Gute Besserung! *I hope you will get well soon!*
best(er-es) *best.*
beständig *constant, permanent, steady; constantly, all the time.*
Beständigkeit *f. constancy, stability.*
bestätigen *to confirm, ratify.*
bestechen *to bribe, corrupt.*
bestechlich *corruptible.*
Bestechung *f. bribery, corruption.*
Besteck *n. silverware.*
bestellen *to arrange, order, tell, cultivate.*
  Waren bestellen *to order goods.*
  zu sich bestellen *to send for.*
BESTIMMEN *to decide, fix, intend, define, induce.*
  bestimmen über *to dispose of.*
  Bestimmt! *Agreed!*
Bestimmtheit *f. certainty, precision.*
bestrafen *to punish.*
Bestrafung *f. punishment.*
BESUCH *m. visit, company, attendance.*
BESUCHEN *to visit, attend.*
Besucher *m. visitor, spectator, audience.*

beteiligen to give a share, take part, take an interest.
    beteiligt sein   to participate.
Beteiligung f. share, participation.
betonen f. to stress, accent, emphasize.
Betonung f. stress, emphasis.
beträchtlich considerable.
(sich) betragen to behave.
betreffen to concern.
    was mich betrifft   so far as I am concerned.
betreten to tread on.
    Betreten des Rasens verboten!   Keep off the grass!
Betrieb m. management, plant, factory.
    in Betrieb sein   to be working.
    ausser Betrieb   not working, closed.
    in Betrieb setzen   to set in motion.
(sich) betrinken to get drunk.
betrüben to grieve, distress.
Betrug m. deception, fraud, swindle.
betrügen to deceive, defraud, trick.
BETT n. bed.
    das Bett hüten   to be confined in bed.
    früh zu Bett gehen   to go to bed early.
Bettdecke f. blanket, bedspread.
betteln to beg.
Bettlaken n. sheet.
Bettler m. beggar.
Bettwäsche f. bed linen.
beugen to bend, bow.
beunruhigen to disturb, alarm, upset.
beurlauben to grant leave, take leave.
    beurlaubt   absent on leave.
Beutel m. bag, purse.
bevollmächtigen to empower, authorize.
BEVOR before.
bewachen to watch over.
bewältigen to master.
bewegen to move, stir.
Beweggrund m. motive.
    Was war der Beweggrund des Verbrechens?   What was the motive of the crime?
beweglich movable, mobile, quick, lively.
BEWEGUNG f. movement, agitation, motion.
    Einer politischen Bewegung angehören   to belong to a political party.
Beweis m. proof, evidence.
beweisen to prove, demonstrate.
Beweisführung f. demonstration.
bewerben to apply for, compete.
    sich bewerben um   to apply oneself for.
    Er bewarb sich um eine neue Stellung.   He applied for a new job (position).
Bewerber m. applicant, candidate.
Bewerbung f. application, courtship.

bewilligen to consent, concede.
bewusst conscious.
    sich einer Sache bewusst sein   to be conscious or aware of something.
bewusstlos unconscious.
BEZAHLEN to pay.
sich bezahlt machen to pay for itself (be lucrative).
bezaubernd charming.
Bezug m. covering, cover, case.
    in Bezug auf   in regard to.
    Bezug nehmen auf   to refer to.
    unter Bezugnahme auf   with reference to.
Bibel f. Bible.
Bibliothek f. library.
Bibliothekar m. librarian.
Biene f. bee.
Bier n. beer.
BIETEN to offer.
    sich alles bieten lassen   to put up with everything.
BILD n. image, picture, illustration, portrait, likeness.
BILDEN to form, shape, educate.
    Der Präsident hat ein neues Kabinett gebildet.   The president has formed a new cabinet.
    die bildenden Künste   fine arts.
Bildseite f. face, head (coin).
Bildung f. formation, constitution.
billig just, reasonable, fair, moderate.
binden to bind, tie.
BIS until, as far as, about.
    zwei bis drei Pfund.   About two or three pounds.
    bis an (acc.) up to.
    bis in alle Ewigkeit   till the end of time.
    bis dann/dahin   until then.
bis auf (acc.) except for.
    Mir gefällt der Film bis auf das Ende.   I like the film except for the ending.
    alle bis weiteres   until further notice.
    bis zu (dat.) (down) to.
    von dem Kopf bis zu den Füssen   from head to foot.
    bis jetzt   so far.
    bisher   till now.
    bisweilen   sometimes.
Bischof m. bishop.
bisschen a bit, a little, a while.
    Das ist ein bisschen stark.   That's going a bit too far.
    Er kam ein bisschen spät.   He came a little late.
Bissen m. bite, mouthful.
Bitte f. request, prayer.
BITTE please.
    bitte, bitte schön, bitte sehr.   (In response to a request: Here you are. In

response to thanks: *You are welcome; don't mention it.*)

Wie, bitte? *I beg your pardon?*

BITTEN *to ask, beg, implore.*

Ich bitte um Entschuldigung. *I beg your pardon, I am sorry.*

bitter *bitter.*

blamieren *to expose to ridicule.*

sich blamieren *to make a fool of oneself.*

BLATT *n. leaf, petal, blade, sheet.*

sich kein Blatt vor den Mund nehmen *to speak plainly.*

blättern *to leaf through the pages of a book.*

BLAU *blue.*

Blech *n. tin.*

Blei *n. lead.*

BLEIBEN *to stay, remain, keep, last.*

bleiben lassen *to leave alone.*

Das bleibt unter uns. *That's between you and me.*

Es bleibt dabei *Agreed.*

sich gleich bleiben *to remain the same.*

stehen bleiben *to stop, stand still.*

bleibend *permanent, lasting.*

bleich *pale, faded, faint.*

bleichen *to bleach.*

Bleistift *m. pencil.*

blenden *to blind, dazzle.*

BLICK *m. glance, look, gaze.*

auf den ersten Blick *at first sight.*

Er warf ihm einen bösen Blick zu. *He gave him a dirty look.*

blind *blind, false.*

ein blinder Alarm *a false alarm.*

Blindheit *f. blindness.*

blinken *to glitter, glimpse, twinkle, signal.*

Blitz *m. lightning, flash.*

blitzen *to lighten, flash, sparkle.*

Block *m. block, log, pad, stocks.*

blond *blond, fair.*

BLOSS *bare, naked, uncovered; merely, only.*

Ich tue es bloss ihnen zu gefallen. *I am only doing it to please you.*

blühen *to bloom.*

BLUME *f. flower.*

Lasst Blumen sprechen! *Say it with flowers!*

Blumenkohl *m. cauliflower.*

Bluse *f. blouse.*

BLUT *n. blood, race, parentage.*

blutarm *anemic.*

Blutdruck *m. blood pressure.*

bluten *to bleed.*

Blutprobe *f. blood-test.*

Blutvergiftung *f. blood-poisoning.*

Boden *m. floor, ground, soil, attic.*

Bogen *m. bow, curve, arch.*

BOHNE *f. bean.*

grüne Bohnen *string beans.*

weisse Bohnen *dried beans.*

Bombardement *n. bombardment.*

bombardieren *to bomb.*

Bombe *f. bomb.*

Atombombe *f. atomic bomb.*

Bonbon *m. & n. candy.*

BOOT *n. boat.*

Bootsfahrt *f. boatride.*

Börse *f. purse, stock exchange.*

Börsenmakler *m. stockbroker.*

bösartig *ill-natured, wicked, malicious.*

BÖSE *bad, angry, evil.*

boshaft *malicious, mischievous.*

Bote *m. messenger.*

Botschaft *f. news.*

Botschafter *m. ambassador.*

boxen *to box.*

Brand *m. burning, fire, conflagration.*

in Brand geraten *to catch fire.*

Brandschaden *m. damage by fire.*

BRATEN *m. roast.*

Brathuhn *n. roast chicken.*

Bratkartoffeln *pl. fried potatoes.*

Bratapfel *m. baked apple.*

BRATEN *to roast, grill, fry.*

Brauch *m. usage, use, custom.*

brauchbar *useful, practicable.*

BRAUCHEN *to use, employ, need.*

Wie lange werden Sie noch brauchen? *How much more time will it take you?*

Brauhaus *n. brewery, tavern.*

BRAUN *brown.*

Brause *f. shower, douche, spray.*

brausen *to storm, rage, roar, rush.*

sich abbrausen *to take a shower.*

Braut *f. fiancee.*

Brautführer *m. best man.*

Brautjungfer *f. bridesmaid.*

Brautkleid *n. wedding dress.*

Brautpaar *n. engaged couple.*

Bräutigam *m. bridegroom.*

brav *good, honest, excellent.*

BRECHEN *to break, pick.*

Er spricht ein gebrochenes Deutsch. *He speaks broken German.*

BREIT *broad, wide, flat.*

weit und breit *high and low.*

Breite *f. breadth, width, latitude.*

Bremse *f. brake.*

bremsen *to put the brakes on.*

BRENNEN *to burn, brand, bake, roast.*

darauf brennen *to be anxious.*

Es brennt in der Stadt. *There is a fire in town.*

Brett *n. board, plank, shelf, stage.*

am schwarzen Brett *on the board.*

BRIEF *m. letter*

Briefkasten *m. letter-box.*
Briefmappe *f. attaché case.*
Briefmarke *f. stamp.*
Briefpapier *n. stationery.*
Brieftasche *f. wallet, pocket-book.*
Briefträger *m. mailman.*
Briefumschlag *m. envelope.*
Brille *f. glasses.*
BRINGEN *to bring, fetch, carry, put, take.*
  dazu bringen   *to induce to.*
  Er hat sich ums Leben gebracht.   *He has*
    committed suicide.
  es zu etwas bringen   *to achieve something.*
  Ich werde das in Ordnung bringen.   *I'll*
    straighten that out.
  Sie hat es auf neunzig Jahre
    gebracht.   *She turned ninety years*
    old.
britisch *British*
BROT *n. bread.*
  Brötchen   *roll.*
  sein Brot verdienen   *to earn one's living.*
Brötchen *n. roll.*
Bruch *m. break, fracture, fraction.*
Bruchteil *m. fraction*
BRÜCKE *f. bridge (also dental).*
  Er hat alle Brücken hinter sich
    abgebrochen.   *He has burnt his*
    bridges behind him.
BRUDER *m. brother.*
  Brüderschaft   *f. fraternity.*
Brunnen *m. spring, well, fountain.*
Brust *f. breast, chest, bosom.*
Bube *m. boy, jack of cards.*
BUCH *n. book.*
Buchdeckel *m. cover, binding.*
Buchführung *f. bookkeeping.*
Buchhaltung *f. bookkeeping.*
Buchhändler *m. bookseller.*
Buchhandlung *f. bookshop.*
Büchse *f. can.*
Büchsenöffner *m. can opener.*
Buchstabe *m. letter, character.*
Buchumschlag *m. jacket (book).*
Bügelbrett *n. ironing board.*
Bügeleisen *n. iron (for pressing).*
bügeln *to press.*
Bühne *f. stage, platform.*
Bund *m. league, confederation.*
Bündel *m. bundle.*
bunt *colored, lively, gay.*
  Das ist mir zu bunt.   *I'm fed up with it.*
Burg *f. castle, citadel.*
Bürge *f. bail.*
bürgen *to guarantee, vouch for.*
Bürger *m. citizen, townsman.*
Bürgerkrieg *m. civil war.*
Bürgermeister *m. mayor.*
Bürgersteig *m. pavement.*

BÜRO *n. office.*
bürokratisch *bureaucratic.*
Bursch *m. youth, lad, fellow.*
Burschenschaft *f. students' association.*
Bürste *f. brush.*
bürsten *to brush.*
Busch *m. bush.*
Busse *f. penitence, repentance.*
  Busse tun   *to do penance.*
büssen *to suffer for, expiate.*
Büste *f. bust.*
Büstenhalter *m. brassiere, bra.*
BUTTER *f. butter.*
Butterbrot *n. slice of bread and butter.*

Café *n. café.*
Cello *n. cello.*
Cellist *m. cellist.*
Champagner *m. champagne.*
Charakter *m. character, disposition.*
charakteristisch *characteristic.*
Chauffeur *m. chauffeur.*
Chef *m. head, boss, chief.*
Chemie *f. chemistry.*
chemisch *chemical.*
Chinese *m., -in, f. Chinese (person).*
chinesisch *Chinese.*
Chirurg *m. surgeon.*
Chor *m. choir, chorus.*
Choral *m. chorale.*
Chorgesang *m. choir singing.*
Choristin *f. chorus-girl.*
Chorknabe *m. choir-boy.*
Christ *m. Christian.*
Christenheit *f. Christendom.*
Christentum *n. Christianity.*
Chronik *f. chronicle.*
Commonwealth Unabhängiger Nationen *n.*
    Commonwealth of Independent States
    (former U.S.S.R.)
Cousin *m. (Vetter m.) cousin (man).*
Cousine *f. (Kusine) cousin (woman).*
Creme *m. cream (cosmetic).*

DA 1. *adv. there, here.*
  2. *conj. when, because, as, since.*
  da sein   *to be present.*
  da stehen   *to stand near, stand by.*
DABEI *near, near by, close to, along,*
    moreover.
  Dabei bleibt es   *there the matter ends.*
  Er hat kein Geld dabei.   *He has no money*
    on him.
dableiben *to stay, remain.*

Dach *n. roof.*
  unter Dach und Fach *safe.*
Dachkammer *f. attic.*
DADURCH *through it, by it, thereby.*
  dadurch dass *through the fact that.*
  Er ist dadurch berühmt geworden. *That made him famous.*
DAFÜR *for that, for it, instead of it.*
  dafür sein *to be in favor of.*
  Ich kann nichts dafür. *It is not my fault.*
DAGEGEN 1. *adv. against it.*
  nichts dagegen haben *to have no objection.*
  2. *conj. on the other hand.*
DAHEIM *at home.*
DAHER *from there.*
  Ich komme gerade daher. *I am just coming from there.*
DAHIN *to there.*
  bis dahin *by then.*
  Ich gehe sofort dahin. *I am going there right now.*
dahinten *behind.*
damalig *then, of that time.*
Dame *f. lady, queen (cards), checkers.*
  eine Partie Dame spielen *to play a game of checkers.*
DAMIT 1. *adv. with it, by it.*
  Was wollte er damit sagen? *What does he mean by that?*
  2. *conj. so that, in order to.*
  Ich sage es noch einmal, damit Sie es nicht vergessen. *I say it once more so that you won't forget it.*
  damit nicht *for fear that.*
Dämmerlicht *n. dusk.*
Dämmerung *f. twilight, dawn.*
Dampf *m. vapor, steam.*
Dampfbad *n. steam bath.*
dämpfen *to damp, tone down, extinguish, steam (cooking).*
Dampfer *m. steamer.*
DANACH *afterwards, after that, thereafter.*
  Es sieht danach aus. *It looks like it.*
daneben 1. *adv. near it, next to it, close by.*
  2. *conj. besides, moreover, at the same time, also.*
DANK *m. thanks, gratitude, reward.*
  Gott sei Dank! *Thank God!*
  zum Dank *as a reward.*
DANKBAR *grateful, thankful.*
DANKE *thank you*
  Danke schön! *Thank you very much!*
DANKEN *to thank.*
  Nichts zu danken. *Not at all, don't mention it.*
DANN *then, thereupon.*
  dann und wann *now and then.*
DARAN (dran) *at it, of that, in it, in that.*

  Ich glaube daran. *I believe in it.*
  nahe daran sein *to be near, on the point of.*
  Wer ist dran? *Whose turn is it?*
DARAUF (drauf) *on, upon it, after that, thereupon.*
  Es kommt darauf an. *It all depends.*
  Ich lege keinen Wert darauf. *I'm not interested in it.*
DARAUS (draus) *of it, of that, from this, from that.*
  Daraus ist nichts geworden. *Nothing came of it.*
darbieten *to offer, present.*
Darbietung *f. entertainment, offering.*
DAREIN (drein) *into it, therein.*
DARIN (drin) *in it, in that.*
  Es ist nichts darin. *There is nothing to it.*
darlegen *to explain.*
Darlegung *f. explanation, exposition.*
Darlehen *n. loan.*
DARÜBER (drüber) 1. *adv. over it, above it, about it.*
  Darüber besteht kein Zweifel. *There is no doubt about that.*
  darüber hinaus *beyond that.*
  2. *conj. meanwhile.*
DARUM (drum) *round it, for it, about it.*
  Ich kann mich nicht darum kümmern. *I can't take care of that.*
DARUNTER (drunter) *under it, underneath, among them, by that.*
  Was verstehen Sie darunter? *What do you mean by that?*
DAS 1. *neuter article (nom. and acc.). the.*
  2. *demons. pron. that.*
  3. *rel. pron. which, that.*
  dasjenige das *the one which.*
  dasselbe *the same.*
dasein *to exist, be present.*
Dasein *n. existence, life.*
  Der Kämpf für das Dasein *struggle for life.*
DASS *conj. that.*
  dass doch *if only.*
Datum *n. date.*
Dauer *f. length, duration.*
  auf die Dauer *for long.*
DAUERN *to last, continue.*
  lange dauern *to take a long time.*
Dauerwelle *f. permanent wave.*
Daumen *m. thumb.*
DAVON *for it, from this, from that, of it, of that.*
  Was halten Sie davon? *What do you think of it?*
  Geben Sie mir ein Paar davon. *Give me a pair of them.*
  Das hängt davon ab. *It depends.*

DAVOR *in front of it, of it, of that.*
  Sie stehen direkt davor. *They stand right in front of it.*
DAZU *to it, for it, for that putpose.*
  Es ist schon zu spät dazu. *It is already too late for that.*
  dazu gehören *to belong to it.*
dazwischen *in between.*
Decke *f. cover, blanket, ceiling.*
Deckel *m. cover, lid.*
DECKEN *to protect, cover, guard, secure.*
Deckung *f. cover, shelter, protection.*
  in Deckung gehen *to take cover.*
Defekt *m. defect, deficiency.*
Degen *m. sword.*
DEIN *(poss. adj. fam. form.) your.*
DEIN *(-er, -e, -es) (poss. pron. fam. form.) yours.*
DEM *dat, sing of der and das to the, to this, to whom, to which.*
  demnach *then.*
  demnächst *soon, shortly.*
  demzufolge *accordingly.*
  Wie dem auch sei *be that as it may.*
Demokrat *m. democrat.*
Demokratie *f. democracy.*
Demut *f. humility.*
demütig *humble.*
demütigen *to humiliate.*
Demütigung *f. humiliation.*
DEN *acc. sing. of der; dat. pl. of die. the, this, to them, whom, that.*
DENEN *dat. pl. of die (rel. pron.) to whom, to which.*
DENKEN *to think, intend, mean.*
  Was denken Sie zu tun? *What do you intend to do?*
  denken an *to remember, think of.*
  sich denken *to imagine.*
  Das kann ich mir schon denken. *I can well imagine.*
Denker *m. thinker.*
DENN *for, because, then.*
  es sei denn, dass *unless.*
dennoch *nevertheless.*
deponieren *to deposit.*
DER *1. masc. article (nom.) the; (fem.) (gen. & dat.) of the, to the; pl. (gen.) of the.*
  2. demons. pron. this.
  3. rel. pron. which, who, that.
  derjenige der *the one who, he who.*
  derselbe *the same.*
DEREN *gen. fem. and pl. of die, (rel. pron.) whose.*
DES *yen. sing. of der and das of the.*
DESHALB *therefore, for that reason.*
DESSEN *gen. sing. of der and das pron. whose.*

Detektiv *m. detective.*
deuten *to point out, explain, interpret.*
deutlich *distinct, clear; distinctly, clearly.*
Deutlichkeit *f. distinctness, clearness.*
DEUTSCH *German.*
DEUTSCHE *m. & f. German (person)*
DEUTSCHLAND *n. Germany.*
Deutung *f. interpretation, explanation.*
Devise *f. foreign bill, motto.*
DEZEMBER *m. December.*
Dialekt *m. dialect.*
Diamant *m. diamond.*
Diät *f. diet.*
  Diät leben *to diet.*
DICH *acc. of du. (fam. form) you.*
DICHT *thick, dense, tight, close.*
dichten *to compose, write poetry, invent.*
Dichter *m. poet.*
Dichtung *f. poetry, fiction.*
DICK *thick, stout, fat.*
  Er ist dick geworden. *He got fat.*
Dickkopf *m. blockhead.*
DIE *1. fem. article (nom. and acc.), the. pl. article (noun. and acc.), the.*
  2. demons. pron. this.
  3. rel. pron. who, which, that.
diejenige die *she who, the one which.*
  dieselbe *the same.*
DIEB *m. thief, burglar.*
  Halten Sie den Dieb! *Stop the thief!*
Diebstahl *m. theft.*
DIENEN *to serve.*
  Womit kann ich dienen? *Can I help you?*
Diener *m. servant.*
Dienerin *f. maid.*
dienlich *serviceable.*
Dienst *m. service, duty, situation, employment.*
  ausser Dienst *off duty.*
  zu Diensten stehen *to be at a person's disposal.*
DIENSTAG *m. Tuesday.*
diensteifrig *zealous.*
Dienstmädchen *n. maid.*
Dienstelle *f. headquarters.*
DIES *(-er, -e, -es) this, that.*
DIESMAL *this time.*
DIESSEITS *(gen.) on this side.*
Diktat *n. dictation, treaty.*
DING *n. thing, object.*
  guter Dinge sein *to be in high spirits.*
  vor allen Dingen *first of all.*
Diplom *n. diploma, certificate.*
Diplomatie *f. diplomacy.*
diplomatisch *diplomatic.*
DIR *dat. of du (fam. form) you, to you.*
direkt *direct.*
Direktor *m. director.*
Dirigent *m. conductor.*

dirigieren *to conduct, direct.*

diskret *discreet, tactful.*

Diskretion *f. discretion.*

diskutieren *to discuss.*

Distanz *f. distance.*

DOCH *however, anyway, nevertheless, but, still, yet; surely, of course, yes (in answer to a negative question); indicates a well-known fact.*

Willst du nicht kommen? Doch. *Won't you come? Of course.*

Ich habe doch gewusst, dass er schwer krank war. *I knew (very well) he was very ill.*

Ich werde doch gehen. *I will go anyhow.*

Ja doch! *Of course.*

Sie werden doch zugeben, dass er recht hatte. *But you will admit he was right.*

Und doch ist es nicht so traurig, wie Sie denken. *And still it is not so sad as you think.*

DOKTOR *m. doctor.*

den Doktor machen *to take the degree of doctor.*

Doktorarbeit *f. thesis for doctorate.*

Dokument *n. document.*

dokumentieren *to prove.*

Dolch *m. dagger.*

dolmetschen *to interpret.*

Dolmetscher *m. interpreter.*

Dom *m. cathedral.*

Donner *m. thunder.*

vom Donner gerührt *thunderstruck.*

donnern *to thunder.*

Donnerschlag *m. thunderbolt.*

DONNERSTAG *m. Thursday.*

Donnerwetter *n. thunderstorm.*

Donnerwetter! *Good heavens!*

doppeldeutig *ambiguous.*

Doppelpunkt *m. colon.*

doppelt *double.*

Doppelbett, *n. double bed.*

Doppelzimmer, *n. room with twin beds.*

DORF *n. village.*

Dorn *m. thorn.*

DORT *there, yonder.*

dorther *from there.*

dorthin *there, that way, over there.*

Dose *f. box, can, dose, amount.*

DRAHT *m. wire, cable, line.*

Drängen *to push, press, hurry, urge.*

Nicht drängen! *Do not push!*

draussen *outside, outdoors, abroad.*

drehen *to turn, rotate, revolve.*

DREI *three.*

Dreieck *n. triangle.*

DREISSIG *thirty.*

DREISSIGSTE *thirtieth.*

DREIZEHN *thirteen.*

DREIZEHNTE *thirteenth.*

dringen *to enter, get in, penetrate.*

dringen auf *to insist on.*

dringend *urgent.*

DRITTE *third.*

Droge *f. drug.*

Drogerie *f. chemist's shop.*

drüben *over there, yonder.*

Druck *m. pressure, compression.*

in Druck gehen *to go to press.*

drucken *to print.*

Druckknopf *m. push button.*

Druckfehler *m. misprint.*

Dschungel *f. jungle.*

DU *pers. pron. fam. form. you.*

Duft *m. scent, smell, fragrance.*

DUFTEN *to smell sweet, be fragrant.*

duftig *sweet-smelling, fragrant.*

dulden *to endure, bear, suffer.*

dumm *stupid, dull, ignorant.*

Sei nicht so dumm! *Don't be so stupid!*

Es wurde mir zu dumm. *I got sick and tired of it.*

Dummheit *f. stupidity, blunder.*

Dummkopf *m. stupid fellow, dunce.*

düngen *to fertilize.*

Dünger *m. fertilizer, manure.*

dunkel *dark, gloomy, vaguely.*

Ich erinnere mich dunkel ... *I vaguely remember ...*

Dunkelheit *f. darkness, obscurity.*

dunkeln *to get dark.*

dünn *thin, weak, rare.*

DURCH 1. *prep. (acc.) through, across, by, by means of, because of.*

Ich ging durch den Wald. *I walked through the forest.*

Durch den Krieg wurden viele Städte zerstört. *Many cities were destroyed because of the war.*

Er bestand die Prüfung durch viel Arbeit. *He passed the examination by working hard. (through much work.)*

Er schickt es durch die Post. *He sends it by mail.*

die ganze Zeit durch *all the time.*

durch and durch *through and through.*

2. *prefix,*

a) *inseparable, through, across, around.*

Die Milchstrasse durchzieht den Himmel. *The milky way goes across the sky.*

b) *separable, implies the idea of accomplishment.*

Ich lese das Buch durch. *I read the book to the end.*

durcharbeiten *to work through, study thoroughly.*

durchaus *thoroughly, absolutely.*

durchaus nicht *not at all, not in the least.*

durcheinander *confusedly, in disorder.*

durchfahren *to drive through (without stopping).*

Durchfahrt *f. thoroughfare, passage.*
Keine Durchfahrt! *No thoroughfare!*

durchfechten *to fight out.*

durchfinden *to find one's way through.*

durchführbar *to carry out, accomplish, execute.*

Durchführung *f. accomplishment, execution, performance.*

Durchgang *m. passageway.*
Kein Durchgang! *No trespassing!*

durchgehen *to go through, pass through, run away.*

durchhalten *to hold out, carry through.*

durchmachen *to go through, suffer.*
Sie haben viel durchgemacht. *They have gone through a lot.*

Durchmesser *m. diameter.*

durchnehmen *to work through, go over.*

Durchreise *f. journey through, passing through, transit.*

durchreisen *to travel through, cross.*

Durchreisevisum *n. transit visa.*

durchschauen *to look through.*

Durchschlag *m. colander, strainer, carbon copy.*

durchschlagend *powerful.*

Durchschlagpapier *n. carbon paper.*

durchschneiden *to cut through.*

durchsetzen *to achieve, carry out, bring about.*

durchsuchen *to search through.*

Durchsuchung *f. search, police raid.*

Durchzug *m. march through, passage through.*

DÜRFEN *to be allowed to, be permitted.*
Darf ich, bitte? *May I, please?*
Darf ich um den nächsten Tanz bitten? *May I have the next dance?*
Darf man hier rauchen? *Is smoking allowed here?*

dürftig *poor, needy, indigent.*

DÜRR *dry, parched, dried, lean, skinny.*
dürres Holz *dry wood.*

DÜRRE *f. dryness, drought.*

Durst *m. thirst.*
Das macht Durst. *That makes (one) thirsty.*

dürsten *to be thirsty, long for, crave.*

durstig *thirsty.*

Dusche *f. shower-bath.*

duschen *(sich) to take a shower.*

Düsenflugzeug *n. jet plane.*

Dutzend *n. dozen.*
dutzendmal *dozens of times.*

E

Ebbe *f. ebb, low tide.*
die Ebbe und die Flut *the ebb and flow.*

EBEN *even, flat, smooth, just.*
eben erst *just now.*
eben deshalb *for that very reason.*
ebenfalls *likewise, too, also.*
ebenmässig *symmetrical, proportional.*
ebenso *just as, just so, quite as.*
Es geschiet dir eben recht. *It just serves you right.*

Ebene *f. plain.*

ebnen *to level, smooth.*

Echo *n. echo.*

ECHT *genuine, true, real, legitimate.*

Echtheit *f. legitimacy.*

Ecke *f. corner, angle.*

eckig *triangular, cornered.*

edel *noble, well-born, generous.*

Efeu *n. ivy.*

Effekt *m. effect, stocks.*

Effekthascherei *f. showing off.*

effektvoll *effective.*

Egoismus *m. egoism.*

Egoist *m. egoist.*

egoistisch *egoistic.*

egozentrisch *egocentric.*

EHE *before, until.*
ehemals *formerly.*
eher *sooner, rather.*

Ehe *f. matrimony, marriage.*

Ehefrau *f. wife, spouse.*

Ehegatte *m. husband.*

Ehepaar *n. married couple.*

ehelich *matrimonial, conjugal.*

Ehescheidung *f. divorce.*

Ehescheidungsklage *f. divorce suit.*

Eheschliessung *f. marriage.*

EHRE *f. honor, reputation, respect.*
Meine Ehre steht auf dem Spiel. *My honor is at stake.*

ehren *to honor.*

ehrenamtlich *honorary.*

Ehrenbezeigung *f. mark of respect.*

Ehrenwort *n. word of honor.*

ehrerbietig *respectful.*

Ehrerbietung *f. deference, respect.*

Ehrfurcht *f. respect, awe, reverence.*

Ehrgefühl *n. sense of honor, self-respect.*

Ehrgeiz *m. ambition.*

ehrlich *honorably.*
ehrlich gesagt *to tell the truth.*
Ehrlich gesagt, glaube ich ihm nicht. *To tell (you) the truth, I don't believe him.*

ehrgeizig *ambitious.*

Ehrlichkeit *f. honesty.*

Ehrlosigkeit *f. dishonesty, infamy.*
Ei *n. (pl. Eier) egg.*
   Eigelb *n. egg yolk.*
   Eiweiss *n. egg white.*
   Rühreier *scrambled eggs.*
   Spiegeleier *fried eggs.*
   weiche Eier *soft-boiled eggs.*
Eiche *f. oak.*
Eichhörnchen *n. squirrel.*
Eifer *m. zeal, ardor.*
Eifersucht *f. jealousy.*
eifersüchtig *jealous.*
eifrig *eager, keen, zealous.*
EIGEN *own, proper, particular, special,*
   choosy.
   Er ist sehr eigen im Essen. *He is very*
   fussy about his food.
eigenartig *odd, peculiar, strange, queer.*
eigensinnig *stubborn, obstinate.*
eigentlich *real, actual; actually, really,*
   exactly, just, as a matter of fact,
   indeed.
   Was heisst das eigentlich? *What does it*
   actually mean?
Eigentum *n. property.*
eigentümlich *queer, odd, peculiar.*
(sich) eignen *to be suited, qualified.*
EILE *f. hurry, haste, speed.*
   Es hat keine Eile. *There's no hurry about*
   it.
   Eile mit Weile. *Haste makes waste.*
EILEN *(sich) to hurry.*
   Das eilt sehr. *This is very urgent.*
   Das eilt nicht. *There's no hurry.*
eilig *fast, hasty.*
   es eilig haben *to be in a hurry.*
Eilzug *m. fast train, express.*
EIN, eine, ein 1. *indefinite article. a, an.*
   2. *number. one.*
   3. *pron. one.*
   Eines Tages *some day.*
   ein für allemal *once for all.*
   4. *separable prefix (implies the idea of*
   entrance or reduction in volume).
   Die Lehrerin trat in das Schulzimmer ein.
   The teacher (fem.) entered the
   classroom.
   Läuft dieser Stoff ein? *Does this material*
   shrink?
EINANDER *each other, one another.*
   Wir haben einander jahrelang nicht
   gesehen. *We have not seen each*
   other for years.
einarbeiten *to get used to, familiarize with.*
einatmen *to inhale.*
Einbahnstrasse *f. one-way street.*
einbiegen *to turn into.*
   Biegen Sie in diese Strasse ein! *Turn into*
   this street.

(sich) einbilden *to imagine; fancy, think,*
   believe.
Einbildung *f. imagination, conceit,*
   presumption.
einbrechen *to break open, through.*
   Heute Nacht ist ein Dieb bei ihm
   eingebrochen. *Last night a thief*
   broke into his house.
Einbrecher *m. burglar.*
Einbruch *m. house-breaking, burglary.*
EINDRUCK *m. impression.*
   Er tut es bloss, um Eindruck zu machen.
   He does it only to show off.
EINFACH *simple, plain, single; simply,*
   plainly, elementary.
   einfache (Fahrt) *one-way (ticket).*
Einfall *m. idea, collapse, whim.*
   Wie kommen Sie auf den Einfall? *What*
   gave you the idea?
einfältig *simple.*
Einfluss *m. influence.*
einflussreich *influential.*
Einfuhr *f. importation, import.*
einführen *to introduce, import.*
Einführung *f. importation.*
Einfuhrzoll *m. import duty.*
Eingabe *f. petition, memorial.*
EINGANG *m. entrance.*
   Kein Eingang. *No entrance.*
   Verbotener Eingang! *Keep out!*
Eingemachtes *n. preserves.*
eingebildet *conceited.*
Eingebung *f. inspiration.*
eingestehen *to admit, confess.*
eingewöhnen *to accustom.*
Einhalt *m. stop.*
   Einhalt gebieten *to put a stop to.*
einhalten *to observe, follow, keep to, meet.*
   Wird er den Termin einhalten? *Will he*
   meet the deadline?
Einheit *f. unity, union, unit.*
einheitlich *uniform.*
einholen *to bring in, collect, gather, make*
   up.
   einholen gehen *to go shopping.*
einig *in agreement, united, unanimous.*
einigemal *several times.*
einigen *to unite, unify.*
   sich einigen *to come to terms, agree.*
einig (-er,-e,-es) *some, any, a few.*
einigermassen *to some extent, somewhat.*
Einigkeit *f. harmony.*
Einigung *f. agreement.*
einjagen *to alarm, frighten.*
EINKAUF *m. purchase, buying.*
EINKAUFEN *to buy, purchase, shop.*
   Einkaufspreis *m. price of purchase.*
Einkommen *n. income.*
Einkommensteuer *f. income tax.*

einladen to invite.

EINLADUNG f. invitation.

Einlass m. entrance, admission.

einlassen to admit, let in.

einleben to settle down, familiarize oneself.

einleiten to begin, initiate, introduce, institute.

Einleitung f. introduction.

einmachen to preserve.

Einmachglas n. preserves jar.

EINMAL once, formerly.

    auf einmal all at once.

    Es war einmal . . .   Once upon a time there was . . .

    noch einmal   once more.

(sich) einmischen to interfere, to meddle.

einmütig unanimous.

Einnahme f. occupation, capture, conquest.

einnehmen to collect, engage, occupy, receive, captivate.

einnehmend captivating.

einordnen to arrange, classify, file.

einpacken to wrap up.

einpflanzen to plant, inculcate.

einrahmen to frame.

einreden to persuade, talk someone into.

einreichen to hand in, deliver, present.

einreihen to insert, include, arrange.

Einreise f. entry into a country.

Einreiseerlaubnis f. permit to enter a country.

einrichten to arrange, prepare, manage, furnish.

    sich einrichten   to plan.

Einrichtung f. furniture, layout.

EINS one, the same.

    Es kommt auf eins hinaus.   It comes to the same thing.

EINSAM lonely, solitary, lonesome.

Einsamkeit f. loneliness, solitude.

einschläfern to lull to sleep.

einschalten to insert, put in.

einschenken to pour in.

einschlafen to fall asleep.

einschlagen to drive in (nail), break, wrap up.

    Schlagen Sie mir das, bitte, ein.   Will you please wrap that for me?

einschliessen to lock up, enclose.

einschliesslich inclusive.

Einschreibebrief m. registered letter.

einschreiben to enter, note down, register.

einschüchtern to intimidate.

EINSEITIG one-sided, partial.

einsetzen to put in, insert.

    sich einsetzen für   to speak on behalf of.

Einspruch m. protest, objection.

    Einspruch erheben   to object to, protest against.

EINST once, one day.

    einstmals   once, formerly.

    einsteilen   meanwhile, for the present.

    einstweilig   temporary.

einsteigen to get in.

    Nach Düsseldorf einsteigen!   (Passengers) to Düsseldorf, all aboard!

einstellen to put on, adjust, stop, cease.

    Arbeit einstellen   to strike.

    Betrieb einstellen   to close down.

    sich einstellen auf   to be prepared.

Einstellung f. adjustment, enlistment, attitude.

    Ich verstehe Ihre Einstellung nicht.   I don't understand your attitude.

einstimmen to join in.

einstimmig unanimous.

einstudieren to study, rehearse.

einteilen to divide, plan, distribute.

Einteilung f. division, distribution, arrangement.

eintönig monotonous.

Eintönigkeit f. monotony.

Eintracht f. harmony, union, concord.

(sich) eintragen to register.

eintreffen to arrive, happen.

    Was ich befürchtete, ist eingetroffen.   What I was afraid of has happened.

EINTRETEN to go in, enter.

    Bitte, treten Sie ein!   Won't you come in, please!

    eintreten für   to intercede.

    eintreten in   to join.

EINTRITT entrance, entry.

    Eintritt verboten! No admission!

    Eintritt frei!   Admission free!

Eintrittsgeld n. admission fee.

Eintrittskarte f. ticket.

EINVERSTANDEN agreed.

    einverstanden sein   to agree.

Einverständnis n. agreement, consent.

Einwand m. objection, protest.

einwandfrei faultless, perfect.

Einwanderer m. immigrant.

einwandern to immigrate.

Einwanderung f. immigration.

einwechseln to change money.

einwenden to object.

einwilligen to consent.

Einwilligung f. consent.

Einwurf m. slit, slot.

Einzahl f. singular.

einzahlen to pay in.

Einzahlung f. payment.

EINZELN individual, particular, separate, single.

    Kann man jeden Band einzeln kaufen?   Can I buy each volume separately?

    jeder einzelne *each and every one.*
einziehen *to pull in, draw, move in.*
    Sie sind schon in ihre neue Wohnung
      eingezogen. *They have already
      moved into their new apartment.*
EINZIG *only, sole, unique.*
    einzig und allein *solely, entirely.*
    Er ist das einzige Kind. *He is the only
      child.*
Einzug *m. entry, entrance, moving in.*
EIS *n. ice, ice cream.*
    Eisbahn *f. rink.*
    Eisschrank *m. refrigerator.*
    eisig *icy.*
EISEN *n. iron.*
    zum alten Eisen werfen *to junk.*
Eisenbahn *f. railway.*
    Eisenbahnwagen *m. railway car.*
Eisenwaren *pl. hardware.*
eisern (er,-e,-es) *of iron, inflexible.*
    der eiserne Vorhang *the iron curtain.*
    Er hat einen eisernen Willen. *He has an
      iron will.*
eitel *vain, conceited, idle.*
Eitelkeit *f. vanity, conceit.*
Elefant *m. elephant.*
elegant *elegant.*
Eleganz *f. elegance.*
Elektriker *m. electrician.*
elektrisch *electric.*
elektrisieren *to electrify.*
Elektrizität *f. electricity.*
Element *n. element.*
elementar *elementary.*
Elend *n. misery, misfortune, distress.*
elend *miserable, ill; miserably.*
Elfenbein *n. ivory.*
ELFTE *eleventh.*
Ellenbogen *m. elbow.*
elterlich *parental.*
ELTERN *pl. parents.*
elternlos *orphaned.*
Emigrant *m. emigrant.*
Empfang *m. receipt, reception.*
EMPFANGEN *to receive, welcome.*
Empfänger *m. receiver, addressee.*
empfänglich *receptive.*
Empfangsnahme *f. receipt (paper).*
empfehlen *to recommend.*
empfinden *to experience, feel, perceive.*
empfindlich *sensitive; susceptible.*
Empfindlichkeit *f. sensitiveness.*
empören *to rouse, excite, shock.*
sich empören *to be furious; rebel.*
Empörung *f. rebellion.*
ENDE *n. end, result, conclusion, extremity.*
    am Ende *in the end, after all.*
    Ende gut, alles gut. *All is well that ends
      well.*

    letzten Endes *finally.*
    zu Ende führen *to finish.*
    zu Ende gehen *to come to an end.*
ENDEN *to end, finish, stop, die.*
Endergebnis *n. final result.*
endgültig *final, definite.*
endlos *endless.*
Endstation *f. terminus.*
Energie *f. energy.*
energisch *energetic, vigorous.*
ENG *narrow, tight, close, intimate.*
    engherzig *narrow-minded.*
engagieren *to engage.*
Engel *m. angel.*
Engländer *m. Englishman.*
Engländerin *f. Englishwoman.*
Englisch *n. English.*
    auf Englisch *in English.*
Enkel *m. 1. ankle. 2. grandson.*
Enkelkind *n. grandchild.*
Enkeltochter *f. (Enkelin) granddaughter.*
entbehren *to be without, lack, miss.*
entbehrlich *superfluous, spare.*
Entbehrung *f. privation, want.*
entdecken *to discover, find out, detect.*
Entdecker *m. discoverer.*
Entdeckung *f. discovery.*
Ente *f. duck.*
entehren *to dishonor.*
enteignen *to expropriate, dispossess.*
Enteignung *f. expropriation.*
enterben *to disinherit.*
entfalten *to unfold, develop, display.*
entfernen *to remove, take away, depart.*
    sich entfernen *to leave.*
entfernt *far off, far away, distant.*
Entfernung *f. distance.*
entfliehen *to run away, escape.*
entfremden *to estrange, alienate.*
Entfremdung *f. estrangement, alienation.*
entführen *to carry off, elope, to abduct.*
Entführung *f. abduction, elopement,
    kidnapping.*
entgegen *toward, opposed to, contrary to.*
entgegen arbeiten *to work against,
    counteract.*
entgegengehen *to go to meet, face.*
entgegengesetzt *opposite.*
entgegenhalten *to object, contrast.*
entgegenkommen *to come to meet.*
    auf halbem Weg entgegenkommen
      to meet halfway.
entgegenkommend *obliging, kind, helpful.*
entgegennehmen *to accept, receive.*
entgegensetzen (entgegenstellen) *to oppose,
    contrast.*
entgegentreten *to advance toward, oppose.*
entgegnen *to reply, answer.*
Entgegnung *f. reply.*

entgehen *to escape, elude.*
enthalten *to contain, hold, include.*
  enthalten sein   *to be included.*
  sich enthalten   *to refrain.*
entkommen *to escape.*
entladen *to unload, discharge.*
Entladung *f. discharge.*
entlassen *to dismiss.*
Entlassung *f. dismissal.*
entmutigen *to discourage, dishearten.*
entnehmen *to take from, gather,*
  understand.
enträtseln *to solve, decipher.*
entrüsten *to provoke, irritate, make angry.*
Entrüstung *f. anger, indignation.*
entsagen *to renounce, abandon,*
  dem Thron entsagen   *to abdicate.*
Entscheid *m. answer.*
entscheiden *to decide, make up one's mind.*
  Entscheiden Sie das. *You decide that.*
entscheidend *decisive, critical.*
Entscheidung *f. decision, judgment, sentence,*
  award.
entscheiden *decided, firm, resolute.*
Entschiedenheit *f. determination, certainty.*
entschliessen *to decide, make up one's mind.*
  Ich habe mich anders entschlossen. *I've*
  changed my mind.
Entschlossenheit *f. determination.*
Entschluss *m. resolution, decision.*
entschuldbar *excusable.*
ENTSCHULDIGEN *to excuse.*
  Entschuldigen Sie, bitte! *Please excuse*
  me!
  Ich bitte vielmals um Entschuldigung. *I am*
  awfully sorry.
  sich entschuldigen *to apologize.*
entschwinden *to vanish, disappear.*
entsetzen *to frighten, dismiss from, relieve.*
entsetzlich *terrible, dreadful.*
(sich) entsinnen *to remember, recollect,*
  recall.
entspannen *to relax.*
Entspannung *f. relaxation, rest, recreation.*
entstehen *to arise, originate.*
Entstehung *f. origin, formation.*
entstellen *to distort, misrepresent.*
enttäuschen *to disappoint.*
Enttäuschung *f. disappointment.*
ENTWEDER ... ODER *either ... or.*
entwerfen *to draw up, design.*
entwerten *to depreciate.*
ENTWICKELN *to develop, explain.*
  einen Film entwickeln *to develop a film*
  (photographic).
Entwicklung *f. development.*
Entwicklungsjahre *pl. adolescence.*
entwürdigen *to degrade, disgrace.*
Entwurf *m. sketch, draft.*

entziehen *to deprive of, take away from,*
  withdraw.
entzücken *to delight, charm, enchant.*
entzückend *charming, delightful.*
entzwei *in two, torn, broken.*
Episode *f. episode.*
Epoche *f. epoch, era.*
ER *he.*
  er selbst *himself.*
(sich) erarbeiten *to get through hard work.*
erbarmen *to feel pity, have mercy.*
erbärmlich *pitiful, miserable.*
erbarmungslos *merciless, pitiless.*
Erbe *m. heir.*
Erbe *n. heritage.*
erben *to inherit.*
Erbfolge *f. succession.*
(sich) erbieten *to offer, volunteer.*
erblassen *to turn pale.*
erblicken *to catch sight of, perceive.*
erbrechen *to break open.*
  sich erbrechen *to vomit.*
Erbschaft *f. inheritance, legacy.*
Erbse *f. pea.*
Erbstück *n. heirloom.*
Erbteil *n. portion of inheritance.*
Erdbeben *n. earthquake.*
Erdbeere *f. strawberry.*
Erdboden *m. ground, soil, earth.*
ERDE *f. earth, ground, soil.*
  auf der Erde *on earth.*
Erdgeschoss *n. ground floor.*
  zu ebener Erde *on the ground floor.*
Erdkunde *f. geography.*
erdolchen *to stab.*
Erdteil *m. continent.*
(sich) ereignen *to happen, occur, pass.*
  Wann hat sich das ereignet? *When did that*
  happen?
Ereignis *n. event, occurrence, incident.*
erfahren *to learn, experience.*
  Wo kann ich das erfahren? *Where can I get*
  this information?
Erfahrung *f. experience, information.*
  aus Erfahrung *by experience.*
  erfahrungsgemäss *from experience.*
erfinden *to find out, discover, invent.*
Erfinder *m. inventor.*
Erfindung *f. invention.*
Erfolg *m. success, result, outcome.*
erfolgen *to result, follow.*
erfolglos *unsuccessful, fruitless.*
erfolgreich *successful.*
erforderlich *necessary, requisite.*
erforschen *to explore, investigate.*
Erforschung *f. exploration, investigation.*
ERFREUEN *to give pleasure, gladden, be*
  pleased, rejoice.
sich erfreuen *to enjoy.*

erfreulich *delightful, gratifying, satisfactory.*

ERFREUT *glad, pleased, delighted.*

Sehr erfreut (*in social introductions*). *How do you do?* (*Delighted.*)

erfrieren *to die of cold, freeze to death.*

erfrischen *to refresh.*

Erfrischung *f. refreshment.*

ergänzen *to complete, restore.*

Ergänzung *f. completion, restoration.*

ergeben *to produce, yield, result in.*

ergeben *devoted.*

Ihr ergebener *yours faithfully.*

ergreifen *to seize, take hold of.*

ergreifend *moving, touching.*

Ergriffenheit *f. emotion.*

erhalten *to receive, obtain, preserve.*

Erhalter *m. supporter, preserver.*

erhältlich *obtainable.*

Erhaltungszustand *m. condition, state of preservation.*

erheben *to raise, lift up, collect.*

erhebend *elevating, impressive.*

erheblich *considerable.*

Erhebung *f. raising, elevation, revolt.*

erhitzen *to heat, warm.*

(sich) erholen *to recover, get better.*

Erholung *f. recovery, rest, recreation.*

ERINNERN *to remind.*

Erinneren Sie mich später daran. *Remind me about it later.*

sich erinnern an *to remember, recall.*

Ich kann mich nicht mehr daran erinnern. *I can't remember it any more.*

Erinnerung *f. remembrance, recollection, memory.*

Erinnerung wachrufen *to evoke memories.*

zur Erinnerung an *in memory of.*

erkälten *to chill.*

sich erkälten *to catch a cold.*

erkämpfen *to win by fighting.*

erkennbar *recognizable.*

ERKENNEN *to recognize, perceive, realize.*

zu erkennen geben *to show, indicate.*

erkenntlich *recognizable, grateful.*

Erkenntnis *f. knowledge, perception, understanding.*

ERKLÄREN *to explain, account for, declare.*

ERKLÄRUNG *f. explanation, interpretation, declaration.*

erkranken *to fall ill, be taken ill.*

Erkrankung *f. illness.*

(sich) erkundigen *to inquire, make inquiries.*

Erkundigung *f. inquiry.*

ERLAUBEN *to allow, permit, presume.*

Erlauben Sie, bitte! *Allow me, please!*

Erlaubnis *f. permission, leave, license.*

erleben *to experience.*

Erlebnis *n. event.*

erledigen *to carry through, wind up, dispatch.*

erledigt sein *to be dead tired.*

erleichtern *to facilitate, ease, relieve.*

Erleichterung *f. facilitation, relief.*

erlogen *false, untrue, fabricated.*

erlösen *to save, redeem, deliver.*

Erlösung *f. redemption, release, deliverance.*

ermächtigen *to empower, authorize.*

Ermahnung *f. exhortation, admonition.*

ermässigen *to reduce, abate.*

Ermässigte Preise *reduced prices.*

ermöglichen *to make possible, enable.*

ermorden *to murder, assassinate.*

Ermordung *f. murder, assassination.*

ermüden *to tire out, weary.*

Ermüdung *f. fatigue, weariness.*

ermutigen *to encourage.*

ernähren *to nourish, feed, support.*

Ernährung *f. nourishment, food, support, maintenance.*

ernennen *to nominate, appoint.*

Ernennung *f. nomination, appointment.*

erneuern *to renew, renovate, replace.*

Erneuerung *f. renewal, renovation.*

erniedrigen *to humiliate, depress.*

Erniedrigung *f. humiliation, degradation.*

ERNST *serious, severe, grave, seriously.*

Sie nimmt die Sache ernst. *She takes the matter seriously.*

ernst meinen *to be serious about something.*

Ernst *m. seriousness, earnestness, gravity.*

Ernst machen mit *to put into practice.*

Ernstfall *m. emergency.*

Ernte *f. harvest, crop.*

Erntearbeit *f. harvesting.*

ernten *to harvest.*

erobern *to conquer, capture.*

eröffnen *to open, start, disclose.*

erörtern *to discuss.*

Erörterung *f. discussion.*

erpressen *to extort, blackmail.*

Erpressung *f. extortion, blackmail.*

erraten *to guess.*

erregbar *excitable, irritable.*

erregen *to excite, stir up.*

Erregung *f. excitement, agitation.*

erreichbar *attainable, within reach.*

erreichen *to reach, attain, get.*

ERSATZ *m. substitute, equivalent, spare.*

Ersatzreifen *m. spare tire.*

Ersatzteil *m. spare part.*

erscheinen *to appear, come out.*

Erscheinung *f. appearance, figure, apparition.*

erschiessen *to shoot; to kill by shooting.*

Erschliessung *f. execution by gunfire.*

erschöpfen *to exhaust.*

erschöpfend *exhaustive.*

Erschöpfung *f. exhaustion.*

erschrecken *to frighten.*

erschrocken *frightened.*

erschüttern *to shake, upset, shock.*

  Die Nachricht hat uns erschüttert. *We were shocked by the news.*

erschweren *to make more difficult, aggravate.*

ersetzen *to replace, compensate, restore.*

ersparen *to save, economize.*

ERST *first, at first, only.*

  der erste beste *the first that comes.*

  eben erst *just now.*

  erst als *not till.*

  erst recht nicht *certainly not.*

  Erst die Arbeit, dann das Spiel. *Business before pleasure.*

Erstaufführung *f. opening night.*

erstaunen *to astonish.*

erstaunlich *astonishing.*

erstenmal (zum) *for the first time.*

erstens *firstly.*

erstgeboren *first-born.*

ersticken *to suffocate.*

erstmalig *first, for the first time.*

Ertrag *m. produce, yield, profit, returns.*

erträglich *bearable, endurable.*

ertränken *to drown.*

ertrinken *to be drowned.*

erübrigen *to save, spare.*

erwachen *to awake.*

erwachsen *to grow up.*

  die Erwachsenen *the grown-ups, adults.*

erwägen *to consider, weigh.*

erwähnen *to mention.*

ERWARTEN *to wait for, await, expect.*

Erwartung *f. expectation, hope.*

  in Erwartung Ihrer Antwort *looking forward to your reply.*

erwartungsvoll *expectant, full of hope.*

erweitern *to widen, expand.*

Erweiterung *f. widening, expansion.*

Erwerb *m. acquisition, gain, profit.*

erwerben *to acquire, gain.*

erwerbslos *unemployed, out of work.*

Erwerbslosenunterstützung *f. unemployment relief.*

ERZÄHLEN *to tell, relate, narrate.*

Erzählung *f. story, tale, narrative.*

erzeugen *to breed, produce, procreate.*

Erzeugnis *n. product.*

  Deutsches Erzeugnis. *Made in Germany.*

Erzeugung *f. procreation, production.*

erziehen *to raise, educate, train.*

erzieherisch *educational.*

Erziehung *f. education, upbringing.*

Erziehungswesen *n. educational system.*

erzwingen *to force, extort.*

ES *it.*

essbar *edible.*

ESSEN *to eat, dine.*

Essen *n. food, dinner, meal.*

Essenszeit *f. mealtime.*

Essig *m. vinegar.*

Esslöffel *m. tablespoon.*

Esswaren *pl. provisions, victuals.*

Esszimmer *n. dining room.*

Etage *f. floor.*

ETWA *nearly, about, by chance.*

ETWAS *some, something, any, anything, a bit, somewhat.*

EUCH *acc. and dat. of ihr (fam. form pl.) you, to you.*

EUER *poss. adj. (fam. pl. form) your.*

EUER(ER,-E,-ES) *poss. pron. (pl. fam. form) yours.*

eurerseits *on your part.*

euresgleichen *like you, of your kind.*

euretwegen *for your sake, on account of you.*

Europa *n. Europe.*

evakuieren *to evacuate.*

evangelisch *Protestant.*

Evangelium *n. Gospel.*

EWIG *eternal, forever, all the time.*

Ewigkeit *f. eternity.*

exakt *exact.*

Examen *n. examination.*

examinieren *to examine.*

Excellenz *f. Excellency.*

Exemplar *n. sample.*

exemplarisch *exemplary.*

Existenz *f. existence.*

existieren *to exist, live.*

Experiment *n. experiment.*

experimentieren *to experiment.*

Export *m. export.*

Exporteur *m. exporter.*

exportieren *to export.*

Extrablatt *n. special edition.*

Extrakt *m. extract.*

exzentrisch *eccentric.*

F

Fabel *f. fable, story, plot.*

fabelhaft *fabulous.*

Fabrik *f. factory, mill, plant.*

Fabrikanlage *f. plant.*

Fabrikant *m. manufacturer.*

Fabrikarbeiter *m. factory worker.*

Fabrikat *n. product (manufactured).*

Fabrikation *f. making.*

fabrizieren *to manufacture.*

Fach *n. compartment, shelf, drawer.*

  Was ist Ihr Fach? *What's your line?*

Fachkenntnis *f. technical knowledge.*

Fachmann m. expert, specialist.

Fackel f. torch.

Faden m. thread.

    an einem Faden hängen   to hang by a thread.

FÄHIG able.

    fähig sein to be able, capable.

Fähigkeit f. capability.

Fahne f. flag, banner.

Fahrbahn f. road, track.

fahrbar passable, navigable.

Fähre f. ferry.

FAHREN to drive, ride, go, travel.

    Fahren Sie rechts! Keep to the right!

    mit dem Schiff fahren   to sail.

    spazieren fahren   to go for a ride.

Fahrer m. driver.

Fahrgast m. passenger.

Fahrgeld n. fare.

Fahrkarte f. ticket (transportation).

Fahrkartenschalter m. ticket window.

fahrlässig careless, negligent.

Fahrlässigkeit f. carelessness, negligence.

Fahrplan m. timetable.

Fahrrad n. bicycle.

Fahrschein m. transportation ticket (bus).

Fahrstrasse f. highway.

Fahrstuhl m. lift, elevator.

    Fahrstuhlführer.   m. elevator boy, attendant.

FAHRT f. ride, journey, trip.

    Hin-und Rückfahrt   round trip.

    in voller Fahrt   at full speed.

    Was kostet die Fahrt, bitte? How much is the fare, please?

Fahrzeug n. vehicle.

Fakultät f. faculty.

FALL m. fall, drop, case, accident.

    auf jeden Fall, auf alle Fälle   in any case.

    auf keinen Fall!   On no account!

Falle f. trap.

FALLEN to fall.

    fallen lassen   to let fall, drop.

    im Krieg fallen   to be killed in action.

    in den Rücken fallen   to attack from behind.

    in Ohnmacht fallen   to faint.

    Das Fest fällt auf einen Sonntag.   The holiday falls on a Sunday.

    Das fällt nicht weiter ins Gewicht.   That is of no further consequence.

falls in case, in the event.

Fallschirm m. parachute.

FALSCH wrong, incorrect, false.

    Sie hat falsche Zähne. She has false teeth.

    Das Geld ist falsch.   The money is counterfeit.

    falsch verstehen   to misunderstand.

fälschen to falsify, forge.

Fälscher m. forger.

Falschheit f. falseness, falsehood.

Falschspieler m. cheat (at cards).

Fälschung f. forgery.

Falte f. pleat, fold, wrinkle.

falten to fold.

familiär familiar, intimate.

FAMILIE f. family.

Familienname m. last name.

Fanatiker m. fanatic.

Fang m. catch, capture, prey.

fangen to catch, capture.

FARBE f. color, paint.

    farbenblind   color blind.

färben to color, dye.

    sich die Haare färben   to dye one's hair.

farbig colored.

farblos colorless, pale.

Fasching m. carnival.

Fass n. barrel, cask.

    Das schlägt dem Fass den Boden aus.   That's the last straw.

Fassade f. front (of a building).

FASSEN to catch, seize, hold, apprehend, grasp, comprehend.

    Fassen Sie sich kurz! Make it short!

    ins Auge fassen   to consider, to keep in mind.

    einen Entschluss fassen   to make a decision.

Fassung f. setting, composure.

    aus der Fassung bringen   to upset, disconcert.

fast almost, nearly.

faul lazy, rotten, lazy.

    Das ist eine faule Sache. This is a shady business.

faulen to rot, be lazy.

Faulheit laziness.

Faulpelz m. idler, lazybones.

Faust f. fist.

    auf eigene Faust   on one own's responsibility.

    faustdick hinter den Ohren haben   to be sly.

Fausthandschuh m. mitten, boxing glove.

fax m. fax.

faxen to fax (colloq.).

FEBRUAR m. February.

FEDER f. pen, feather.

    Federhalter   m. penholder.

    federleicht   light as a feather.

fegen to sweep.

FEHLEN to miss, make a mistake, lack, be absent.

    es an nichts fehlen lassen   to spare no pains.

    Sie werden mir sehr fehlen. I'll miss you very much.

Was fehlt Ihnen? *What's the matter with you?*

FEHLER *m.* fault, defect, mistake, blunder.
   Das ist mein Fehler. *That is my fault.*

Fehlschlag *failure.*

Feier *f.* festival, celebration, ceremony, party.

Feierabend *time for the workday to end.*
   Wir machen jetzt Feierabend. *Let's call it a day.*

feierlich *solemn, festive, ceremonious.*

Feierlichkeit *f.* solemnity, ceremony.

feiern *to celebrate.*
   Sie feiern ihre goldene Hochzeit. *They are celebrating their golden anniversary.*

Feierstunde *f.* leisure hour, festive hour.

Feiertag *m.* holiday.

feige *cowardly.*

Feigheit *f.* cowardice.

feil *for sale, mercenary.*
   feil bieten *to offer for sale.*
   feil halten *to have for sale.*

FEIN *fine, thin, delicate, refined, distinguished, elegant.*

Feind *m.* enemy.

feindlich *hostile.*

feinfühlig *sensitive.*

Feingefühl *n.* sensitivity.

Feinheit *f.* fineness, grace, elegance, refinement, subtlety.

Feinschmecker *m.* gourmet.

FELD *n.* field, plain, ground, square.
   Schlachtfeld, *n. battlefield.*

Feldstecher *m. binoculars.*

Feldzug *m. campaign.*

Fell *n.* skin, hide, coat, fur (*animals*).
   Diese Katze hat ein schönes Fell. *This cat has a beautiful fur.*

Fels *m.* rock, cliff.
   felsenfest *firm as a rock.*

felsig *rocky, craggy.*

FENSTER *n.* window.

Fensterbank *f.* window-sill.

Fensterrahmen *m.* window-frame.

Fensterscheibe *f.* window pane.

Ferien *pl.* holidays, vacation.
   in die Ferien gehen *to go on vacation.*

FERN *far, distant, remote.*
   von fern *from afar, from a distance.*

Ferne *f.* distance.

ferner *further, furthermore, besides.*

Ferngespräch *n.* long-distance phone call.

Fernglas *n.* binoculars, field glass.

fernmündlich *by telephone, over the telephone.*
   Das Telegramm wurde mir fernmündlich durchgegeben. *The telegram was given to me over the phone.*

Fernsehen *n.* television.

Fernsprechbuch *n.* telephone directory.

Fernsprecher *m.* telephone.

Fernsprechstelle *f.* telephone booth.

FERTIG *ready, ready-made, finished, done.*
   fertigbringen *to bring about, accomplish.*
   sich fertig machen *to get ready.*
   Werden Sie damit fertig werden? *Will you be able to manage this by yourself?*

FEST *n.* festival, feast.

FEST *firm, hard, rigid, steady, solid, stiff, stable, firmly, stiffly, fully.*
   eine feste Stellung *a permanent post.*
   fester Schlaf *sound sleep.*

festbinden *to tie, bind, fasten.*

Festessen *n.* banquet.

festfahren *to get stuck.*

Festhalle *f.* banqueting hall.

festhalten *to hold tight.*
   sich festhalten an *to hold on to.*

festigen *to make firm.*

Festigkeit *f.* solidity, firmness.

festlegen *to fix, lay down.*

festlich *festive, solemn.*

Festlichkeit *f.* festivity.

festmachen *to fasten, attach, fix, settle.*

Festnahme *f.* arrest, seizure.

festsetzen *to fix, set, settle.*
   Der Preis wird auf hundert Mark festgesetzt. *The price has been fixed at one hundred marks.*

festsitzen *to be stuck, fit tightly.*

Festspiel *n.* festival performance.

Feststellung *f.* statement, determination, identification.

Festtag *m.* holiday, feast.

Festung *f.* fortress, stronghold.

FETT *fat, plump, fertile, rich, greasy.*

Fett *n.* grease, fat.

fettig *fatty, greasy.*

FEUCHT *damp, humid, muggy.*

FEUER *n.* fire, firing, bombardment.
   Feuer! *Fire!*
   Feuer fangen *to catch fire.*
   Feuer geben *to give a light.*

feuerfest *fireproof.*

Feuergefahr *f.* danger of fire.

feuergefährlich *inflammable.*

Feuerlöscher *m.* fire-extinguisher.

Feuerung *f.* fuel.

Feuerversicherung *f.* fire insurance.

Feuerwache *f.* fire station.

Feuerwerk *n.* firework.

Feuerzeug *n.* lighter.

Fieber *n.* fever, temperature.
   Fieber messen *to take one's temperature.*

fieberhaft *feverish.*

fiebern *to be feverish, have a temperature.*

Fieberthermometer *n.* clinical thermometer.

Fieberwahn *m. delirium.*

Figur *f. figure, form, shape.*

Filiale *f. branch.*

FILM *m. film, picture, movie.*

Filmaufnahme *f. shooting of film.*

filmen *to film.*

Filmstreifen *m. filmstrip.*

Filter *m. filter.*

filtern *to filter, strain.*

Filz *m. felt.*

filzig *stingy.*

Finanz *f. finance.*

Finanzamt *n. revenue office.*

finanziell *financial.*

finanzieren *to finance, support.*

FINDEN *to find, discover, meet with, think,*
    consider.

Finder *m. finder.*

findig *clever, ingenious.*

Findigkeit *f. cleverness.*

FINGER *m. finger.*

Fingerabdruck *m. fingerprint.*

Fingerfertigkeit *f. dexterity, skill.*

Fingerhut *m. thimble.*

Fingerspitze *f. tip of the finger.*

Fingerspitzengefühl *n. instinct; intuition.*

Fingerzeig *m. hint, tip.*

finster *dark, gloomy, obscure.*

Finte *f. feint, trick.*

Firma *f. firm, business.*

FISCH *m. fish.*

FISCHEN *to fish.*

Fischer *m. fisherman.*

Fischerei *f. fishing, fishery.*

Fischgräte *f. fish-bone.*

Fischhändler *m. fishmonger.*

FLACH *flat, plain, level.*

Fläche *f. surface, plain, area.*

Flachland *n. flat country, plain.*

Flagge *f. flag.*

flaggen *to deck with flags.*

Flamme *f. flame.*

FLASCHE *f. bottle.*

Flaschenbier *n. bottled beer.*

Flaschenöffner *m. bottle opener.*

flatterhaft *fickle, inconsistent.*

flattern *to flutter; wave.*

FLECK *m. place, spot, stain.*
    vom Fleck kommen *to get on, make*
    headway.

Flecken *m. spot, stain.*

fleckenlos *spotless.*

fleckig *spotted, stained.*

Flegel *m. boor, impertinent person.*

flegelhaft *rude, insolent.*

Flegeljahre *pl. teenage years.*

flehen *to implore, beseech.*

FLEISCH *n. flesh, meat, pulp.*

Fleischbrühe *f. meat broth.*

Fleischer *m. butcher.*

fleischig *fleshy, plump.*

fleischlos *meatless.*

FLEISS *m. diligence, industry.*
    mit Fleiss *on purpose.*

fleissig *diligent, industrious.*

flicken *to patch, mend, repair.*

Fliege *f. fly.*

FLIEGEN *to fly, rush.*
    in die Luft fliegen *to blow up.*

Flieger *m. airman, aviator, pilot.*

fliehen *to run away, flee.*

fliessen *to flow, run.*
    fliessendes Wasser *running water.*
    fliessend sprechen *to speak fluently.*

flink *quick, agile, nimble.*

Flinte *f. shotgun, rifle.*
    die Flinte in das Korn werfen *to give up.*

Flirt *m. flirtation.*

flirten *to flirt.*

Flitterwochen *pl. honeymoon.*

Floh *m. flea.*

Flöte *f. flute.*

flöten *to play the flute.*

flott *afloat, floating.*

Flotte *f. fleet, navy.*

Fluch *m. curse, imprecation.*

fluchen *to curse, swear.*

Flucht *f. flight, escape.*

flüchten *to flee, escape.*

flüchtig *careless, passing, superficial.*
    Er ist nur ein flüchtiger Bekannter. *He is*
    only a passing acquaintance.

Flüchtling *m. fugitive.*

FLUG *m. flight (aerial).*

Flugblatt *n. pamphlet.*

Fluggast *m. air passenger.*

Flughafen *m. airport.*

Flugplatz *m. airfield, airport.*

Flugzeug *n. airplane*

Flugzeugträger *m. aircraft carrier.*

Flur *f. field, meadow.*

Flur *m. hall, corridor.*

FLUSS *m. river.*

flüssig *liquid, fluid.*

Flüssigkeit *f. fluidity.*

Flusslauf *m. course of a river.*

flüstern *to whisper.*

Flut *f. tide, flood.*

fluten *to stream, flow.*

FOLGE *f. sequence, succession.*
    Folge leisten *to comply with.*

Folgeerscheinung *f. consequence, effect.*

FOLGEN *to follow, succeed, obey, mind.*
    daraus folgt *hence follows.*

folgendermassen *as follows.*

folgern *to infer, conclude, deduce.*

Folgerung *f. inference, conclusion, deduction.*

folglich *consequently.*

folgsam *obedient, docile.*
Folgsamkeit *f. obedience, docility.*
foltern *to torture.*
fordern *to demand, ask, claim, require.*
Forderung *f. demand, claim, challenge.*
Form *f. form, shape.*
Formalität *f. formality.*
Format *n. size, weight, importance.*
Formel *f. formula.*
formell *formal.*
formen *to form, shape.*
förmlich *formal, ceremonious, regular.*
Formlosigkeit *f. formlessness, shapelessness.*
Formular *n. form.*
formulieren *to formulate, define.*
formvollendet *perfect in form.*
forschen *to investigate, search.*
Forschung *f. inquiry, investigation.*
Förster *m. forester, gamekeeper.*
FORT *adv. and separable prefix (implies*
    movement away from speaker, or
    continuation). away, off, gone, on
    (going on).
  und so fort *and so forth.*
fortan *henceforth, from this time.*
Fortbildung *f. further study.*
fortfahren *to drive away, remove, continue.*
  Er ist gestern fortgefahren. *He left*
    yesterday.
fortführen *to lead away, go on, continue.*
fortgehen *to go away.*
fortgesetzt *continuous, incessant.*
fortschreiten *to advance, proceed, make*
    progress.
Fortschritt *m. progress.*
fortschrittlich *progressive.*
fortsetzen *to continue, carry on, pursue.*
Fortsetzung *f. continuation, pursuit.*
  Fortsetzung folgt *to be continued.*
Fracht *f. freight.*
Frachtdampfer *m. freighter.*
FRAGE *f. question, inquiry, problem.*
  das ist noch die Frage *that remains to be*
    seen.
  eine Frage stellen *to ask a question.*
  ohne Frage *undoubtedly.*
FRAGEN *to ask, inquire.*
  fragen nach *to ask for.*
  nichts danach fragen *not to care about*
    something.
  sich fragen *to wonder.*
  Es fragt sich, ob es der Mühe wert ist. *It*
    is a question whether it is worth the
    trouble.
Fragezeichen *n. question mark.*
fraglich *in question, questionable, doubtful.*
fraglos *unquestionable.*
Franzose, -n *n. Frenchman.*
Französin, -nen *f. Frenchwoman.*

französisch *French.*
FRAU *f. woman, wife, Mrs.*
  gnädige Frau *Madam.*
  Ihre Frau (Gemahlin) *your wife.*
Frauenarzt *m. gynecologist.*
FRÄULEIN *n. young lady, girl, Miss.*
fraulich *womanly.*
frech *impudent, insolent.*
Frechheit *f. impudence, insolence.*
FREI *free, vacant, open, liberal,*
    spontaneous, frank; freely, frankly, at
    ease.
  die freie Zeit *leisure, spare time.*
  Es ist mein freier Tag. *This is my day off.*
  Ist dieser Platz frei? *Is this seat taken?*
  unter freiem Himmel, im Freien *outside,*
    in the open air.
Freibillet *n. complimentary ticket.*
Freidenker *m. freethinker.*
freigeben *to set free, release, open (to the*
    public).
freigebig *liberal, generous.*
Freigebigkeit *f. liberality, generosity.*
Freigeist *m. freethinker.*
freihalten *to hold, treat.*
Freiheit *f. freedom.*
freilassen *to release, set free.*
Freilassung *f. release.*
Freimut *m. frankness, candor.*
freimütig *frank, candid.*
freisprechen *to acquit, absolve.*
Freispruch *m. acquittal.*
Freistelle *f. scholarship, free place.*
FREITAG *m. Friday.*
Freizeit *f. leisure time.*
freiwillig *voluntary, spontaneous.*
Freiwillige *m. volunteer.*
FREMD *strange, foreign, unknown, exotic.*
  fremdes Gut *other people's property.*
fremdartig *strange, odd.*
FREMDE *m. foreigner, tourist, foreign*
    country.
  in der Fremde (im Ausland) *abroad.*
Fremdenführer *m. tourist guide.*
Fremdenverkehr *m. tourist traffic.*
Fremdsprache *f. foreign language.*
Frendwort *n. foreign word.*
Fressen *n. animal food, feed.*
fressen *to eat (animals), feed.*
FREUDE *f. joy, delight, pleasure, cheer.*
  Freude haben an *to enjoy, delight in.*
  freudestrahlend *beaming with joy.*
freudelos *joyless, cheerless.*
freudig *joyful, cheerful.*
freuen *to please, delight.*
  sich freuen *to be pleased, rejoice.*
  Es freut mich sehr, Sie kennenzulernen.
    I am very glad to meet you.
  sich freuen auf *to look forward to.*

FREUND m. -in f. friend.
FREUNDLICH friendly, kind, obliging, pleasant.
Freundlichkeit f. friendliness.
Freundschaft f. friendship.
freundschaftlich friendly, serviceable.
FRIEDE m. peace.
Friedensbruch m. breach of peace.
Friedensvertrag m. peace treaty.
Friedhof m. churchyard, cemetery.
friedlich peaceful.
friedliebend peace-loving.
frieren to freeze, be cold, get cold.
  Die Füsse frieren mir. *My feet are freezing.*
  Mich friert (es). *I am cold.*
FRISCH fresh, bright, lively, new.
  frisch gestrichen *wet paint.*
  frische Eier *fresh eggs.*
  frische Wäsche *clean linen.*
FRISÖR m. barber, hairdresser.
Friseuse f. hairdresser (female).
frisieren to fix one's hair.
  sich frisieren lassen *to have one's hair done.*
Frisur f. hairdressing, hairdo.
froh glad, happy.
frohgemut cheerful.
FRÖHLICH merry, happy.
  Fröhliche Weihnachten! *Merry Christmas!*
Fröhlichkeit f. cheerfulness.
Frohsinn m. cheerfulness.
fromm pious, religious, godly.
Front f. front (military).
Frosch m. frog.
Frost m. frost, cold, chill.
frösteln to shiver, feel chilly.
FRUCHT f. fruit, crop, produce.
fruchtbar fruitful, fertile.
Fruchtbarkeit f. fruitfulness, fertility.
fruchtbringend fruit-bearing, productive, fertile.
fruchten to bear fruit, to have effect.
Fruchtsaft m. fruit juice.
FRÜH early in the morning.
  heute früh *this morning.*
  morgen früh *tomorrow morning.*
Frühe f. morning, dawn.
  in aller Frühe *very early.*
früher earlier, sooner, former.
  früher oder später *sooner or later.*
frühestens at the earliest.
FRÜHLING m. Spring.
FRÜHSTÜCK n. breakfast.
frühstücken to breakfast.
Fuchs m. fox.
fügen to join, put together, add, submit.
fügsam yielding, submissive.
Fügung f. dispensation, coincidence.

fühlbar tangible, perceptible.
FÜHLEN to feel, sense, be sensitive to.
  sich gut fühlen *to feel well.*
FÜHREN to lead, conduct, direct, handle, carry.
  ein Gespräch führen *to have a conversation.*
  Wer führt? *Who is ahead?*
  Er führt immer das grosse Wort. *He is always bragging.*
  Er führt etwas im Schilde. *He is up to something.*
Führer m. leader, driver, pilot, guidebook.
Führerschein m. driving license.
Führung f. leadership, command, direction, management, behavior, conduct.
FÜLLEN to fill, stuff.
  sich füllen *to fill up.*
  Das Stadion füllt sich langsam. *The stadium is slowly filling up.*
Fund m. finding.
Fundament n. foundation.
fundieren to lay a foundation.
FÜNF five.
FÜNFTE fifth.
FÜNFZEHN fifteen.
FÜNFZEHNTE fifteenth.
FÜNFZIG fifty.
FÜNFZIGSTE fiftieth.
Funk m. wireless, radio (communications medium).
Funke m. spark.
funkeln to sparkle.
Funker m. telegraphist.
FÜR prep. (acc.) for, by, to.
  ein für allemal *once for all.*
  Er geht Schritt für Schritt vorwärts. *He walks forward step by step.*
  Ich arbeite für mich. *I work for myself.*
  Ich habe Karten für das Theater. *I have tickets for the theater.*
  Stück für Stück *piece by piece.*
  Tag für Tag *day by day*
  Was für ein? *what kind of?*
FURCHT f. fear, fright, dread, anxiety.
furchtbar awful, horrible, terrible: awfully, terribly.
fürchten to fear.
fürchterlich terrible, horrible, frightful.
furchtlos fearless, intrepid.
Furchtlosigkeit f. fearlessness, intrepidity.
furchtsam timid, nervous.
Furchtsamkeit f. timidity.
Fürst m. (-in f.) prince(ss).
Fürwort n. pronoun.
FUSS m. foot, base, bottom.
  auf eigenen Füssen stehen *to be independent.*
  auf freien Fuss setzen *to set at liberty.*

Er lebt auf grossem Fuss. *He is living in grand style.*

Ich stehe mit ihm auf gutem Fuss. *I am on good terms with him.*

zu Fuss *on foot.*

Fussball *m. soccer.*

Fussbank *f. footstool.*

Fussgänger *m. pedestrian.*

nor für Fussgänger *for pedestrians only.*

Fusspur *f. footprint.*

Fusstapfe *f. footstep.*

Fusstritt *m. kick.*

Futter *n.* 1. *food, feed (animals).* 2. *sheath, lining.*

Futterseide *f. silk for lining.*

Gabe *f. present, gift, talent.*

Gabel *f. fork.*

gähnen *to yawn, gape.*

GANG *m. walk, stroll, walk, aisle, course, gear, hall, errand.*

in Gang setzen *to start, set.*

in vollem Gang *in full swing.*

die Sache nimmt ihren Gang *the matter takes/runs its course.*

Gans *f. goose.*

Gänseblümchen *n. daisy.*

ganz *all, whole, entire, complete; in full, wholly, entirely, thoroughly, altogether.*

die ganze Stadt *the whole town.*

ganz anders *quite different.*

ganz besonders *more especially.*

ganz gleich *all the same, no matter.*

ganz und gar *wholly.*

ganz und gar nicht *not at all.*

im ganzen *on the whole.*

im grossen und ganzen *on the whole.*

von ganzem Herzen *with all my heart.*

gar *done, cooked through; fully, very, quite, even.*

gar kein . . . *no . . . whatsoever.*

gar nicht *not at all.*

gar nichts *nothing at all.*

Garage *f. garage.*

Garderobe *f. wardrobe, cloakroom.*

Garderobenmarke *f. check (cloakroom).*

Garderobennummer *f. check (cloakroom).*

Gardine *f. curtain*

Garn *n. yarn, thread.*

garnieren *to trim, garnish.*

Garnitur *f. trimming, outfit.*

garstig *nasty, ugly.*

GARTEN *m. garden.*

Gartenhaus *n. summer house.*

Gartenlaube *f. garden house (pavilion).*

Gärtner *m. gardener.*

Gas *n. gas.*

Gashahn *m. gas tap.*

Gasleitung *f. gas pipes, gas supply.*

Gasse *f. narrow street, alley.*

GAST *m. visitor, guest.*

gastfreundich *hospitable.*

Gastfreundschaft *f. hospitality.*

Gastgeber *m. host*

Gasthaus *n. inn, hotel.*

Gasthof *m. inn, hotel.*

gastlich *hospitable.*

Gastspiel *n. guest performance.*

Gastwirt *m. innkeeper.*

Gasuhr *f. gas meter.*

Gatte *m. husband.*

Gattin *f. wife.*

Gaumen *m. palate.*

Geächtete *m. outlaw.*

Gebäck *n. pastry, cookie.*

Gebärde *f. gesture, movement.*

(sich) gebärden *to behave, conduct oneself.*

Gebäude *n. building, structure, edifice.*

GEBEN *to give, present, produce, yield.*

Das gibt mir zu denken. *That makes me wonder.*

es gibt *there is, there are*

Was gibt es zum Mittagessen? *What are they having for lunch?*

gegeben werden *to play (in theater).*

Was wird heute im Theater gegeben? *What's playing tonight at the theater?*

Gebet *n. prayer.*

Gebiet *n. district, territory, area, field.*

gebieten *to order, command.*

Gebirge *n. mountain chain.*

gebirgig *mountainous.*

Gebiss *n. set of teeth, denture.*

Gebot *n. order, command, law.*

Gebrauch *m. use, customs, rites.*

gebrauchen *to use, make use of.*

gebräuchlich *usual, in use.*

Gebühr *f. duty, tax, fee, rate.*

gebühren *to be due.*

sich gebühren *to be proper.*

gebührenfrei *tax-free*

gebührenpflichtig *taxable.*

gebührlich *suitable, proper.*

GEBURT *f. birth, origin, extraction.*

Geburtshelferin *f. midwife.*

Geburtjahr *n. year of birth.*

Geburtsschein *m. birth certificate.*

Geburtstag *m. birthday.*

Gedächtnis *n. memory, remembrance.*

aus dem Gedächtnis *from memory.*

GEDANKE *m. thought, idea.*

sich Gedanken machen *to worry.*

Wie kommen Sie auf den

Gedanken? *What gives you that idea?*
gedankenlos *thoughtless.*
Gedankenlosigkeit *f. thoughtlessness.*
Gedeck *n. cover (at table), set of table linens.*
gedeihen *to grow, develop, succeed.*
gedenken *to intend, think of*
Gedenkfeier *f. commemoration.*
Gedicht *n. poem.*
Gedränge *n. crowd, throng.*
gedruckt *printed.*
Geduld *f. patience, endurance.*
(sich) gedulden *to have patience.*
geduldig *patient.*
Gefahr *f. danger, risk.*
gefährden *to endanger, expose to danger.*
gefährlich *dangerous, perilous.*
gefahrlos *safe, secure, without danger.*
gefahrvoll *dangerous, perilous.*
GEFALLEN *to please, suit.*
　Das gefällt mir. *I like that.*
　sich gefallen lassen *to submit, put up with.*
gefällig *pleasant, agreeable.*
Gefangene *m. prisoner, captive.*
　Kriegsgefangene *m. prisoner of war.*
Gefangenschaft *f. captivity, confinement.*
Gefangensetzung *f. capture, arrest.*
Gefängnis *n. prison, jail.*
Gefäss *n. container, receptacle.*
gefasst *composed, collected, calm.*
　sich gefasstmachen auf *to be prepared for.*
Geflügel *n. birds, poultry, fowl.*
Geflüster *n. whispering.*
Gefolge *n. suite, entourage.*
GEFÜHL *n. feeling, sentiment, sense, emotion, sensation.*
gefühllos *numb, heartless.*
Gefühllosigkeit *f. numbness, heartlessness.*
gefühlvoll *tender, sentimental.*
GEGEN *prep. (acc.) against, about, around, toward, for, to, compared with.*
　Die Soldaten kämpfen gegen den Feind. *The soldiers fight against the enemy.*
　Er schwamm gegen den Strom. *He swam against the current.*
　Es ist gegen neun Uhr. *It is about nine o'clock.*
　gegen voriges Jahr *compared with last year.*
　gegeneinander *against each other.*
　Waren gegen Geld tauschen *to exchange goods for money.*
GEGEND *f. country, region, district.*
Gegenseite *f. opposite side.*
gegenseitig *reciprocal, mutual.*

Gegenstand *m. subject.*
gegenstandlos *pointless.*
Gegenteil *n. contrary, opposite.*
　im Gegenteil *on the contrary.*
gegenüber *opposite.*
Gegenwart *f. present, presence.*
gegenwärtig *present.*
Gegenwert *m. equivalent.*
Gegner *m. opponent, adversary, enemy.*
Gehalt *m. content.*
Gehalt *n. salary.*
gehaltlos *worthless.*
gehaltvoll *valuable, substantial.*
gehässig *spiteful, malicious.*
Gehässigkeit *f. spite, malice.*
geheim *conceal, hidden, clandestine.*
GEHEIMNIS *n. secret, mystery.*
geheimnisvoll *mysterious.*
Geheimpolizei *f. secret police.*
GEHEN *to go, walk, pass, move, leave; run, work (machinery).*
　an die Arbeit gehen *to go to work.*
　Das geht nicht. *That won't do.*
　Es geht mir gut, danke. *I am fine, thank you.*
　Es geht nichts über gutes Bier. *There is nothing like good beer.*
　Es geht um Tod und Leben. *It is a matter of life and death.*
　gehen auf (nach) *to face on, look out on.*
　Das Fenster geht auf den Hof. *The window faces the courtyard.*
　gehen lassen *to let go, give up.*
　sich gehen lassen *to let oneself go.*
　Wie geht es Ihnen? *How are you?*
Gehilfe *m. assistant, clerk, helper.*
Gehirn *n. brain.*
GEHÖR *n. hearing; ear (mus.).*
gehorchen *to obey.*
GEHÖREN *to belong to, be owned by.*
　Es gehört ihm. *It belongs to him.*
　Das gehört nicht zur Sache. *That's beside the point.*
　Dazu gehört Zeit. *That takes time.*
gehorsam *obedient.*
Geige *f. violin.*
geigen *to play the violin.*
GEIST *m. spirit, genius, mind.*
geistesabwesend *absent-minded.*
Geistesgegenwart *f. presence of mind.*
geisteskrank *of unsound mind, insane.*
geistesschwach *feeble-minded.*
geistig *spiritual, intellectual, mental.*
geistlich *religious, spiritual.*
geistlos *spiritless, lifeless, dull.*
geistreich *ingenious, spiritual, witty.*
Geiz *m. stinginess, avarice.*
geizig *avaricious, stingy.*
Gelände *n. country, countryside.*

Geländer *n. railing, banister.*

gelangen *to reach, arrive, attain to.*

gelassen *calm, collected.*

Gelassenheit *f. calmness, composure.*

geläufig *fluent, familiar, current.*

gelaunt *disposed.*

    gut gelaunt   *in good humour.*

    schlecht gelaunt   *cross, bad-tempered.*

Geläute *n. chime, ringing of bells.*

GELB *yellow.*

gelblich *yellowish.*

Gelbsucht *f. jaundice.*

GELD *n. money.*

    Bargeld   *n. cash.*

    Kleingeld   *n. change.*

Geldentwertung *f. inflation, devaluation.*

Geldschein *m. paper money, bill.*

Geldschrank *m. safe.*

Geldstück *n. coin.*

Geldtasche *f. purse.*

Gelee *m. jelly.*

gelegen *1. situated. 2. convenient.*

    Er kam gerade zu gelegener Zeit.   *He came just at the right time.*

Gelegenheit *f. opportunity, occasion, chance.*

Gelegenheitskauf *m. bargain.*

gelegentlich *occasional, accidental.*

gelehrig *docile, teachable.*

Gelehrsamkeit *f. learning, erudition.*

gelehrt *learned, scholarly, erudite.*

Gelehrte *m. scholar, savant.*

Geleise *n. track.*

Geleit *n. escort, convoy.*

geleiten *to accompany, escort, convoy.*

Geleitwort *n. motto.*

Gelenk *n. joint, articulation.*

Geliebte *m. & f. lover, mistress, beloved.*

gelingen *to succeed, manage.*

gelten *to matter, mean, be worth, have influence, be valid.*

    Das gilt nicht.   *That does not count.*

    gelten als   *to be considered as.*

Geltungsdauer *f. period of validity.*

gemächlich *comfortable.*

Gemahl *m. husband.*

Gemahlin *f. wife.*

gemäss *suitable.*

GEMEIN *ordinary, general, low, vulgar, common.*

    Es war gemein von ihm.   *It was mean of him.*

    gemeinhaben mit   *to have in common with.*

Gemeinde *f. community, congregation, parish, municipality.*

Gemeinheit *f. vulgarity, baseness, bad trick.*

gemeinnützig *beneficial to the community.*

Gemeinschaft *f. community.*

    in Gemeinschaft mit   *together with.*

GEMÜSE *n. vegetables.*

Gemüsehändler *m. greengrocer.*

Gemüt *n. soul, mind, heart, feelings.*

Gemütlich *good-natured, cozy.*

Gemütlichkeit *f. comfort, coziness.*

GENAU *close, tight, exact, accurate.*

    Er nimmt es sehr genau.   *He. is very particular.*

    Nehmen Sie es nicht zu genau!   *Don't take it too literally!*

Genauigkeit *f. exactness, accuracy, precision.*

General *m. general.*

genesen *to recover, get better.*

Genesung. *f. recovery, convalescence.*

genial *full of genius.*

Genialität *f. genius, originality.*

Genick *n. nape (of neck).*

Genie *n. genius.*

genieren *to trouble, inconvenience, bother.*

geniessbar *eatable, drinkable.*

geniessen *to eat, enjoy, have the benefit of.*

Genosse *m. companion, colleague.*

GENUG *sufficient, enough.*

Genugtuung *f. satisfaction, compensation.*

Geographie *f. geography.*

GEPÄCK *n. luggage, baggage.*

Gepäckabfertigung *f. luggage dispatch office.*

Gepäckannahme *m. luggage counter.*

Gepäckaufbewahrung *f. left luggage office.*

Gepäckausgabe *f. luggage office.*

Gepäckschein *m. receipt for registered baggage.*

Gepäckstück *n. bag, parcel.*

Gepäckträger *m. porter.*

GERADE *direct, upright, straight, honest; just, exactly, directly.*

    nun gerade   *now move than ever.*

    geradeus   *straight on.*

Gerät *n. tool, implement, utensil.*

geraten *to succeed, turn out well.*

    sich in die Harre geraten   *to come to blows.*

    Ihm gerät nichts.   *He never succeeds in anything.*

    in Brand geraten   *to catch fire.*

geräumig *roomy, spacious.*

Geräusch *n. noise.*

geräuschvoll *noisy.*

GERECHT *just, fair, equitable.*

Gerechtigkeit *f. justice, righteousness, fairness.*

Gerede *n. talk, rumor, gossip.*

Gereiztheit *f. irritation.*

Gericht *n. dish, course, judgment.*

    Jüngstes Gericht   *Last Judgment.*

    vor Gericht   *in court.*

Gerichtshof *m. court of law.*

gering *small, little, unimportant.*

   nicht im geringsten *not in the least.*

   geringfügig *unimportant.*

Gerippe *n. skeleton.*

GERN *gladly, with pleasure, readily, easily.*

   gern essen *to like (to eat something).*

   Gern geschehen! *Don't mention it!*

   gern haben *to like (a person or object).*

   gern tun *(or any verb of action) to like (to do something).*

   Ich esse gern Eisbein mit Sauerkraut. *I like pig's knuckles with sauerkraut.*

   Sie hat ihn gern. *She likes him.*

   Tanzen Sie gern? *Do you like to dance?*

Geruch *m. smell, scent, odor.*

geruchlos *odorless.*

Gerücht *n. rumor, report.*

Gerüst *n. scaffold, stage.*

GESANG *m. song, singing.*

   Gesanglehrer *m. singing teacher.*

GESCHÄFT *n. business, transaction, commerce, commerical firm, store.*

geschäftlich *commercial.*

Geschäftsführer *m. manager.*

Geschäftsmann *m. business man.*

geschäftsmässig *commercial.*

Geschäftsviertel *n. shopping district.*

Geschäftszeit *f. office hours;* **Sprechzeit** *f. doctor's office hours.*

GESCHEHEN *to happen, occur, be done.*

   Es geschieht ihm recht. *It serves him right.*

   Es ist um mich geschehen. *I am done for.*

   geschehen lassen *to allow, permit, let happen.*

gescheit *clever, intelligent, sensible.*

Geschenk *n. present, gift.*

GESCHICHTE *f. story, history.*

Geschichtsbuch *n. history book.*

Geschick *n. fate, destiny.*

geschickt *clever, capable.*

Geschirr *n. crockery, dishes, china, tableware.*

GESCHLECHT *n. sex, gender, kind, species, race, family, stock.*

geschlechtlich *sexual.*

GESCHMACK *m. taste, flavor.*

   Geschmack finden an *to like.*

geschmacklos *insipid, in bad taste.*

Geschmacklosigkeit *f. bad taste.*

geschmackvoll *tasteful.*

Geschrei *n. shouting, screaming, clamor.*

Geschwätz *n. idle talk.*

geschwätzig *talkative, verbose.*

geschwind *quick, fast, swift, prompt, speedy.*

Geschwindigkeit *f. quickness, rapidity.*

   Geschwindigkeitsgrenze 60 km. *Speed limit 60 kilometers.*

Geschwister *pl. brother(s) and sister(s).*

Geselle *m. fellow, companion, journeyman.*

Geselligkeit *f. sociability, social life.*

GESELLSCHAFT *f. society, association, company.*

   (jemanden) Gesellschaft leisten *to keep (someone) company.*

   in Gesellschaft *socially.*

Gesellschafter *m. partner.*

Gesellschaftsanzug *m. evening clothes.*

Gesellschaftskleidung *f. evening dress.*

   Gesellschaftskleidung erwünscht. *Evening dress requested.*

Gesellschaftsspiel *n. party game*

Gesetz *n. law, statute.*

Gesetzbuch *n. code*

gesetzlich *legal, lawful.*

gesetzwidrig *unlawful, illegal.*

GESICHT *n. vision, sight, hallucination, appearance, face.*

   Das steht Ihnen gut (zu Gesicht). *It is very becoming to you.*

   Gesichter schneiden *to make faces*

   Sie lachte übers ganze Gesicht. *She was all smiles.*

Gesichtszug *m. feature.*

Gesinnung *f. mind, way of thinking.*

gesinnungslos *unprincipled.*

gesinnungstreu *loyal*

Gesinnugswechsel *m. change of opinion.*

gesittet *well-mannered.*

gespannt *stretched, strained.*

Gespenst *n. ghost.*

gespenstig *ghostly*

Gespött *n. mockery, derision.*

GESPRÄCH *n talk, conversation, discourse.*

gesprächig *talkative.*

Gesprächsstoff *m. topic of conversation.*

Gestalt *f. form, figure, shape, build, frame, manner, fashion.*

gestalten *to form.*

Geständnis *n. confession.*

   ein Geständnis ablegen über *to make a confession.*

gestehen *to confess, admit.*

Gesträuch *n. shrubs, bushes, shrubbery.*

Gesuch *n. application, petition, request.*

GESUND *healthy, well, sound, natural.*

   gesunder Menschenverstand *common sense*

Gesundheit *f. health*

   Gesundheit! *God bless you!*

gesundheitlich *hygienic, sanitary.*

gesundheitshalber *for the sake of health.*

Getränk *n. drink, beverage.*

Getreide *n. grain.*

Getreidespeicher *m. granary.*

Getümmel *n. bustle, tumult.*

Gewächs *n. plant, growth, produce.*

gewachsen *equal to*

Er ist der Arbeit gewachsen. *He is equal to the task.*

Er ist seinem Gegner gewachsen. *He is a match for his opponent.*

Gewächshaus *n. conservatory (greenhouse).*

gewagt *risky.*

Gewähr *f. security, surety.*

gewähren *to grant.*

jemanden gewähren lassen *to let a person do as he pleases.*

GEWALT *f. power, authority, force. violence.*

in der Gewalt haben *to have command of, master.*

mit aller Gewalt *with all one's might.*

sich in der Gewalt haben *to have self-control.*

Gewaltherrschaft *f. despotism.*

gewaltsam *violent.*

gewalttätig *brutal, violent.*

gewandt *agile, skillful, clever.*

gewärtig *expecting, expectant.*

Gewebe *n. weaving, web, tissue, fabric.*

Gewehr *n. rifle, weapon.*

Gewerbe *n. trade, business, profession.*

Gewerbeschein *m. trade license.*

Gewerbeschule *f. trade, technical school.*

gewerbsmässig *professional.*

Gewicht *n. weight.*

ins Gewicht fallen *to weigh with.*

gewichtig *weighty, important.*

Gewinn *m. winning.*

Gewinnanteil *m. dividend.*

gewinnbringend *profitable, lucrative.*

GEWINNEN *to gain, earn, win, produce, extract.*

es über sich gewinnen *to bring oneself to.*

Gewinner *m. winner.*

gewinnsüchtig *greedy (for victory).*

Gewirr *n. confusion, mess*

GEWISS *certain, sure, fixed; certainly, indeed, of course, no doubt.*

Gewiss! *Surely!*

In gewissem Sinne hat er recht. *In a sense he is right.*

gewissenlos *unscrupulous.*

gewissermassen *to some extent, so to speak, as it were.*

Gewissheit *f. certainty.*

Gewitter *n. thunderstorm.*

gewittern *to thunder.*

Gewitterregen *m. deluge.*

GEWÖHNEN *to accustom.*

sich an etwas gewöhnen *to get used to something.*

Gewohnheit *f. habit.*

gewöhnlich *usual, ordinary, common.*

gewöhnt *accustomed.*

Gewölbe *n. vault.*

Gewühl *n. turmoil, crowd.*

Gewürz *n. spice, seasoning, condiment.*

gewürzig *spiced.*

geziert *affected.*

giessen *to pour, water, spill.*

Gift *n. poison.*

giftig *poisonous, venomous.*

Gipfel *m. summit, peak, top.*

Gipfelpunkt *m. limit.*

Giraffe *f. giraffe.*

Gitter *n. railing, fence, grating.*

Gianz *m. brightness, glamour.*

glänzen *to shine, glitter, gleam.*

glänzend *shining, lustrous.*

Glanzleistung *f. (top) record, achievement.*

glanzvoll *brilliant, splendid, glorious.*

GLAS *n. glass, jar, pitcher.*

gläsern *of glass, vitreous.*

GLATT *even, smooth, slippery, flat; smoothly, slippery.*

Glatteis *n. slippery ice.*

Glauben *m. faith, confidence, trust, belief.*

GLAUBEN *to believe, trust, think, suppose.*

Sie können ihm aufs Wort glauben. *You can take his word for it.*

glaubhaft *credible, likely, probable.*

gläubig *believing, faithful.*

gläublich *credible, likely.*

glaubwürdig *credible, reliable, authentic.*

Glaubwürdigkeit *f. credibility, authenticity.*

GLEICH *same, similar, alike, even, level, direct, equal, like, equivalent; equally, just, at once, immediately.*

es einem gleich tun *to rival a person.*

Es ist mir gleich. *It is all the same to me.*

gleich darauf *immediately afterwards.*

Gleich und gleich gesellt sich gern. *Birds of a feather flock together.*

gleichberechtigt *entitled to the same rights.*

GLEICHEN *to be equal, resemble.*

gleichfalls *likewise.*

gleichförmig *uniform.*

gleichgesinnt *congenial.*

Gleichgewicht *n. equilibrium, balance, poise.*

gleichgültig *indifferent, unconcerned.*

Gleichgültigkeit *f. indifference.*

Gleichheit *f. equality, identity, similarity.*

gleichmässig *proportional.*

Gleichstrom *m. direct current.*

gleichviel *no matter, just the same.*

gleichwertig *equivalent.*

gleichzeitig *simultaneous.*

Gletscher *m. glacier.*

Glied *n. limb, member.*

gliedern *to articulate, arrange, classify.*

glitzern *to glitter, glisten, twinkle.*

Globus *m. globe.*

Glocke *f. bell, clock.*

Glockenspiel n. chime.

Glockenturm m. steeple.

GLÜCK n. fortune, good luck, prosperity.

etwas auf gut Glück tun to take a chance on something.

Glück haben to be lucky.

Glück im Spiel, Unglück in der Liebe. Lucky at cards, unlucky in love.

Glück wünschen to congratulate.

Viel Glück! Good luck! Many happy returns!

zu meinem Glück fortunately.

glücken to succeed, be lucky.

GLÜCKLICH fortunate.

Glückliche Reise! Have a pleasant trip!

glücklicherweise fortunately.

Glücksfall m. chance.

Glücksspeil n. game of chance.

Glückwunsch m. congratulations, good wishes.

Glühbirne f. electric bulb.

glühen to glow.

glühend glowing, fervent.

Glühwurm m. glowworm.

Glut f. glow, heat.

Gnade f. favor, mercy.

auf Gnade und Ungnade at discretion.

Gnadengesuch n. petition for clemency.

GNÄDIG merciful, gracious.

gnädige Frau Madam.

GOLD n. gold.

golden gold, of gold, golden.

Goldgrube f. gold mine.

goldig shining like gold.

jedes Wort auf die Goldwaage legen to weigh one's words carefully.

Golf m. golf.

gönnen to wish well, allow, permit; not to begrudge.

Gotik f. Gothic.

GOTT m. God.

Gott sei Dank! Thank God!

Um Gottes willen! For Heaven's sake!

Gott behüte! God forbid!

in Gottes Name! for heaven's sake!

Götterdämmerung f. twilight of the Gods.

Gottesdienst m. public worship, service (church).

göttlich divine, godlike.

Grab n. tomb, grave.

Grabstein m. tombstone.

Grad m. degree.

Graf m. count.

Gräfin f. countess.

Gram m. sorrow, grief.

grämen to grieve, worry.

Gramm n. gram. (1,000 grams equal 1 kilogram.)

Grammatik f. grammar.

GRAS n. grass.

grässlich terrible, horrible.

Gräte f. fish-bone.

Gratulant m. congratulator, well-wisher.

gratulieren to congratulate.

GRAU gray.

grauen to be afraid, shudder, dread.

Es graut mir vor. I am afraid.

grauenhaft horrible, ghastly.

grauenvoll awful, dreadful.

Grauhaar n. gray hair.

grausam cruel.

Grausamkeit f. cruelty.

grausig gruesome, ghastly.

Grazie f. grace, charm.

graziös gracious.

greifbar tangible, palpable.

greifen to seize, grasp, catch, touch, strike.

ineinander greifen to interlock.

Greis m. old man.

Greisenalter n. old age.

Greisin f. old woman.

Grenze f. frontier, boundary, limit.

grenzenlos boundless, infinite.

Grenzverkehr m. traffic at or across the frontier, frontier trading.

Griff m. grip, grasp, hold, catch.

Grimm m. anger, rage.

grimmlg furious, grim.

Grippe f. grippe.

grob thick, rough, coarse, clumsy.

Grobheit f. coarseness, rudeness.

Groll m. resentment, anger.

grollen to be resentful, angry.

GROSS big, tall, large, great, huge, grand.

die grossen Ferien the summer vacation.

gross tun to boast.

gross ziehen to bring up.

grosse Kinder grown-up children.

grosser Buchstabe capital letter.

im grossen und ganzen on the whole.

das grosse Publikum the general public.

eine grosse Zahl von a great many (of).

gross auftreten to assume airs.

grossartig great, grand.

GRÖSSE f. size, dimension, largeness, tallness, celebrity, star.

Grosseltern pl. grandparents.

Grosshandel m. wholesale trade.

grossjährig of age.

Grossmacht f. great power.

grossmütig generous, magnanimous.

Grossmutter f. grandmother.

grosspurig arrogant.

Grosstadt f. metropolis

Grosstädter m. inhabitant of a large town.

grösstenteils for the most part, largely.

Grossvater m. grandfather.

grosszügig *generous, on a large scale.*

Grün *n. green, verdure.*

GRÜN *green (adj.).*
  im Grünen *in country surroundings.*
  vom grünen Tisch aus *only in theory.*

GRUND *m. ground, bottom, cause, reason.*
  im Grunde *after all.*
  auf den Grund gehen *to investigate.*
  Aus welchem Grund? *For what reason?*

Grundbesitz *m. real estate.*

gründen *to found, establish, promote.*

Grundgedanke *m. fundamental idea.*

Grundlage *f. foundation.*

grundlegend *fundamental.*

gründlich *thorough, solid, profound.*

Gründlichkeit *f. thoroughness, solidity.*

Grundsatz *m. principle.*

grundsätzlich *fundamental.*

Grundstück *n. piece of land, lot.*

Gründung *f. foundation, establishment.*

grünen *to grow green, sprout.*

Gruppe *f. group.*

GRUSS *m. greeting; salute (military).*

GRÜSSEN *to greet, salute.*
  grüssen lassen *to send one's regards.*

gültig *valid, available, good, current.*

Gültigkeit *f. validity; currency (monetary).*

Gummi *m. rubber, eraser.*

Gummiabsatz *m. rubber heel.*

Gummiband *n. rubber band.*

Gummischuh *m. galosh.*

Gummiwaren *pl. rubber goods.*

Gunst *f. kindness, favor.*
  zu Gunsten von *in favor of.*

günstig *kind, favorable.*

Gurke *f. cucumber.*

Gürtel *m. belt, girdle.*

Guss *m. torrent, downpour.*

Gut *n. property, good, estate, farm.*

GUT *good, pleasant, kind, full; well, pleasantly, kindly*
  es gut haben *to be well off.*
  Gute Besserung! *I hope you get well soon!*
  Guten Morgen! *Good morning!*
  kurz und gut *in short.*
  Schon gut! *All right!*

Gutachten *n. expert opinion, estimate.*

Gutachter *m. assessor, surveyor, consultant.*

gutartig *good-natured.*

Güte *f. kindness.*

Güterzug *m. freight train.*

gutgelaunt *in a good temper, in good spirits.*

gutgläubig *credulous.*

Guthaben *n. balance, credit.*

gutheissen *to approve, sanction.*

gutherzig *kind-hearted; warmhearted.*

gütig *kind, good.*

gutmachen *to make amends for.*

gutmütig *good-natured.*

Gutmütigkeit *f. good nature.*

Gutsbesitzer *m. landowner, gentleman farmer.*

Gutschein *m. token, voucher.*

gutwillig *willing, voluntary.*

Gymnasialbildung *f. classical education.*

Gymnasiast *m. high-school boy.*

Gymnasium *n. high-school.*

Gymnastik *f. gymnastics.*

HAAR *n. (Haare pl.) hair.*
  sich die Haare machen *to do one's hair.*
  sich die Haare schneiden lassen *to get a haircut.*
  Haare auf den Zähnen haben *to stand up (to opponents).*
  um ein Haar *nearly, narrowly.*
  kein gutes Haar an einem lassen *to pull a person to pieces.*
  sich in die Haare geraten *to come to blows.*
  Lassen Sie sich darüber keine grauen Haare wachsen! *Don't let that give you gray hair!*

Haarnadel *f. hairpin.*

Haarspalterei *f. hair-splitting.*

Haarwasser *n. hair tonic.*

Habe *f. property, belongings.*
  Hab und Gut *good and chattel.*
  habhaft werden *to obtain possession.*

HABEN *to have, own, possess, get.*
  Den wievielten haben wir heute? *What is the date today?*
  nichts auf sich haben *to be of no consequence.*
  Recht haben *to be right.*
  unter sich haben *to be in charge of.*
  Was hast du? *What is the matter with you?*
  zu haben sein *to be obtainable.*

Habgier *f. greed, avarice.*

habgierig *greedy, avaricious.*

hacken *to chop, mince.*

Hafen *m. port, harbor.*

Hafenstadt *f. seaport.*

Haft *f. custody, arrest, detention.*

haftbar *responsible, liable.*

haften *to stick to, cling to.*
  haften für *to answer for (bear the responsibility).*

Häftling *m. prisoner.*

haftpflichtig *liable, responsible.*
  mit beschränkter Haftung *with limited liability.*

Haftung *f. liability, responsibility.*

Hagel *m. hail.*

Hagelschlag *m. hailstorm.*

HAHN *m. rooster, cock.*

Hai *m. shark.*

Haken *m. hook, mark.*

Halb *half.*

auf halbem Wege *midway, halfway.*

ein halbes Pfund *half a pound.*

halb durchgebraten *medium done* (*meat*).

halb so viel *half as much.*

halb zwei *half past one.*

halb geschenkt *practically given away.*

halbieren *to halve, bisect.*

Halbinsel *f. peninsula.*

Halbmond *m. crescent moon, half-moon.*

Hälfte *f. half.*

Kinder zahlen die Hälfte. *Children pay half price.*

Halle *f. hall, hangar.*

HALS *m. neck, throat.*

Es hängt mir schon zum Hals heraus. *I am sick and tired of it already.*

Hals über Kopf *headlong.*

um den Hals fallen *to embrace.*

Es geht um den Hals. *It's a matter of life and death.*

Halsband *n. necklace.*

halsbrecherisch *dangerous.*

Halsschmerzen *pl. sore throat.*

Halstuch *n. scarf.*

Halt *m. stop, halt, hold, footing.*

Halt! *Stop!*

haltbar *tenable, lasting, durable.*

Haltbarkeit *f. durability, defensibility.*

HALTEN *to hold, support, observe, keep, celebrate, last, stop, endure, continue, follow.*

an sich halten *to restrain oneself.*

Er hält sich für sehr klug. *He thinks he is very clever.*

halt machen *to stop.*

halten für *to consider, to think.*

es halten mit *to side with.*

Halten Sie sich rechts! *Keep to the right!*

halten von *to think of.*

Was halten Sie von ihr? *What do you think of her?*

schwer halten *to be difficult.*

sein Wort halten *to keep one's word.*

viel halten auf *to think highly of.*

Haltestelle *f. stop, station.*

haltlos *without support, unsteady, unprincipled.*

Haltung *f. behavior, attitude, self-control.*

Hammer *m. hammer.*

HAND *f. hand, palm.*

an der Hand führen *to lead someone.*

ihn auf den Händen tragen *to treat him with every consideration.*

aus zweiter Hand kaufen *to buy something secondhand.*

die Hände voll zu tun haben *to be very busy.*

eine Hand wäscht die andere *a good turn deserves another.*

bei der Hand sein *to be ready.*

die Hand im Spiel haben *to have a finger in the pie.*

einem die Hand geben *to shake hands with someone.*

Hand und Fuss haben *to be to the purpose.*

mit Händen und Füssen *with might and main* (*tooth and nail*).

unter der Hand *secretly.*

von der Hand gehen *to work well.*

von der Hand weisen *to decline.*

zur Hand *handy.*

Handarbeit *f. manual work, labor.*

HANDEL *m. trade, business, affair.*

Handel treiben *to trade.*

handelseinig werden *to come to terms.*

handeln *to act, do.*

handeln mit *to trade with.*

handeln von *to deal with.*

sich handeln um *to be about, be a matter of.*

Handelskammer *f. chamber of commerce.*

Handfertigkeit *f. manual skill.*

Handgelenk *n. wrist.*

Handgepäck *n. hand luggage.*

handgreiflich *obvious, manifest.*

handgreiflich werden *to use one's fists.*

handhaben *to handle, manage.*

Handkoffer *m. suitcase.*

Händler *m. trader, dealer.*

handlich *handy.*

Handlung *f. act, action, deed, business.*

Handlungsweise *f. way of acting, method of dealing.*

Handschrift *f. handwriting.*

Handschuh *m. glove.*

Handstreich *m. surprise attack.*

Handtasche *f. handbag.*

Handtuch *n. towel.*

Handwerk *n. handicraft, trade.*

einem das Handwerk legen *to stop a person's activities.*

hängen *to hang, suspend, fix, attach.*

hängen bleiben *to be caught.*

hänseln *to tease.*

Harm *m. grief, sorrow, insult, injury.*

harmlos *harmless.*

Harmlosigkeit *f. harmlessness, innocence.*

Harmonie *f. harmony.*

harmonieren *to harmonize, agree.*

HART *hard, firm, solid.*

hartherzig *hard-hearted.*

harthörig *hard of hearing.*

Härte *f. hardness, roughness, cruelty, severity.*

hartnäckig *obstinate, stubborn.*

Hase *m. hare.*

Hasenbraten *m. roast hare.*

Hass *m. hate, hatred.*

hassen *to hate.*

hässlich *ugly, nasty.*

Hässligkeit *f. ugliness.*

Hast *f. hurry, haste.*

hastig *hurried, hasty.*

Haube *f. hood, cap.*
  unter die Haube bringen *to marry off.*

Hauch *m. breath, slight breeze.*

hauchen *to breathe.*

Haufen *m. heap, pile.*

häufen *to heap, pile, accumulate.*

häufig *frequent, abundant.*

HAUPT *n. chief, head; principal.*

Hauptbahnhof *m. main station.*

Hauptmann *m. captain.*

Hauptperson *f. principal person, leading character (theater).*

Hauptpostamt *n. general post office.*

Hauptquartier *n. headquarters.*

Hauptsache *f. main thing.*

hauptsächlich *principal.*

Hauptstadt *f. capital.*

Hauptverkehrszeit *f. rush hour.*

Hauptwort *n. substantive, noun.*

HAUS *n. house, home, building.*
  bei uns zu Hause *where I come from.*
  das Haus hüten *to be confined to the house.*
  nach Hause gehen *to go home.*
  von Haus aus *originally.*
  zu Hause *at home.*

Hausangestellte *m. & f. servant.*

Hausarbeit *f. housework.*

Hausaufgabe *f. homework.*

Häuschen *n. small house.*

Hausflur *m. hall, corridor.*

Hausfrau *f. housewife.*

Haushalt *m. household.*

haushalten *to keep house, to economize.*

Haushälterin *f. housekeeper.*

Hausherr *m. master.*

Hauslehrer *m. private tutor.*

häuslich *domestic.*

Häuslichkeit *f. family life, domesticity.*

Hausmeister *m. janitor.*

Hausschuh *m. slipper.*

Haussuchung *f. police raid.*

Haustier *n. domestic animal*

Haustür *f. front door.*

Hauswirt *m. landlord.*

HAUT *f. skin, hide, coat.*

aus der Haut fahren *to lose one's patience.*

sich seiner Haut wehren *to defend oneself.*

Hautfarbe *f. complexion.*

heben *to lift, raise.*

Heer *n. army.*

Hefe *f. yeast.*

Heft *n. notebook, pamphlet.*

heften *to pin, fasten, stitch, fix.*

heftig *violent, strong.*

Heftigkeit *f. violence, vehemence, intensity.*

heikel *delicate, ticklish, difficult.*

HEIL *unhurt, intact, safe, cured.*

heilbar *curable.*

heilen *to cure.*

heilig *holy, godly, sacred.*
  Heiligabend *Christmas Eve.*
  heilighalten *to hold sacred.*

heilkräftig *curative.*

Heilmittel *n. remedy.*

heilsam *curative.*

Heilsarmee *f. Salvation Army.*

Heilung *f. healing, cure.*

Heilverfahren *n. medical treatment.*

HEIM *n. home.*

heim *homeward.*

Heimat *f. native country, homeland.*

heimatlos *homeless.*

Heimatstadt *f. home town.*

Heimkehr(-kunft) *f. homecoming.*

heimlich *secret, private, comfortable; secretly, privately.*

Heimsuchung *f. trial, misfortune.*

Heimtücke *f. malice.*

heimtückisch *malicious, insidious.*

Heimweg *m. way home, return.*

Heimweh *n. homesickness.*
  Heimweh haben *to be homesick.*

HEIRAT *f. marriage.*

heiraten *to marry, get married.*

Heiratsantrag *m. proposal.*

heiser *hoarse.*
  heiser sein *to be hoarse, have a sore throat.*

Heiserkeit *f. hoarseness, sore throat.*

HEISS *hot.*

HEISSEN *to call, name, be called.*
  das heisst *that is.*
  es heisst *they say.*
  Ich heisse Anna. *My name is Ann.*
  Wie heisst das auf Englisch? *What is that called in English?*
  jemand willkommen heissen *to bid someone welcome.*

heiter *gay, cheerful.*

Heiterkeit *f. brightness, clearness, serenity, cheerfulness.*

heizbar *with heating*

heizen to heat.

Heizkissen n. electric pad.

Heizung f. heating, firing, radiator.

Held m. hero.

HELFEN to support, help, assist.

Ich kann mir nicht helfen.   I can't help it.

Helfer m. helper, assistant.

Helfershelfer m. accomplice ("helper's helper")

HELL bright, shining, clear, light, fair, pale, sheer.

Helle f. clearness, brightness.

hellhörig keen of hearing.

Helm m. helmet.

HEMD n. shirt.

hemmen to check, stop, hinder, restrain.

Hemmung f. inhibition, check, stoppage restraint

hemmungslos free, unrestrained.

HER 1. adv. here, from, since, ago.

von Alters her   of old, long ago.

2. separable prefix (implies the idea of a movement toward the speaker)

Kommen Sie her!   Come here!

herab down, downward.

herablassen to lower, let down, to stoop.

Herablassung f. condescension.

herabsehen to look down upon.

herabsetzen to lower, degrade, reduce (price).

Herabsetzung f. lowering, degradation; reduction (price).

heran on, up, near, along.

heranbilden to train, educate.

herankommen to come near.

die Dinge an sich herankommen lassen   to bide one's time.

heranwachsen to grow up.

HERAUF up, upwards.

heraufgehen to go up.

Kommen Sie herauf!   Come up!

HERAUS out, from within.

Sie kommen heraus.   They are coming out.

herausbekommen to get back (money); find out.

herausnehmen to take out, extract.

herausstellen to turn out, appear.

herbei here, near, hither.

herbeischaffen to bring near, procure, produce.

HERBST m. autumn.

herbstlich autumnal.

Herd m. hearth, fireplace.

Herdplatte f. hot plate.

HEREIN in.

Kommen Sie herein (Herein!)   Come in!

Hier herein, bitte!   This way, please!

hereinfallen to be taken in, disappointed.

herkommen to come near, approach, originate.

Herkunft f. origin, descent.

HERR m. master, gentleman, lord, sir, Mr.

Meine Damen und Herren   Ladies and gentlemen.

Ist der Herr Doktor zu sprechen?   Can I see the doctor?

eigener Herr sein   to stand on one's own feet.

Herr werden   to master, overcome.

Herr im Hause sein   to be the master of the house.

herrichten to arrange.

herrisch imperious, dictatorial.

Herrschaft f. power, rule, command, master and mistress (of an estate).

herrschen to rule, govern, prevail, exist.

Herrscher m. ruler, tyrant, dictator.

herrschsüchtig fond of power, tyrannical.

herüber across, to this side.

herüberkommen to come over.

HERUM around, round, near, about.

rundherum   all around.

herumdrehen to turn round.

herumführen to lead.

herumreichen to hand around.

(sich) herumtreiben to run around.

HERUNTER down, off.

herunterkommen to come down.

Komm gleich herunter!   Come down right away!

heruntersetzen to lower.

hervor out, forth.

hervorbringen to produce, yield.

hervorheben to make prominent.

hervorragen to stand out, project.

hervorragend prominent, excellent.

(sich) hervortun to distinguish oneself.

Herz n. heart, feeling, mind, courage.

ans Herz legen   to recommend to someone's care.

ins Herz schliessen   to become fond of.

sich ein Herz fassen   to take courage.

sich zu Herzen nehmen   to take to heart.

von Herzen gern   with the greatest pleasure.

Was haben Sie auf dem Herzen?   What's on your mind?

herzleidend suffering from heart trouble.

herzlich hearty, cordial.

mit herzlichen Grüssen   with kindest regards.

herzlos heartless.

Herzschlag m. heart beat, heart failure.

Heu n. hay.

Heufieber n. hay fever.

Heuchelei f. hypocrisy.

heucheln to feign, pretend.

Heuchler m. hypocrite.

HEUTE today.

   heute abend   tonight.

   heute früh; heute morgen   this morning.

   heute vor acht Tagen   a week ago.

   heutzutage   nowadays.

Hexe f. witch.

HIER here.

   hier und da   here and there.

hierauf hereupon.

hierdurch through this, this way, thereby.

hierher here, hither.

hierherum hereabout.

hiermit herewith, with this.

hiernach after this, thereupon.

hierüber over here, about this.

hiervon hereof, from this.

hierzu to this, moreover.

HILFE f. help, assistance, support, relief.

   Hilfe leisten   to help, assist.

   erste Hilfe   first aid.

hilflos helpless.

hilfreich helpful, charitable.

hilfsbedürftig indigent, needing help.

HIMMEL m. sky, heaven.

   aus allen Himmeln fallen   to be bitterly disappointed.

   Himmel und Menschen   a throng; many people.

Himmelsrichtung f. quarter, direction, point of compass.

himmlisch heavenly, celestial.

HIN 1. adv. there, thither.

   hin und her   to and fro.

   hin und her überlegen   to turn over in one's mind.

   hin und wieder   now and then.

   2. separable prefix (implies the idea of a movement away from the speaker).

   Gehen Sie hinaus!   Go out.

hinab down, downward.

HINAUF up, upward.

   hinaufarbeiten   to work one's way up.

   Er geht die Treppe hinauf.   He goes up the stairs.

HINAUS out, outside, past.

   darüber hinaus   beyond that.

   Ich schicke die Kinder hinaus.   I am sending the children outside.

hinausgehen to go out.

hinauskommen to come out.

   auf eins hinauskommen   to come to the same thing.

hinausschieben to defer, postpone, put off.

hinauswerfen to throw out, expel.

   hoch hinauswollen   to aim high.

hinausziehen to draw out, put off.

Hinblick m. look at or toward.

   im Hinblick auf   with regard to.

hinbringen to take, bring, carry.

hinderlich in the way, hindering, obstructive.

hindern to prevent, hinder, hamper.

hindurch through, throughout, across.

HINEIN in, into.

   Ich gehe in das Zimmer hinein.   I go into the room.

hineingehen to go into.

hinfahren to carry, drive to.

Hinfahrt f. trip there.

hinfallen to fall down.

hinfällig frail, weak.

   hinfällig werden   to fail, come to nothing.

hinfort henceforth, in the future.

Hingabe f. surrender, devotion.

hinhalten to put off.

hinlänglich sufficient, adequate.

hinnehmen to take, accept.

hinsehen to look at.

(sich) hinsetzen to set down, sit down.

hinsichtlich with regard to.

hinstellen to place, put down.

hinten behind, in the rear, at the back.

HINTER 1. prep. (dat. when answering question, Wo?; acc. when answering question, Wohin? and depending on the idiom) behind, back, after.

   Hinter dem Haus ist eine Garage.   There is a garage behind the house.

   Sie hat schon viel hinter sich.   She has been through a lot.

   hinter sich bringen   to get over, cover.

Hinterbliebene m. & f. survivor.

hintereinander one after the other.

   zwei Tage hintereinander   two days running.

Hintergedanke m. underlying thought, unacknowledged motive.

Hintergrund m. background.

Hinterhalt m. ambush.

hinterhältig malicious, devious.

hinterher behind, afterwards.

hinterlassen to leave, leave behind.

   Hat er keine Nachricht für mich hinterlassen?   Hasn't he left a message for me?

hinterlistig artful, cunning.

Hinterrad n. backwheel.

hinters hinter das behind.

HINÜBER over, across, over there, to the other side.

HINUNTER down, downward, downstairs.

   Sie geht die Treppe hinunter.   She walks down the stairs.

Hinweg m. way there.

hinweg away, off.

hinwegkommen (über) to get over.

hinwegsetzen (über) to disregard.

Hinweis m. indication, hint, reference, direction.

hinweisen to show, indicate, refer.

hinwerfen to throw down.

hinzu to, near, there.

hinzufügen to add.

hinzuziehen to include, consult.

Hirn n. brain.

Hitze f. heat.

hitzig hot, hot-headed.

HOCH high, tall, lofty, great, noble.

    Es geht hoch her.   *Things are getting pretty lively.*

    Hände hoch!   *Hands up!*

    hoch anrechnen   *to value greatly.*

    Hoch leben . . . !   *Long live. . . !*

    hochleben lassen   *to toast.*

hochachten to esteem, respect.

Hochachtung f. esteem, respect.

    hochachtungsvoll   *yours respectfully.*

Hochbetrieb m. intense activity.

Hochdeutsch n. high German, standard German.

hochhalten to cherish, raise.

Hochhaus n. skyscraper.

hochherzig high-minded, magnanimous.

Hochmut m. pride, arrogance.

hochmütig arrogant, proud.

Hochschule f. university, college.

Hochsommer m. midsummer.

Hochspannung f. high tension.

    Vorsicht! Hochspannung!   *Caution! High tension wires!*

HÖCHST highest, utmost, extreme, maximum; very, extremely.

Hochstapelei f. swindling.

Hochstapler m. swindler.

höchstens at best, at most.

Höchstgeschwindigkeit f. top speed, speed limit.

Höchstgrenze f. limit.

Höchstleistung f. maximum output, record performance.

höchstwahrscheinlich most likely.

hochtrabend high-sounding.

Hochverrat m. high treason.

Hochzeit f. wedding, marriage.

Hochzeitsreise f. honeymoon trip.

HOF m. yard, court, farm.

    den Hof machen   *to pay court to.*

HOFFEN to hope.

    hoffen auf   *to hope for.*

hoffentlich it is to be hoped.

Hoffnung f. hope.

    sich falsche Hoffnungen machen   *to have illusions.*

hoffnungslos hopeless.

hoffnungsvoll hopeful.

HÖHE f. height, altitude, latitude, top, summit, amount.

    auf der Höhe sein   *to be up to date, to be in top form.*

    auf gleicher Höhe mit   *on the same level with.*

    sich nicht auf der Höhe fühlen   *not to feel up to par.*

    auf der Höhe von   *at the altitude of.*

    aus der Höhe   *from on high.*

    Das ist die Höhe.   *That is the limit.*

    in (der) Höhe von   *in the amount of.*

Höhenstrahlen pl. cosmic rays.

höher higher, superior.

HOHL hollow, concave, dull.

Höhle f. hole, cave.

Hohlraum m. empty space, cavity.

Hohn m. scorn, sneer, mockery, insult.

höhnen to mock, defy.

höhnisch scornful, sneering.

HOLEN to get, take, fetch.

    sich Rat holen   *to consult.*

    sich eine Erkaltung holen   *to catch a cold.*

    Atem holen   *to catch one's breath.*

HÖLLE f. hell.

höllisch hellish, infernal.

HOLZ n. wood, timber, lumber.

hölzern wooden.

Honig m. honey.

horchen to listen, lend an ear, listen in, spy.

    Es horcht jemand.   *Somebody is listening in.*

HÖREN to hear, listen, attend, obey, understand.

    schwer hören   *to be hard of hearing.*

Horizont m. horizon.

Horn n. horn, bugle.

Horoskop n. horoscope.

    ein Horoskop stellen   *to cast horoscope.*

Hörspiel n. radio play.

Hose f. trousers, pants.

    Sie hat die Hosen an.   *She wears the pants.*

Hosenträger pl. suspenders.

Hotel n. hotel, inn.

hübsch pretty, charming, nice.

Huf m. hoof.

Hügel m. hill.

HUHN n. hen.

    gebratenes Hühnchen   *roast chicken.*

    junges Huhn   *young chicken.*

Huld f. grace, favor, charm.

huldigen to pay homage.

Humor m. sense of humor.

humoristisch humorous.

HUND m. dog.

Hundert n. hundred.

zu Hunderten *by hundreds.*
HUNDERT *one hundred (adj.)*
HUNGER *m. hunger.*
  Hunger haben *to be hungry.*
hungern *to be hungry, starve.*
Hungersnot *f. famine.*
hungrig *hungry.*
husten *to cough.*
  Hustensirup *m. cough syrup.*
HUT *m. hat.*
  unter einen Hut bringen *to reconcile.*
hüten *to guard, keep, beware.*
  das Zimmer hüten *to be confined to one's*
  room.
Hütte *f. hut.*

I

ICH *I, self, ego.*
Ideal *n. ideal.*
Idealist *m. idealist.*
Idee *f. idea, notion.*
identifizieren *to identify.*
identisch *identical.*
IHM *dat. of* er, es. *(pers. pron., masc. and*
  neut.) to him, to it.
IHN *acc. of* er *(pers. pron. masc.) him, it.*
IHNEN (ihnen) *dat. of* sie *(pers. pron. pl).*
  to them.
IHNEN (ihnen) *dat. of* Sie *(pers. pron. sing,*
  polite form) to you.
IHR *dat. of* sie *(pers. pron. fem.) to her, to*
  it.
IHR (ihr) *poss. adj. (fem. and pl.) her, its,*
  their.
IHR (ihr) *poss. adj. (sing. polite form) your.*
IHR(ER,-E,-ES) *poss. pron. (fem. and pl.)*
  hers, its, theirs.
  poss. pron.(sing. polite form) your.
ihretwegen *on her (its, their) account, for*
  her sake.
Ihretwegen *on your account, for your sake.*
illustrieren *to illustrate.*
imitieren *to imitate.*
IMMER *always, ever.*
  auf immer *forever.*
  immer mehr *more and more.*
  immer wieder *again and again.*
  immerfort *continually, constantly.*
  wer auch immer *whoever.*
immerhin *for all that, still, nevertheless.*
immerzu *all the time, continually.*
imponieren *to impress.*
Import *m. imports, importation.*
Impuls *m. impulse.*
impulsiv *impulsive.*
IN *prep. (dat. answering question, Wo?; acc.*

  answering question, Wohin?) in, into,
  to, at.
Die Besucher gehen in die Oper. *The*
  spectators go to the opera.
Der Lehrer sitzt in dem Zimmer. *The*
  teacher is sitting in the room.
Der Lehrer tritt in das Zimmer ein. *The*
  teacher goes into the room.
Der Sänger singt in der Oper. *The singer*
  sings in the opera.
Goethe wurde in Frankfurt geboren. *Goethe*
  was born in Frankfort.
im Februar *in February.*
im Kreise *in a circle.*
Inbegriff *m. embodiment, essence.*
inbegriffen *including, inclusive, included.*
INDEM *while, by, on, since.*
indirekt *indirect.*
indiskret *indiscreet, tactless.*
Indiskretion *f. indiscretion.*
Industrie *f. industry.*
Industrielle *m. manufacturer, producer.*
Infektionskrankheit *f. infectious disease.*
infolge *in consequence of, as a result of.*
  infolgedessen *because of that,*
  consequently, hence.
Ingenieur(-in) *m. (f.) engineer.*
Inhaber *m. proprietor.*
Inhalt *m. contents, area, extent, volume,*
  capacity.
inhaltlich *with regard to the contents.*
Inhaltsangabe *f. summary, table of contents.*
inhaltsleer *empty, meaningless.*
inhaltsreich *full of meaning, significant.*
Inhaltsverzeichnis *n. contents, table of*
  contents, index.
inmitten *in the midst of.*
innen *within, inside, in.*
INNER *interior, internal, inner.*
innerhalb *within, inside.*
innerlich *inward, internal, interior.*
innig *hearty, intimate.*
Innigkeit *f. intimacy, cordiality.*
ins *in das.*
insbesondere *particularly.*
Inschrift *f. inscription, legend.*
Insekt *n. insect.*
INSEL *f. island.*
Inserat *n. advertisement.*
inserieren *to advertise.*
insgesamt *all together, collectively.*
insofern *in so far, as far as that goes.*
insoweit *in so far.*
Instandhaltung *f. upkeep.*
inständig *instant, urgent.*
Instinkt *m. instinct.*
instruieren *to instruct, brief.*
Instrument *n. instrument.*
Intelligent *intelligent.*

Intelligenz *f. intelligence, understanding, intellect.*
interessant *interesting.*
Interesse *n. interest, advantage.*
interessieren *to interest.*
   sich interessieren (für) *to be interested in.*
international *international.*
interviewen *to interview.*
Inventar *n. inventory, stock.*
investieren *to invest.*
inzwischen *in between, in the meantime.*
IRGEND *any, some.*
   wenn irgend möglich *if at all possible.*
irgendetwas *something.*
irgendjemand *somebody, anybody.*
irgendwann *sometime.*
irgendwie *somehow.*
irgendwo *somewhere.*
irgendwoher *from some place or other.*
irgendwohin *to somewhere or other.*
ironisch *ironical.*
irre *astray, wrong, confused, insane.*
   irre werden an *to lose confidence in.*
IRRE *f. wandering, mistaken course.*
   in die Irre gehen *to lose one's way, go astray.*
   Irre machen *to confuse.*
irren *to err, wander, lose one's way, be mistaken, be wrong.*
   sich irren *to be mistaken.*
   irren ist menschlich *To err is human.*
Irrenanstalt *f. lunatic asylum.*
irrereden *to talk incoherently, to rave.*
irritieren *to irritate.*
Irrsinn *m. madness, insanity.*
irrsinnig *mad, insane.*
Irrtum *m. error, mistake*
   Sie sind im Irrtum. *You are mistaken.*
irrtümlich *erroneous, wrong.*
Israeli *m. Israeli (person).*
israelisch *Israeli.*
Italiener *m. Italian (person).*
Italienisch *n. Italian (language).*
italienisch *Italian.*

J

JA *yes, really, indeed, certainly.*
   Da sie Sie ja! *So there you are!*
   Sie wissen ja, dass ich nicht gehen kann. *But you know that I can't go.*
   ja sogar *even.*
Jacke *f. jacket.*
Jackenkleid *n. lady's suit.*
JAGD *f. hunt, pursuit, hunting, shooting.*
   auf die Jagd gehen *to go hunting.*
Jadgschein *m. hunting license.*

jagen *to chase, pursue.*
Jäger *m. hunter, huntsman, sportsman.*
jäh *sudden, quick, steep.*
JAHR *n. year.*
   ein halbes Jahr *six months.*
Jahrestag *m. anniversary.*
Jahreswende *f. New Year, turn of the year.*
JAHRESZEIT *f. season.*
Jahrhundert *n. century.*
jährlich *yearly, annual.*
Jahrmarkt *m. fair.*
Jahrtausend *n. thousand years, millennium.*
Jahrzehnt *n. decade.*
Jähzorn *m. sudden anger, violent temper.*
jähzornig *hot-tempered, irascible.*
Jammer *m. misery, wailing.*
   Was für ein Jammer! *What a pity!*
jammern *to lament, wail, moan.*
JANUAR *m. January.*
Japaner *m. Japanese (person).*
japanisch *Japanese (language).*
jauchzen *to exult, shout, rejoice.*
JAWOHL *of course, indeed.*
JE *each, ever, at all times.*
   je zwei *two at a time.*
   Sie erhielten je ein Pfund. *They received a pound each.*
   je nach *according to*
   je nachdem *according as*
   Je eher umso (desto) besser. *The sooner, the better.*
jedenfalls *at all events, in any case.*
JEDER (jede, jedes) *every, each, either, any.*
jedermann *everyone, everybody.*
jederzeit *at any time, always.*
jedesmal *every time.*
   jedesmal wenn *whenever, as often as.*
jedoch *however, nevertheless.*
jeher *von jeher at all times, from times immemorial.*
jemals *at any time.*
jemand *somebody, someone.*
JENER (jene, jenes) *that, that one, the former, the other.*
   jenseitig *opposite, on the opposite side.*
JENSEITS 1. *adv. beyond, on the other side, yonder.*
   2. *prep. (gen.) that side, on the other side.*
   Er wohnt jenseits des Flusses. *He lives on the other side of the river.*
jetzig *present, actual.*
JETZT *now, at present.*
Joch *n. yoke.*
Jod *n. iodine.*
Journalist *m. journalist.*
Jubel *m. rejoicing, jubilation.*
Jude *m. Jew.*
jüdisch *Jewish.*

JUGEND f. youth, young people.
Jugendfreund m. friend of youth.
jugendlich youthful.
Jugendliche m. & f. young boy or girl.
Jugendliebe f. first love.
Jugendzeit f. youth, young days.
JULI m. July.
JUNG young, youthful.
Junge m. boy, lad.
jungenhaft boyish.
jünger younger.
Jungfrau f. virgin, maid, maiden.
  alte Jungfer   old maid.
Junggeselle m. bachelor.
Jüngling m. young man.
JUNI m. June.
Jura pl. law.
  Jura studieren   to study law.
Jurist m. law-student, lawyer.
Justiz f. administration of the law.
Juwel n. jewel.
Juwelier m. jeweler.

K

Kabarett n. cabaret.
Kabine f. cabin.
Kachel f. glazed tile.
KAFFEE m. coffee.
Kaffeekanne f. coffee-pot.
Käfig m. cage.
kahl bald, bare, naked.
kahlköpfig bald-headed.
Kai m. wharf.
Kaiser m. emperor.
Kalb n. calf.
Kalbfleisch n. veal.
  Kalbsbraten   m. roast veal.
Kalender m. calendar.
kalkulieren to calculate.
KALT cold, indifferent.
kaltblütig cold-blooded.
Kälte f. coldness, indifference.
Kamel, n. camel.
Kamera f. camera
Kamerad m. friend, comrade, fellow.
Kameradschaft f. fellowship, comradeship.
Kamin m. chimney, fireplace.
Kamm m. comb.
kämmen to comb.
Kammer f. small room, chamber
  (government).
Kammermusik f. chamber music.
KAMPF m. fight, combat, conflict, struggle.
  Kampf ums Dasein   struggle for a living.
KÄMPFEN to fight.
Kanadier m. Canadian (person).
kanadisch Canadian.

Kanal m. canal, sewer.
Kanarienvogel m. canary bird.
Kandidat m. candidate.
kandidieren to be a candidate.
Kaninchen n. rabbit.
Kanne f. jug, pot, pitcher.
Kanone f. cannon.
Kante f. edge, corner.
kantig edged, angular.
Kantine f. canteen, mess.
Kanzel f. pulpit.
Kapelle f. chapel, band.
Kapital n. capital.
Kapitalsanlage f. investment.
Kapitalismus m. capitalism.
Kapitalist m. capitalist.
kapitalkräftig wealthy.
Kapitän m. captain.
Kapitel n. chapter.
kapitulieren to capitulate.
kaputt broken, ruined, out of order.
Karfreitag m. Good Friday.
Karikatur f. caricature.
Karneval m. carnival.
Karotte f. carrot.
Karriere f. career, gallop.
KARTE f. card, ticket, map, menu.
  Karten legen   to tell one's fortune.
Kartenspiel n. card game, pack of cards.
KARTOFFEL f. potato
  Kartoffelpüree   n. mashed potatoes.
  Bratkartoffeln   pl. fried potatoes.
  Kartoffelsalat   m. potato salad.
Karton m. cardboard, box.
Karwoche f. Passion Week.
KÄSE m. cheese.
Kaserne f. barracks.
Kasse f. cash-box.
  Zahlen Sie, bitte, an der Kasse!   Please
    pay the cashier.
Kassenschein m. receipt.
kassieren to receive money.
Kassierer m. cashier.
Kastanie f. chestnut.
Kasten m. box, chest, mailbox.
Katalog m. catalog.
Katastrophe f. catastrophe.
katastrophal catastrophic.
Katholik m. Roman Catholic.
katholisch Roman Catholic (adj.).
Katze f. cat.
kauen to masticate, chew.
  Kaugummi   n. chewing-gum.
KAUF m. buy, purchase.
  mit in Kauf nehmen   to put up with.
KAUFEN to buy, purchase.
  sich etwas kaufen   to buy oneself
    something.
Käufer m. buyer.

Kaufhaus n. department store, store, warehouse.

Kaufladen m. store, shop.

Kaufmann m. shopkeeper, merchant.

KAUM hardly, scarcely, barely.

Kavalier m. cavalier, gentleman.

keck bold, daring, impudent.

Keckheit f. boldness.

Kegel m. ninepin.

    mit Kind und Kegel with bag and luggage.

kegeln to bowl.

Kehle f. throat.

Kehlkopf m. larynx.

KEHREN turn, to sweep.

    ihm den Rücken kehren to turn one's back to him.

    kehrtmachen to face about, turn back.

KEIN adj. no, not one, not any.

KEIN (ER,-E,-ES) pron. none, neither.

    keiner von beiden neither of them.

keinerlei of no sort.

KEINESWEGS on no account, not at all.

Kelch m. cup, goblet, chalice.

Keller m. cellar.

KELLNER m (-in, f.) waiter, (waitress).

KENNEN to know, be acquainted with.

    kennenlernen to meet, become acquainted with.

Kenner m. connoisseur.

Kennkarte f. identity-card.

kenntlich recognizable, distinguishable.

KENNTNIS f. knowledge, information.

    in Kenntnis setzen to inform.

    zur Kenntnis nehmen to take note of.

Kennzeichen n. identity, mark.

Kern m. kernel, corn, seed, stone (fruit).

Kerze f. candle, sparking plug.

Kessel m. boiler, kettle.

Kette f. chain, necklace.

Kettenhund m. watch dog.

keuchen to pant, puff.

Keuchhusten m. whopping cough.

Keule f. club, leg (of lamb, etc.)

keusch pure, chaste.

Keuschheit f. modesty, purity, chastity.

Kiefer m. jaw.

Kilogramm n. kilogram (2.204 pounds).

Kilometer m. kilometer (.621 miles).

Kilometerzähler m. mileage recorder.

KIND n. child.

    kleines Kind baby (infant).

    von Kind auf from childhood on.

Kinderernährung baby feeding.

Kindergarten m. kindergarten, nursery school.

kinderlos childless.

Kindermädchen n. nursemaid.

Kinderstube f. nursery.

Kinderwagen m. baby carriage.

Kindheit f. childhood.

kindisch childish.

kindlich childlike.

Kinn n. chin.

Kino n. cinema, picture show, movies.

Kirche f. church, service.

Kirchhof m. cemetery.

Kirchtum m. church steeple.

Kirsche f. cherry.

Kissen n. cushion, pillow.

Kissenbezug m. cover, pillow-case.

Kiste f. box, chest, case.

kitzeln to tickle.

kitzlig ticklish.

Klage f. lament, complaint.

klagen to lament, complain, sue.

Kläger m. plaintiff.

kläglich lamentable, deplorable.

klamm numb, stiff, tight.

klammern to fasten, clasp, cling to.

Klang m. sound, tone, ringing of bell.

Klangfarbe f. timbre.

klanglos soundless.

klangvoll sonorous.

Klappstuhl m. folding chair.

Klapptisch m. folding table.

Klaps m. slap.

KLAR clear, limpid, pure, plain, evident.

    klar und deutlich distinctly, plainly.

    klar zum Gefecht ready for action.

    klar legen (stellen) to clear up, explain.

    sich klar darüber sein to realize.

Klarinette f. clarinet.

Klarinettist m. clarinetist.

KLASSE f. class, form, order.

Klassenlehrer m. class-teacher.

Klassenzimmer n. classroom.

Klassik f. classical art, classical period.

Klatsch m. smack, crack, slap.

klatschen to clap, lash, applaud.

    Beifall klatschen to applaud.

Klavier n. piano.

Klavierspieler m. pianist.

kleben to stick, glue.

Klee m. clover, shamrock.

KLEID n. dress, frock, gown.

    die Kleider pl. garments.

kleiden to dress, clothe, suit, become.

    Er ist immer gut gekleidet. He is always well-dressed.

Kleiderbügel m. coathanger.

Kleiderbürste f. clothes brush.

Kleiderschrank m. wardrobe.

Kleidung f. dress, clothes, clothing.

KLEIN little, small, tiny, minor.

    klein schneiden to cut in pieces.

    klein schreiben to write with small letters.

    von klein auf from infancy on.

klein denken *to have narrow views.*
KLEINGELD *n. change (monetary).*
kleingläubig *of little faith.*
Kleinholz *n. sticks, firewood.*
Kleinkram *m. trifle.*
Kleinstadt *f. small provincial town.*
kleinstädtisch *provincial.*
klettern *to climb.*
Klima *n. climate.*
klimatisch *climatic.*
Klingel *f. bell.*
klingeln *to ring.*
Klinke *f. doorknob; handle.*
klipp *snapping sound, snap of the fingers.*
   klipp und klar *quite clear.*
klirren *to clink, jingle.*
klopfen *to beat, knock, tap.*
Kloster *n. monastery, convent.*
Klub. *m. club.*
Klubsessel *m. lounge chair, easy chair.*
KLUG *intelligent, sensible, clever.*
   Ich werde nicht klug daraus. *I can't
     figure it out.*
Klugheit *f. intelligence.*
Klumpen *m. lump.*
KNABE *m. boy, lad.*
Knall *m. bang, detonation, crack.*
knapp *narrow, tight, close, poor.*
   knapp werde *to run short of.*
Knappheit *f. scarcity, shortage.*
Knecht *m. servant, farmhand, slave.*
Knechtschaft *f. servitude, slavery.*
kneifen *to pinch, nip.*
Kneipe *f. tavern, public house.*
Knie *n. knee.*
Kniehosen *pl. breeches, shorts.*
knistern *to rustle, crackle.*
KNOCHEN *m. bone.*
knöchern *of bone, bony.*
Knopf *m. button, knob, head.*
knöpfen *to button.*
Knopfloch *n. buttonhole.*
Knospe *f. bud.*
Knoten *m. knot.*
knurren *to growl, rumble.*
knusprig *crisp.*
Koch *m. cook.*
Kochbuch *n. cookbook.*
KOCHEN *to cook, boil.*
Kochgeschirr *n. pots and pans.*
Köchin *f. cook.*
Kochlöffel *m. ladle.*
Kochtopf *m. saucepan, pot, casserole.*
Koffer *m. trunk, bag, suitcase.*
Kognak *m. cognac, brandy.*
Kohl *m. cabbage.*
Kohle *f. coal, carbon.*
   auf Kohlen sitzen *to be on thorns or
    tenterhooks.*

Kohleneimer *m. coal bucket.*
Koje *f. cabin, berth.*
Kollege *m. colleague.*
Kolonialwaren *pl. groceries.*
Kolonialwarenhandlung *f. grocery store.*
Komiker *m. comedian.*
komisch *comical.*
Komma *n. comma.*
kommandieren *to command, order.*
KOMMEN *to come, arrive, get, result,
    happen, occur.*
   Das kommt davon. *That's the result.*
   Das kommt nicht in Frage. *This is out of
    the question.*
   Es kommt darauf an. *It depends.*
   kommen lassen *to send for.*
   kommen sehen *to foresee.*
   nicht dazu kommen *to have no time to.*
   Wann komme ich an die Reihe? *When
    will it be my turn?*
   Wie kommet es, dass *how is it that.*
   zu sich kommen *to recover.*
kommend *next.*
   kommende Woche *next week.*
Kommentar *m. commentary.*
Kommode *f. chest of drawers.*
Komödiant *m. comedian, hypocrite.*
Komödie *f. comedy.*
Kompass *m. compass.*
komplett *complete; completely.*
Kompliment *n. compliment.*
komponieren *to compose.*
Komponist *m. composer.*
Konditor *m. pastry cook.*
Konditorei *f. pastry-shop, cafe.*
Konfekt *n. candy, chocolates, sweets.*
Konfektion *f. ready-made clothes.*
Konferenz *f. conference.*
Konfession *f. confession.*
Konfitüre *f. preserves, jam.*
Konflikt *m. conflict.*
KÖNIG *m. king.*
königlich *royal.*
Konkurrent *m. rival.*
Konkurrenz *f. competition.*
konkurrieren *to be in competition with,
    compete.*
Konkurs *m. bankruptcy.*
   Konkurs anmelden *to declare bankruptcy.*
KÖNNER *to be able to, be possible,
    understand.*
   Das kann sein. *It may be.*
   Das kann nicht sein. *It is impossible.*
   Ich kann nicht mehr. *I am exhausted.*
   Er kann nichts dafür. *It is not his fault.*
konsequent *consistent.*
Konsequenz *f. consistency.*
konservativ *conservative.*
Konservatorium *n. academy of music.*

Konserve *f. canned goods.*
konstruieren *to construct.*
Konstrukteur *m. constructor.*
Konsul *m. consul.*
Konsulat *n. consulat.*
Kontinent *m. continent.*
Konto *n. account (financial).*
Kontoauszug *m. statement (account).*
Kontrakt *m. contract.*
Kontrast *m. contrast.*
Kontrolle *f. control.*
Kontrolleur *m. controller.*
kontrollieren *to control.*
Kontroverse *f. controversy.*
Konversationslexikon *n. encyclopedia.*
Konzert *n. concert.*
KOPF *m. head, brains, intellect, heading.*
  auf den Kopf stellen *to turn upside down.*
  aus dem Kopf *by heart.*
  einem den Kopf waschen *to give a
      person a dressing-down.*
  Es ist mir über den Kopf gewachsen. *It
      was too much for me.*
  im Kopf behalten *to remember.*
  Kopf oder Schrift *heads or tails.*
  nich auf den Kopf gefallen sein *to be no
      fool.*
  sich den Kopf zerbrechen *to rack one's
      orains.*
  sich etwas aus dem Kopf schlagen *to
      dismiss something from one's mind.*
  sich in den Kopf setzen *to take into one's
      head.*
  vor den Kopf stossen *to hurt, offend.*
  den Kopf verlieren *to lose one's head.*
  ihm über den Kopf wachsen *to be too
      much for him.*
Kopfarbeit *f. brain work.*
Kopfkissen *n. pillow.*
Kopfsalat *m. lettuce.*
kopfscheu *timid.*
Kopfschmerzen *pl. headache.*
  Ich habe Kopfschmerzen. *I have a
      headache.*
Kopfweh *n. headache.*
Korb *m. basket.*
Kork *m. cork, stopper.*
Korkenzieher *m. corkscrew.*
Korn *n. grain.*
  aufs Korn nehmen *to aim at.*
KÖRPER *m. body.*
körperlich *bodily, physical.*
Körperpflege *f. physical culture, care of the
      body.*
Körperwärme *f. body heat.*
korrekt *correct.*
Korrespondenz *f. correspondence.*
Korridor *m. corridor.*
korrigieren *to correct.*

Kosmetik *f. cosmetics.*
Kost *f. food, board.*
kostbar *precious, costly, valuable.*
Kostbarkeit *f. preciousness, object of valor.*
Kosten *f. costs, expenses.*
  auf seine Kosten kommen *to recover
      expenses, be satisfied with the deal.*
KOSTEN *to cost, require, taste.*
Kostenanschlag *m. estimate.*
kostenlos *free.*
kostenpflichtig *liable for the cost.*
Kostenpunkt *f. expenses.*
köstlich *precious, valuable, delicious.*
kostspielig *expensive.*
Kostüm *n. costume, tailored suit.*
Kostümfest *n. fancy dress ball.*
Kotelett *n. cutlet, chop.*
Krabbe *f. shrimp, crab.*
Krach *m. crash, noise, quarrel,*
  mit Ach und Krach *with difficulty, just
      barely.*
KRAFT *f. strength, energy, power.*
  ausser Kraft setzen *to annul, abolish.*
  Das geht über meine Kräfte. *That's too
      much for me.*
  in Kraft treten *to come into force, effect.*
  nach bestem Kräften *to the best of one's
      ability.*
  zu Kräften kommen *to regain one's
      strength.*
kräftig *robust, strong.*
kraftlos *weak, feeble.*
Kragen *m. collar.*
KRANK *ill, sick.*
  sich krank lachen *to split one's sides
      (with laughter).*
  krank werden *to be taken ill.*
Kranke *m. patient.*
Krankenauto *n. ambulance.*
Krankenhaus *n. hospital.*
Krankenschwester *f. nurse.*
Krankheit *f. illness, disease.*
Kranz *m. wreath, garland.*
kraus *crisp, curly.*
  die Stirne krausziehen *to knit one's brow.*
Kraut *n. cabbage.*
Krawatte *f. necktie.*
Krebs *m. crawfish, cancer.*
Kredit *f. credit.*
KREIS *m. circle, social group.*
  einen Kreis ziehen *to describe a circle.*
  sich im Kreise drehen *to turn around,
      rotate.*
  in allen Kreisen des Lebens *in every walk
      of life.*
kreisen *to circle, revolve, circulate.*
Kreislauf *m. circulation, course, revolution.*
KREUZ *n. cross; clubs (cards)*
  das Kreuz schlagen *to cross oneself.*

das Rote Kreuz   the Red Cross.
kreuz und quer   in all directions.
Kreuzung f. crossing.
   Eisenbahnkreuzung.   Railroad crossing.
Kreuzverhör n. cross-examination.
Kreuzworträtsel n. crossword puzzle.
kriechen to creep, crawl.
KRIEG m. war.
   im Krieg   in wartime.
   Krieg führen   to make war.
Kriegsgefangene m. prisoner of war.
Kriegsschauplatz m. theater of war.
Kriminalpolizei f. criminal investigation
      department.
Kriminalroman m. detective-story.
Kritik f. criticism.
Kritiker m. critic.
kritiklos uncritical, undiscriminating.
kritisch critical.
kritisieren to criticize.
Krone f. crown.
Kronleuchter m. chandelier.
Krug m. pitcher, jar.
Krümel n. crumb.
krümeln to crumble.
krumm crooked, curved, bent.
krümmen to bend.
Krümmung f. curve.
Krüppel m. cripple.
Kristall n. crystal.
KÜCHE f. kitchen, cooking.
Kuchen m. cake, pastry.
Küchenherd m. stove.
Kugel f. bullet, ball, globe, sphere.
Kuh f. cow.
   Er ist bekannt wie eine bunte Kuh.   He is
      well-known everywhere ("like a
      colorful cow").
KÜHL cool, fresh, chilly.
Kühlanlage cold storage plant.
Kühle f. coolness, freshness.
kühlen to cool.
Kühler m. radiator (car).
Kühlschrank m. refrigerator.
Kühlung f. cooling, freshness.
kühn bold, daring, audacious.
Kühnheit f. boldness, audacity.
Kulisse f. wing
   hinter den Kulissen   backstage; behind the
      scenes (secretly).
kultivieren to cultivate.
Kultur f. culture.
Kummer m. grief, sorrow.
kummervoll sad, sorrowful.
Kunde f. customer, client, news.
Kundgebung f. announcement.
kundig well-informed, experienced.
kündigen to give notice (to quit).
Kundschaft f. customers.

künftig in the future.
KUNST f. art.
Kunstausstellung f. art exhibition.
Kunstgalerie f. art gallery.
Kunsthandel m. fine art trade.
Kunsthändler m. art dealer.
Künstler m. artist.
künstlich artificial, false.
Kunstseide f. artificial silk.
Kunststoff m. plastics, synthetic material.
Kunststück n. feat, trick.
KUR f. treatment, cure.
Kurgast m. visitor, patient.
Kurhaus n. casino
kurios odd, strange.
Kurort m. health resort.
Kurs m. course, rate of exchange.
Kurve f. curve, bend, turn.
   Gefährliche Kurve!   Dangerous curve!
KURZ short, brief, abrupt; in short, briefly.
   den Kürzem ziehen   to be the loser.
   in kurzem   soon, shortly.
   kurz darauf   shortly after.
   kurz oder lang   sooner or later.
   kurz und bündig   concisely, briefly.
   kurz und gut   in short.
   vor kurzem   recently.
   kurz abfertigen   to dismiss abruptly.
Kürze f. shortness, brevity.
kürzen to shorten, abridge.
kurzgefasst concise; in short.
Kurzgeschichte f. short story.
kürzlich lately, recently.
Kurzschrift f. shorthand.
kurzsichtig shortsighted.
Kürzung f. shortening, abbreviation.
Kuss m. kiss.
   Mit Grüssen und Küssen   With love and
      kisses.
küssen to kiss.
Küste f. coast, shore.
Kuvert n. envelope, cover, wrapping.

L

Laborant m. laboratory assistant.
Laboratorium n. laboratory.
lächeln to smile.
   höhnisch lächeln   to sneer.
Lachen n. laugh, laughter.
LACHEN to laugh.
lächerlich laughable, ridiculous.
   lächerlich machen   to ridicule.
Laden m. shop, store, shutter.
Ladeninhaber m. shopkeeper.
Ladenschluss m. closing time.
Ladentisch m. counter.
Ladeplatz m. loading point, goods platform.

Lage *f. situation, position, site, condition,*
storage.
Lager *n. bed, couch, layer, support.*
Lageraufnahme *f. inventory.*
Lagergeld *n. storage fee.*
Lagerhaus *n. warehouse.*
lagern *to lie down, camp; to be stored.*
lahm *lame, paralyzed.*
Laie *m. layman.*
Laken *n. sheet.*
LAMPE *f. lamp, light.*
Lampenfieber *n. stagefright.*
Lampenschirm *m. lamp-shade.*
LAND *n. land, mainland, ground.*
ans Land steigen   *to land, go ashore.*
aufs Land gehen   *to go to the country.*
ausser Landes gehen   *to go abroad.*
landen *to land, put ashore.*
aus aller Herren Ländern   *from all parts of*
the globe, from all over the world.
Landesbrauch *m. national custom.*
Landesfarben *pl. national colors.*
Landessprache *f. national language.*
Landestracht *f. national costume.*
Landesverrat *m. high treason.*
Landesverweisung *f. expulsion, banishment,*
exile.
Landhaus *n. country house.*
Landkarte *f. map.*
Landschaft *f. landscape, scenery.*
landschaftlich *provincial.*
Landstrasse *f. highway, highroad.*
Landung *f. landing, disembarkation.*
Landwirtschaft *f. farming, agriculture.*
landwirtschaftlich *agricultural.*
LANG *long, tall.*
auf lange Sicht   *long-dated.*
auf die lange Bank schieben   *to put off.*
den lieben langen Tag   *the livelong day.*
einen Tag lang   *for a day.*
Es dauert lange.   *It takes long.*
es ist schon lange her, dass ...   *It's been*
a long time since/that ...
über kurz oder lang   *sooner or later.*
langatmig *long-winded, lengthy.*
Länge *f. length, duration.*
der Länge nach   *lengthwise.*
in die Länge ziehen   *to drag on, spin out.*
langen *to suffice, last, be enough.*
Lange mir den Hut!   *Hand me my hat.*
Längengrad *degree of longitude.*
länger *longer.*
Je länger, je lieber.   *The longer, the better.*
schon länger   *for some time.*
Langeweile *f. boredom.*
langfristig *long-dated.*
LÄNGS *prep. (gen.) along.*
Der Weg läuft längs des Stromes.   *The*
road runs along the river.

langsam *slow, tardy.*
Langsam fahren!   *Slow down!*
Langsamkeit *f. slowness.*
längst *long ago, long since.*
schon längst   *for a very long time.*
am längsten   *the longest.*
längstens   *at the latest, at the most.*
langweilen *to bore.*
sich zu Tode langweilen   *to be bored to*
death.
langweilig *boring.*
Lärm *m. noise, din, row.*
LASSEN *to let, allow, permit, suffer, omit,*
abandon.
aus dem Spiel lassen   *to leave out of the*
question.
Das muss man ihm lassen.   *One must*
credit him with that.
es beim alten lassen   *to let things remain*
as they are.
Lassen Sie von sich hören!   *Let us hear*
from you.
holen lassen   *to send for.*
Lass das!   *Don't!*
Lass nur!   *Never mind!*
Ich habe den Wagen waschen lassen.
I had the car washed.
machen (waschen, reinigen, richten, usw.)
lassen   *to have made (washed,*
cleaned, fixed, etc.).
mit sich reden lassen   *to be reasonable.*
sein Leben lassen   *to lose one's life.*
sich sagen lassen   *to be told, take advice.*
sich Zeit lassen   *to take time.*
warten lassen   *to keep waiting.*
lässig *lazy, idle, indolent.*
Last *f. load, weight, burden, charge.*
lästig *troublesome, annoying, irksome.*
Lastwagen *m. cart, truck, van.*
Laterne *f. lantern, lamp.*
Laub *f. foliage, leaves.*
Laubwerk *m. foliage.*
Lauer *f. ambush.*
lauern *to wait for.*
Lauf *m. race, course, run, current.*
in vollem lauf   *at full gallop.*
freien Lauf lassen   *to give vent to.*
Laufbahn *f. career.*
LAUFEN *to run, flow, go on.*
laufen lassen   *to let things go.*
auf dem laufenden sein   *to be up to date,*
abreast.
Gefahr laufen   *to run the risk.*
laufend *running.*
Laufjunge *m. errand-boy.*
Laune *f. mood, whim.*
guter Laune sein   *to be in good mood.*
launisch *moody.*
Laut *m. sound, tone.*

laut 1. *adj. loud, noisy, audible.*
  laut werden *to become known, get about.*
  2. *prep. (gen.) according to, in accordance with.*
  lut Befehls *by order.*
  laut Rechnung *as per account.*
lauten *to sound.*
läuten *to ring, toll.*
lautlos *silent.*
Lautlosigkeit *f. silence.*
Lautsprecher *m. loudspeaker.*
lauwarm *lukewarm.*
LEBEN *n. life, lifetime, living.*
  am Leben bleiben *to survive.*
  am Leben sein *to be alive.*
  auf Leben und Tod *a matter of life and death.*
  einem Kind das Leben schenken *to give birth to a child.*
  ins Leben rufen *to originate, start.*
  Lebenshaltung Kosten *standard of living.*
LEBEN *to live, be alive, dwell, stay.*
lebendig *living, lively.*
Lebendigkeit *f. liveliness, animation.*
Lebensgefahr *f. danger, risk of one's life.*
lebensgefährlich *highly dangerous.*
Lebenslage *f. position.*
lebenslänglich *for life, perpetual.*
Lebenslauf *n. curriculum vitae, background.*
Lebensmittel *n. food, provisions.*
Lebensmittelgeschäft *food shop.*
lebensmüde *tired of life.*
Lebensraum *m. living space.*
Lebensunterhalt *m. livelihood, living.*
Lebensweise *f. mode of life.*
Leber *f. liver.*
lebhaft *lively, vivacious.*
Leck *n. leak.*
lecken *to lick.*
LEDER *n. leather*
LEER *empty, vacant, blank, idle.*
  mit leeren Händen *with empty hands.*
Leere *f. emptiness, void, vacuum.*
  leerlauf *m. neutral (gear).*
leeren *to empty.*
LEGEN *to put, lay, place.*
  sich legen *to lie down, calm down, subside.*
Lehne *f. back of chair.*
lehnen *to lean against, rest upon.*
  sich lehnen *to lean back.*
Lehnstuhl *m. armchair.*
Lehramt *n. teacher's post.*
Lehrberuf *m. teaching profession.*
Lehrbuch *n. text book.*
Lehre *f. instruction, precept, advice, lesson.*
LEHREN *to teach, instruct.*
LEHRER *m. (-in, f.) teacher.*
Lehrfach *n. subject.*

lehrhaft *didactic.*
Lehrjahre *pl. years of apprenticeship.*
lehrreich *instructive.*
Leib *m. body, belly, womb.*
Leibschmerzen *m. pl. stomach-ache, colic.*
Leiche *f. corpse.*
LEICHT *easy, light, slight, mild, careless, frivolous; easily.*
  etwas leicht nehmen *to take it easy.*
  leicht möglich *very probable.*
leichtfertig *thoughtless, frivolous.*
Leichtfertigkeit *f. thoughtlessness, frivolity.*
leichtgläubig *credulous.*
Leichtsinn *m. carelessness, thoughtlessness.*
leichtsinnig *careless, thoughtless.*
LEID *n. grief, sorrow, pain, harm.*
  Ihm tut mir leid. *I am sorry for him.*
  Es tut mir leid. *I am sorry about it.*
  zu meinem Leid *to my regret.*
leiden *to suffer, bear, endure, stand.*
  leiden können, leiden mögen *to like.*
  Sie leidet schwer darunter. *It's making her very miserable.*
Leidenschaft *f. passion.*
leidenschaftlich *passionately.*
leidenschaftslos *dispassionate.*
leider *unfortunately.*
  leider nicht *unfortunately not.*
Leihbibliothek *f. lending library.*
leihen *to lend.*
Leine *f. leash.*
Leinwand *f. linen, screen.*
leise *soft, gentle, dim.*
  mit leiser Stimme *in a low voice.*
Leiste *f. strip; ledge.*
leisten *to perform, carry out, accomplish.*
  es sich leisten können *to be able to afford something.*
leistungsfähig *capable, fit, efficient.*
Leistungsfähigkeit *f. capacity for work, efficiency, power.*
leiten *to lead, conduct, manage, direct.*
Leiter *m. leader, manager, principal, head.*
Leitung *f. direction, management, guidance, line, pipe.*
Leitungswasser *tap water.*
Lektion *f. lesson (in a book).*
lenkbar *manageable, steerable.*
lenken *to direct, conduct, drive, steer.*
lernbegierig *anxious to learn.*
LERNEN *to learn, study.*
Lesebuch *reader (book).*
LESEN *to read, lecture.*
lesenswert *worth reading.*
Leser *m. reader (person).*
leserlich *legible.*
LETZT *(er, -e, -es) last, latest, final, extreme.*
  in letzter Zeit *lately, recently.*
  letzte Neuheit *latest novelty.*

letzten Endes *after all.*
letzten Sonntag *last Sunday.*
letztes hergeben *to do one's utmost.*
letztens *lately, of late.*
Leuchte *f. lamp, light.*
leuchten *to light, shine, beam, glow.*
Leuchter *m. candlestick.*
Leuchtturm *m. lighthouse.*
Leuchtuhr *f. luminous clock or watch.*
Leuchtzifferblatt *m. luminous dial.*
leugnen *to deny, disavow.*
LEUTE *pl. people, persons, folk.*
Leutnant *m. second lieutenant.*
leutselig *affable.*
Lexikon *n. dictionary.*
LICHT *n. light, candle, illumination.*
  Bitte, machen Sie das Licht an. *Please*
    turn on the light.
  Licht anzünden *to turn on the light.*
  Licht ausmachen *to turn off the light.*
  in ein falsches Licht setzen *to*
    misrepresent.
  Mir ging ein Licht auf. *It dawned on me.*
licht
  am lichten Tage *in broad daylight.*
  lichte Augenblicke *sane moments.*
lichtempfindlich *sensitive to light.*
lichten *to thin out, clear (forest).*
Lichterglanz *m. brightness.*
Lichtreklame *f. luminous sign, illuminated*
  advertisement.
LIEB *dear, nice, beloved, agreeable.*
  Es ist mir lieb. *I am glad.*
  es wäre mir lieb *I should like.*
Liebchen *n. darling, love, sweetheart.*
LIEBE *f. love, affection, charity.*
  aus Liebe *for love.*
  mir zu Liebe *for my sake.*
LIEBEN *to love, like, be in love.*
liebenswürdig *amiable, kind.*
Liebenswürdigkeit *f. amiability, kindness.*
lieber *dearer, rather.*
Liebeserklärung *f. declaration of love.*
Liebesgedicht *n. love poem.*
Liebesgeschichte *f. love story.*
Liebespaar *n. lovers, couple.*
liebgewinnen *to grow fond of.*
liebhaben *to love.*
Liebhaber *m. (-in f.) lover; amateur.*
Liebhaberei *f. fancy, liking, hobby.*
liebkosen *to caress, fondle.*
Liebkosung *f. caress, petting.*
lieblich *lovely, charming.*
Liebling *m. darling, favorite.*
Lieblingsgericht *n. favorite dish.*
Liebreiz *m. charm, attraction.*
Liebschaft *f. love affair.*
Liebste *m. & f. dearest, beloved, lover,*
  sweetheart.

LIED *n. song, air.*
Liederbuch *n. song-book, hymn-book.*
liederlich *slovenly, immoral, dissolute.*
lieferbar *available.*
Lieferfrist *f. term of delivery.*
liefern *to deliver, yield, produce.*
Lieferung *f. delivery, supply.*
LIEGEN *to lie, rest, be situated, stand.*
  Das liegt an mir. *It is my fault.*
  Mir liegt daran. *I am interested in the*
    matter.
  Mir liegt nichts daran. *I don't care for it.*
liegenlassen *to leave behind; to neglect.*
Likör *m. liqueur, cordial.*
Limonade *f. lemonade.*
lindern *to soften, ease, soothe.*
Linderung *f. relief.*
Linie *f. line, descent, branch (of a family).*
  in erster Linie *first of all.*
LINK *left, wrong side of a cloth, reverse of a*
  coin.
linkisch *awkward, clumsy.*
LINKS *to the left, on the left.*
  Gehen Sie nach links! *Go to the left!*
  Sie liess ihn ganz links liegen. *She gave*
    him the cold shoulder.
linkshändig *left-handed.*
Linnen *n. linen.*
Linse *f. lentil.*
Lippe *f. lip.*
Lippenstift *m. lipstick.*
List *f. cunning, craft.*
Liste *f. list, roll, catalogue.*
listig *cunning, crafty, sly, astute.*
Liter *m. liter (1.056 quarts).*
literarisch *literary.*
Literatur *f. literature, letters.*
Litfasssäule *f. billboard.*
Lizenz *f. license, permit.*
Lob *n. praise.*
loben *to praise.*
lobenswert *praiseworthy.*
lobpreisen *to praise.*
Loch *n. hole, gap.*
Locke *f. lock, curl.*
locken *to entice, allure.*
Löffel *m. spoon.*
  Eislöffel *m. tablespoon.*
Loge *f. box (theater).*
Logik *f. logic.*
logisch *logical.*
Lohn *m. compensation, reward, wages.*
Lohnempfänger *m. wage-earner.*
Lohnerhöhung *f. wage increase.*
lohnen *to reward.*
  Es lohnt sich. *It is worthwhile.*
Löhnung *f. pay.*
lokal *local, suburban.*
Lokomotive *f. engine (of a train).*

Los *n. lot, chance.*

LOS 1. *adv. loose, slack, free.*

  Hier ist viel los. *There's plenty going on here.*

  Mit ihm ist nicht viel los. *He is not up to much.*

  Was ist los? What's up?

  2. *separable prefix (implies the idea of separation or quick movement).*

  Du kannst die Hunde losmachen. *You can untie the dogs.*

  Eins, zwei, drei, los! *One, two, three, go!*

losbinden *to untie, unloosen.*

löschen *to put out, extinguish.*

losgehen *to set out, become loose, go off.*

loskommen *to get away.*

loswerden *to get rid of.*

Löwe *m. lion*

LUFT *f. air, breath, breeze.*

  aus der Luft greifen *to invent.*

  frische Luft schöpfen *to take the air.*

  in die Luft sprengen *to blow up.*

  keine Luft bekommen *not to be able to breathe.*

  luftdicht *air-tight.*

  in die Luft fliegen *to blow up.*

  Es liegt etwas in der Luft. *Something is in the wind.*

lüften *to air.*

luftig *airy, breezy.*

Luftkrankheit *f. airsickness.*

  luftkrank sein *to be airsick.*

Luftkurort *m. health resort.*

luftleer *airless.*

  lutleerer Raum *vacuum.*

Luftpost *f. air mail.*

Luftraum *m. atmopshere.*

Lüge *f. lie, untruth, falsehood.*

lügen *to lie (falsify).*

Lunge *f. lung.*

Lungenentzündung *f. pneumonia.*

Lupe *f. magnifying glass.*

Lust *f. pleasure, joy, delight, inclination, lust.*

  Lust haben *to be inclined to.*

  mit Lust und Liebe *with heart and soul.*

lustig *gay, funny, jolly.*

  sich lustig machen über *to make fun of.*

Lustspiel *n. comedy.*

Luxus *m. luxury.*

Lyrik *f. lyrics.*

M

Machart *f. style, description, kind, sort.*

MACHEN *to make, do manufacture, cause, amount to.*

  Das lässt sich machen. *This is feasible.*

  Das macht nichts. *That does not matter.*

  Was macht Ihre Erkältung? *How is your cold?*

  Spass machen *to joke.*

  Anspruch machen auf *to claim.*

MACHT *f. strength, might, power, authority.*

mächtig *strong, mighty, powerful.*

machtlos *powerless.*

MÄDCHEN *n. girl, servant.*

  Mädchen für alles *general servant.*

mädchenhaft *girlish, maidenly.*

Mädchenname *m. maiden name.*

Magen *m. stomach.*

  Ich habe einen verdorbenen Magen. *I have an upset stomach.*

Magenverstimmung *f. stomach upset.*

mager *thin, scanty.*

Magerkeit *f. leanness, skimpiness.*

mähen *to mow, cut, reap.*

MAHL *n. meal.*

mahlen *to grind, mill.*

Mahnbrief *m. request to payment; demand notice.*

mahnen *to remind, admonish, exort.*

Mahnung *f. reminder, warning.*

MAI *m. May.*

Maiglöckchen *n. lily of the valley.*

Mais *m. corn, maize.*

Major *m. major.*

MAL *n.* 1. *landmark, monument, mark.* 2. *time, turn.*

  dieses Mal *for once.*

  ein für alle Mal *once and for all.*

  mit einem Mal *suddenly.*

  zum ersten Mal *for the first time.*

mal *times, once, just.*

  Danke vielmals *thank you very much.*

  Viermal drei ist zwölf *Four times three is twelve.*

malen *to paint, portray, represent.*

  sich malen lassen *to have one's portrait made.*

Maler *m. painter.*

malerisch *pictorial, picturesque.*

MAN *one, they, people, you.*

  man hat mir gesagt, dass. . . . *I was told that. . . .*

  Man spricht hier Deutsch. *They (We) speak German here.*

  Man sagt so. *So they say.*

MANCHE *many, some.*

manch(er,-e,-es) *many a.*

mancherlei *various, diverse.*

manchmal *sometimes*

Mangel *m. need, want, absence, lack.*

  aus Mangel an *for want of.*

mangelhaft *faulty, defective.*

mangeln *to want, be wanting.*

  es mangelt mir an *I am short of.*

Manier *f. manner, style.*

manierlich *polite, civil, mannerly.*

MANN *m. man; husband.*

  mit zweitausend Mann *with 2,000 men (soldiers).*

  ein Mann ein Wort *A man is as good as his word.*

  wenn Not am Mann ist *if the worst comes to the worst.*

Mannesalter *n. manhood.*

mannhaft *manly.*

männlich *male, manly.*

Manschette *f. cuff.*

Manschettenknopf *m. sleeve link.*

MANTEL *m. coat.*

Mappe *f. document case, writing case.*

Märchen *n. fairy tale.*

märchenhaft *fabulous, legendary.*

Marine *f. navy.*

Mark *f. mark (currency).*

markant *characteristic, striking.*

Marke *f. mark, sign, postage stamp, token.*

MARKT *m. market, marketplace.*

Markthalle *f. market-hall.*

Marktplatz *m. marketplace.*

Marmelade *f. jam.*

Marmor *m. marble.*

Marmorplatte *f. marble slab.*

Marsch *m. march.*

marschieren *to march.*

MÄRZ *m. March.*

Marzipan *m. & n. marzipan.*

MASCHINE *f. machine, engine, typewriter.*

  auf der Maschine schreiben *to typewrite.*

Maske *f. mask, disguise.*

Maskenball *m. fancy dress ball.*

Maskerade *f. masquerade.*

MASS *n. measure, dimension, size, degree, proportion, moderation.*

  in hohem Mass *in a high degree.*

  Mass nehmen *to measure.*

  Masse und Gewichte *pl. weights and measurements.*

  nach Mass gemacht *made to measure.*

Massarbeit *f. made to measure (to order).*

MASSE *f. crowd, mass, quantity.*

massenhaft *in large quantities, wholesale.*

massgebend *standard.*

massgeblich *standard.*

masshalten *to observe moderation, keep within limits.*

mässig *reasonable, moderate, poor, mediocre.*

mässigen *to observe moderation, restrain.*

Mässigkeit *f. moderation, frugality.*

masslos *boundless, without limit.*

Massregel *f. measure, step.*

Massstab *m. yard, measure, scale.*

Material *n. material, substance.*

materialisieren *to materialize.*

materialistisch *materialistic.*

Mathematik *f. mathematics.*

Matratze *f. mattress.*

Matrose *m. sailor.*

matt *weak, soft, dull; mate (chess).*

  mattsetzen *to mate (chess).*

Matte *f. mat.*

Mauer *f. wall.*

mauern *to build with stones.*

Maultier *n. mule.*

Maurer *m. mason, bricklayer.*

Maus *f. mouse.*

Mechanik *f. mechanics.*

Mechaniker *m. mechanic.*

mechanisch *mechanical.*

Medikament *n. medicament.*

Medizin *f. medicine, remedy.*

Mediziner *m. medical student.*

MEER *n. sea, seashore.*

Meerenge *f. channel, straights, narrows.*

Meeresspiegel *m. sea-level.*

Mehl *n. flour.*

MEHR *more.*

  desto mehr *all the more.*

  immer mehr *more and more.*

  je mehr . . . desto *the more . . . the more.*

  mehr als *more than.*

  nicht mehr *no more, any more, any longer.*

  nie mehr *never again.*

  nur mehr *only, nothing but.*

  um so mehr als . . . *all the more as.*

Mehrbetrag *m. surplus.*

mehrere *several.*

mehreres *several things.*

mehrfach *manifold, numerous.*

Mehrheit *f. majority.*

mehrmals *several times, again and again.*

Mehrzahl *f. majority, plural.*

Meile *f. mile (1.609 kilometers).*

MEIN *poss. adj. my.*

MEIN(er, –e, –es) *poss. pron. mine.*

MEINEN *to mean, think, believe, suppose.*

  Was meinen Sie damit? *What do you mean by that?*

  So war es nicht gemeint *It wasn't meant that way.*

  Wie meinen Sie das? *How do you mean that?*

meinerseits *for my part, as far as I am concerned.*

meinesgleichen *my equals, people like me.*

meinethalben *for my sake, for all I care.*

meinetwegen *for my sake, for me, on my account, as far as I am concerned.*

meinetwillen (um–) *for my sake.*

MEINUNG *f. meaning, opinion, view.*

  einem die Meinung sagen *to give someone a piece of one's mind.*

meiner Meinung nach   *to my mind, in my opinion.*
meist *most, mostly.*
   die meisten   *most people.*
MEISTENS *mostly.*
MEISTER *m. master.*
   Übung macht den Meister.   *Practice makes perfect.*
Meisterschaft *f. championship.*
Meistersinger *mastersinger.*
Meisterstück *n. masterpiece.*
Meisterwerk *n. masterpiece.*
Meldeamt *n. registration office.*
melden *to report, announce, inform, apply.*
Meldezettel *m. registration form.*
Meldung *f. news, announcement, advice, notification.*
melken *to milk.*
Melodie *f. melody, tune.*
Menge *f. quantity, amount, lots, multitude.*
   in Mengen   *in abundance, plenty of*
mengen *to mix, meddle, interfere.*
MENSCH *m. man, human being, person.*
   Es kam kein Mensch.   *Not a soul came.*
   seit Menschengedenken   *within the memory of man; immemorial.*
   Was für ein Mensch ist er?   *What sort of a person is he?*
Menschenalter *n. generation.*
menschenmöglich *humanly possible.*
Menschheit *f. human race.*
menschlich *human.*
Menschlichkeit *f. human nature.*
merkbar *noticeable.*
merken *to perceive, notice, observe, note.*
   sich merken   *to keep in mind.*
   sich nichts merken lassen   *to appear to know nothing.*
merklich *noticeable.*
Merkmal *n. characteristic, sign, mark.*
merkwürdig *characteristic, strange, peculiar, remarkable.*
merkwürdigerweise *strangely enough, strange to say.*
Merkwürdigkeit *f. strangeness, peculiarity.*
Messe *f. mass; fair; mess (officers').*
MESSEN *to measure, survey, take the temperature (of a patient).*
   Blicken messen   *to eye.*
   messen mit   *to compete with.*
   nicht messen können mit   *to be no match*
MESSER *n. knife.*
Messergriff *m. knife handle.*
Messerstich *m. stab (with a knife).*
Messing *brass.*
Metall *n. metal.*
Meter *n. meter (39.37 inches).*
Metermass *n. tape-measure.*
Methode *f. method.*

Metzger *m. butcher.*
Metzgerei *n. butcher's shop.*
MICH *acc. of ich (pers. pron) me, myself.*
Miene *f. expression (facial), air, countenance.*
   gute Miene zum bösen Spiel machen   *to put up a brave show.*
MIETE *f. rent, lease.*
   Die Miete ist fällig.   *The rent is due.*
   zur Miete wohnen   *to be a tenant, to rent.*
mieten *to rent.*
Mieter *m. tenant.*
mietefrei *rent free.*
Mietshaus *n. apartment house.*
Mietvertrag *m. lease.*
Mikrofon *n. microphone.*
Mikroskop *n. microscope.*
mikroskopisch *microscopic.*
MILCH *f. milk.*
Milchgeschäft *n. dairy.*
Milchgesicht *n. baby face.*
Milchglas *n. opalescent glass.*
Milchladen *m. dairy.*
Milchstrasse *f. Milky Way.*
Milchzahn *m. milk tooth.*
MILD *mild, soft, gentle, mellow, kind.*
MILDE *f. gentleness, kindness.*
mildern *to soften, extenuate.*
   mildernde Umstände   *extenuating circumstances.*
mildtätig *kind, generous.*
Militär *n. army, service.*
Militärdienst *m. active service.*
militärisch *military.*
Militarismus *m. militarism.*
MILLIARDE *f. billion.*
MILLION *f. million.*
Millionär *m. millionaire.*
MINDER *less, minor, inferior.*
minderbemittelt *of moderate means.*
Minderheit *f. minority.*
minderjährig *minor (age).*
   minderjährig sein   *to be a minor.*
Minderjährigkeit *f. minority (age).*
minderwertig *inferior.*
Minderwertigkeitsgefühl *n. inferiority complex.*
MINDEST *least.*
   nicht im mindesten   *not in the least, by no means.*
mindestens *at least.*
Mindestlohn *m. minimum wage.*
Mine *f. mine.*
Mineral *n. mineral.*
Minister *m. minister.*
Ministerium *n. ministry.*
Ministerpräsident *m. prime minister.*
MINUTE *f. minute.*
   minutenlang   *for several minutes.*

MIR *dat. of ich (pers. pron.) to me, me, myself.*

mischen *to blend, mix, meddle, shuffle (cards).*

   sich einmischen *to interfere.*

Mischung *f. blend, mix.*

missachten *to disregard, disdain.*

Missachtung *f. disregard, disdain.*

missbilligen *to disapprove.*

Missbilligung *f. disapproval.*

missbrauchen *to misuse, abuse.*

missen *to do without.*

Misserfolg *m. failure.*

Missetat *f. misdeed, crime.*

Missetäter *m. criminal.*

missfallen *to displease.*

Missgeschick *n. bad luck, misfortune.*

missglücken *to fail.*

missgönnen *to grudge.*

missgünstig *envious, jealous.*

Misstrauen *n. distrust, mistrust.*

misstrauen *to distrust, mistrust.*

misstrauisch *suspicious.*

missvergnügt *displeased.*

missverstehen *to misunderstand.*

MIT *prep. (dat.) with, at, by.*

   Der Patient hat mit gutem Appetit gegessen. *The patient has eaten with a good appetite.*

   mit anderen Worten *in other words.*

   mit der Post *by post.*

   mit der Zeit *gradually.*

   Die Kosten sind mitberechnet. *The costs are included.*

   Mit fünf Jahren spielte er schon Klavier. *At the age of five, he already played the piano.*

   Wir sind mit der Eisenbahn gereist. *We traveled by train.*

   2. *separable prefix (implies accompaniment or participation).*

   Kommen Sie mit? *Are you coming along?*

mitarbeiten *to collaborate, cooperate, contribute.*

Mitarbeiter *m. collaborator.*

Mitbesitzer *m. joint proprietor.*

mitbringen *to bring along.*

Mitbürger *m. fellow citizen.*

miteinander *with each other, together, jointly.*

mitempfinden *to sympathize with.*

Mitgefühl *n. sympathy.*

Mitgift *f. dowry.*

Mitglied *n. member.*

mitkommen *to accompany, come along, keep up.*

Mitleid *n. sympathy, pity, mercy.*

Mitleidenschaft *f. compassion.*

   in Mitleidenschaft ziehen *to affect.*

mitleidig *compassionate.*

mitleidlos *pitiless.*

mitmachen *to take part in, go through.*

   Sie hat sehr viel mitgemacht. *She went through a lot.*

mitnehmen *to take along, affect.*

   Ihr Tod hat ihn sehr mitgenommen. *Her death affected him deeply.*

mitschuldig *implicated (in a crime).*

Mitschuldige *m. & f. accomplice.*

mitspielen *to join in a game; to accompany (music).*

MITTAG *m. noon, midday; south.*

   zu Mittag essen *to have lunch.*

Mittagessen *n. lunch.*

mittags *at noon.*

Mittagspause *f. lunch hour.*

MITTE *f. middle, centre, mean, medium.*

   Er ist Mitte dreissig. *He is in his middle thirties.*

   goldene Mitte *golden mean.*

mitteilen *to impart, communicate.*

Mitteilung *f. information, communication, intelligence.*

Mittel *n. means; remedy, cure, medicine.*

   Er ist ohne irgendwelche Mittel. *He is penniless.*

   als Mittel zum Zweck *as a means to an end.*

Mittelalter *n. Middle Ages.*

Mitteleuropa *n. Central Europe.*

mittellos *without means.*

mittelmässig *average, mediocre.*

Mittelmeer *n. Mediterranean.*

Mittelstand *m. middle class.*

MITTEN *midway, in the middle of.*

   mitten auf (in) *in the midst of.*

   mittendrin *right in the middle of.*

   mittendurch *right across, right through.*

   mitten auf der Strasse *in/on the open street.*

   mitten in der Nacht *in the middle of the night.*

MITTERNACHT *f. midnight.*

mitternachts *at midnight.*

mittlerweile *meanwhile, in the meantime.*

MITTWOCH *m. Wednesday.*

mitunter *sometimes, now and then.*

Mitwelt *f. our age, our generation.*

Mitwisser *m. confident, one in on the secret.*

MÖBEL *n. piece of furniture.*

Möbel *pl. furniture.*

Möbelhändler *m. furniture dealer.*

Möbelstück *n. piece of furniture.*

möblieren *to furnish.*

Mode *f. fashion.*

Modell *n. model, pattern, mold.*

modern *modern.*

Modenschau *f. fashion show.*
modisch *fashionable.*
MÖGEN *to want, wish, be able, be allowed; to like, care for.*
  Das mag ich nicht. *I don't like that.*
  Das mag sein *that may be so.*
  Er ist faul, er mag nicht lernen. *He is lazy, he does not want to learn.*
  Ich möchte nicht. *I don't want to.*
  Ich möchte wissen. *I'd like to know.*
  wie dern auch sein mag *be that as it may.*
  lieber mögen *to prefer.*
  Ich möchte lieber auf dem Land leben. *I'd rather live in the country.*
möglich *possible, practicable, feasible, likely.*
  alles mögliche *all sorts of things, everything possible.*
  möglichst wenig *as little as possible.*
  möglichst schnell *as quickly as possible.*
  Nicht möglich! *It can't be!*
  sein möglichstes tun *to do one's utmost.*
möglicherweise *possibly, perhaps.*
Möglichkeit *f. possibility, chance.*
Moment *m. moment.*
  Einen Moment! *One moment!*
Momentaufnahme *f. snapshot.*
Monarchie *f. monarchy.*
MONAT *m. month.*
monatelang *for months.*
monatlich *monthly.*
Mönch *m. monk.*
MOND *m. moon.*
Mondschein *m. moonlight.*
Monolog *m. monologue.*
MONTAG *m. Monday.*
Moor *n. swamp.*
Moos *n. moss.*
Mop *m. mop.*
moppen *to mop.*
Moral *f. morality, morals, moral.*
moralisch *moral.*
moralisieren *to moralize.*
Mord *m. murder.*
  Selbstmord *m. suicide.*
Mordanschlag *m. murderous attack.*
Mörder *m. murderer.*
MORGEN *m. morning, dawn, daybreak; the following day.*
  früh morgens *early in the morning.*
  Guten Morgen. *Good morning.*
  heute morgen *this morning.*
  morgens *in the morning.*
morgen *tomorrow.*
  morgen früh *tomorrow morning.*
  morgen in acht Tagen *a week from tomorrow.*
  Morgen ist auch ein Tag. *Tomorrow is another day.*

Morgengrauen *n. dawn of the day, break of the day.*
morgenländisch *eastern, oriental.*
Morgenrock *m. robe.*
Motor *m. motor, engine.*
Motorboot *n. motor boat.*
Motorpanne *f. engine trouble.*
Motorrad *n. motorcycle.*
Matte *f. moth.*
Mücke *f. mosquito (gnat).*
Mückenstich *m. mosquito bite.*
MÜDE *tired, weary.*
  müde werden *to get tired.*
Müdigkeit *f. weariness, fatigue.*
MÜHE *f. labor, toil, effort.*
  sich Mühe geben *to take pains.*
  der Mühe wert *worthwhile.*
  mit Müh und Not *only just, barely.*
  Mühe machen *to give troubles.*
  machen Sie sich keine Mühe! *Don't bother.*
mühelos *easy, effortless.*
Mühevoll *laborious, difficult.*
Mühle *f. mill.*
Müller *m. miller.*
MUND *m. mouth.*
  den Mund halten *to keep one's mouth shut.*
  den Mund vollnehmen *to brag.*
  Er ist nicht auf den Mund gefallen. *He has a ready tongue.*
  nach dem Mund reden *to flatter.*
  Sie leben von der Hand in den Mund. *They live from hand to mouth.*
Mundwinkel *m. corner of the mouth.*
Munition *f. ammunition.*
munter *alive, wide-awake, gay.*
Münze *f. coin, medal.*
  Sie nimmt alles für bare Münze. *She takes everything at its face value.*
mürrisch *morose, sullen.*
Museum *n. museum.*
Musik *f. music.*
musikalisch *musical.*
Muskel *m. muscle.*
Muskelkater *m. stiffness and soreness.*
MÜSSEN *to have to, be obliged to, must, ought to.*
  Alle Menschen müssen sterben. *All human beings must die.*
  Man müsste es ihr eigentlich sagen. *Somebody really ought to tell her.*
  Sie müssen nicht, wenn Sie nicht wollen. *You don't have to if you don't want to.*
Muster *n. sample, model, design, pattern.*
musterhaft *exemplary, standard.*
mustern *to examine.*

Musterung f. examination.

MUT m. courage, fortitude, state of mind.

jemandem den Mut nehmen   to discourage
someone.

Mut fassen   to summon up courage.

Mut machen   to encourage.

den Mut verlieren   to lose one's courage.

mutig brave.

mutlos despondent, disheartened.

MUTTER f. mother.

Muttermal n. birthmark.

Muttersprache f. mother tongue.

Mütze f. cap.

N

NACH 1. prep. (with dat.) after, toward,
according to, like, past, by, in.

dem Namen nach kennen   to know by
name.

der Sage nach   according to the legend.

Der Vater schickt die Kinder nach
Hause.   The father sends the children
home.

einer nach dem anderen   one after
another, one at a time.

Es ist zehn nach fünf.   It is ten after five.

Es sieht nach Schnee aus.   It looks like
snow.

Gehen Sie nach links!   Turn left.

meiner Meinung nach   in my opinion.

Nach dem Essen ruht er sich aus.   He
rests after meals.

nach und nach   little by little

2. adv. after, toward, according to.

3. separable prefix (implies coming after,
following, imitation).

Der Schutzmann lief dem Dieb nach.   The
policeman ran after the thief.

Kannst du diese Arbeit nachmachen?   Can
you copy this work?

nachahmen to imitate.

nachahmenswert worthy of imitation.

Nachahmung f. imitation.

Nachbar m. neighbor.

Nachbarschaft f. neighborhood.

nachdem conj. after.

Nachdem er sie verlassen hatte, weinte
sie.   After he had left, she cried.

nachdenken to reflect, think.

nachdenken über   to think over.

nachdenklich thoughtful.

Nachdruck m. stress, emphasis, reprint,
reproduction.

Nachdruck verboten.   Reproduction
forbidden.

nachdrücklich strong, emphatic.

nacheifern to emulate.

nachforschen to inquire into, investigate.

Nachfrage f. inquiry, demand.

nachgeben to yield, give way.

nachgehen to follow, investigate, inquire.

Nachgeschmack m. after-taste.

nachher afterwards, later.

Nachhilfe f. aid, help, coaching.

nachkommen to come later, follow on.

Nachkriegszeit f. postwar period.

nachlässig negligent, careless.

Nachlässigkeit f. negligence, carelessness.

nachlaufen to run after.

nachlesen to look up (in a book).

nachmachen to imitate, copy, counterfeit,
duplicate.

NACHMITTAG m. afternoon.

nachmittags afternoons, in the afternoon.

Nachnahme f. cash on delivery.

Nachname m. surname.

nachprüfen to test, check, verify.

Nachricht f. news, information, account,
report, message.

Ist eine Nachricht für mich da?   Is there a
message for me?

nachsagen to repeat after.

nachsehen to revise, check, examine.

nachsenden to send after.

Nachsicht f. indulgence.

nachsichtig (-sichtsvoll) indulgent, lenient.

nächst nearest, next, closest, following. prep.
(dat.) next to, next after.

Nächstenliebe f. love for one's fellow men;
charity.

NACHT f. night.

bei Nacht, des Nachts   at night.

bis in die Nacht arbeiten   to burn the
midnight oil.

über Nacht   during the night.

über Nacht bleiben   to stay overnight.

Nachteil m. disadvantage, loss, damage,
injury.

im Nachteil sein   to be at a
disadvantage.

Nachthemd n. nightgown.

Nachtigall f. nightingale.

Nachtisch m. dessert.

Nachtrag m. supplement.

nachtragen to add.

nachträglich additional, further.

Nachweis m. proof, evidence.

nachweisen to prove.

Nachwirkung f. after-effect.

Nachwuchs m. after-crop, rising generation.

Nacken m. nape of the neck.

nackt naked, nude, bare, plain.

Nadel f. needle, pin.

NAGEL m. nail.

Es brennt mir auf den Nägeln.   The matter
is urgent.

den Nagel auf den Kopf treffen *to hit the nail on the head.*

Nagelfeile *f. nail file.*

Nähe *f. nearness, proximity, vicinity.*

in der Nähe *near to, close at hand.*

NAHE *near, close to, imminent, approaching.*

nahe daran sein *to be about.*

zu nahe treten *to hurt one's feelings, offend.*

nahen *to draw near, approach.*

nähen *to sew, stitch.*

näher *nearer, closer, more intimate, further.*

Nähere *n. details, particulars.*

Näherin *f. seamstress.*

nähern *to bring near, place near.*

nahestehen *to be closely connected, be friends with.*

Nähgarn *n. sewing thread.*

Nähmaschine *f. sewing machine.*

Nähnadel *f. sewing needle.*

Nährboden *m. fertile soil.*

nähren *to feed, nurse, nourish.*

sich nähren von *to live on.*

Nahrung *f. nourishment, food.*

Nahrungsmittel *pl. food, foodstuffs.*

NAME *m. name, appellation, character.*

dem Namen nach *by name.*

im Namen *(with gen.) on behalf of.*

namenlos *nameless.*

Namenstag *m. saint's day, name day.*

nämlich *namely, same, very.*

Narbe *f. scar.*

Narkose *f. anesthetic.*

Narr *m. fool, jester.*

zum Narren halten *to make a fool of.*

narren *to fool.*

NASE *f. nose.*

Der Zug fuhr mir vor der Nase weg. *I missed the train by a hair (nose).*

Sie schlug ihm die Tür vor der Nase zu. *She slammed the door in his face.*

NASS *wet, damp.*

Die Strasse ist nass. *The street is wet.*

Bei Nässe glatt. *Slippery when wet.*

nass werden *to get wet.*

Nation *f. nation.*

national *national.*

Nationalhymne *f. national anthem.*

NATUR *f. nature, disposition, constitution.*

Naturalismus *m. naturalism.*

naturalistisch *naturalistic.*

Naturgeschichte *f. natural science.*

natürlich *natural, unaffected.*

Natürlich! *Of course!*

Natürlichkeit *f. naturalness, simplicity.*

Naturschutzgebiet *n. national park.*

naturtreu *lifelike.*

Nebel *m. fog, mist, haze.*

nebelhaft *nebulous.*

nebelig (neblig) *misty, foggy.*

Nebelregen *m. drizzle.*

Nebelwetter *n. foggy weather.*

NEBEN 1. *prep. (dat. when answering question, Wo?, acc. when answering question, Wohin?). next, next to, beside, among, besides.*

2. *adv. next to, beside, among.*

Setzen Sie sich neben mich! *Sit down next to me!*

Er sass neben dem Mädchen. *He was seated next to the girl.*

neben anderen Dingen *among other things.*

nebenan *next door.*

Nebenanschluss *m. extension (telephone).*

Nebenbegriff *m. subordinate idea.*

nebenbei *on the side, by the way, adjoining.*

nebenbei bemerkt (gesagt) *by the way, incidentally.*

Nebenberuf *m. additional occupation, side-line.*

nebeneinander *next to each other, side by side.*

Nebeneingang *m. side entrance.*

Nebeneinnahme *f. additional income.*

Nebenerzeugnis *n. by-product.*

Nebenfluss *m. tributary.*

Nebengebäude *n. additional building, annex.*

Nebengedanke *m. subordinate idea, mental reservation.*

nebenher (nebenhin) *by the side of.*

Nebenkosten *f. incidentals, extra.*

Nebenlinie *f. branch, secondary railroad line.*

Nebenmensch *m. fellow-creature.*

Nebenperson *f. secondary character (theater).*

Nebenrolle *f. secondary part (theater).*

Nebensache *f. matter of secondary importance.*

nebensächlich *unimportant, immaterial.*

Nebensatz *m. subordinate clause (grammar).*

Nebenstrasse *f. side-street.*

Nebenzimmer *n. next room.*

necken *to tease.*

Neffe *m. nephew.*

Neger *m. (–in, f.) black (person).*

negieren *to deny.*

NEHMEN *to take, accept, receive.*

Abschied nehmen *to say good-bye.*

Anstoss nehmen *to object.*

es sich nicht nehmen lassen *to insist on something.*

es genau nehmen *to be pedantic.*

etwas zu sich nehmen *to eat something.*

genau genommen *strictly speaking.*

Nehmen Sie Platz! *Sit down!*

sich in Acht nehmen *to be careful.*

ihm beim Worte nehmen *to take him at his word.*

streng genommen *strictly speaking.*

eine Stellung nehmen *to express one's view about*

Neid *m. envy, jealousy.*

neidisch *jealous, envious.*

Neige *f. slope, decline.*

zur Neige gehen *to be on the decline, come to an end.*

neigen *to incline, bow.*

geneigt sein *to be inclined.*

Neigung *f. slope, declivity, inclination, taste.*

NEIN *no.*

Nektar *m. nectar.*

Nelke *f. carnation.*

NENNEN *to name, call, mention.*

ein Ding beim rechten Namen nennen *to call a spade a spade.*

nennenswert *worth mentioning.*

Nennwort *n. noun.*

Nerv *m. nerve.*

auf die Nerven fallen *to get on one's nerves.*

Nervenheilanstalt *f. mental hospital.*

nervenkrank *neurotic, neurasthenic.*

Nervenschwäche *f. nervous debility, neurasthenia.*

nervös *nervous.*

Nervosität *f. nervousness.*

Nerz *m. mink.*

Nest *n. nest.*

NETT *nice, neat, pretty.*

Netz *n. net, network.*

NEU *new, fresh, recent, modern, latest.*

Was gibt's Neues? *What's new?*

Neubau *m. new building, reconstruction.*

neuerdings *recently, lately.*

Neuerung *f. innovation, change.*

Neugier *f. curiosity.*

neugierig *curious.*

Neuheit *f. novelty.*

Neuhochdeutsch *n. modern high German.*

Neuigkeit *f. news.*

NEUJAHR *n. New Year.*

Glückliches Neujahr! *Happy New Year!*

neulich *recently, the other day.*

NEUN *nine.*

NEUNTE *ninth.*

NEUNZEHN *nineteen.*

NEUNZEHNTE *nineteenth.*

NEUNZIG *ninety.*

NEUNZIGSTE *ninetieth.*

neutral *neutral.*

Neuzeit *f. modern times.*

neuzeitlich *modern.*

NICHT *not.*

auch nicht *not even.*

ganz und gar nicht *not in the least.*

gar nicht *not at all.*

nicht einmal *not even.*

nicht mehr *no longer, no more.*

nicht wahr? *isn't it?*

noch nicht *not yet.*

Nichtachtung *f. disregard.*

Nichte *f. niece.*

NICHTS *nothing, not anything.*

gar nichts *nothing at all.*

Es macht nichts. *It doesn't matter.*

Ich will nichts mehr davon hören. *I don't want to hear another word about that.*

mir nichts, dir nichts *quite coolly.*

nichts als *nothing but.*

nichts anderes *nothing else.*

durchaus nicht *not at all.*

nichtsdestoweniger *nevertheless.*

nichtssagend *meaningless, insignificant.*

Nichtstuer *m. idler.*

Nichtstun *n. idling.*

nie (mals) *never.*

fast nie *hardly ever.*

NIEDER *down, low, mean.*

auf und nieder *up and down.*

niedergeschlagen *downhearted, depressed.*

Niedergeschlagenheit *f. depression.*

Niederlage *f. defeat.*

niedertreten *to trample.*

niedrig *low, inferior, humble.*

NIEMAND *nobody.*

Niere *f. kidney.*

nimmer *never.*

nimmermehr *nevermore, by no means.*

nirgends *nowhere.*

nirgendwo *nowhere.*

NOCH *still, yet, besides.*

noch dazu *in addition.*

noch ein *another.*

noch einmal *once more.*

noch einmal so *twice as.*

noch etwas *something else.*

noch immer *still.*

noch nicht *not yet.*

noch nie *never before.*

weder . . . noch *neither . . . nor.*

nochmals *once again.*

Norden *m. North.*

nach Norden *in the direction of the North.*

nordisch *nordic, northern.*

nördlich *northern.*

nordöstlich *northeastern.*

Nordpol *m. North Pole.*

Nordsee *f. North Sea.*

Norm *f. standard, rule.*

normal *normal.*

NOT *f. distress, want.*

aus Not *from necessity.*
Not bricht Eisen. *Necessity is the mother of invention.*
ohne Not *without real cause.*
seine liebe Not haben mit *to have a hard time with.*
zur Not *if need be.*
Notar *m. notary.*
notariell *attested by a notary.*
Notausgang *m. emergency exit.*
Notbehelf *m. expedient.*
Notbremse *f. emergency brake.*
Note *f. note (music, bank, dipl.); mark (school); (–n, pl., music).*
Notfall *m. emergency.*
notgedrungen *compulsory, forced.*
nötig *necessary, needful.*
nötig haben *to need.*
nötigenfalls *if need be.*
notleidend *poor, distressed.*
Notlüge *f. white lie.*
notwendig *necessary.*
Notwendigkeit *f. necessity.*
Novelle *f. short story, short novel.*
NOVEMBER *m. November.*
nüchtern *empty, sober, insipid.*
Nüchternheit *f. emptiness, sobriety, insipidity.*
null *null.*
null und nichtig *null and void.*
Null *f. zero.*
numerieren *to number.*
numerierter Platz *m. reserved seat.*
NUMMER *f. number, part, ticket, size, issue.*
Seine Nummer ist besetzt. *His line is busy.*
Welche Nummer tragen Sie? *What size do you wear?*
die letzte Nummer *the last issue (magazine).*
NUN *now, well, then.*
von nun an *henceforth, from now on.*
NUR *only, sole, merely, just, possibly.*
nur mehr *still more.*
Nur zu! *Go on!*
wenn nur *if only.*
wer nur immer *whoever.*
Lass mich nur machen! *Let me do it!*
nicht nur . . . sondern auch *not only . . . but also.*
Nuss *f. nut.*
Nussbaum *m. walnut tree.*
Nussknacker *m. nutcracker.*
nutzbar *useful, necessary.*
nutzbringend *profitable.*
Nutzen *m. profit, benefit.*
nützen *to be of use, be profitable, serve.*
Es nützt nichts! *It's no use!*
nützlich *useful.*

Nützlichkeit *f. usefulness, utility.*
nutzlos *useless.*
Nutzlosigkeit *f. uselessness, futility.*
Nylon *n. nylon.*

O

OB *whether, if.*
Wir möchten wissen, ob sie kommen. *We want to know whether they are coming.*
als ob *as if, as though.*
OBEN *above, up, upstairs, on top.*
auf . . . oben *at the top of.*
dort oben *up there.*
nach oben *upwards.*
oben auf *on top of.*
von oben bis unten *from top to bottom.*
von oben herab behandeln *to treat in a condescending manner.*
obendrein *into the bargain, in addition.*
ober *upper, supreme, above.*
das obere Bett *the upper berth.*
Ober *m. waiter.*
Herr Ober! *Waiter!*
Oberbefehlshaber *m. commander-in-chief.*
Oberfläche *f. surface, area.*
oberflächlich *superficial, superficially.*
oberhalb *above.*
Oberhemd *n. shirt.*
Oberkellner *m. headwaiter.*
Oberkörper *m. upper part of the body.*
Oberlippe *f. upper lip.*
Oberschule *f. high school.*
Oberst *m. colonel.*
oberst *highest, uppermost.*
Oberstleutnant *m. lieutenant colonel.*
obgleich *although.*
Oboe *f. oboe.*
Obrigkeit *f. authority.*
obschon *although.*
Obst *n. fruit.*
Obstgarten *m. orchard.*
Ochs *m. ox.*
ochsen *to grind, cram, work hard (slang).*
öde *dull, empty.*
ODER *or.*
oder aber *instead.*
entweder oder *either or.*
Ofen *m. stove, furnace.*
offen *open, free, vacant, frank, sincere.*
auf offener Strecke *on the road.*
offen gestanden *frankly.*
offene Rechnung *current account.*
einen offenen Sinn für eine Sache haben *to be receptive to something.*
offenbar *obvious, evident.*
Offenbarung *f. disclosure, revelation.*

Offenheit f. frankness, sincerity.
offenherzig frank, sincere.
offensichtlich obvious, apparent.
öffentlich public.
Öffentlichkeit f. publicity.
offiziell official.
Offizier m. officer.
öffnen to open, dissect.
Öffnung f. opening, gap, dissection.
OFT often, frequently.
öfter more often
    je öfter ... desto   the more ... the more.
    des öfteren   frequently.
öfters quite often.
oftmals often, frequently.
OHNE prep. (acc.) without, but, for, except.
    Er ging ohne ein Wort zu sagen.   He left
      without saying a word.
    ohne Arbeit   out of work.
    ohne dass   without (conj.).
    ohne dass er mich angeredet hatte   without
      his having spoken to me.
    ohne weiteres   right off.
    ohne zu   without (before verb).
    ohne zu antworten   without answering.
    ohnehin   besides, apart.
Ohnmacht f. faintness, unconsciousness,
    faint.
ohnmächtig powerless, unconscious, helpless.
    ohnmächtig werden   to faint.
OHR n. ear, hearing.
    die Ohren steif halten   to keep one's
      courage.
    ganz Ohr sein   to be all ears.
Ohrring m. earring.
OKTOBER m. October.
ÖL n. oil.
Ölbaum m. olive tree.
Ölbild n. oil painting.
ölen to oil, lubricate.
Ölfarbe f. paint.
ölig oily.
Olive f. olive.
Omelett(e) n. omelet.
ONKEL m. uncle.
OPER f. opera, opera house.
Operation f. operation.
Operette f. operetta.
Opfer n. sacrifice, martyr, victim.
opfern to sacrifice.
Opferung f. sacrifice.
Optiker m. optician.
Optimismus m. optimism.
optimistisch optimistic.
Orange f. orange.
Orchester n. orchestra.
Orden m. order, decoration.
ordentlich in order, neat, tidy.
ordnen to put in order, arrange.

ORDNUNG f. order, arrangement.
    Das finde ich ganz in Ordnung.   I think it
      is quite all right.
    in Ordnung bringen   to settle, straighten
      out.
    Ist alles in Ordnung?   Is everything all
      right?
    nicht in Ordnung   out of order.
    zur Ordnung rufen   to call to order.
Organ n. organ (body).
organisieren to organize.
organisch organic.
Organist m. organist.
Orgel f. organ (music).
original original.
ORT m. place, spot, locality.
    Wir fanden alles wieder an Ort und
      Stelle.   We found everything back in
      place.
örtlich local.
Osten m. East, Orient.
    nach Osten   in the direction of the East.
Osterfest n. Easter.
Ostern n. East.
Österreicher m. Austrian.
österreichisch Austrian.
östlich eastern.
Ostsee f. Baltic sea.
ostwärts eastward.
Ozean m. ocean.

P

Paar n. pair, couple.
    mit ein Paar Worten   in a few words.
    ein Paar Strümpfe   a pair of socks.
paar few, some, even, matching.
    ein paar   a few, several.
    ein paarmal   several times.
paaren to pair, couple.
Pächter m. farmer, tenant, householder.
Päckchen n. small parcel.
packen to seize, grasp, pack.
packend thrilling, absorbing.
Packung f. package, packet.
Paddelboot n. canoe.
paddeln to paddle.
Paket n. parcel.
Paketannahme f. parcel-receiving office.
Pakt m. pact, agreement.
Palast m. palace.
Palme f. palm.
panieren to coat with breadcrumbs.
Panik f. panic.
Panne f. breakdown, trouble (motor).
Pantoffel m. slipper, mule.
Pantoffelheld m. henpecked husband.
Panzer m. armor, tank,

panzern *to armor, plate.*

Pagagei *m. parrot.*

PAPIER *n. paper, identification paper, document.*

  zu Papier bringen *to write down, put on paper.*

Papierbogen *m. sheet of paper.*

Papiergeld *n. paper money.*

Papierhandlung *f. stationery store.*

Papierkorb *m. wastepaper basket.*

Pappe *f. cardboard.*

Papst *m. Pope.*

Parade *f. parade, review.*

Paradies *n. paradise.*

paradiesisch *paradisiacal.*

parallel *parallel.*

Parfum or **Parfüm** *n. perfume.*

PARK *n. park, grounds.*

parken *to park.*

  Parkverbot! *No parking!*

Parkplatz *m. parking place.*

Parlament. *n. parliament.*

Parodie *f. parody.*

Partei *f. party, faction, tenant, side.*

  Partei nehmen für *to take the side of.*

Parterre *n. ground floor.*

Partie *f. part, section.*

  eine Partie Schach *a game of chess.*

Partner *m. partner.*

Partnerschaft *f. partnership.*

Pass *m. pass, passage, passport.*

Passagier *m. passenger.*

Passamt *n. passport division.*

Passant *m. passer-by.*

PASSEN *to fit, suit, be convenient, be suitable.*

  zueinander passen *to match, harmonize.*

PASSEND *suitable, convenient.*

passieren *to happen, go through, pass, cross.*

  Was ist passiert? *What happened? (What's the trouble?)*

passiv *passive.*

Passkontrolle *f. examination of passport.*

Pastete *f. pie, pastry.*

Pastor *m. pastor, minister, clergyman.*

Pate *m. godfather.*

Patenkind *n. godchild.*

Patent *n. (letters) patent.*

Patentamt *n. patent office.*

pathetisch *pathetic.*

Patient *m. patient.*

Patin *f. godmother.*

Patriot *m. patriot.*

patriotisch *patriotic.*

Pauke *f. kettledrum.*

Pause *f. pause, interval, break, rest (music).*

pausieren *to pause.*

Pech *n. bad luck, pitch.*

pechschwarz *pitch-black.*

Pechvogel *m. unlucky person.*

Pedal *n. pedal.*

Pedant *m. pedant.*

pedantisch *pedantic.*

Pein *f. pain, agony, torture.*

peinigen *to torment, harass.*

Peiniger *m. tormentor.*

Peinigung *f. torment, torture.*

peinlich *painful, embarrassing.*

Peinlichkeit *f. painfulness; carefulness, embarrassment.*

Peitsche *f. whip, lash.*

Pellkartoffeln *pl. potatoes in their jackets.*

PELZ *m. fur, pelt, skin, hide, fur coat.*

Pelzhändler *m. furrier.*

Pelzmantel *m. fur coat.*

Pension *f. pension; boarding-house.*

  Er erhält eine Pension. *He receives a pension.*

  in Pension sein *to board.*

Pensionat *n. boarding-school.*

pensionieren *to pension off.*

per *per.*

  per Post *by post.*

  per Adresse *(in) care of.*

Periode *f. period.*

Perle *f. pearl, bead.*

perlen *to sparkle, glisten.*

Perlenkette *f. pearl necklace, string of pearls.*

PERSON *f. person, personage, character (theater).*

  in Person *in person.*

Personal *n. staff, employees, personnel.*

Personalbeschreibung *f. personal description of a person.*

Personalien *pl. particulars about a person, data.*

Personenaufzug *m. passenger elevator.*

Personenkraftwagen *m. motor-car.*

Personenzug *m. passenger train.*

persönlich *personal; personally.*

Persönlichkeit *f. personality.*

Perücke *f. wig.*

pessimistisch *pessimistic.*

Pest *f. plague, pestilence, epidemic.*

Petersilie *f. parsley.*

Pfad *m. path.*

Pfadfinder *m. (–in, f.) boy (girl) scout.*

Pfahl *m. pole, stake, pile, post.*

Pfand *m. pledge, security, forfeit.*

pfänden *to seize, take in pledge.*

Pfandhaus *n. pawnshop.*

Pfandleiher *m. pawnbroker.*

Pfandschein *m. pawn ticket.*

Pfanne *f. pan.*

Pfannkuchen *m. pancake.*

Pfarrer *m. priest, pastor, minister.*

Pfarrgemeinde *f. parish.*

Pfau m. peacock.
PFEFFER m. pepper
Pfefferkuchen m. spiced cakes, gingerbread.
Pfefferminz n. & f. peppermint.
pfeffern to season with pepper.
Pfeife f. pipe, whistle.
pfeifen to whistle, pipe.
Pfeil m. arrow.
Pfeiler m. pillar, post.
PFERD n. horse.
Pfiff m. whistle, whistling, trick.
Pfingsten n. & f. Pentecost, Whitsuntide.
Pfirsich m. peach.
PFLANZE f. plant.
pflanzen to plant.
Pflanzenkunde f. botany.
Pflaster n. plaster, pavement.
Pflasterstein m. paving-stone.
PFLAUME f. plum.
    gedörrte Pflaume   f. prune.
Pflaumenmus n. plum jam.
PFLEGE f. care, attention, nursing.
Pflegeeltern pl. foster parents.
Pflegekind n. foster child.
pflegen to care for, cherish, nurse, cultivate.
PFLICHT f. duty, obligation.
Pflichteifer m. zeal.
Pflichtgefühl n. sense of duty.
pflichtgemäss obligatory.
pflücken to pick, gather, pluck.
Pflug m. plough.
pflügen to plough.
Pförtner m. gatekeeper.
Pfote f. paw.
Pfui! Shame!
Pfund n. pound.
Pfütze f. puddle.
Phänomen n. phenomenon.
Phantasie f. imagination, fancy.
phantasieren to daydream, imagine.
Phantast m. dreamer, visionary.
phantastisch fantastic, fanciful.
Philosoph m. philosopher.
Philosophie f. philosophy.
philosophieren to philosophize.
Photoapparat m. camera.
Photograph m. photographer.
Photographie f. photography.
photographieren to photograph.
Physik f. physics.
Pianist m. pianist.
Piano n. piano.
Picknick n. picnic.
Pietät f. reverence, piety.
pietätlos irreverent.
Pikkoloflöte f. piccolo.
Pilger m. pilgrim.
pilgern to go on a pilgrimage.
Pille f. pill.

Pilot m. pilot.
Pilz m. mushroom.
    Giftpilz   m. poisonous mushroom.
Pinsel m. brush, paintbrush.
pinseln to paint (art).
Pirat m. pirate.
Pistole f. pistol.
Plage f. plague.
plagen to plague, torment.
    sich plagen   to struggle, overwork oneself.
Plakat placard, poster.
    Keine Plakate.   Post no bills.
Plakatsäule f. sign post.
Plan m. plan, map, design; intention.
planen to plan, scheme.
Planet m. planet.
planlos without any fixed plan.
planmässig according to plan; methodical.
Planung f. planning, plan.
Planwirtschaft f. economic planning.
Plastik f. plastic art, sculpture.
plastisch plastic.
Platin n. platinum.
plätschern to splash.
PLATT flat, level, insipid, dull.
Plattdeutsch n. Low German.
Platte f. plate, tray; record (phonograph)
    kalte Platte   cold meats.
PLATZ m. place, spot, room, seat; square
    (street).
    Platz machen   to make room.
    Bitte, nehmen Sie Platz.   Please have a
        seat.
    am Platz sein   to be opportune.
Platzanweiser m. (–in, f.) usher.
Plätzchen n. little place; cookie.
platzen to burst, explode, crack.
Platzmangel m. lack of space.
Plauderei f. chat, small talk, conversation.
PLAUDERN to chat, talk, gossip.
PLÖTZLICH sudden; suddenly.
plump heavy, shapeless, tactless, clumsy.
Plumpheit f. shapelessness, heaviness,
        clumsiness.
plumpsen to plump down.
plündern to plunder, pillage.
Plünderung f. plundering, sack.
Plural m. plural.
Pöbel m. mob, populace.
pöbelhaft vulgar, low.
pochen to knock, beat, throb.
Pocken f. pl. smallpox.
Pockenimpfung f. smallpox vaccination.
Podium n. platform, rostrum.
Poesie f. poetry.
Poet m. poet.
poetisch poetical.
Pol m. pole.
polar polar, arctic.

Polarforscher m. polar explorer.
Pole m. Pole (native of Poland).
polieren to polish.
Poliermittel n. polish.
Politik f. politics, policy.
Politiker m. politician.
politisch political.
politisieren to talk politics.
Politur f. polish, gloss, refinement.
POLIZEI f. police.
    Rufen Sie die Polizei!   Call the police!
    Polizeibehörde   police authorities.
Polizeiamt n. police-station.
Polizeiaufsicht f. police control.
polizeilich of the police.
Polizeistreife f. police raid.
Polizeistunde f. curfew.
polizeiwidrig contrary to police regulations.
Polizist m. policeman, constable.
polnisch Polish.
Polster n. cushion, pillow, bolster, pad.
Polstermöbel pl. upholstered furniture.
Polstersessel m. easy chair.
Polsterung f. upholstery, padding, stuffing.
Pomade f. pomade, hair gel.
Pomp m. pomp.
pomphaft pompous, magnificent.
pompös pompous, magnificent.
populär popular
Pore f. pore.
porös porous.
Portemonnaie n. purse.
Portion f. portion, helping, ration, order.
Porto n. postage.
portofrei postfree, prepaid.
portopflichtig liable to postage fee.
Porträt n. portrait, likeness.
porträtieren to portray, paint a portrait.
Porträtmaler m. portrait painter.
Porzellan porcelain, china.
Porzellanservice n. set of china.
positiv positive.
POST f. post, mail, post office.
Postfach n. post-office box.
Postamt n. post office.
Postanweisung f. money order.
Postbeamte m. post-office clerk.
Postbote m. postman.
Posten m. post, situation.
    auf dem Posten sein   to feel well.
Postkarte f. postcard.
postlagernd general delivery (USA).
postlich postal.
Postschliessfach n. post-office box.
postwendend by return mail.
Pracht f. splendor.
Prachtausgabe f. deluxe edition.
prächtig magnificent, splendid, lovely.
prachtvoll splendid, gorgeous, magnificent.

prahlen to brag, boast.
Prahlerei f. boasting, bragging.
prahlerisch boastful, ostentatious.
praktisch clever, handy, useful.
    praktischer Arzt   general practitioner.
praktizieren to practice (a profession).
prall blazing, tight, tense.
    in der prallen Sonne   in the full glare of
      the sun.
Prämie f. premium.
prämieren to award a prize to.
Präposition f. preposition.
präsentieren to present.
Präsident m. president.
Präsidium n. chair, presidency.
prassen to feast, revel.
präzis precise, exact, punctual.
Präzision f. precision.
predigen to preach.
Prediger m. preacher, minister.
Predigt f. sermon, lecture.
PREIS m. price, cost, rate, praise.
    um jeden Preis   at any cost.
    um keinen Preis   not at any price.
    zu festem Preis   at fixed price.
    den Preis davontragen   to take the prize.
Preisangabe f. quotation of prices.
Preisausschreiben n. prize competition.
Preisbewerber m. competitor.
Preiselbeere f. cranberry.
preisen to praise, extol, glorify.
Preiserhöhung f. rise in prices.
Preisgabe f. surrender, abandonment.
preisgeben to surrender, give up, abandon,
      sacrifice.
Preislage f. price range.
Preisrichter m. arbiter, judge.
Preissturz m. fall in prices.
Preisträger m. prize-winner.
Preistreiberei f. forcing up of prices.
preiswert reasonable, cheap.
Premiere f. first night.
Presse f. press.
Pressestimme f. press comment, review.
Priester m. priest.
Prima f. highest class of secondary school.
prima prime, first-rate, great.
primitiv primitive.
Prinz m. (–essin, f.) prince(ss).
Prinzip n. principle.
    aus Prinzip   as a matter of principle.
prinzipiell on principle.
PRIVAT private, privately.
Privatrecht n. civil law.
Probe f. trial, experiment, test, probation;
      rehearsal (theater).
    auf die Probe stellen   to put to the test.
    Probe ablegen   to give proof of.
    die Probe bestehen   to pass the test.

zur Probe *as a sample; on approval.*
Proben halten *to have a rehearsal.*
Probeabzug *m. proof.*
proben *to rehearse.*
probeweise *on approval, on trial.*
Probezeit *f. time of probation.*
probieren *to try, taste.*
Darf ich das anprobieren? *May I try this on?*
Er probiert die Suppe *He tastes the soup.*
Problem *n. problem.*
problematisch *problematic.*
Produkt *n. product.*
Produktion *f. production.*
Produzent *m. producer, manufacturer.*
produzieren *to produce, show off, exhibit.*
Professor *m. professor.*
Prognose *f. forecast, prognosis.*
Programm *n. program.*
Projekt *n. project.*
Projektionsapparat *m. projector.*
Proklamation *f. proclamation.*
Prokura *f. procuration, power of attorney.*
prolongieren *to prolong.*
Promenade *f. promenade.*
Propaganda *f. propaganda.*
Prophet *m. prophet.*
prophetisch *prophetic.*
prophezeien *to prophesy.*
Prophezeiung *f. prophecy.*
Proportion *f. proportion.*
Prosa *f. prose.*
Prosit! *To your health!*
Prospekt *m. prospect.*
Protest *m. protest.*
Protest erheben *to protest.*
Protestant *m. Protestant.*
protestantisch *Protestant.*
Protestantismus *m. Protestantism.*
protestieren *to protest.*
Protokoll *n. protocol; proceedings.*
Proviant *m. provisions (mil.)*
Provinz *f. province.*
provinziell *provincial.*
Provision *f. brokerage.*
Prozent *n. per cent.*
Prozentsatz *m. percentage.*
prozentual *expressed as percentage.*
PROZESS *m. lawsuit, process, proceedings, trial.*
im Prozess liegen *to be involved in a law suit.*
kurzen Prozess machen mit *to dispose of quickly.*
prozessieren *to be involved in a lawsuit.*
Prozession *f. procession.*
PRÜFEN *to test, investigate, inspect, examine.*
Prüfer *m. examiner.*

Prüfling *m. examinee.*
PRÜFUNG *f. investigation, examination.*
eine Prüfung ablegen *to take an examination.*
Prunk *m. splendor, ostentation.*
prunkvoll *gorgeous, splendid.*
Psychiater *m. psychiatrist.*
Psychiatrie *f. psychiatry.*
psychisch *psychic.*
Psychologe *m. psychologist.*
Psychologie *f. psychology.*
psychologisch *psychological.*
Psychopath *m. psychopath.*
Publikum *n. public.*
Pudel *m. poodle.*
pudelnass *drenched, soaked.*
Puder *m. toilet powder.*
pudern *to powder.*
Puls *m. pulse.*
Pulsschlag *m. pulse-beat.*
Pult *n. desk.*
Pulver *n. powder, gunpowder.*
Pulverfass *n. powder barrel.*
auf dem Pulverfass sitzen *to sit on top of a volcano.*
PUNKT *m. point, dot, spot.*
der springende Punkt *the salient point.*
Punkt ein Uhr *at one o'clock sharp.*
Ausgangspunkt *point of departure.*
pünktlich *on time, punctual, prompt.*
Pünktlichkeit *f. punctuality.*
Puppe *f. doll, puppet.*
Putz *m. trimming, ornament, dress.*
putzen *to clean, polish.*
Putzfrau *f. charwoman, cleaning lady.*
Putzlappen *m. duster, flannel, polishing cloth.*
Pyjama *n. & m. pajamas*

Quadrat *n. square.*
Quäker *m. Quaker.*
Qual *f. torment, torture, pain.*
Quälen *to torment, worry, torture, bother.*
Quäler *m. tormentor.*
Quälerei *f. tormenting, torture.*
Quälgeist *m. nuisance (person).*
qualifizieren *to qualify.*
Qualität *f. quality.*
qualitativ *qualitative.*
Qualitätsware *f. high-class article.*
Qualm *m. dense smoke.*
qualmen *to smoke (chimney).*
qualmig *smoky.*
qualvoll *very painful, agonizing.*
Quarantäne *f. quarantine.*
unter Quarantäne stellen *to quarantine.*

Quecksilber *n. mercury.*
Quelle *f. spring, fountain.*
quellen *to gush, well, flow.*
Quellwasser *n. spring water.*
quer *cross, lateral, oblique; across, obliquely.*
   kreuz unter quer *all over.*
querfeldein *across country.*
Querschnitt *m. cross-section.*
Querstrasse *f. crossroad.*
quetschen *to squeeze, smash.*
Quetschung *f. contusion.*
Quetschwunde *f. bruise.*
quietschen *to scream, squeal.*
quittieren *to receipt.*
Quittung *f. receipt.*
Quote *f. quota, share.*

Rabatt *m. discount.*
Rabbiner *m. rabbi.*
Rache *f. revenge.*
rächen *to revenge, avenge.*
   sich rächen *take revenge, get revenge.*
   Deine Faulheit wird sich an dir rächen. *You will have to suffer for your laziness.*
Rachsucht *f. thirst for revenge.*
rachsüchtig *revengeful.*
RAD *n. wheel, bicycle.*
radfahren *to cycle.*
Radfahrer *m. cyclist.*
Radfahrweg *m. cycle track.*
Radiergummi *m. eraser.*
Radierung *f. etching.*
Radio *n. radio.*
Radreifen *m. bicycle tire.*
raffiniert *refined, cunning.*
Rahm *m. cream.*
Rahmen *m. frame.*
Rakete *f. rocket.*
Rampe *f. ramp, platform; limelight.*
RAND *m. edge, brim, border, margin.*
   ausser Rand und Band sein *to be out of hand.*
   Schreiben Sie es an den Rand! *Write it in the margin!*
Randbemerkung *f. marginal note.*
Rang *m. rank, order, quality, class.*
   den Rang ablaufen *to get the better of.*
   ersten Ranges *first class, first rate.*
   erster Rang *first balcony, dress circle.*
   zweiter Rang *second balcony, upper circle.*
Rangabzeichen *n. badge of rank.*
Rangordnung *f. order of precedence.*
Rangstufe *f. degree.*

rar *rare, scarce.*
Rarität *f. rarity, curiosity.*
rasch *quick, swift, speedy.*
rascheln *to rustle.*
rasen *to rave, rage, speed (coll.)*
rasend *raving, raging, frantic.*
   rasend machen *to make mad, enrage.*
Raserei *f. raving, fury; rage.*
Rasierapparat *m. safety razor.*
   elektrischer Rasierapparat *electric razor.*
rasieren *to shave.*
   sich rasieren *to shave (oneself).*
   sich rasieren lassen *to get shaved.*
Rasierklinge *f. razor blade.*
Rasiermesser *n. razor.*
Rasierpinsel *m. shaving brush.*
Rasierzeug *n. shaving things.*
Rasse *f. race, breed.*
rassig *thoroughbred.*
rassisch *racial.*
Rast *f. resting, recreation, rest, repose.*
rasten *to rest.*
rastlos *restless, indefatigable.*
Rastlosigkeit *f. restlessness.*
RAT *m. counsel, advice, consultation, remedy.*
   Rat schaffen *to devise means.*
   um Rat fragen *to ask advice.*
   zu Rat ziehen *to consult.*
   etwas zu Rate halten *to economize.*
   mit Rat und Tat *by word and deed.*
   ihm Rat erteilen *to give him advice.*
Rate *f. installment.*
raten *to advise, guess, solve.*
ratenweise *by installments.*
Ratgeber *m. adviser.*
Ration *f. ration.*
rationell *rational; economical.*
ratlos *at a loss, helpless.*
Ratlosigkeit *f. helplessness, perplexity.*
Ratschläge *m. counsel, advice.*
Rätsel *n. riddle, enigma, puzzle.*
   Es ist mir ein Rätsel. *It puzzles me.*
rätselhaft *mysterious, enigmatic.*
Ratte *f. rat.*
Raub *m. robbery, plundering.*
   auf Raub ausgehen *to go on the prowl.*
rauben *to rob, plunder.*
Räuber *m. robber, thief.*
Raubmord *m. murder and robbery.*
Raubtier *n. beast of prey.*
Raubvogel *m. bird of prey.*
Rauch *m. smoke.*
RAUCHEN *to smoke.*
   Rauchen Verboten! *No Smoking!*
Raucher *m. smoker.*
räuchern *to smoke, cure, fumigate.*
Räucherwaren *pl. smoked meats and fish.*
Rauchtabak *m. tobacco.*

Rauchzimmer n. smoking room.

RAUH uneven, rough, raw, hoarse, harsh.

Rauheit f. roughness, harshness.

RAUM m. place, room, space.

  Raum geben to give way, indulge.

räumen to clear away, remove, clean, evacuate.

Rauminhalt m. volume, capacity.

räumlich relating to space, spatial.

Räumlichkeit f. room, premises, space.

Raummangel m. lack of room.

Räumung f. removal, evacuation.

Raupe f. caterpillar.

Raupenschlepper m. caterpillar tractor.

Rausch m. intoxication, frenzy, drunkenness.

rauschen to rustle, rush, roar.

Rauschgift n. narcotic, drug.

Reaktion f. reaction.

Rebe f. grape, vine.

Rebell m. rebel.

rebellieren to rebel.

Rechen m. rake.

Rechenmaschine f. calculating machine.

RECHNEN to count, reckon, calculate.

RECHNUNG f. sum, account, bill, calculation.

  auf eigene Rechnung at one's own risk.

  auf Rechnung setzen to charge, put to one's account.

  in Rechnung ziehen to take into account.

  laut Rechnung as per invoice.

  Die Rechnung, bitte. Please bring me the check.

  Sind Sie auf Ihre Rechnung gekommen? Did you get your money's worth? (Was it worth while?)

  die Rechnung führen to keep accounts.

Rechnungsprüfer m. auditor.

RECHT n. right, privilege, title, claim, law.

  alle Rechte vorbehalten all rights reserved.

  an den Rechten kommen to meet one's match.

  mit vollem Recht for good reasons.

  nach dem Rechten sehen to see to things.

  Recht behalten to be right in the end.

  Recht geben to agree with.

  Recht haben to be right.

  Recht sprechen to administer justice.

  von Rechts wegen by rights, according to the law.

  zu Recht bestehen to be valid.

RECHT right, all right, right-hand, correct, proper, genuine, lawful.

  Das ist mir recht. That's all right with me.

  Das ist nur recht und billig. That's only fair.

  die rechte Hand the right hand.

  erst recht all the more now, now more than ever.

  Es geschieht ihm recht. It serves him right.

  es recht machen to suit, please.

  Man kann es nicht allen recht machen. You cannot please everybody.

  schlecht und recht not bad.

  zur rechten Zeit in time.

  rechtzeitig on time.

  bürgerliches Recht civil law.

  wenn es Ihnen recht ist ... if it's agreeable to you ...

Rechteck n. rectangle.

rechteckig rectangular.

rechterhand on the right hand.

rechtfertigen to justify, to exculpate.

  sich rechtfertigen to justify oneself.

Rechtfertigung f. justification.

rechthaberisch dogmatic, obstinate.

rechtlich just, lawful, legitimate.

Rechtlichkeit f. integrity, honesty.

rechtmässig lawful, legitimate.

RECHTS to the right, on the right.

  Biegen Sie rechts ab! Turn to the right!

  nach rechts to the right.

  Nehmen Sie die erste Strasse rechts. Take the first turn to your right.

  Rechts halten! Keep to the right!

  Rechts um! Right turn!

Rechtsanspruch m. legal claim.

Rechtsanwalt m. lawyer, counsel.

rechtschaffen honest, upright; very, extremely, thoroughly.

Rechtschreibung f. spelling.

Rechtsfall m. lawsuit.

Rechtsgelehrte m. jurist.

rechtsgültig legal, valid.

Rechtsspruch m. verdict.

rechtsungültig illegal, invalid.

rechtsverbindlich legally, binding.

Rechtsweg m. legal proceedings, law.

rechtswidrig illegal.

Rechtswissenschaft f. jurisprudence.

rechtzeitig in good time.

recken to stretch, extend.

  die Glieder recken to stretch one's limbs.

Redakteur m. editor.

Redaktion f. editors, editorial staff; wording.

redaktionell editorial.

REDE f. talk, discourse, speech, conversation, rumor.

  Davon ist keine Rede! That's out of the question!

  Davon ist nicht dir Rede! That's not the point!

  eine Rede halten to make a speech.

  in die Rede fallen to interrupt.

nicht der Rede wert   *not worth mentioning.*
Rede stehen   *to answer for.*
Wovon ist die Rede?   *What is it all about?*
zur Rede stellen   *to call to account, to take to task.*
Redefreiheit *f. freedom of speech.*
redegewandt *fluent, eloquent.*
REDEN *to talk, speak, converse, make a speech.*
begeistert reden   *to rave, enthuse.*
mit sich reden lassen   *to listen to reason.*
nicht zu reden von   *to say nothing of.*
von sich reden machen   *to cause a stir.*
Redensart *f. phrase, idiom, nonsense.*
Redner *m. orator, speaker.*
reduzieren *to reduce.*
Reederei *f. steamship company.*
Referenz *f. reference.*
reformieren *to reform.*
Regal *n. shelf.*
rege *active, brisk.*
Regel *f. rule, regulation, principle.*
in der Regel   *as a rule.*
regelmässig *regular, proportional.*
regeln *to arrange, regulate.*
geregelt   *regular, well ordered.*
regelrecht *regular, correct, proper.*
REGEN *m. rain, precipitation.*
Auf Regen folgt Sonnenschein.   *The calm follows the storm. ("After rain follows sunshine.")*
Regenbogen *m. rainbow.*
regendicht *waterproof.*
Regenmantel *m. raincoat.*
Regenschirm *m. umbrella.*
Regenzeit *f. rainy season.*
Regie *f. production (theater); administration, management.*
regieren *to rule, govern, reign.*
Regierung *f. government, reign, rule.*
Regierungsbeamte *n. government official.*
Regiment *n. regiment, government.*
Regisseur *m. stage manager.*
Register *n. register, index, table of contents.*
registrieren *to register.*
REGNEN *to rain*
Es regnet in Strömen.   *It's raining cats and dogs.*
regnerisch *rainy.*
regsam *active, agile, quick.*
Regsamkeit *f. agility, activity, quickness.*
Regung *f. movement.*
Reh *n. deer.*
Rehbraten *m. roast venison.*
Reibeisen *n. grater.*
Reiben *to rub, grate, grind.*
sich wundreiben   *to chafe oneself.*

REICH *rich, wealthy, well off, plentiful, abundant.*
Reich *n. empire, kingdom.*
Deutsches Reich   *n. Germany.*
Österreich   *n. Austria.*
reichen *to give, present, hand.*
reichhaltig *full, rich, abundant.*
Reichhaltigkeit *f. fullness, richness.*
reichlich *plentiful, abundant, copious.*
Reichsautobahn *f. state road.*
Reichtum *m. wealth, abundance.*
Reichweite *f. range, reach.*
Reif *m. frost.*
REIF *ripe, mature, mellow.*
Reifen *m. tire.*
reifen *to ripen, mature.*
Reifenpanne *f. flat tire, blowout.*
Reifenschaden *m. flat tire, blowout.*
Reifeprüfung *f. final comprehensive examination.*
Reifezeugnis *n. final certificate, diploma.*
reiflich *maturely, carefully.*
REIHE *f. row, range, series, sequence.*
ausser der Reihe   *out of one's mind.*
der Reihe nach   *successively, in rotation.*
Er ist an der Reihe.   *It is his turn.*
Reihenfolge *f. succession, sequence.*
reihenweise *in rows.*
Reim *m. rhyme.*
reimen *to rhyme.*
REIN *clean, plain, sheer, pure, genuine, tidy.*
aus reinem Trotz   *out of sheer obstinacy.*
reine Bahn machen   *to clear the way.*
reiner Gewinn   *net profit.*
reiner Zufall   *sheer luck, pure chance.*
aus reinem Mitleid   *out of sheer compassion.*
Reingewinn *m. net profit.*
Reinheit *f. purity, pureness.*
REINIGEN *to clean, cleanse, purify.*
Reinigung *f. cleaning, cleansing, cleaners.*
reinlich *clean, neat, tidy.*
Reinlichkeit *f. cleanliness, neatness, tidiness.*
Reis *m. rice.*
REISE *f. trip, journey, voyage.*
Glückliche Reise!   *Have a nice trip!*
eine Reise machen   *to take a trip.*
Reiseandenken   *n. souvenir (from a trip).*
Reisebüro *n. tourist office.*
Reiseführer *m. guidebook.*
REISEN *to travel.*
REISENDE *m. passenger, traveler.*
Reisescheck *m. traveler's check.*
reissen *to tear, pull, drag.*
an sich reissen   *to seize, hold up, snatch up.*
in Stücke reissen   *to tear to pieces.*
sich reissen um   *to fight for.*
reissend *ravenous, rapid, torrential.*

der reissende Strom *m. torrent.*
Reissverschluss *m. zipper.*
reiten *to ride a horse.*
Reiter *m. horseman, cavalryman.*
Reithose *f. riding pants.*
Reitschule *f. riding school.*
REIZ *m. charm, attraction; irritation; incentive.*
reizbar *sensitive, irritable, excitable.*
reizen *to irritate, excite, provoke, tempt.*
reizend *charming.*
reizlos *unattractive.*
reizvoll *charming, attractive.*
REKLAME *f. publicity, advertisement.*
     Reklame machen *to advertise.*
rekonstruieren *to reconstruct.*
Rekord *m. record, competition.*
Rektor *m. university president.*
relativ *relative, relating to.*
Religion *f. religion.*
religiös *religious.*
Rennbahn *f. racecourse.*
RENNEN *to run, race.*
Rennfahrer *m. racing cyclist.*
Rennstall *m. racing stable.*
renovieren *to renovate, redecorate.*
Rentamt *n. revenue office.*
Rente *f. pension, revenue.*
Reparation *f. reparation.*
Reparatur *f. repair.*
     Wegen Reparatur geschlossen. *Closed for repairs.*
Reparaturwerkstätte *f. repair shop.*
Reportage *f. commentary, eye-witness account.*
repräsentieren *to represent.*
Republik *f. republic.*
Republikaner *m. Republican.*
republikanisch *republican.*
Reserve *f. reserve.*
Reserverad *n. spare wheel.*
reservieren *to reserve.*
Respekt *m. respect.*
respektabel *respectable.*
respektieren *to respect.*
respektlos *without respect, irreverent.*
respektvoll *respectful.*
Rest *m. rest, remains, remnant.*
restaurieren *to repair, restore (work of art).*
Restbestand *m. remainder, residue.*
restlos *complete, without anything left over.*
Resultat *n. result, answer.*
retten *to save, preserve, rescue, deliver.*
Rettung *f. rescue, saving, escape.*
Rettungsboot *n. lifeboat.*
Rettungsgürtel *m. lifebelt.*
Reue *f. repentance.*
reuen *to repent, regret.*
     Es reut mich. *I regret.*

reumütig *repentant, penitent.*
Revier *n. hunting ground, district.*
     Polizeirevier *n. district police station.*
Revolte *f. revolt, insurrection.*
Revolution *f. revolution.*
revolutionär *revolutionary.*
Revolver *m. revolver.*
Rezept *n. recipe, prescription.*
rezitieren *to recite.*
Rheumatismus *m. rheumatism.*
rhythmisch *rhythmical.*
Richter *m. judge.*
RICHTIG *right, correct, true, real, straight.*
     Das ist nicht sein richtiger Name. *That's not his real name.*
     Meine Uhr geht richtig. *My watch is right.*
     Richtig! *Quite right!*
Richtigstellung *f. rectification.*
Richtlinie *f. guiding principle, rule.*
Richtung *f. direction, line, course, tendency.*
riechen *to smell.*
Riemen *m. strap.*
Riese *m. giant.*
riesenhaft *gigantic, colossal.*
Rind *n. ox, cow, cattle.*
Rinde *f. bark, rind of cheese, crust.*
Rinderbraten *m. roast beef.*
Rindfleisch *n. beef.*
Ring *m. ring, circle.*
ringen *to struggle, wrestle.*
Ringkampf *m. wrestling match.*
Ringkämpfer *m. wrestler.*
Ringrichter *m. umpire, referee.*
rings *round, around.*
ringsum *(–her) all around.*
Rinne *f. gutter, channel.*
rinnen *to flow, run.*
Rinnstein *m. gutter.*
Rippe *f. rib.*
riskant *risky.*
riskieren *to risk.*
Riss *m. tear, hole, gap, crack.*
Ritter *m. knight, cavalier.*
Rittergut *n. estate, manor.*
ritterlich *chivalrous, gallant.*
Rivale *m. rival.*
Rock *m. coat (man's); skirt.*
rodeln *to sled.*
Rodelschlitten *m. sled.*
roden *to root out, clear (forest, garden).*
ROH *raw, crude, coarse, rare (steak).*
Rohmaterial *n. raw material.*
Rohr *n. pipe, oven.*
Röhre *f. tube, valve.*
Rolle *f. roll, cylinder; part (theater).*
     aus der Rolle fallen *to misbehave.*
     die Rollen verteilen *to cast (a play).*
     eine Rolle spielen *to be important.*

Rollenbesetzung f. cast.
Rollmops m. pickled herring.
Rollschuh m. rollerskate.
   Rollschuh laufen   to rollerskate.
Rollstuhl m. wheelchair.
Rolltreppe f. escalator.
Roman m. novel.
Romanschriftsteller m. novelist.
Romantik f. Romanticism.
Romantiker m. romanticist.
romantisch romantic.
röntgen to x-ray.
Röntgenaufnahme f. X-ray photograph.
Röntgenbild n. X-ray photograph.
Röntgenstrahlen pl. X-rays.
rosa pink, rose-colored.
Rose f. rose.
Rosenkohl m. Brussels spouts.
Rosine f. raisin.
Rost m. 1. rust.
   2. grate.
Rostbraten m. roast beef.
Röstbrot toast.
rösten to roast, grill, toast.
Rostfleck m. ironmold.
rostfrei stainless
   rostfreier Stahl   stainless steel.
rostig rusty.
ROT red, ruddy.
   rot werden   to blush.
rotblond auburn.
Röte f. red, redness, blush.
Rotkohl m. red cabbage.
Rotstift m. red pencil.
Rotwein m. red wine.
Rübe f. sugar beet.
   weisse Rübe   turnip
   gelbe Rübe   carrot
Rubin m. ruby.
Rückantwort f. reply.
Rückblick m. glance back, retrospect.
RÜCKEN m. back, rear.
   den Rücken kehren   to turn one's back.
   in den Rücken fallen   to attack from the
     rear.
   Rücken gegen Rücken   back to back.
   Es läuft mir kalt über den Rücken. A
     shiver runs down my spine.
rücken to move, push, move away.
Rückendeckung f. rear, cover, protection.
rückerstatten to refund, reimburse.
Rückfahrkarte f. return ticket.
Rückfahrt f. return trip.
Rückfall m. relapse.
rückfällig relapsing.
Rückflug m. return flight.
Rückfrage f. query, search back; further
   inquiry.
Rückgabe f. return.

Rückgang m. decline, falling off.
rückgängig retrogressive.
   rückgängig machen   to cancel.
Rückgrat spine, backbone.
rückhaltlos unreserved, without reserve.
Rückkehr f. return.
Rücklehne f. back (of chair).
Rückmarsch m. retreat.
Rückporto n. return postage.
Rückreise f. return trip.
Rückschlag m. reverse, setback, reaction,
     recoil (of a gun).
Rückschritt m. step back, relapse.
Rückseite f. back, reverse side.
Rücksicht f. regard, consideration.
   Rücksicht nehmen auf   to be considerate
     of.
rücksichtslos inconsiderate, reckless.
rücksichtsvoll considerate.
Rücksitz m. back seat.
Rücksprache f. discussion, consultation.
   Rücksprache nehmen   to discuss, talk
     over.
Rückstand m. arrears, residue.
rückständig backward, old-fashioned.
Rückstelltaste back-spacer (on a typewriter).
Rücktritt m. retirement, resignation.
Rückwand f. back wall.
rückwärts backwards; back.
Rückwärtsgang m. reverse gear.
Rückweg m. way back, return.
rückwirkend retroactive, retrospective.
Rückwirkung f. reaction, retroaction.
Rückzahlung f. repayment.
Rückzug m. withdrawal, retreat.
Ruder n. oar, rudder, helm.
   ans Ruder kommen   to come into power.
Ruderboot n. rowboat.
rudern to row.
Ruf m. reputation, cry, call.
   in gutem Rufe stehen mit   to have a good
     reputation with.
RUFEN to call, shout.
   Soll ich Sie rufen lassen? Shall I send for
     her?
   wie gerufen kommen   to come at the right
     moment.
Rufname m. Christian name.
RUHE f. rest, repose, calm.
   Angenehme Ruhe! Sleep well!
   in aller Ruhe very calmly.
   Lassen Sie mich in Ruhe! Leave me
     alone!
   Nichts bringt ihn aus der Ruhe. Nothing
     upsets him.
   Ruhe! Silence! Quiet!
   sich zur Ruhe setzen   to retire.
   keine Ruhe haben   to have no peace.
ruhelos restless.

RUHEN *to rest, sleep, stand still.*
  ruhen auf   *to rest on, be based on.*
Ruhestätte *f. resting-place.*
Ruhestellung *f. at-ease position (standing).*
Ruhestörer *m. brawler, rioter.*
RUHIG *still, quiet, silent, calm, composed.*
  Bleiben Sie ruhig sitzen! *Don't get up!*
  Seien Sie ruhig! *Be quiet!*
Ruhm *m. fame, glory.*
rühmen *to praise.*
  sich rühmen *to boast, brag.*
rühmlich *glorious, praiseworthy.*
ruhmlos *inglorious, obscure.*
Rührei *n. scrambled egg.*
rühren *to move, stir.*
  sich rühren *to touch, move.*
  zu Tränen rühren *to move to tears.*
rührend *touching, moving, pathetic.*
rührig *active, quick.*
Rührung *f. emotion, feeling.*
Ruine *f. ruin.*
ruinieren *to ruin.*
RUND *round, circular, plump.*
  rund heraus *flatly.*
  rund (her)um *all around.*
Rundblick *m. panorama.*
RUNDE *f. circle, lap, beat.*
  die Runde machen *to be passed around.*
runden *to make round, round.*
Rundfahrt *f. circular tour.*
Rundfrage *f. inquiry, questionnaire.*
RUNDFUNK *m. radio, wireless,*
    broadcasting.
  im Rundfunk gehört *heard over the*
    radio.
Rundfunkgerät *n. wireless set.*
Rundfunkhörer *m. listener (radio).*
Rundgang *m. stroll, round (military).*
rundlich *round, rounded.*
Rundschreiben *n. circular letter.*
Russe *m. (Russin f.) Russian (person).*
russig *sooty.*
russisch *Russian.*
Russische *n. Russian (language).*
rüsten *to arm, prepare for war.*
rüstig *strong, robust, vigorous.*
Rüstung *f. preparation, equipment, armor.*
Rutsch *m. slide, glide, landslip.*
rutschen *to slide, slip, skid.*
rutschig *slippery.*

Saal *m. large room, hall.*
Saat *f. seed.*
Säbel *m. saber.*
sabotieren *to sabotage.*
Sachbearbeiter *m. expert.*

sachdienlich *relevant, pertinent.*
SACHE *f. thing, subject, business, case,*
    circumstances, cause, point, subject.
  bie der Sache sein *to pay attention.*
  gemeinsame Sache machen *to make*
    common cause with.
  zur Sache *to the point.*
Sachen *pl. things, clothes.*
  seine sieben Sachen *all one's belongings.*
sachgemäss *appropriate, suitable.*
Sachkunde *f. expert knowledge.*
sachkundig *expert, competent.*
Sachlage *f. state of affairs.*
sachlich *factual, essential, objective.*
Sachlichkeit *f. reality, objectivity.*
Sachschaden *m. damage to property.*
sachte *soft, gentle.*
Sachverhalt *m. facts of the case.*
Sack *m. sack, bag, pocket, purse.*
Sackgasse *f. blind alley, dead end.*
säen *to sow.*
Saft *m. juice, liquid, sap.*
  Apfelsinensaft *m. orange juice.*
saftig *juicy, succulent.*
saftlos *dry, sapless.*
Sage *f. legend, tale.*
Säge *f. saw.*
SAGEN *to say, tell, mean.*
  Das hat nichts zu sagen. *That does not*
    matter.
  Das ist leichter gesagt als getan. *That's*
    easier said than done.
  Er hat es mir ins Ohr gesagt. *He*
    whispered it in my ear.
  Gesagt, getan. *No sooner said than done.*
  man sagt *they say.*
  sagen lassen *to send word.*
  sage und schreibe *precisely.*
  sich etwas gesagt sein lassen *to be*
    warned.
  unter uns gesagt *between you and me.*
  ihm gehörig die Meinung sagen *to give*
    him a piece of one's mind.
  er lässt sich nichts sagen *he won't listen*
    to reason.
  auf alles etwas zu sagen wissen *to have*
    an answer for everything.
  ihr sagen lassen *to let her know.*
  Dank sagen *to express thanks.*
  Was sagen Sie dazu? *What do you say to*
    that?
  Was wollen Sie damit sagen? *What do*
    you mean by that?
sagenhaft *legendary, fabulous, mythical.*
Sägewerk *n. sawmill.*
Sahne *f. cream.*
Saison *f. season.*
Saisonausverkauf *m. clearance sale.*
Saite *f. string, chord.*

Saiteninstrument *n. stringed instrument.*
Salat *m. salad.*
  grüner Salat *lettuce.*
Salbe *f. salve, ointment.*
salben *to anoint.*
Salon *m. drawing room, parlor.*
salutieren *to salute.*
SALZ *m. salt.*
salzen *to salt, season.*
Salzgurke *f. pickled cucumber.*
salzhaltig *containing salt.*
salzig *salted, salty.*
Same *m. seed.*
SAMMELN *to collect, gather, accumulate.*
Sammelplatz *m. assembly point, meeting*
    place.
Sammelstelle *f. assembly point, meeting*
    place.
Sammler *m. collector.*
Sammlung *f. collection.*
SAMSTAG *m. Saturday.*
Samt *m. velvet.*
samt *together with.*
  samt und sonders *one and all.*
sämtlich *altogether, complete.*
Sanatorium *n. sanatorium.*
SAND *m. sand.*
Sandale *f. sandal.*
Sandboden *m. sandy soil.*
sandig *sandy.*
SANFT *soft, tender, delicate, gentle, smooth.*
Sanftheit *f. softness.*
sänftigen *to soften, appease.*
Sanftmut *f. gentleness.*
sanftmütig *gentle, meek.*
Sänger *m. (-in, f.) singer.*
Sanitäter *m. medical aid (person).*
Sardelle *f. anchovy.*
Sardine *f. sardine.*
Sarg *m. coffin.*
sarkastisch *sarcastic.*
Satiriker *m. satirist.*
satirisch *satirical.*
SATT *full, satisfied, saturated.*
  Ich habe es satt. *I've enough of it, I'm fed*
    up with it.
Sattel *m. saddle.*
  in allen Sätteln gerecht sein *to be good at*
    everything.
satteln *to saddle.*
sättigen *to satisfy.*
Satz *m. set, clause, sentence (grammar);*
  proposition (philo.); phrase (music);
  sediment.
Satzbau *m. sentence structure.*
Satzzeichen *n. punctuation mark.*
sauber *clean, neat, tidy.*
Sauberkeit *f. tidiness, cleanliness.*
säuberlich *clean, neat.*

säubern *to clean, clear.*
Säuberung *f. cleaning.*
Sauce *f. sauce, gravy.*
SAUER *sour, acid, pickled.*
Sauerbraten *m. sauerbraten.*
Sauerkraut *n. sauerkraut.*
säuerlich *acid, acidulous.*
säuern *to make sour.*
Sauerstoff *m. oxygen.*
Sauerstoffgerät *n. oxygen apparatus.*
saugen *to suck, absorb.*
säugen *to suckle, nurse.*
Säugling *m. infant, baby.*
Säule *f. pillar, column.*
Saum *m. edge, border, hem.*
Säure *f. acid, sourness, tartness, acidity.*
säurehaltig *containing acid.*
Saxophon *n. saxophone.*
schäbig *shabby, worn out.*
Schäbigkeit *f. shabbiness.*
Schach *n. chess.*
  Schach bieten *to defy.*
Schachbrett *n. chessboard.*
Schachfeld *n. square of a chessboard.*
schachmatt *checkmate.*
Schachpartie *f. chess game.*
Schachtel *f. box.*
SCHADE *too bad.*
  Es ist schade! *It is a pity!*
  Wie schade! *What a pity!*
  zu schade für *too good to.*
Schaden *m. damage, harm, injury, bias.*
  Durch Schaden wird man klug. *You learn*
    by your mistakes.
  zu Schaden kommen *to suffer damage.*
  Schaden anrichten *to do damage.*
  zu Schaden kommen *to come to harm.*
  Durch Schaden wird man klug. *Once*
    bitten, twice shy.
SCHADEN *to hurt, damage, injure,*
  prejudice.
  Es schadet nichts. *It doesn't matter.*
Schadenersatz *m. compensation.*
Schadenfreude *f. malicious joy.*
schadenfroh *rejoicing over another's*
  misfortune.
schadhaft *damaged, defective, dilapidated.*
  sich schadlos halten *to get even with.*
schädlich *harmful, bad.*
Schaf *n. sheep.*
Schäfchen *n. lamb.*
  sein Schäfchen ins Trockene bringen *to*
    feather one's nest.
Schäfer *m. shepherd.*
Schäferhund *m. sheep-dog.*
schaffen *to create, produce, accomplish,*
  make, do.
  sich zu schaffen machen *to be busy.*
  wie geschaffen für *as though cut out for.*

schaffend *creative, working.*
Schaffner *m. conductor,* (*train*) *guard.*
Schal *m. shawl, scarf.*
Schale *f. skin, peel, rind, shell; bowl.*
schälen *to peel, shell, bark, skin.*
Schall *m. sound.*
schalldicht *soundproof.*
Schalleffekt *m. sound effect.*
schallen *to sound, resound.*
Schallplatte *f. record* (*phonograph*).
Schaltanlage *f. switch, gear.*
schalten *to deal with, use, direct, change gears.*
Schalter *m. switch, ticket-window.*
Schaltjahr *n. leap year.*
Schaltung *f. gear change, connection.*
Scham *f. shame, modesty.*
(**sich**) **schämen** *to be ashamed.*
Schamgefühl *n. sense of shame.*
schamhaft *modest, bashful.*
schamlos *shameless, impudent.*
Schamlosigkeit *f. shamelessness, impudence.*
schamrot *blushing red.*
Schamröte *f. blush.*
schandbar *infamous.*
Schande *f. shame, disgrace.*
schänden *to spoil, disfigure, dishonor, rape.*
schändlich *shameful, disgraceful.*
Schändlichkeit *f. infamy.*
Schandtat *f. crime, misdeed.*
SCHARF *sharp, keen, harsh, pointed, piercing, acute, strong, quick.*
  Behalten Sie ihn scharf im Auge! *Keep a sharp eye on him!*
  Ich bin nicht so scharf darauf. *I am not so keen on that.*
Scharfblick *m. penetrating glance.*
Schärfe *f. sharpness, rigor, acuteness.*
schärfen *to sharpen.*
scharfkantig *sharp-edged.*
Scharfsicht *f. keenness of sight, perspicacity.*
scharfsichtig *keen-sighted, penetrating.*
Scharlach *m. scarlet fever.*
SCHATTEN *m. shadow, shade, spirit, phantom.*
  in den Schatten stellen *to overshadow.*
  Sie folgt mir wie ein Schatten. *She follows me like a shadow.*
Schattenseite *f. shady side.*
schattieren *to shade.*
schattig *shady.*
Schatz *m. treasure.*
Schatzamt *n. treasury.*
Schatzanweisungen *f. treasury bonds.*
schätzen *to value, estimate, judge.*
schätzenswert *estimable.*
Schatzmeister *m. treasurer.*
Schätzung *f. estimate, taxation.*
schätzungsweise *approximately.*

SCHAU *f. sight, view, show, exhibition.*
  zur Schau stellen *to exhibit, display.*
Schauder *m. shudder, shivering, horror, terror, fright.*
schauen *to see, behold, gaze, view.*
Schauer *m. horror, terror, awe, thrill.*
schauerlich *awful.*
schauern *to shudder, shiver.*
  mich schaudert bei *I shudder at.*
Schauerroman *m. thriller.*
Schaufel *f. shovel, scoop.*
schaufeln *to shovel.*
Schaufenster *n. show-window.*
Schaukasten *m. show case.*
Schaukel *f. swing.*
schaukeln *to swing, rock.*
Schaukelstuhl *m. rocking chair.*
schaulustig *curious.*
SCHAUSPIEL *n. spectacle, scene, play, drama.*
Schauspieler *m* (**–in,** *f.*) *actor* (*actress*).
Schauspielkunst *f. dramatic art.*
Schaustellung *f. exhibition.*
Schaustück *n. specimen; showpiece.*
Schaum *m. foam.*
  zu Schaum schlagen *to beat up* (*food*).
schäumen *to foam.*
schaumig *foamy, frothy.*
Scheck *m. check.*
Scheckbuch *n. check book.*
Scheckformular *n. blank check.*
Scheckinhaber *m. bearer.*
Scheibe *f.* (*window*) *pane, disk, slice, target.*
Scheibenwischer *m. window-wiper.*
scheiden *to separate, divide, part, divorce.*
  sich scheiden lassen *to get a divorce.*
Scheidewand *f. partition.*
Scheidung *f. separation, divorce.*
Scheidungsklage *f. divorce suit.*
SCHEIN *m. appearance, air, look; shine; ticket, receipt.*
  Der Schein trügt. *Appearances are deceiving.*
scheinbar *apparent*(*ly*).
Scheinbild *n. phantom, illusion.*
SCHEINEN *to shine; seem; look.*
scheinheilig *hypocritical, sanctimonious.*
Scheintod *m. suspended animation, trance.*
Scheinwerfer *m. reflector, search light, headlight* (*car*).
Scheitel *m. top, crown, summit; parting of the hair.*
scheitern *to fail.*
Schelle *f. door bell, little bell.*
Schema *n. order, arrangement, model.*
schematisch *systematic, mechanical.*
Schenkel *m. thigh.*
schenken *to give, present with, grant.*
  geschenkt bekommen *to get as a present.*

Schenker *m. donor.*

Schenkung *f. donation, gift.*

Schere *f. scissors.*

Scherz *m. joke, jest, pleasantry.*

scherzen *to joke.*

scherzhaft *joking.*

SCHEU *shy, timid.*

  scheu werden *to become shy, to take fright.*

scheuen *to avoid, shun.*

  sich scheuen *to shy away.*

scheuern *to scrub, rub, clean, chafe.*

Schicht *f. layer, bed, coat, shift, stratum*

Schichtwechsel *m. change of shift.*

Schick *m. elegance, smartness, chic.*

SCHICKEN *to send, dispatch.*

  schicken nach *to send for.*

  sich schicken in *conform, adapt oneself to.*

  Waren ins Haus schicken *to deliver goods to the door.*

  zuschicken *to send by mail.*

schicklich *proper, decent.*

Schicksal *n. fate, destiny, lot.*

SCHIEBEN *to move, push, shove.*

  schieben auf *to lay the blame on.*

  etwas auf die lange Bank schieben *to postpone a thing.*

Schiebetür *f. sliding door.*

Schiebung *f. profiteering, graft.*

Schiedsrichter *m. umpire.*

schief *oblique, crooked, askance.*

Schiefer *m. slate, splinter.*

Schieferdach *n. slate roof.*

Schiene *f. rail, track, splint.*

schiessen *to shoot, flash, fire.*

  einen Blick schiessen auf *to shoot a glance at.*

  ein Tor schiessen *to score a goal.*

SCHIFF *n. boat, ship, vessel.*

  zu Schiff *on board, by boat.*

schiffbar *navigable.*

Schiffbruch *m. shipwreck.*

Schiffchen *n. small boat, shuttle.*

schiffen *to ship, sail.*

Schiffer *m. sailor.*

Schiffsbesatzung *f. crew.*

Schiffskörper *m. hull.*

Schiffsladung *f. cargo, freight.*

Schiffswerft *m. wharf, dock.*

Schild *m. shield, coat of arms, sign.*

  im Schilde führen *to have something up one's sleeve.*

schildern *to relate, describe.*

Schilderung *f. description.*

Schimmel *m. mold, mildew.*

schimmelig *moldy.*

Schimmer *m. glitter.*

schimmern *to glitter, gleam.*

Schimpf *m. disgrace, insult.*

schimpfen *to kick, gripe, scold.*

  schimpfen mit *to scold.*

schimpflich *disgraceful.*

Schimpfwort *n. rude name; term of abuse.*

SCHINKEN *m. ham.*

  Eier mit Schinken *ham and eggs.*

Schirm *m. umbrella, shelter, lampshade.*

Schlacht *f. combat, battle.*

schlachten *to slaughter, kill, butcher.*

Schlächter *m. butcher.*

Schlachtfeld *n. battlefield.*

Schlachthaus *n. slaughterhouse.*

Schlachtschiff *n. battleship.*

SCHLAF *m. sleep.*

  im Schlaf liegen *to be asleep.*

Schlafanzug *m. pajamas.*

Schläfchen *n. nap.*

SCHLAFEN *to sleep.*

  schlafen gehen *to go to bed.*

Schlafenszeit *m. bedtime.*

schlaff *slack, loose, relaxed.*

Schlaffheit *f. laxity.*

Schlafkrankheit *f. sleeping sickness.*

schlaflos *sleepless.*

Schlaflosigkeit *f. insomnia.*

Schlafmittel *m. narcotic.*

schläfrig *sleepy.*

Schlafsaal *m. dormitory.*

Schlafwagen *m. sleeping-car.*

Schlafwandler *m. sleepwalker.*

Schlafzimmer *n. bedroom.*

SCHLAG *m. blow, stroke, striking (clock).*

  zwei Fliegen auf einen Schlag treffen *to kill two birds with one stone.*

Schlagader *f. artery.*

Schlaganfall *m. stroke, fit.*

SCHLAGEN *to beat, knock, hit, strike, throb.*

  sich schlagen *to fight.*

  sich geschlagen geben *to give up.*

  schlagen nach *to take after.*

  eine geschlagene Stunde *a whole hour.*

  etwas aus dem Kopfe schlagen *to dismiss something from one's thoughts.*

  die Schanze schlagen *to risk one's life.*

  einen Rekord schlagen *to set a record.*

  Die Uhr schlägt zehn. *The clock strikes ten.*

  seine Unkosten auf die Ware schlagen *to add one's expenses to the price of the goods.*

schlagfertig *quick at repartee.*

Schlagfertigkeit *f. quickness at repartee.*

Schlagsahne *f. whipped cream.*

Schlagwort *n. slogan.*

Schlagzeile *f. headline.*

Schlagzeug *n. percussion instrument.*

Schlamm *m. mud, ooze.*

schlammig *muddy, oozy.*

Schlange *f. snake.*

    Schlange stehen *to stand in line; to make a line.*

Schlangenbiss *m. snake bite.*

schlank *slim, slender.*

Schlankheit *f. slimness, slenderness.*

schlapp *weak, tired, limp, flabby.*

    schlapp machen *to collapse.*

schlau *sly, cunning.*

Schlauberger *m. sly fox.*

Schlauch *m. hose, tube.*

Schlauheit *f. slyness, cunning.*

Schlaukopf *m. sly fox.*

SCHLECHT *bad, poor, inferior, ill, wicked.*

    mir ist schlecht *I feel sick.*

    schlecht machen *to run down.*

    schlecht und recht *somehow.*

    schlecht werden *to spoil (food).*

schlechtgelaunt *in a bad temper.*

Schlechtigkeit *f. badness, wickedness.*

schleichen *to creep, drag, sneak.*

    sich davon schleichen *to steal away.*

    wie die Katze um den heissen Brei schleichen *to beat around the bush ("to creep like the car around the hot roast")*

schlicht *simple, plain, even.*

schlichten *to make simple, smooth.*

Schlichtheit *f. simplicity.*

Schliesse *f. clasp, fastening.*

SCHLIESSEN *to close, lock, shut, break up.*

    in die Arme schliessen *to embrace.*

    geschlossen *enclosed.*

    die Ehe schliessen *to get married.*

Schliessfach *n. locker.*

schliesslich *final, finally, after all.*

Schliessung *f. closing.*

schlimm *bad, sore.*

    schlimmstenfalls *if the worst comes to the worst.*

Schlips *m. necktie (coll.).*

Schlitten *m. sled, sleigh.*

Schlittenfahrt *f. sleigh driving.*

Schlittschuh *m. skate.*

    Schlittschuh laufen *to skate.*

Schlittschuhläufer *m. skater.*

SCHLOSS *n. castle, lock.*

Schlosser *m. locksmith.*

Schluck *m. gulp, draught.*

Schluckauf *m. hiccup.*

schlucken *to gulp, swallow.*

Schlucker *m. hiccup.*

    armer Schlucker *poor wretch.*

Schlummer *m. slumber.*

schlummern *to slumber.*

Schlüpfer *m. panties.*

SCHLUSS *m. closing, shutting, conclusion.*

Schlüssel *m. key, code.*

Schlüsselbund *m. bunch of keys.*

Schlüsselloch *m. keyhole.*

Schlusslicht *n. tail light.*

Schlusswort *n. summary, last word.*

Schmach *f. disgrace, dishonor, humiliation.*

schmachten *to languish.*

schmachvoll *disgraceful, humiliating.*

schmackhaft *tasty, savory.*

schmähen *to abuse.*

schmählich *disgraceful.*

SCHMAL *narrow, thin, slender, poor.*

schmälern *to diminish, lessen.*

Schmalz *n. drippings.*

SCHMECKEN *to taste, try.*

    Es schmeckt gut. *It tastes good.*

    Es schmeckt mir nicht. *I don't like it.*

    schmecken nach *to taste of.*

    Wie schmeckt's? *How do you like it?*

Schmeichelei *f. flattery.*

schmeichelhaft *flattering.*

Schmeichelkatze *f. wheedler, flatterer.*

schmeicheln *to flatter.*

Schmeichler *m. flatterer.*

schmeichlerisch *flattering.*

schmelzen *to melt.*

SCHMERZ *m. pain, ache, hurt, sorrow.*

SCHMERZEN *to hurt, pain, grieve.*

Schmerzensgeld *n. smart money, compensation.*

schmerzerfüllt *deeply affected.*

schmerzhaft *painful.*

schmerzlich *grievous, sad.*

schmerzlos *painless.*

schmerzstillend *soothing.*

Schmetterling *m. butterfly.*

Schmied *m. blacksmith.*

Schmiede *f. forge.*

schmieden *to forge, hammer.*

    Pläne schmieden *to devise plans.*

schmiegen *to bend.*

schmiegsam *flexible, supple.*

Schmiegsamkeit *f. flexibility.*

schmieren *to spread, grease, smear.*

Schminke *f. rouge, paint, make up.*

schminken *to make up, paint the face.*

Schmorbraten *m. stewed steak.*

SCHMUCK *m. jewelry, ornament, decoration.*

schmücken *to decorate, adorn.*

Schmuckstück *n. piece of jewelry.*

Schmuggel *m. smuggling.*

schmuggeln *to smuggle.*

schmunzeln *to grin, to smirk.*

Schmutz *m. dirt, mud.*

schmutzen *to dirty.*

Schmutzfleck *m. stain, spot.*

schmutzig *dirty.*

Schnabel *m. beak, bill.*

schnarchen *to snore.*

schnaufen *to breathe heavily, pant.*
Schnecke *f. snail.*
  wie eine Schnecke kriechen   *to go at a*
    snail's pace.
SCHNEE *m. snow.*
Schneeball *m. snowball.*
Schneedecke *f. blanket of snow.*
Schneefall *m. snowfall.*
Schneeflocke *f. snowflake.*
Schneekette *f. non-skid chain (automobile).*
Schneeschuh *m. snow shoe, ski.*
Schneetreiben *n. blizzard.*
schneeweiss *snow-white.*
SCHNEIDEN *to cut, carve.*
  sich schneiden   *to cut oneself.*
schneidend *sharp, bitter.*
Schneider *m. tailor.*
schneien *to snow.*
SCHNELL *quick, fast, swift, prompt, speedy.*
Schnelligkeit *f. rapidity, velocity.*
Schnellzug *m. express train.*
(sich) schneuzen *to blow one's nose.*
Schnippchen *n. snap of the fingers.*
  ein Schnippchen schlagen   *to play a trick.*
Schnitt *m. cut, cutting, incision.*
Schnittblumen *pl. cut flowers.*
Schnittmuster *n. cut pattern.*
Schnittwunde *f. cut.*
schnitzen *to carve, cut.*
Schnupfen *m. (head) cold.*
  sich einen Schnupfen holen   *to get a*
    (head) cold.
schnupfen *to sniff.*
Schnur *f. string, cord.*
  Über die Schnur hauen   *to kick over the*
    traces.
Schnurrbart *m. moustache.*
schnurren *to hum, buzz, purr.*
Schnürsenkel *m. shoelaces.*
Schock *m. shock.*
Schokolade *f. chocolate.*
SCHON *already, all right, very, yet, even,*
    indeed, certainly.
  Schon gut!   *All right!*
  Wenn schon!   *So what!*
  Haben Sie es schon einmal gesehen?   *Did*
    you ever see it before?
SCHÖN *beautiful, handsome, fine, nice, fair,*
    noble.
  Danke schön (Schönen Dank).   *Thanks.*
  Das wäre noch schöner!   *That's all we*
    need!
  die Schönen Künste   *the fine arts.*
  schön tun   *to flatter.*
  Schönen Gruss an Ihre Frau.   *Best regards*
    to your wife.
  Schönsten Dank.   *Many thanks.*
  sich schön machen.   *to smarten oneself.*
schonen *to spare, save, look after, preserve.*

schonend *careful, considerate.*
Schöngeist *m. wit; esthete.*
schöngeistig *esthetical.*
Schönheit *f. beauty.*
Schönheitsmittel *n. cosmetic.*
Schönheitspflege *f. beauty treatment.*
Schonung *f. indulgence.*
schonungslos *pitiless.*
schöpfen *to draw, create.*
Schöpferkraft *f. power, creative.*
Schöpflöffel *m. scoop, dipper.*
Schornstein *m. chimney.*
Schoss *m. lap.*
Schotte *m. Scotsman.*
schottisch *Scottish.*
schräg *diagonally.*
Schräge *f. slant, slope.*
Schramme *f. scratch, scar.*
schrammen *to scratch.*
Schrank *m. wardrobe.*
Schranke *f. fencing, enclosure, gate.*
  sich in Schranken halten   *to keep within*
    bounds.
schrankenlos *boundless, without limits.*
Schrankkoffer *m. wardrobe trunk.*
Schraube *f. screw, propeller, bolt.*
schrauben *to screw, turn, wheel.*
Schraubenschlüssel *m. wrench.*
Schraubenzieher *m. screwdriver.*
SCHRECK (EN) *m. scare, fright, fear,*
    dread, horror.
  in Schrecken setzen   *to terrify.*
schrecken *to frighten.*
Schreckgespenst *n. terrible vision.*
schreckhaft *timid, easily frightened.*
schrecklich *terrible, awful.*
Schreckschuss *m. warning shot.*
Schrei *m. scream, cry.*
SCHREIBEN *to write, spell.*
  auf der Maschine schreiben   *to type.*
  die Zeitung schreibt   *the paper says.*
  Schreiben Sie sich das hinter die
    Ohren.   *to make a special note of it;*
    to take it to heart.
Schreiberei *f. writing, correspondence.*
Schreibfehler *m. slip of the pen.*
Schreibmappe *f. writing case, portfolio,*
    blotter.
Schreibmaschine *f. typewriter.*
Schreibpapier *n. note paper.*
Schreibstube *f. office.*
Schreibwaren *pl. stationery.*
Schreibwarengeschäft *n. stationery store.*
Schreibwarenhändler *m. stationer.*
Schreibwarenhandlung *f. stationery store.*
SCHREIEN *to scream, shout, yell.*
schreiend *loud, gaudy.*
Schreier *m. shouter, bawler.*
Schreiner *m. carpenter, cabinetmaker.*

Schreinerei *f. cabinetmaker's shop.*
SCHRIFT *f. writing, handwriting, script.*
schriftlich *in writing, written.*
Schriftführer *m. secretary (association or politics).*
Schriftsteller *m. writer (author).*
SCHRITT *m. step, stride.*
    auf Schritt und Tritt *everywhere, all the time.*
    Schritt fahren! *Drive slowly!*
    Schritt für Schritt *step by step.*
    Schritt halten *to keep pace with.*
schroff *rugged, rough, uncouth.*
schrubben *to scrub.*
Schrubber *m. scrubber.*
schrumpfen *to shrink, contract.*
Schrumpfung *f. shrinking, contraction.*
Schublade *f. drawer.*
schüchtern *bashful, timid.*
Schüchternheit *f. bashfulness, timidity.*
Schuft *m. scoundrel.*
SCHUH *m. shoe.*
    einem etwas in die Schuhe schieben *to put the blame on someone.*
Schuhanzieher *m. shoehorn.*
Schuhkrem *f. shoe-polish.*
Schuhmacher *m. shoemaker.*
Schuhputzer *m. bootblack.*
Schuhriemen *m. shoelace.*
Schuhsohle *f. sole of a shoe.*
Schularbeit *f. lesson, homework.*
Schulbesuch *m. attendance at school.*
Schulbildung *f. schooling, education.*
SCHULD *f. obligation, debt, cause, blame.*
    in jemandes Schuld stehen *to have an obligation.*
    Schuld sein an *to be guilty of.*
    Schulden machen *to incur debts.*
    Schuld geben *to accuse.*
schuldbewusst *guilt-conscious.*
schulden *to owe.*
Schuldenmacher *m. contractor of debts.*
schuldig *owing, due, obliged, guilty.*
    schuldig sein *to be indebted.*
    Geld schuldig sein *to owe money.*
    keine Antwort schuldig bleiben *never to be at a loss for an answer.*
Schuldigkeit *f. duty, obligation.*
schuldlos *innocent.*
Schuldner *m. debtor.*
Schuldschein *m. bond, promissory note.*
SCHULE *f. school, academy, courses.*
    die Schule schwänzen *to cut classes.*
    Schule machen *to find followers.*
schulen *to school, train, teach.*
Schüler *m. student, pupil.*
Schulferien *pl. m. school holidays.*
schulfrei *having a holiday, off from school.*
Schulfreund *m. school friend.*

Schulgeld *n. school fees.*
Schulmappe *f. schoolbag, satchel.*
Schulmeister *m. schoolmaster, teacher.*
schulmeistern *to censure, to be pedantic.*
Schulstunde *f. school lesson.*
Schulter *f. shoulder.*
Schulung *f. school training.*
Schulzeugnis *n. school certificates, report card*
Schuppe *f. scale (fish).*
Schürze *f. apron.*
Schuss *m. shot, report, round.*
schussbereit *ready to shoot.*
Schusswaffe *f. firearm.*
Schussweite *f. range.*
Schusswunde *f. bullet wound.*
schütteln *to shake.*
schütten *to pour in, to spill, to shed.*
SCHUTZ *m. shelter, protection, refuge.*
    im Schutz der Nacht *under cover of the night.*
    in Schutz nehmen *to defend.*
    Schutz suchen *to take shelter.*
Schutzbrille *f. safety goggles.*
Schützen *to protect.*
    sich schützen *to protect oneself.*
Schutzengel *m. guardian angel.*
Schutzhaft *f. protective custody.*
Schutzimpfung *f. vaccination.*
schutzlos *defenseless, unprotected.*
Schutzmann *n. policeman.*
Schutzpockenimpfung *f. vaccination against smallpox.*
SCHWACH *weak, frail, faint, feeble.*
Schwäche *f. weakness, debility, frailty.*
schwächen *to weaken.*
    schwachen Besuch *poor attendance.*
Schwächheit *f. weakness, feebleness.*
schwächlich *weak, delicate.*
Schwächlichkeit *f. delicacy, infirmity.*
Schwachsinn *m. imbecility.*
schwachsinnig *imbecile.*
Schwager *m. brother-in-law.*
Schwägerin *f. sister-in-law.*
Schwalbe *f. swallow.*
Schwamm *m. sponge, mushroom.*
Schwan *m. swan.*
schwanger *pregnant.*
schwanken *to rock, toss, sway.*
Schwankung *f. variation.*
Schwanz *m. tail, end.*
Schwarm *m. crowd, multitude.*
schwärmen *to swarm, riot.*
Schwärmer *m. enthusiast, fanatic.*
Schwärmerei *f. enthusiasm.*
schwärmerisch *enthusiastic, fanatic.*
Schwarte *f. rind, skin.*
SCHWARZ *black, dark, dirty, gloomy.*
    ins Schwarze treffen *to hit the bull's eye.*

schwarz auf weiss *in black and white.*
Sie sieht immer alles schwarz *She always sees the dark side of things.*
Schwarzbrot *n. black bread.*
Schwarze *m. black (person).*
Schwarzhandel *m. black market.*
Schwarzwald *m. Black Forest.*
Schwatz *m. chat, talk.*
Schwatzbase *f. chatterbox.*
schwatzen, schwätzen *to chatter, gossip.*
Schwätzer *m (–in, f.) gossip.*
schwatzhaft *talkative.*
Schwatzhaftigkeit *f. loquacity.*
Schwebe *f. state of suspense.*
in der Schwebe sein *to be undecided, to be pending.*
Schwebebahn *f. suspension railway.*
schweben *to be suspended, pending.*
auf der Zunge schweben *to have on the tip of the tongue.*
in Gefahr schweben *to be in danger.*
Schwede *m. Swede.*
schwedisch *Swedish.*
Schwefel *m. sulphur.*
schweigen *n. silence.*
schweigsam *silent, taciturn.*
Schweigsamkeit *f. taciturnity.*
Schwein *n. pig, hog.*
Schweinebraten *m. roast pork.*
Schweinefleisch *n. pork.*
Schweiss *m. sweat, perspiration.*
Schweisstropfen *m. bead of perspiration.*
Schweizer *m. Swiss.*
schweizerisch *Swiss.*
schweigen *to keep silent.*
Schwelle *f. threshold.*
schwellen *to swell, rise, grow.*
Schwellung *f. swelling, tumor, growth.*
SCHWER *heavy, hard, difficult, serious, strong; heavily, seriously, strongly.*
etwas schwer nehmen *to take something to heart.*
schwer fallen (halten) *to be difficult.*
ein schweres Geld kosten *to cost a lot of money.*
schweren Herzens *with a heavy heart.*
schwer beleidigen *to deeply offend.*
schwerblütig *melancholy.*
schwerfällig *phlegmatic*
Schwerfälligkeit *f. heaviness, clumsiness.*
Schwergewicht *n. heavyweight.*
schwerhörig *hard of hearing.*
Schwerhörigkeit *f. deafness.*
Schwerkraft *f. force of gravity.*
Schwerkriegsbeschädigte *m. disabled soldier.*
schwerlich *hardly, scarcely, with difficulty.*
Schwermut *f. melancholy, sadness.*
schwermütig *melancholy, sad.*

Schwerpunkt *m. center of gravity.*
Schwert *n. sword.*
Schwerverbrecher *m. criminal, gangster.*
schwerwiegend *serious, grave.*
SCHWESTER *f. sister, hospital nurse.*
schwesterlich *sisterly.*
Schwiegereltern *pl. parents-in-law.*
Schwiegermutter *f. mother-in-law.*
Schwiegersohn *m. son-in-law.*
Schwiegertochter *f. daughter-in-law.*
Schwiegervater *m. father-in-law.*
schwierig *difficult.*
Schwierigkeit *f. difficulty.*
Schwimmanstalt *f. swimming-pool.*
SCHWIMMEN *to swim, float, sail.*
Schwimmhose *f. swimming trunks.*
Schwimmweste *f. life jacket.*
Schwindel *m. swindle; fraud; dizziness.*
Schwindelanfall *m. fit of dizziness.*
schwindeln *to swindle, cheat; be dizzy, to tell a lie.*
Mir schwindelt. *I feel dizzy.*
Schwindler *m. swindler.*
schwindlig *dizzy.*
schwingen *to swing, sway, oscillate, vibrate.*
Schwingung *f. oscillation.*
Schwips *m. Smack! Slap!*
einen Schwips haben *to be tipsy.*
schwören *to swear, take an oath.*
schwül *sultry, muggy.*
Schwung *f. swing (push), vault.*
in Schwung bringen *to set going.*
im Schwung sein *to be in full swing.*
schwungvoll *energetic.*
Schwur *m. oath.*
Schwur leisten *to take an oath.*
SECHS *six.*
SECHSTE *sixth.*
SECHZEHN *sixteen.*
SECHZEHNTE *sixteenth.*
SECHZIG *sixty.*
SECHZIGSTE *sixtieth.*
See *m. lake.*
SEE *f. sea, seaside.*
an die See gehen *to go to the seaside.*
in See stechen *or* gehen *to set sail; to put to sea.*
Seebad *n. seaside resort.*
seefest *seaworthy.*
seefest sein *to be a good sailor.*
Seehund *m. seal.*
seekrank *seasick.*
seekrank sein *to be seasick.*
Seekrankheit *f. seasickness.*
SEELE *f. soul, mind, spirit.*
jemandem aus der Seele sprechen *to express a person's thoughts.*
Sie sind mit Leib und Seele dabei. *They are in it with heart and soul.*

seelisch *spiritual, mental, emotional.*
Seemann *m. sailor.*
Seemeile *f. nautical mile (1.852 kilometers).*
Seenot *f. distress (at sea).*
Seewasser *n. sea-water.*
Segel *n. sail, canvas.*
Segelboot *n. sailboat.*
Segelflugzeug *n. glider.*
segeln *to sail.*
Segelschiff *n. sailboat.*
Segen *m. blessing.*
segnen *to bless.*
SEHEN *to see, look, behold, contemplate.*
   darauf sehen *to watch carefully.*
   gut sehen *to have good eyesight.*
   Ich kenne sie nur vom Sehen. *I know her
      only by sight.*
   schlecht sehen *to have poor eyesight.*
   sehen nach *to look after.*
   sich sehen lassen *to appear.*
   Ich kann sie nicht sehen. *I can't stand the
      sight of her.*
   ihm auf die Finger sehen *to watch him
      closely.*
   nach der Uhr sehen *to look at the clock.*
   sehen auf *to look at, to look over, to face,
      to see it.*
sehenswert *worth seeing, remarkable.*
Sehenswürdigkeit *f. point of interest.*
Sehkraft *f. eyesight.*
Sehne *f. sinew, ligament.*
SEHNEN *to long, yearn for.*
   sich sehnen nach *to yearn for.*
sehnlich *ardent, longing.*
Sehnsucht *f. longing, yearning.*
sehnsüchtig *longing, yearning.*
SEHR *very; very much.*
   Bitte sehr. *You are quite welcome.*
seicht *shallow.*
SEIDE *f. silk.*
Seidenpapier *n. tissue paper.*
Seidenraupe *f. silkworm.*
seidig *silky.*
Seife *f. soap.*
Seifenflocken *pl. soapflakes.*
Seifenpulver *n. soap powder.*
Seil *n. rope, line.*
Seilbahn *f. cable.*
Sein *n. being.*
SEIN *to be, exist.*
   es sei denn, dass . . . *unless.*
SEIN *poss. adj. his, her, its.*
SEIN(ER, -E, -ES) *poss. pron. his, hers.*
   die Seinen *one's own people.*
seinetwegen *because of him, for his sake.*
SEIT *prep. (with dat.) since, for.*
   Ich warte seit einer Stunde. *I have been
      waiting for an hour.*
   seit kurzer Zeit *lately.*

   seit meiner Ankunft *since my return.*
   Seit Wann? *Since when?*
Seitdem *conj. since, since that time.*
SEITE *f. side, page, party, member.*
   auf die Seite *aside, away.*
   auf die Seite gehen *to step aside.*
   Schwache Seite *weakness.*
   Seite an Seite *side by side.*
   zur Seite stehen *to stand by, help.*
   auf dieser Seite *on this side.*
   auf meiner Seite stehen *to be on my side.*
   nach allen Seiten *in all directions.*
Seitenflügel *m. side, aisle, wing.*
Seitenstrasse *f. side street.*
Seitenzahl *f. number of pages.*
seither *since then.*
seitlich *lateral, collateral.*
seitwärts *sideways, aside.*
Sekt *m. champagne.*
Sekretär *m. (–in, f.) secretary.*
SEKUNDE *f. second (time, music, fencing).*
Sekundenzeiger *m. second hand (on clocks).*
selbe (der, die, das) *same.*
selber *self.*
   ich selber *myself.*
SELBST 1. *adj. or pron. self.*
   Ich habe es selbst getan. *I did it myself.*
   Das versteht sich von selbst. *That goes
      without saying.*
   2. *adv. even.*
   Ich habe alles zu Hause gelassen, selbst
      mein Geld. *I left everything at home,
      even my money.*
selbständig *independent.*
Selbstbeherrschung *f. self-control.*
selbstbewusst *self-assured.*
Selbstbewusstsein *n. self-assurance.*
Selbsterhaltung *f. self-preservation.*
Selbsterkenntnis *f. self-knowledge.*
selbstgefällig *self-satisfied, complacent.*
Selbstgefühl *n. self-respect.*
Selbstgespräch *m. monologue, soliloquy.*
selbstherrlich *autocratic.*
Selbstkostenpreis *m. cost price.*
selbstlos *unselfish, disinterested.*
Selbstlosigkeit *f. unselfishness.*
Selbstmörder *m. suicide.*
selbstredend *self-evident, obvious.*
Selbstsucht *f. selfishness, egoism.*
selbstsüchtig *selfish, egoistic.*
SELBSTVERSTÄNDLICH *evident.*
Selbstvertrauen *n. self-confidence.*
selbstzufrieden *self-satisfied.*
selig *blessed.*
Seligkeit *f. happiness, bliss.*
Sellerie *f. celery.*
SELTEN *rare, unusual.*
Seltenheit *f. rarity, scarcity.*
SELTSAM *strange, unusual, odd.*

Selterwasser *n. soda-water.*
Semester *n. term, session.*
Seminar *n. training college.*
Senat *m. senate.*
senden *to send, broadcast, transmit.*
Sender *m. transmitter.*
Senderaum *m. studio.*
Sendung *f. mission, transmission.*
Senf *m. mustard.*
Senkel *m. lace (shoe).*
senken *to lower, dip, sink.*
  sich senken *to settle.*
sensationell *sensational.*
Sensationslust *f. desire to cause a sensation.*
Sentimentalität *f. sentimentality.*
SEPTEMBER *m. September.*
Serie *f. series, issue.*
Service *n. service set, attendance.*
Servierbrett *n. tray.*
servieren *to serve, wait at a table.*
Serviette *f. table napkin.*
Sessel *m. armchair.*
sesshaft *settled, established.*
SETZEN *to put, set, place, fix, erect.*
  sich setzen *to sit down.*
  alles daran setzen *to risk everything.*
  gesetzt den Fall, dass *suppose that.*
  in Freiheit setzen *to set free.*
  Setzen Sie sich! *Sit down!*
  sich etwas in den Kopf setzen *to get an
    idea into one's head.*
  sich in Verbindung setzen mit *to get in
    touch with.*
  unter Druck setzen *to put pressure on.*
  ausser Gebrauch setzen *to supersede,
    discard.*
  ausser Kraft setzen *to invalidate.*
  in Bewegung setzen *to set into motion.*
  in die Zeitung setzen *to advertise in the
    newspapers.*
  übers Wasser setzen *to ferry across.*
  sich zur Ruhe setzen *to retire.*
Seuche *f. epidemic, pestilence.*
seufzen *to sigh.*
sezieren *to dissect.*
SICH *oneself, himself, herself, itself, yourself,
  yourselves, themselves, each other,
  one another.*
  sich selbst *itself, oneself, etc.*
SICHER *secure, safe, certain, positive,
  surely.*
  aus sicherer Hand *on good authority.*
  seiner Sache sicher sein *to be certain of a
    thing.*
  sicher gehen *to be on the safe side.*
  sicher rechnen auf *to have complete
    confidence in.*
  sicher stellen *to put in safe keeping.*
  sicher wissen *to know for certain.*

Sicherheit *f. safety, security.*
  in Sicherheit bringen *to secure.*
  Sicherheit leisten *to give security.*
sicherheitshalber *for safety's sake.*
Sicherheitsnadel *f. safety-pin.*
Sicherheitsschloss *n. safety-lock.*
sicherlich *surely, certainly.*
sichern *to protect.*
Sicherung *f. protection.*
SICHT *f. sight, visibility.*
  sichtbar *visible, apparent.*
sichten *to sight; to sift, sort.*
SIE (sie) *pers. pron. 3rd pers. sing. (fem.
  nom. & acc.); 3rd pers. pl. (m., f., n.,
  nom. & acc.) she, her, it; they, them.*
Sieb *n. colander, strainer.*
sieben *to sift, strain.*
SIEBEN *seven.*
SIEBENTE *seventh.*
SIEBZEHNTE *seventeenth.*
SIEBZIG *seventy.*
siebzigst *seventieth.*
siech *sickly, ailing, infirm.*
siedeln *to settle, colonize.*
SIEG *m. victory, triumph.*
Siegel *n. seal.*
Sieger *m. victor, winner.*
siegesgewiss *certain or confident of victory.*
siegreich *victorious.*
Signal *n. signal.*
Signalanlage *f. signaling system.*
Signalhupe *f. siren.*
signalisieren *to signal.*
Signatur *f. mark, sign, characteristic, stamp.*
Silbe *f. syllable.*
Silber *n. silver.*
Silbergeschirr *n. silver plate, silverware.*
Silberpapier *n. silver paper, tin foil.*
Silvesterabend *m. New Year's Eve.*
SINGEN *to sing.*
Singstimme *f. singing voice, vocal part.*
sinken *to sink, drop, fall.*
SINN *m. sense, faculty, mind, understanding,
  intellect.*
  anderen Sinnes werden *to change one's
    mind.*
  in gewissem Sinn *in a way, in a sense.*
  im Sinn haben *to intend.*
  sich etwas aus dem Sinn schlagen *to
    dismiss a thing from one's mind.*
Sinnbild *n. symbol, emblem, allegory.*
sinnbildlich *symbolic.*
sinnen *to think, reflect, meditate.*
  sinnen auf *to plot, devise.*
sinnlich *sensual, sensuous, material.*
sinnlos *senseless, absurd.*
Sinnlosigkeit *f. senselessness, foolishness.*
sinnreich *sensible, clever.*
Sirene *f. siren.*

Sitte *f. custom, habit.*
Sittengesetz *n. moral law, moral code.*
Sittenlehre *f. moral, philosophy, ethics.*
sittenlos *immoral, dissolute.*
sittlich *moral.*
sittsam *modest.*
Sittsamkeit *f. modesty, decency.*
SITZ *m. seat, residence.*
SITZEN *to sit, fit, adhere.*
   etwas auf sich sitzen lassen *to put up with.*
   sitzen bleiben *to remain seated; to be left back (school).*
   sitzen lassen *to leave.*
   im Gefängnis sitzen *to be in jail.*
Sitzgelegenheit *f. seating accommodation.*
Sitzplatz *m. seat.*
Skandal *m. scandal.*
Skelett *n. skeleton.*
skeptisch *sceptical.*
Ski *m. ski.*
   skilaufen *to ski.*
Skiläufer *m. skier.*
Skispringen *n. ski-jumping.*
Skizze *f. sketch.*
skizzieren *to sketch.*
Sklave *m. slave.*
sklavisch *slavish, servile.*
Skrupel *m. scruple.*
SO *so, thus, in this way, like that, anyhow.*
   Ach so! *Oh, I see!*
   So? *Is that so? Indeed? Really?*
   so . . . auch, *however.*
   so bald als *as soon as.*
   so . . . doch *yet, nevertheless.*
   so ein *such a.*
   so etwas *a thing like that.*
   so gut wie *as if, practically.*
   so oder so *this way or that way.*
   so . . . so *though . . . yet.*
   so wie *as, the way*
Socke *f. sock.*
sodann *then.*
sodass *so that.*
soeben *just, just now.*
sofern *so far as.*
sofort *immediately, at once.*
sogar *even.*
sogenannt *so-called.*
sogleich *at once, immediately.*
Sohle *f. sole.*
sohlen *to resole.*
SOHN *m. son.*
solange *so, as long as.*
SOLCH *such, the same.*
   solch ein *such a.*
Soldat *m. soldier.*
Solist (–in) *m. soloist. (female)*
SOLLEN *ought, shall, to have to, must, be supposed to, be said to.*
   Du sollst nicht töten. *Thou shalt not kill.*
   Die Schüler sollen fleissig sein. *Students must be industrious.*
   Er soll ein Millionär sein. *They say he is a millionaire.*
   Sollte er nicht zu Hause sein? *Is it possible that he is not at home?*
   Sollte er telefonieren? *Should he telephone?*
   Was soll das heissen? *What is the meaning of that?*
   Was soll es bedeuten? *What does that mean?*
   Was sollte ich dagegen machen? *How could I help it?*
somit *consequently.*
SOMMER *m. summer.*
   Sommernachtstraum *m. Midsummer Night's Dream*
Sommerfrische *f. health-resort.*
Sommersprosse *f. freckle.*
Sommerzeit *f. summertime.*
Sonderausgabe *f. special edition.*
SONDERBAR *strange, peculiar.*
sonderbarenweise *strange to say.*
sondergleichen *unequaled, unique.*
Sonderling *m. strange character.*
Sondermeldung *f. special announcement.*
SONDERN *but (in a negative sentence).*
   Ich wollte niche ausgehen, sondern zu Hause bleiben. *I did not want to go out but to stay home.*
   nicht nur . . . sondern auch *not only . . . but also.*
   Sie war nicht nur schön, sondern auch gut. *She was not only beautiful but kind as well.*
SONNABEND *m. Saturday.*
SONNE *f. sun.*
(sich) sonnen *to sun oneself, bask.*
Sonnenaufgang *m. sunrise.*
Sonnenblume *f. sunflower.*
Sonnenbrand *m. sunburn.*
Sonnenbrille *f. sunglasses.*
Sonnenstrahl *m. sunbeam.*
Sonnenuntergang *m. sunset.*
sonnig *sunny.*
SONNTAG *m. Sunday.*
sonntags *on Sunday.*
SONST *else, moreover, besides, otherwise, formerly.*
   Sonst noch etwas? *Anything else?*
   sonst jemand *anybody else.*
   sonst nichts *nothing else.*
   Sonst niemand? *No one else?*
   sonst und jetzt *formerly and now.*
   Was konnte ich sonst tun? *What else could I do?*

Wenn es sonst nichts wäre! *If that were all it was!*

wie sonst *as usual.*

sonstwie *in some other way.*

sonstwo *elsewhere.*

Sopran *m. soprano.*

Sopranistin *f. soprano singer.*

SORGE *f. grief, sorrow, anxiety, worry, trouble, care.*

einem Sorgen machen *to worry someone.*

sich Sorgen machen *to worry.*

Sorge tragen *to see about something.*

SORGEN *to care for, look after, take care of, provide.*

sich sorgen um *to be concerned about; to see to, to take responsibility.*

sorgen für *to look after.*

Sorgenkind *n. problem child.*

sorgenvoll *worried.*

Sorgfalt *f. carefulness, care, accuracy.*

sorgfältig *careful, painstaking.*

sorglich *thoughtful.*

sorglos *carefree, careless.*

Sorglosigkeit *f. lightheartedness, thoughtlessness.*

SORTE *f. kind, sort, brand, grade.*

sortieren *to sort, arrange.*

SOVIEL *as much as, so far as.*

soweit *as far as.*

sowenig *as little as.*

sowie *as soon as.*

sowieso *anyway, anyhow.*

sozial *social.*

Sozialismus *m. Socialism.*

Sozialist *m. Socialist.*

sozialistisch *socialistic.*

Sozialwissenschaft *f. sociology.*

Sozius *m. partner.*

spähen *to be on the look out, patrol.*

Spalier bilden/stehen *to form an honor guard; to line.*

Spalt *m. crack, slot, gap.*

spalten *to split, divide.*

sich spalten *to split.*

Spaltholz *n. firewood sticks.*

Spange *f. buckle, brooch.*

Spanier *m (–in, f.) Spaniard*

spanisch *Spanish.*

Spanisch *n. Spanish (language).*

Spanne *f. short space of time, margin.*

SPANNEN *to put up, stretch, pull, tighten, grip, clamp.*

gespannt sein *to be anxious, curious.*

Ich bin auf die Antwort gespannt. *I am curious to know the answer.*

das Pferd hinter den Wagen spannen. *to put the cart before the horse.*

spannend *fascinating, absorbing, thrilling.*

Spannung *f. tension, strain, suspense, voltage.*

Sparbüchse *f. money-box (piggy bank).*

Spareinlage *f. savings deposit.*

Spargel *m. asparagus.*

Sparkasse *f. savings bank.*

spärlich *scarce, frugal, thin, scanty.*

Spärlichkeit *f. scarcity.*

SPARSAM *economical, thrifty.*

Sparsamkeit *f. economy, thrift.*

Spass *m. joke, fun.*

zum Spass *for fun.*

spassen *to joke.*

Spassmacher *m. joker.*

SPÄT *late, belated, backward.*

Besser spät als nie. *Better late than never.*

zu spät kommen *to be late.*

Wie spät ist es? *What time is it?*

Spaten *m. spade.*

später *later, afterwards.*

späterhin *later on.*

spätestens *at the latest.*

Spatz *m. sparrow.*

SPAZIEREN *to walk about, stroll.*

spazieren gehen *to go for a walk.*

Spazierfahrt *f. drive, pleasure trip*

Spaziergang *m. walk.*

Spaziergänger *m. walker, stroller.*

Speck *m. bacon.*

Speckschwarte *f. rind of bacon.*

Spediteur *m. mover, shipper, forwarding agent.*

Speicher *m. silo, granary, warehouse.*

speichern *to store.*

SPEISE *f. food, meal.*

Speiseeis *n. ice cream.*

Speisekarte *f. menu.*

Speisesaal *m. dining room.*

Speisewagen *m. dining car.*

Spekulant *m. speculator.*

spekulieren *to speculate.*

Spende *f. gift, present, donation.*

spenden *to dispense, bestow, administer.*

Spender *m. giver, donor, benefactor.*

spendieren *to give freely, lavishly.*

Sperre *f. gate, closing, barrier.*

sperrangelweit *wide open.*

sperren *to close, shut, block, barricade.*

ins Gefängnis sperren *to put in prison.*

Sperrklinke *f. safety catch.*

Sperrholz *n. plywood.*

Spesen *f. pl. charges, expenses.*

Spezialarzt *n. specialist.*

spezialisieren *to specialize.*

speziell *special, particular.*

spezifisch *specific.*

spezifizieren *to specify.*

Spiegel *m. mirror.*

Spiegelbild n. reflected image.

spiegelglatt smooth as a mirror.

spiegeln to shine, glitter.

  sich spiegeln to be reflected.

SPIEL n. game, deck of cards, playing, play, sport, touch (music).

  auf dem Spiel stehen to be at stake.

  aufs Spiel setzen to risk.

  Lassen Sie mich aus dem Spiel. Leave me out of this.

  leichtes Spiel haben to have no difficulties.

  seine Hand im Spiel haben to have a finger in the pie.

  sein Spiel treiben mit to make game of.

  Ich bin am Spiel. It's my turn.

  ihm freies Spiel lassen to give him a (free) hand.

Spielautomat m. gambling machine.

Spielbank f. gambling casino.

Spielergebnis n. score (result of play).

Spieldose f. musical box.

SPIELEN to play, act, perform, gamble, pretend.

  Was spielt man heute abend? What's playing tonight?

Spielerei f. trifle.

Spielplan m. program, repertory.

Spielsachen pl. toys.

Spielverderber m. kill-joy.

Spielzeug n. toy.

Spiess m. lance, spear, pike.

Spiessbürger m. bourgeois, narrow minded, commonplace.

Spinat m. spinach.

Spinne f. spider.

spinnen to spin.

Spinngewebe n. cobweb.

Spinnrad n. spinning wheel.

Spion m. spy.

Spionage f. spying, espionage.

Spionageabwehr f. counterespionage.

spionieren to spy.

Spiritus m. spirits, alcohol.

Spital n. hospital.

SPITZ pointed, sharp, acute, caustic.

Spitze f. point, tip (tongue), top, head, lace, sarcasm.

  etwas auf die Spitze treiben to carry to extremes.

SPITZEN to sharpen, point.

  seine Ohren spitzen to prick one's ears.

Spitzenleistung f. record, maximum.

Spitzenlohn m. maximum pay.

spitzfindig pointed, sharp, sarcastic, subtle.

Spitzfindigkeit f. subtlety.

spitzig pointed, sharp, sarcastic.

Spitzname m. nickname.

Splitter m. splinter, chip, fragment.

splittern to splinter, split.

spontan spontaneous.

Sporn m. spur.

Sport m. sport

  Sport treiben to go in for sports.

Sportfunk m. radio sports news.

Sportler (–in) m. sportsman (woman).

sportlich sporting, athletic.

Sportname m. nickname.

Spott m. mockery, ridicule.

spotten to mock, make fun, defy.

spöttisch mocking, scoffing, sarcastic.

SPRACHE f. language, speech, talk.

  zur Sprache bringen to bring up a subject.

  zur Sprache kommen to be mentioned.

  gehobene Sprache elevated diction.

Sprachfertigkeit f. fluency (of speech).

sprachgewandt fluent

sprachkundig proficient in languages.

Sprachlehre f. grammar.

sprachlich linguistic.

sprachlos speechless.

Sprachschatz m. vocabulary.

Sprachschnitzer m. grammatical blunder, mistake.

Sprachstörung f. speech defect.

SPRECHEN to speak, talk, say, converse, discuss.

  Der Herr Doktor ist nicht zu sprechen. The doctor is busy.

  gut zu sprechen sein auf to be kindly disposed to.

  Ich bin für niemanden zu sprechen. I am in to no one.

  sich herumsprechen to be whispered about town.

  Sie sprechen nicht miteinander. They are not on speaking terms.

  Sprechen Sie Deutsch? Do you speak German?

  Sprechen Sie langsam, bitte. Please speak slowly.

  unter uns gesprochen between us.

  das Urteil sprechen to pronounce judgment.

  zu sprechen kommen auf to come to speak of.

  Wen wünschen Sie zu sprechen? Whom do you want to see?

Sprecher m. speaker.

Sprechstunde f. office hours, office (doctor).

Sprechstundenhilfe f. doctor's receptionist.

Sprechweise f. diction.

Sprechzimmer n. consulting room.

sprengen to burst, blow up, blast, spray.

Sprengung f. blowing up, explosion.

Sprichwort n. proverb.

Springbrunnen m. fountain.

SPRINGEN *to jump, skip, spring, play.*
> Das ist der springende Punkt. *That is the crucial point.*
> in die Augen springen *to be obvious.*

spritzen *to spray, splash, sprinkle.*

spröde *brittle, hard, inflexible.*

Sprosse *f. sprout, sprig, offspring.*

Sprössling *m. sprout, shoot, offshoot, son (heir).*

Spruch *m. aphorism, saying.*

spruchreif *ripe for decision.*

sprudeln *to bubble up.*

sprühen *to spark.*

Sprühregen *m. drizzle, drizzling rain.*

SPRUNG *m. leap, jump, crack.*
> Es ist nur ein Sprung von meinem Haus. *It is only a stone's throw from my house.*
> Ich war auf dem Sprung auszugehen. *I was just going to leave.*

Sprungschanze *f. ski-jump.*

spucken *to spit.*
> Spucken Verboten! *No spitting!*

Spülbecken *n. washtub.*

spülen *to rinse.*

Spülwasser *n. dishwater.*

SPUR *f. trace, trail, track, footprint.*
> einem auf die Spur kommen *to be on a person's tracks.*
> Keine Spur! *Not in the least!*
> keine Spur von *no trace of.*

spüren *to feel, perceive, experience.*
> spüren nach *to track, follow.*

spurlos *trackless.*

Spürsinn haben *to have a flair.*

(sich) sputen *to hurry up.*

STAAT *m. state, government, pomp, parade, show.*
> in vollem Staat *in full dress.*
> Staat machen *to show off.*

staatlich *public, political.*

Staatsaktion *f. government undertaking.*

Staatsangehörige *m. & f. subject, national.*

Staatsangehörigkeit *f. nationality, citizenship.*

Staatsanwalt *m. public prosecutor.*

Staatsbeamte(r) *m. civil servant.*

Staatsbesitz *m. state/public property.*

Staatsgebäude *n. public building.*

Staatsdienst *m. civil service.*

Staatsmann *m. statesman, politician.*

staatsmännisch *statesmanlike.*

Stab *m. stick, rod, bat, condemn.*
> den Stab brechen über *to condemn.*

stabil *stable.*

stabilisieren *to stabilize.*

Stachel *m. thorn, prickle, sting, spur.*

Stachelbeere *f. gooseberry.*

Stacheldraht *m. barbed wire.*

Stadion *n. stadium, arena.*

Stadium *n. phase, stage.*

STADT *f. town, city.*

Stadtbahn *f. city railway.*

stadtbekannt *known all over town.*

Städter (-in) *m. townsman (woman)*

Stadtgespräch *n. local call.*

städtisch *municipal, urban.*

Stadtteil *m. quarter (of a town).*

Stahl *m. steel.*

stählern *of steel.*

Stahlguss *m. steel.*

Stall *m. stable.*

Stamm *m. stem, root, trunk.*

Stammbaum *m. genealogical tree.*

stammeln *to stammer.*

stammen *to spring from, come from.*

Stammgast *m. regular customer.*

Stammhalter *m. eldest son and heir.*

stämmig *sturdy, strong, vigorous.*

stampfen *to stamp, mash, crush.*

Stand *m. standing position.*
> einen schweren Stand haben *to have a tough job.*
> einen guten Stand haben *to be well thought of.*
> Stand der Dinge *State of affairs.*

Standbild *n. statute.*

Ständchen *n. serenade.*

Standesamt *n. registrar's office.*

Standesbeamte *m. registrar.*

Standesehe *f. marriage for position or rank.*

standesgemäss *in accordance with one's rank.*

Standesgericht *n. court martial.*

Standesunterschied *m. difference of class.*

standhaft *steady, constant.*

standhalten *to hold firm.*

ständig *permanent.*

Standort *m. station, position.*

Standpunkt *m. point of view.*

Standuhr *f. grandfather's clock.*

Stange *f. pole, bar, perch.*
> eine Stange Gold *a bar of gold.*
> von der Stange *ready-made.*
> ein Anzug von der Stange *a suit off the rack.*

Stanze *f. stanza.*

stanzen *to stamp.*

STARK *strong, stout, considerable, hard.*
> Das ist denn doch zu stark! *That is too much!*
> stark auftragen *to exaggerate, boast.*
> starke Erkältung *bad cold.*
> starkes Gedächtnis *good memory.*
> starker Regen *heavy rain.*
> stark besetzt *well attended.*
> stark übertrieben *grossly exaggerated.*

Stärke *f. strength, force, vigor, intensity, energy, violence.*

stärken *to strengthen, fortify, starch, confirm.*

Starkstrom *m. power current.*

Starkstromleitung *f. power-circuit.*

starr *stiff, hard, paralyzed.*

   starren vor Staunen   *to be dumbfounded.*

starren *to stare, be numb.*

starrköpfig *stubborn.*

Starrsinn *m. obstinacy.*

Start *m. start.*

Startbahn *f. runway.*

starten *to start.*

Station *f. station, stop, ward.*

   freie Station   *free board and lodging.*

Stationsarzt *m. resident physician.*

Stationsvorsteher *m. station master.*

Statistik *f. statistics.*

statistisch *statistical.*

STÄTTE *f. place, spot.*

STATT (anstatt) *prep. (gen.) instead of.*

stattfinden *to take place.*

stattgeben *to permit, allow.*

statthaft *admissible, legal.*

stattlich *stately, magnificent, imposing.*

Stattlichkeit *f. dignity, magnificence.*

Statue *f. statute.*

Staub *m. dust, powder.*

   in den Staub ziehen   *to depreciate.*

   Staub wischen   *to dust.*

staubig *dusty.*

Staublappen *m. duster.*

Staubsauger *m. vacuum-cleaner.*

staunen *to be surprised.*

STECHEN *to stick, bite, sting.*

   sich stechen   *to prick oneself.*

   in die Augen stechen   *to take one's fancy.*

Stechfliege *f. horse-fly.*

Steckdose *f. wall-plug, socket.*

STECKEN *to stick, pin up, fasten, fix, plant, stuff.*

   Dahinter steckt etwas.   *There is something behind this.*

   in Brand stecken   *to set fire.*

steckenbleiben *to be stuck.*

Steckenpferd *n. hobby, pet project.*

Stecker *m. plug.*

Stecknadel *f. pin.*

STEHEN *to stand, stop, be, suit, become.*

   gut stehen   *to be becoming.* (Rot steht ihr. *Red is becoming to her.*)

   gut stehen mit   *to be on good terms with*

   geschrieben stehen   *to be written.*

   Das Thermometer steht auf Null.   *The thermometer reads zero.*

   Es steht bei ihr.   *It's up to her.*

   im Verdacht stehen   *to be under suspicion.*

   in einem Amte stehen   *to hold an office.*

stehenbleiben *to stop, remain standing.*

stehend *standing, stationary, permanent.*

   stehenden Fusses   *at once.*

stehenlassen *to leave (standing).*

Stehlampe *f. floor lamp.*

STEHLEN *to steal, rob, take away.*

steif *stiff.*

Steig *m. path.*

STEIGEN *to climb, go up, ascend, rise, increase.*

   zu Kopf steigen   *to go to one's head.*

steigend *growing, increasing.*

steigern *to raise, increase, intensify.*

   sich steigern in   *to intensify, work up.*

Steigerung *f. raising, increase, gradation, climax.*

steil *steep, precipitous.*

Steilhang *m. steep slope.*

STEIN *m. stone, rock, jewel.*

   Das hat den Stein ins Rollen gebracht.   *That started the ball rolling.*

   Das ist nur ein Tropfen auf den heissen Stein.   *That's only a drop in the bucket.*

   einen Stein im Brett haben bei   *to be in favor with.*

   Mit fällt ein Stein vom Herzen!   *I feel so relieved!*

   Stein des Anstosses   *stumbling block.*

   Stein und Bein schwören   *to swear by all the gods.*

Steinbruch *m. quarry.*

steinern *of stone.*

steinhart *as hard as stone.*

steinig *stony, rocky.*

steinreich *very wealthy.*

Steinzeit *f. Stone Age.*

STELLE *f. spot, place, position, situation, passage.*

   auf der Stelle   *on the spot.*

   offene Stelle   *vacancy.*

   von der Stelle kommen   *to make progress.*

   zur Stelle sein   *to be present.*

   an Stelle von   *instead of.*

STELLEN *to put, place, set, arrange, regulate, provide, furnish.*

   auf den Kopf stellen   *to turn upside down.*

   auf sich selbst gestellt sein   *to be dependent on oneself.*

   eine Bedingung stellen   *to make a condition.*

   eine Frage stellen   *to ask a question.*

   Er ist sehr gut gestellt.   *He is very well off.*

   Antrag stellen auf   *to apply for.*

   in Dienst stellen   *to put into service.*

   auf die Probe stellen   *to put to the test.*

etwas in Aussicht stellen *to hold out the prospect of something.*

sich stellen gegen *to oppose.*

sich stellen *to stand.*

kalt stellen *to put in a cool place.*

sich gut stellen mit *to be on good terms with.*

sich stellen zu *to behave toward.*

zur Verfügung stellen *to place at one's disposal.*

Stellenangebot *n. job offer; vacancy.*

Stellengesuch *n. application for a position, situations wanted.*

stellenlos *unemployed.*

Stellennachweis *m. employment reference.*

Stellenvermittlung *f. employment agency.*

STELLUNG *f. position, situation, stand, job.*

Stellung nehmen zu *to express one's opinion.*

Stellungnahme *f. opinion, comment, point of view.*

Stellungsgesuch *n. application for a position.*

stellungslos *unemployed.*

Stellungswechsel *m. change of position.*

Stellvertreter *m. representative.*

Stempel *m. stamp, postmark.*

Stempelkissen *n. ink-pad.*

stempeln *to stamp, mark.*

stenografieren *to write in shorthand.*

stenografisch *stenographic.*

Stenogramm *n. shorthand.*

Stenogramm aufnehmen *to take down in shorthand.*

Stenotypist *m. (–in, f.) stenotypist.*

Steppdecke *f. quilt.*

Sterbebett *n. deathbed.*

Sterben *n. death.*

im Sterben liegen *to be dying.*

STERBEN *to die.*

sterblich *mortal.*

sterblich verliebt *madly in love.*

Sterblichkeit *f. death rate.*

steril *sterile.*

sterilisieren *to sterilize.*

Stern *m. star.*

Sternbild *n. constellation.*

Sterndeuter *m. astrologer.*

Sternhimmel *m. starry sky.*

stets *always, forever.*

Steuer *n. rudder, helm, steering wheel.*

Steuer *f. tax.*

Steueraufschlag *m. supplementary tax.*

steuerfrei *tax-free.*

steuern *to steer, pilot, drive.*

steuerpflichtig *subject to taxation.*

Steuerrad *n. steering wheel.*

Steuerzahler *m. taxpayer.*

Stich *m. sting, prick, stitch.*

im Stich lassen *to forsake.*

einen Stich haben *to have a screw loose (coll.).*

Stichtag *m. fixed day.*

Stichwort *n. catchword, cue.*

Stiefbruder *m. stepbrother.*

Stiefmutter *f. stepmother.*

Stiefmütterchen *n. pansy.*

Stiefschwester *f. stepsister.*

Stiefsohn *m. stepson.*

Stieftochter *f. stepdaughter.*

Stiefvater *m. stepfather.*

Stier *m. bull.*

Stierkämpfer *m. bullfighter.*

Stift *m. pencil, crayon; charitable institution.*

stiften *to donate; to found, establish.*

Stifter *m. founder; donor.*

Stiftung *f. foundation.*

Stil *m. style, manner.*

Stilgefühl *n. stylish sense.*

STILL *still, quiet, silent, secret.*

Seien Sie still! *Be quiet!*

stille Jahreszeit *off-season, slow season.*

stille Liebe *secret love.*

bei stiller Nacht *in the dead of the night.*

sich still verhalten *to keep still/quiet.*

STILLE *f. silence, calm, quietude, peace.*

im Stillen *secretly.*

in aller Stille *privately, secretly.*

stillen *to quiet, appease, satisfy, quench, nurse.*

stillhalten *to keep still.*

Stilleben *n. still life (art).*

stilllegen *to shut down, close, discontinue.*

stillschweigen *to be silent.*

stillschweigend *silent.*

Stillstand *m. standstill, stop.*

stillstehen *to stand still, stop.*

Still gestanden! *Attention!*

stilvoll *in good style, taste.*

Stimmabgabe *f. vote, voting.*

stimmberechtigt *entitled to vote.*

STIMME *f. voice, part, comment, vote.*

Stimme abgeben *to vote.*

STIMMEN *to tune, vote, be correct, impress someone, influence someone's mood.*

Das stimmt! *That is correct!*

Werden Sie für oder dagegen stimmen? *Are you going to vote for or against?*

Stimmrecht *n. right to vote.*

STIMMUNG *f. tuning, pitch, key, mood, humor, impression, atmosphere.*

Stimmung machen für *to create a mood for, to make propaganda for.*

Stimmungsmensch *m. moody person.*

stimmungsvoll *impressive, appealing.*

Stimmzettel *m. ballot.*

Stirn *f. forehead, front, imprudence.*

die Stirn runzeln *to frown.*

einem die Stirne bieten   *to show a bold front.*

Stock *m. stick, rod, cane, floor (story).*
  über Stock und Stein   *up hill and down dale.*
  Welcher Stock?   *What floor?*
stockdumm *utterly stupid.*
stocken *to stop, stand still.*
  ins Stocken geraten   *to get tied up.*
  im Reden stocken   *to break down, hesitate.*
  stock dunkel   *pitch dark.*
stockfinster *pitch-dark.*
Stockfisch *m. dried cod.*
Stockwerk *n. story, floor.*
Stoff *m. matter, substance.*
stöhnen *to groan.*
stolpern *to stumble, trip over.*
stolz *proud.*
  stolz sein auf   *to be proud of.*
stopfen *to darn, fill, stuff.*
Stopfgarn *n. darning thread.*
Stopfnadel *f. darning needle.*
stoppen *to stop.*
Stoppuhr *f. stop-watch.*
Stöpsel *m. stopper, cork.*
stöpseln *to cork.*
Storch *m. stork.*
STÖREN *to disturb, trouble, inconvenience.*
  Nicht stören!   *Do not disturb!*
  gestörte Leitung   *faulty electrical line.*
störrisch *stubborn.*
Störung *f. disturbance, upset.*
  geistige Störung   *mental disorder.*
Stoss *m. push, poke, pile, jerk, shock.*
stossen *to push, shove, hit, kick, knock.*
  stossen auf   *to run into.*
Stossstange *f. bumper (on a car).*
stottern *to shutter, stammer.*
Strafanstalt *f. penitentiary.*
strafbar *liable to punishment.*
Strafe *f. punishment, penalty, fine.*
  bei Strafe von   *on pain of.*
strafen *to punish.*
Straferlass *m. amnesty.*
straff *stretched, tense, tight, strict.*
straffällig *punishable.*
straffen *to tighten.*
straffrei *exempt from punishment, unpunished.*
Strafgefangene *m. convict.*
Strafgericht *n. criminal court.*
sträflich *criminal, punishable.*
Strafmassnahme *f. sanction.*
Strafporto *n. extra postage, surcharge.*
Strafprozess *m. criminal case.*
strafwürdig *punishable.*
STRAHL *m. ray, beam, stream.*
strahlen *to radiate, beam, shine.*

stramm *tight, close.*
  stramm stehen   *to stand at attention.*
STRAND *m. seashore, beach, strand.*
Strandbad *n. seaside, resort.*
stranden *to run around or ashore.*
Strandschuhe *pl. beach shoes.*
STRANG *m. rope, cord, line.*
  am gleichen Strang ziehen   *to act in concert.*
  an einem Strang ziehen   *to act together.*
  über die Stränge schlagen   *to kick over the traces.*
  wenn alle Stränge reissen   *if the worst comes to the worst.*
Strapaze *f. fatigue.*
strapazieren *to tire, exhaust.*
STRASSE *f. street, highway, road.*
  an der Strasse   *by the wayside.*
  auf der Strasse   *in the street.*
Strassenarbeiter *m. roadman.*
Strassenbahn *f. tram, streetcar.*
Strassenfeger *m. street cleaner.*
Strassenübergang *m. pedestrian crossing.*
Strassenverstopfung *f. traffic congestion, traffic jam.*
sträuben *to ruffle up, bristle.*
Strauch *m. shrub, bush.*
streben *to endeavor, aspire, aim at.*
Streber *m. climber, careerist.*
Strecke *f. distance, way, route, tract.*
  auf freier Strecke   *on the road.*
strecken *to stretch, extend, stretch out.*
  die Waffen strecken   *to lay down arms.*
  sich strecken   *to stretch.*
Streich *m. stroke, blow.*
  einem einen Streich spielen   *to play a trick on a person.*
streichen *to spread, rub, strike, erase, cancel, paint, wander, stroll, migrate.*
  Frisch gestrichen!   *Wet paint!*
Streichholz *n. match.*
Streichmusik *f. string music.*
Streichquartett *n. string quartet.*
Streifen *m. stripe, marking.*
streifen *to touch lightly, stripe, brush, wander.*
Streik *m. strike.*
  in den Streik treten   *to go on strike.*
streiken *to strike.*
STREIT *m. fight, quarrel, dispute.*
streiten *to fight.*
  sich streiten   *to quarrel.*
Streitfall *m. quarrel, controversy.*
Streitfrage *f. matter in dispute.*
  einem etwas streitig machen   *to contest a person's right to a thing.*
STRENG *strict, stern, severe.*
  streng genommen   *strictly speaking.*
Strenge *f. severity, strictness.*

strengläubig *orthodox.*
streuen *to strew, scatter, spread.*
Strich *m. dash, stroke, line, compass point.*
  gegen den Strich *against the grain.*
  Machen wir einen Strich darunter! *Let's put an end to that.*
  nach Strich und Faden *thoroughly.*
Strichpunkt *m. semicolon.*
Strick *m. cord, rope.*
  wenn alle Stricke reissen *if everything else fails.*
stricken *to knit.*
Stroh *n. straw.*
Strohhalm *m. straw (for drinking).*
STROM *m. large river, stream, current.*
  Es regnet in Strömen. *It's pouring.*
stromabwärts *downstream.*
stromaufwärts *upstream.*
strömen *to stream, flow, pour.*
Strömung *f. current, stream.*
Stromzähler *electric meter.*
Strudel *m. whirlpool; type of pastry.*
Strumpf *m. stocking, sock.*
Strumpfband *n. garter.*
Strumpfhalter *m. garter (woman's).*
struppig *bristly, unkempt.*
STUBE *f. room, chamber, living room.*
Stubenhocker *m. stay-at-home.*
stubenrein *housebroken (of dogs).*
STÜCK *n. piece, play, extract, morsel.*
  aus einem Stück *all of a piece.*
  aus freien Stücken *of one's own free will.*
  ein starkes Stück *a bit stiff.*
  ein Stück Arbeit *a stiff job.*
  ein Stück mitnehmen *to give a lift.*
  Er hält grosse Stücke auf ihn. *He thinks a lot of him.*
  in allen Stücken *in every respect.*
  zwanzig Stück Vieh *twenty head of cattle.*
stückweise *piece by piece, by the piece.*
Student *m. (-in, f.) student.*
Studie *f. study, sketch (art).*
studieren *to study.*
Studium *n. study, university education.*
Stufe *f. step, stair, level.*
  auf gleicher Stufe mit *on a level with.*
stufenweise *by degrees, gradually.*
STUHL *m. chair, seat.*
stumm *dumb, silent, mute.*
Stummheit *f. dumbness.*
stumpf *blunt, obtuse, dull.*
  mit Stumpf und Stiehl *root and branch.*
Stumpfsinn *m. stupidity.*
stumpfsinnig *stupid, dull.*
STUNDE *f. hour; lesson, period.*
stundenlang *for hours.*
Stundenplan *m. timetable.*
Stundenzeiger *m. hour-hand.*

ständlich *hourly.*
STURM *m. storm, gale.*
stürmen *to take by storm.*
stürmisch *stormy, impetuous.*
Sturz *m. fall, crash, tumble, overthrow, collapse.*
  zurn Sturz bringen *to overthrow.*
stürzen *to overthrown, throw down, fall down, plunge into, crash.*
  Nicht stürzen! *Handle with care!*
Stütze *f. stay, support, help.*
stutzen *to trim, cut short, stop short.*
stützen *to support, base, prop up.*
Stutzer *m. dandy, fop.*
Stützpfeiler *m. pillar, support.*
Stützpunkt *m. base, strong point.*
Subjekt *m. subject.*
Substantiv *n. substantive, noun.*
Substanz *f. substance.*
substrahieren *to subtract.*
Suche *f. search, quest.*
  auf die Suche gehen *to go in search of.*
  auf der Suche sein nach *in search of.*
SUCHEN *to look for, try, seek.*
  das Weite suchen *to run away.*
  nach Worten suchen *to be at a loss for words.*
  Sie hat hier nichts zu suchen. *She has no business here.*
Sucht *f. passion, rage.*
Süden *m. south.*
Südfrüchte *pl. tropical fruits.*
südlich *southern, (to the) south.*
Südpol *m. south pole.*
Sühne *f. expiation, atonement.*
sühnen *to expiate, atone.*
Summe *f. sum, amount.*
summieren *to add up.*
Sumpf *m. swamp, marsh.*
Sünde *f. sin.*
Sünder *m (-in. f.) sinner.*
süundhaft *sinful.*
sündigen *to sin.*
Suppe *f. soup, broth.*
Suppenanlage *f. things (that are) added to the soup.*
suspendieren *to suspend.*
SÜSS *sweet, fresh, lovely.*
Süsse *f. sweetness.*
Süssigkeit *f. sweetness, sweets.*
süsslich *sweetish, mawkish.*
Symbol *n. symbol.*
symbolisch *symbolical.*
Sympathie *f. sympathy.*
sympathisch *nice, likable, congenial.*
Symphonie *f. symphony.*
Symptom *n. symptom.*
Synagoge *f. synagogue.*
System *n. system.*

Szene *f. scene.*
Szenerie *f. scenery, settings.*

T

Tabak *m. tobacco.*
Tabelle *f. table, index, schedule.*
Tablett *n. tray.*
Tablette *f. tablet.*
Tadel *m. reprimand, blame.*
tadellos *excellent, perfect.*
tadeln *to blame, find fault.*
TAFEL *f. board, blackboard, bar, plate, table.*
   sich von der Tafel aufheben *to rise from the table.*
TAG *m. day, daylight, life (one's days).*
   alle acht Tage *every week.*
   alle Tage *every day.*
   am Tag *during the day, in the daytime.*
   an den Tag bringen *to bring to light.*
   auf ein paar Tage *for a few days.*
   auf seine alten Tage *in his old age.*
   bei Tage *in the daytime.*
   den ganzen Tag *all day long.*
   dieser Tage *one of these days.*
   eines Tages *some day.*
   Er lebt in den Tag hinein. *He lives from hand to mouth.*
   Guten Tag! *Good morning!*
   in acht Tagen *in a week.*
   Tag aus, Tag ein *day in, day out.*
   Tag für Tag *day by day.*
   einen Tag um den andern *every other day.*
   Man soll den Tag nicht von dem Abend loben. *Don't count your chickens before they hatch.*
   vierzehn Tage *two weeks.*
   vor acht Tagen *a week ago.*
Tagebuch *n. diary.*
tagelang *for days on end.*
Tagesbericht *m. daily report, bulletin.*
Tageseinnahme *f. day's earnings.*
Tagesgespräch *n. topic of the day.*
Tageswerk *n. day's work.*
Tageszeit *f. time of day.*
Tageszeitung *f. daily paper.*
taghell *as light as day.*
täglich *daily.*
tagsüber *during the day.*
Tagung *f. conference, meeting.*
Taille *f. waist.*
Takt *m. time measure (music).*
Taktgefühl *n. tact.*
Taktik *f. tactics.*
taktisch *tactical.*
taktlos *tactless.*

Taktlosigkeit *f. tactlessness, indiscretion.*
taktvoll *tactful, discreet.*
Tal *n. valley.*
Talent *n. talent, ability.*
talentiert *talented.*
Talk *m. talcum powder.*
Talsperre *f. river dam.*
talwärts *downhill.*
Tank *m. tank (car).*
tanken *to fill up (car).*
Tanne *f. fir tree.*
Tannenadeln *pl. fir needles.*
Tannenbaum *m. fir tree.*
Tannenzapfen *m. fir cone.*
Tante *f. aunt.*
Tanz *m. dance, ball.*
   Darf ich um den nächsten Tanz bitten? *May I have the next dance?*
TANZEN *to dance.*
Tänzer *m. (–in, f.) dance partner.*
Tapete *f. wallpaper.*
Tapezier *m. paperhanger, upholsterer.*
tapezieren *to paper.*
tapfer *brave, gallant.*
Tapferkeit *f. bravery, gallantry.*
Tarif *m. rate, tariff.*
tarifmässig *in accordance with the tariff.*
tarnen *to camouflage, disguise.*
Tarnung *f. camouflage.*
TASCHE *f. pocket, bag, purse.*
   jemandem auf der Tasche liegen *to be a financial drain to a person.*
Taschenausgabe *f. pocket book edition.*
Taschengeld *n. change.*
Taschenbuch *n. pocketbook.*
Taschendieb *m. pickpocket.*
Taschenlampe *f. flashlight.*
Taschenmesser *n. pocket knife.*
Taschentuch *n. handkerchief.*
Taschenuhr *f. pocket-watch.*
TASSE *f. cup.*
   eine Tasse Kaffee *a cup of coffee.*
Taste *f. key (music and typewriter).*
tasten *to touch, feel.*
TAT *f. deed, act, fact, achievement, feat.*
   auf frischer Tat *in the very act.*
   in der Tat *indeed, as a matter of fact.*
tatenlos *inactive, idle.*
Täter *m. perpetrator, doer.*
tätig *active.*
   tätig sein *to be active, hard at work.*
Tätigkeit *f. activity, job.*
tatkräftig *energetic, active.*
Tatsache *f. fact.*
tatsächlich *real, actual.*
Tau *m. dew.*
Tau *n. rope.*
taub *deaf, empty, hollow.*
Taube *f. pigeon.*

Taubheit *f. deafness.*
taubstumm *deaf and dumb.*
Taubstumme(r) *m. deaf-mute.*
tauchen *to dive, dip, plunge.*
Taucher *m. diver.*
tauen *to thaw.*
Taufe *f. baptism, christening.*
    aus der Taufe heben   *to be godfather (or*
       godmother).
taufen *to baptize.*
Taufname *m. Christian name.*
taugen *to be of use.*
Taugenichts *m. good-for-nothing.*
Tauglichkeit *f. fitness, suitability.*
Tausch *m. exchange.*
tauschen *to exchange, swap.*
täuschen *to delude, deceive, disappoint.*
    Mich können Sie nicht täuschen.   *You*
       can't fool me.
    Der Schein täuscht
    sich täuschen lassen   *to let oneself be*
       fooled.
Täuschung *f. deception.*
TAUSEND *thousand.*
tausendmal *a thousand times.*
Tauwetter *n. thaw.*
Taxe *f. tax, rate, duty.*
Taxi *n. taxi.*
    ein Taxi holen   *to call a cab.*
taxieren *to appraise, value.*
Technik *f. technology.*
Techniker *m. technician.*
technisch *technical.*
Tee *m. tea.*
Teelöffel *m. teaspoon.*
Teer *n. tar.*
Teich *m. pond.*
Teig *m. dough.*
TEIL *m. & n. part, share, portion.*
    ich für mein Teil   *as for me.*
    sich sein Teil denken   *to have one's own*
       ideas.
    zum Teil   *partly.*
    zum grössten Teil   *for the most part.*
teilbar *divisible.*
Teilbeschäftigung *f. part-time work.*
Teilchen *n. particle.*
TEILEN *to divide, share, distribute, deal*
    out.
    geteilte Gefühle   *mixed feelings.*
    geteilter Meinung sein   *to be of a different*
       opinion.
    sich teilen lassen durch   *to be divisible by*
Teilhaber *m. partner, participant.*
Teilhaberschaft *f. partnership.*
Teilnahme *f. participation, condolences.*
    Meine aufrichtige Teilnahme   *my sincere*
       condolences.
teilnahmslos *indifferent.*

teilnahmsvoll *sympathetic.*
teilnehmen *to take part in.*
Teilnehmer *m. participant, subscriber.*
teilweise *partial.*
Teilzahlung *f. part-payment, installment.*
Telekopierer *m. fax*
telekopieren *to fax.*
Telefax *m. facsimile, fax.*
    einen Telefax übersenden   *to send a fax.*
    Ich möchte etwas faxen (colloq.).   *I'd like*
       to fax (something).
TELEFON *n. telephone.*
Telefonanruf *m. telephone call.*
Telefonbuch *n. telephone directory.*
TELEFONIEREN *to telephone.*
telefonisch *telephonic, by telephone.*
Telefonist *m. (–in, f.) telephone operator.*
Telefonnummer *f. telephone number.*
Telefonzelle *f. telephone booth.*
Telefonzentrale *f. telephone exchange.*
Telegrafie *f. telegraphy.*
TELEGRAFIEREN *to telegraph.*
telegrafisch *by telegram.*
TELEGRAMM *n. telegram.*
Telegrammformular *n. telegraph form.*
Teller *m. plate.*
Temperament *n. temperament, character,*
    disposition.
temperamentvoll *high spirited, impetuous.*
Temperatur *f. temperature.*
Temperaturanstieg *m. rise in temperature*
Temperaturschwankungen *pl. variations in*
    temperature.
Temperatursturz *m. fall/drop in*
    temperature.
Tempo *n. time, measure, speed.*
Tendenz *f. tendency, inclination.*
Tennis *n. tennis.*
Tennisplatz *m. tennis court.*
Tennisschläger *m. tennis racket.*
Tenor *m. tenor.*
Teppich *m. carpet.*
Termin *m. deadline.*
Terrasse *f. terrace.*
Territorium *n. territory.*
Testament *n. testament.*
TEUER *expensive, high, costly.*
Teuerung *f. dearness, scarcity, high cost of*
    living.
Teufel *m. devil.*
    den Teufel an die Wand malen.   *speak of*
       the devil.
teuflisch *devilish, diabolical.*
Text *m. text, libretto.*
    aus dem Text kommen   *to lose the thread.*
Textbuch *n. words, libretto.*
Textilien *pl. textiles.*
Textilwaren *pl. textiles.*
THEATER *n. theater, stage.*

Theaterbesuch *m. playgoing.*
Theaterbesucher *m. theatergoer.*
Theaterdirektor *m. manager of a theater.*
Theaterkasse *f. box office.*
theatralisch *theatrical.*
Theke *f. counter, bar.*
Thema *n. theme, subject.*
Theologe *m. theologian.*
Theoretiker *m. theoretician.*
Thermometer *n. thermometer.*
Thermometerstand *m. thermometer reading.*
Thron *m. throne.*
Thronbesteigung *f. accession to the throne.*
TIEF *deep, low, deeply, far.*
  Das lässt tief blicken. *That gives food for thought.*
  in tiefer Nacht *late at night.*
  aus tiefstem Herzen *from the bottom of my heart.*
  tiefe Einsicht *profound insight.*
  im tiefsten Winter *in the dead of winter.*
Tiefe *f. depth, profundity.*
tiefgründig *deep, profound.*
tiefliegend *sunken.*
Tiefsee *f. deep sea.*
tiefsinnig *profound, pensive, melancholy.*
Tiefstand *m. lowness, low level.*
TIER *n. animal, beast.*
Tierarzt *m. veterinarian.*
Tiergarten *m. zoo.*
Tiger *m. tiger.*
Tinte *f. ink.*
  in der Tinte sitzen *to be in a mess.*
Tintenfass *n. inkwell.*
Tintenfleck *m. blot, ink spot.*
TISCH *m. table.*
  bei Tisch *during the meal.*
  Bitte, zu Tisch! *Dinner is ready!*
  Er ist gerade zu Tisch gegangen. *He has just gone out to lunch.*
  reinen Tisch machen *to make a clean sweep.*
  unter den Tisch fallen *to be ignored.*
Tischdecke *f. tablecloth.*
Tischler *m. cabinet-maker.*
Tischplatte *f. table top.*
Tischrede *f. after-dinner talk.*
Tischtennis *n. table tennis, ping-pong.*
Tischtuch *n. tablecloth.*
Tischzeit *f. dinner-time.*
Titel *m. title, claim.*
Titelbild *n. frontispiece.*
Titelblatt *n. title page.*
Titelhalter *m. title-holder.*
Toast *m. toast.*
toasten *to drink toasts.*
toben *to rage, rave.*
Tobsucht *f. raving madness.*
tobsüchtig *raving mad.*

TOCHTER *f. daughter.*
TOD *m. death, decease.*
  des Todes sein *to be doomed.*
  sich den Tod holen *to catch one's death of a cold.*
  Es geht um Leben und Tod. *It's a matter of life and death.*
Todesanzeige *f. death notice.*
Todeskampf *m. death agony.*
Todesstrafe *f. capital punishment, death penalty.*
Todestag *m. death anniversary.*
todkrank *very ill.*
tödlich *fatal, deadly, mortal.*
todmüde *dead tired.*
Toilette *f. toilet, dress, dressing table, lavatory.*
  Toilette machen *to dress, get dressed.*
tolerant *tolerant.*
toll *mad, insane, raving, awful.*
tölpisch *clumsy.*
Ton *m. sound, note, stress, accent.*
tönen *to sound, resound.*
Tonfall *m. musical intonation, cadence.*
Tonfilm *m. sound film.*
tonlos *soundless, voiceless.*
Tonne *f. barrel, ton.*
Tönung *shading.*
Topf *m. pot.*
Tor *n. gate.*
Tor *m. fool.*
Torheit *f. foolishness, folly.*
töricht *foolish, silly.*
Torte *f. layer cake.*
tosen *to rage, roar.*
TOT *dead, dull.*
  tote Zeit *dead season.*
  toter Punkt *deadlock.*
(sich) totarbeiten *to kill oneself with work.*
Tote(r) *m. dead person, deceased.*
TÖTEN *to kill.*
  sich töten *to commit suicide.*
  sich totlachen *to die laughing.*
Totenbett *n. deathbead.*
totenbleich *deadly pale.*
totenstill *still as death.*
Tötung *f. killing, slaying.*
Tour *f. tour, excursion.*
  in einer Tour *without stopping.*
Tournee *f. tour (theater).*
Trab *m. trot.*
  im Trab *quickly.*
Tracht *f. dress, costume.*
trachten *to strive, seek after.*
traditionell *traditional.*
TRAGEN *to carry, bear, wear, take, endure, suffer, produce.*
  die Schuld tragen an *to carry the blame for.*

Sie trägt Trauer. *She is in mourning.*
TRÄGER *m. porter.*
Tragfähigkeit *f. capacity.*
Tragflügel *m. wing of aircraft.*
tragisch *tragic.*
Tragödie *f. tragedy.*
trainieren *to train.*
Träne *f. tear.*
Trank *m. drink.*
tränken *to water, soak.*
transpirieren *to perspire.*
Transport *m. transport.*
Traube *f. grape, bunch of grapes.*
Traubenlese *f. grape harvest.*
Traubenmost *m. grape juice.*
trauen *to marry, give in marriage, join, trust, rely.*
  Ich traue ihm alles zu. *I trust him completely.*
  sich trauen lassen *to get married.*
Trauer *f. sorrow, grief, affliction.*
Traueranzeige *f. announcement of a death.*
Trauermarsch *m. funeral march.*
trauern *to mourn, grieve.*
Trauerspiel *n. tragedy.*
träufeln *to drop.*
traulich *intimate, cosy.*
TRAUM *m. dream, fancy, illusion.*
  Träume sind Schäume. *All dreams are lies.*
träumen *to dream.*
Träumer *m. dreamer.*
träumerisch *dreamy.*
traumhaft *dreamlike.*
TRAURIG *sad, sorrowful, mournful.*
Traurigkeit *f. sadness.*
Trauschein *m. marriage certificate.*
Trauung *f. marriage ceremony.*
Trauzeuge *m. witness to a marriage.*
TREFFEN *to meet, hit, strike, affect, touch, fall upon.*
  Alle nötigen Vorbereitungen sind getroffen worden. *All the necessary arrangements have been made.*
  sich getroffen fühlen *to feel hurt.*
  sich gut treffen *to be lucky.*
  sich treffen *to meet.*
  Vorsichtsmassregeln treffen *to take all the necessary precautions.*
  Wen trifft die Schuld? *Who is to blame?*
treffend *to the point.*
Treffer *m. target, luck, winning ticket, prize.*
trefflich *excellent, admirable.*
Trefflichkeit *f. excellence.*
treiben *to drive, set in motion, float, drift.*
  Wintersport treiben *to practice winter sports.*
Treibhaus *n. conservatory, hothouse.*
trennbar *separable, divisible.*

TRENNEN *to separate, divide, dissolve.*
  getrennt leben *to live separately.*
  sich trennen *to part.*
  sich trennen von *to part from.*
Trennung *f. separation.*
Treppe *f. stairway, stairs.*
Treppenabsatz *m. landing.*
Treppengeländer *n. banisters, railing.*
Tresor *m. treasury.*
TRETEN *to step, tread, walk, go.*
  in jemandes Fusstapfen treten *to follow one's footsteps.*
  aus dem Dienste treten *to retire from active service.*
  in Erscheinung treten *to appear.*
  in Kraft treten *to go into effect.*
  mit Füssen treten *to trample under foot.*
  zu nahe treten *to hurt one's feelings.*
TREU *faithful, true, loyal.*
treubrüchig *faithless, perfidious.*
Treue *f. fidelity, faithfulness, loyalty.*
treuherzig *frank, naive.*
treulich *faithfully.*
treulos *unfaithful.*
Treulosigkeit *f. faithlessness.*
Tribüne *f. tribune.*
Trieb *m. sprout, shoot, driving force, motive power.*
trinkbar *drinkable.*
TRINKEN *to drink, absorb.*
Trinker *m. drunkard.*
Trinkgeld *n. tip.*
Trinkspruch *n. toast.*
Tritt *m. step, footstep.*
Trittbrett *n. running board.*
Triumph *m. triumph, victory.*
triumphieren *to triumph.*
trocken *dry, arid, dull.*
  trockener Empfang *cool reception.*
Trockenmilch *f. dry milk.*
trocknen *to dry up.*
Trommel *f. drum.*
trommeln *to beat the drum.*
Trompete *f. trumpet.*
Trompeter *m. trumpeter.*
Tropen *pl. tropics.*
tropfen *to drop, drip.*
tropfenweise *by drops, drop by drop.*
TROST *m. comfort.*
trostbedürftig *in need of consolation.*
trösten *to comfort, console, cheer up.*
  sich trösten *to cheer up.*
tröstlich *consoling, comforting.*
trostlos *discouraged.*
Trostlosigkeit *f. despair, hopelessness.*
trostreich *comforting, consoling.*
Trottoir *m. pavement, sidewalk.*
TROTZ *prep. (gen.) in spite of.*
  Trotz der Kälte ging ich jeden Tag

spazieren. *In spite of the cold, I took a walk every day.*

Trotz *m. obstinacy, stubbornness, defiance.*

jemandem zum Trotz *in defiance of someone.*

Trotz bieten *to defy.*

trotzdem *nevertheless, anyway, although.*

Trotzdem es sehr kalt ist, werde ich spazieren gehen. *Although it is very cold, I shall take a walk.*

trotzen *to defy, be obstinate.*

trotzig *defiant.*

trüb(e) *dark, sad, gloomy.*

trüben *to dim, trouble, spoil.*

Der Himmel trübt sich. *The sky is clouding over.*

Trübsal *f. affliction, misery; sorrow.*

trübselig *sad, gloomy, dreary, troubled.*

trübsinnig *melancholy, dejected.*

trügen *to deceive.*

trügerisch *deceitful.*

Truhe *f. chest, trunk.*

Trümmer *f. ruins, debris.*

in Trümmer gehen *to be shattered.*

Trumpf *m. trump.*

trumpfen *to trump.*

Trunk *m. drink.*

Trunkenheit *f. drunkenness.*

Truppe *f. troop, company.*

Truthahn *m. turkey.*

Tube *f. tube.*

Tuberkulose *f. tuberculosis.*

TUCH *n. cloth, fabric, shawl.*

tüchtig *good, able, fit, qualified, competent, efficient.*

Tüchtigkeit *f. fitness, ability, efficiency.*

Tücke *f. malice, spite.*

tückisch *malicious, spiteful.*

TUGEND *f. virtue.*

tugendhaft *virtuous.*

Tulpe *f. tulip.*

Tumult *m. tumult, commotion.*

TUN *to do, make, act, perform, execute.*

Das tut nichts. *That does not matter.*

des Guten zu viel tun *to overdo something.*

Er tut nur so. *He is only pretending.*

Es tut mir leid. *I am sorry.*

es zu tun bekommen mit *to have trouble with.*

Haben Sie sich weh getan? *Did you hurt yourself?*

Mir ist daran zu tun. *It is very important for me.*

tun als ob *to pretend.*

Tun Sie als ob Sie zu Hause wären! *Make yourself at home.*

Wir haben viel zu tun. *We are very busy.*

Das lässt sich tun. *That can be done.*

in die Schule tun *to send to school.*

Tue ihm nichts! *Don't do anything to him (Don't hurt him)!*

tunlich *feasible, practicable.*

Tunnel *m. tunnel.*

tupfen *to dot, touch lightly, dab.*

TÜR *f. door, doorway.*

ihn vor die Tür setzen *to show him to the door; to throw him out of the house.*

Er wohnt zwei Türen von hier. *He lives next door (one or two houses).*

Türgriff *m. doorknob.*

Türklinke *f. door latch (handle).*

Turm *m. tower, steeple.*

Turmuhr *f. church clock, tower clock.*

Turnen *n. gymnastics.*

turnen *to do gymnastics.*

Turnhalle *f. gymnasium.*

Turnier *n. tournament.*

Tusche *f. watercolor.*

Tüte *f. paper bag.*

typisch *typical.*

Tyrann *m. tyrant.*

tyrannisieren *to tyrannize.*

Übel *n. evil, ailment, misfortune, inconvenience.*

ÜBEL *evil, wrong, bad, ill.*

Das ist nicht übel. *That is not bad.*

Mir ist übel. *I feel sick.*

übel daran sein *to be in a bad way.*

auf ihn übel zu sprechen sein *not to have a good word to say about him.*

übel zumute *ill at ease, uncomfortable.*

übelgelaunt *cross, grumpy.*

übelgesinnt *evil-minded.*

Übelkeit *f. nausea.*

übelnehmen *to take offense.*

übelnehmerisch *touchy, susceptible.*

Übeltäter *m. evil-doer, criminal.*

üben *to exercise, practise.*

ÜBER 1. *prep (dat. when answering question, Wo?; acc. when answering question Wohin?, and depending on the idiom) higher, while, concerning, via.*

den Winter über *the whole winter long.*

Er schwamm über den See. *He swam across the lake.*

Er zog sich die Decke über den Kopf. *He pulled the blanket over his head.*

Ich wundere mich über ihre Einstellung. *I am surprised at her attitude.*

Sie sprach über ihre Sorgen. *She spoke about her sorrows.*

über Bord *overboard.*

Über der Erde ziehen Wolken. *Clouds are floating above the earth.*
über kurz oder lang   *sooner or later.*
über und über   *over and over.*
Seine Liebe geht ihr über alles. *She places his love above everything.*
überall   *all over.*
von Berlin über Strassburg nach Paris   *from Berlin to Paris via Strassburg.*
über den Essen.   *during the meal.*
über den Sommer   *during the course of the summer.*
2. *adv. wholly, completely, in excess.*
3. *prefix* a) *separable (when meaning above).*
Das Flugzeug fliegt über dem Ozean. *The airplane flies above the ocean.*
b) *inseparable (in all uses where it does not mean above).*
Er übersetzt ein Gedicht von Schiller. *He translates a poem by Schiller.*
überaltert *too old.*
überanstrengen *to overwork, overstrain.*
überarbeiten *to review, go over.*
  sich überarbeiten   *to overwork oneself.*
überbelichten *to overexpose (photo).*
überbieten *to excel, surpass.*
Überblick *m. perspective, summary, survey.*
überblicken *to survey, sum up.*
überdauern *to outlast.*
überdies *besides, moreover.*
Überdruss *m. boredom, satiety, disgust.*
überdrüssig *tired of, sick of, bored with.*
Übereifer *m. excess zeal.*
übereignen *to transfer, assign, convey.*
übereilen *to rush, hurry, precipitate.*
  sich übereilen   *to be in a great hurry.*
  Übereilen Sie sich nicht!   *Don't rush!*
Übereilung *f. hastiness, rush.*
übereinkommen *to agree.*
Übereinkunft *f. agreement, arrangement.*
übereinstimmen *to agree, coincide.*
Übereinstimmung *f. agreement, conformity.*
überessen *to overeat.*
überfahren *to overrun (signal) run over.*
Überfahrt *f. crossing.*
Überfall *m. holdup, attack.*
überfallen *to hold up, attack.*
überfällig *overdue.*
überfliegen *to fly over, skim through.*
überfliessen *to overflow, run over.*
Überfluss *m. abundance, profusion.*
  im Überfluss   *abundantly.*
  zum Überfluss   *unnecessarily.*
überflüssig *superfluous, unnecessary.*
überfordern *to overcharge.*
Überfracht *f. excess freight, overweight.*
überführen *to convey, transport.*

Überführung *f. conveying, transfer.*
überfüllen *to overload, crowd.*
Überfüllung *f. overloading.*
Übergabe *f. delivery, surrender.*
Übergang *m. passage, crossing.*
übergeben *to hand over, deliver.*
übergehen *(separable prefix) to cross, pass over.*
übergehen *(separable prefix) to transfer.*
  Das Geschäft ist in andere Hände übergegangen. *This store has changed hands.*
übergehen *(inseparable) to pass over, to omit.*
  Er übergeht diese Frage im Kapital. *He passes over this question in the chapter (but will get back to it).*
Übergewicht *n. overweight, excess weight.*
  das Übergewicht bekommen   *to lose one's balance.*
übergiessen *to spill.*
Überhandnahme *f. increase.*
überhandnehmen *to increase, spread.*
Überhang *m. curtain, hangings.*
überhängen *to hang over.*
ÜBERHAUPT *in general, altogether.*
  überhaupt nicht   *not at all.*
überheben *to save, spare, exempt.*
überheblich *presumptuous.*
Überheblichkeit *f. presumption, arrogance.*
überholen *to pass (car), surpass, overhaul.*
überholt *outdated.*
überhören *to miss, ignore.*
Überkleid *n. overdress, overall.*
überkochen *to boil over.*
überladen *to overload.*
überlassen *to leave, give up, relinquish.*
überlasten *to overload.*
überlaufen *to run over, boil over, desert.*
Überläufer *m. deserter.*
überleben *to survive, outlive.*
  sich überlebt haben   *to be outdated.*
  Er hat sie überlebt. *He outlived her.*
Überlebende *m. survivor.*
überlegen *to reflect, consider.*
  sich überlegen   *to think over, consider.*
  Ich habe es mir anders überlegt. *I've changed my mind.*
überlegen *adj. superior.*
  überlegen sein   *to feel superior to.*
Überlegenheit *f. superiority.*
Überlegung *f. consideration, thought, deliberation.*
überliefern *to deliver, transmit.*
Überlieferung *f. delivery, tradition, surrender.*
ÜBERMACHT *f. superiority, predominance.*
Übermass *n. excess.*
  im Übermass   *to excess, excessive.*

übermässig *excessive, immoderate.*
Übermensch *m. superman.*
übermenschlich *superhuman.*
übermitteln *to transmit, convey.*
Übermittlung *f. transmission, conveyance.*
ÜBERMORGEN *the day after tomorrow.*
übermüden *to overtire.*
Übermüdung *f. over-fatigue.*
Übermut *m. high spirits, bravado.*
übermütig *to be in high spirits.*
übernachten *to stay overnight, spend the night.*
Übernahme *f. taking over, take-over.*
übernatürlich *supernatural.*
übernehmen *to take over, seize.*
   sich übernehmen   *to overstrain oneself.*
überraschen *to surprise.*
Überraschung *f. surprise.*
überreden *to persuade.*
überreichen *to hand over, present.*
überreif *overripe.*
Überrest *m. remainder.*
überschätzen *to overrate, overestimate.*
überschauen *to overlook, survey.*
überschneiden *to intersect, overlap.*
überschreiten *to cross, exceed, overstep.*
Überschreitung *f. crossing, excess, transgression.*
Überschrift *f. heading, title.*
Überschuh *m. overshoe, galosh.*
Überschuss *m. surplus, excess.*
überschüssig *in excess.*
überschwemmen *to inundate.*
Überschwemmung *f. inundation, flood.*
Übersee *f. overseas.*
übersehen *to survey, overlook.*
übersenden *to send, transmit, forward.*
   einen Telefax übersenden   *to send a fax.*
Übersendung *f. transmission.*
übersetzen *to pass across.*
ÜBERSETZEN *to translate.*
Übersetzer *m. translator.*
Übersetzung *f. translation.*
Übersicht *f. view, review, summary.*
übersichtlich *clear, visible.*
Übersichtlichkeit *f. clearness, lucidity.*
übersinnlich *transcendental.*
überspannen *to stretch over, span.*
überspannt *eccentric.*
überspringen *to jump across.*
überstehen *to endure, come through.*
überströmen *to overflow.*
Überstunden *pl. overtime.*
   Überstunden machen   *to work overtime.*
ÜBERSTÜRZEN *to rush, hurry, act hastily.*
   Überstürzen Sie sich nicht!   *Don't rush yourself!*
übertragbar *transferable.*

übertragen *to transfer, give up, entrust with, transmit, broadcast.*
Übertragung *f. transfer, transcription, transmission.*
übertreffen *to excel, surpass.*
übertreiben *to exaggerate.*
Übertreibung *f. exaggeration.*
übertreten *to go over, change over, violate.*
Übertretung *f. violation, transgression.*
übervölkert *overpopulated.*
überwachen *to watch over, supervise.*
Überwachung *f. observation, surprise.*
überwältigen *to overwhelm.*
Überwältigung *f. overwhelming.*
überweisen *to transfer, remit.*
   telegraphisch überweisen   *to send a cable.*
Überweisung *f. transfer, remittance.*
überwiegen *to outweigh.*
überwiegend *preponderant, predominant.*
überwinden *to overcome.*
Überwindung *f. overcoming, conquest.*
Überzahl *f. numerical superiority, majority.*
überzählig *surplus.*
überzeugen *to convince.*
Überzeugung *f. conviction, belief.*
   der Überzeugung sein   *to be convinced.*
überziehen *to cover, re-cover; to overdraw (bank account).*
   das Bett überziehen   *to change the sheets.*
üblich *usual, customary.*
U-Boot *n. submarine.*
ÜBRIG *left over, remaining, other.*
   das Übrige   *the rest.*
   ein übriges tun   *to do more than necessary.*
   Haben Sie ein paar Minuten für uns übrig?   *Can you spare us a few minutes?*
   im Übrigen   *otherwise.*
   nichts übrig haben für   *to care little for.*
   übrig bleiben   *to be left over.*
   übrig lassen   *to leave (over).*
   zu wünschen übrig lassen   *to leave much to be desired.*
ÜBRIGENS *besides, by the way.*
ÜBUNG *f. exercise, practice, drill.*
UFER *n. shore, bank (river).*
UHR *f. hour, clock, watch.*
   nach der Uhr sehen   *to look at the time.*
   um halb fünf Uhr   *at half past five.*
   Um wieviel Uhr?   *At what time?*
   Wieviel Uhr ist es?   *What time is it?*
Uhrmacher *m. watchmaker.*
Uhrzeiger *m. clock hand.*
UM *1. prep. (acc.), at, about, around, because of, for the sake of, for, up.*
   Der Zug verlässt Düsseldorf um drei Uhr.   *The train leaves Düsseldorf at three o'clock.*

Ihre Zeit ist um. *Your time is up.*
Tag um Tag *every day, day after day.*
Wir ängstigen uns um sie. *We worry about her.*
Wir sitzen um den Tisch. *We sit around the table.*
Um Himmels willen! *For God's sake!*
um jeden Preis *not at any cost.*
um keinen Preis *not at any price.*
um so besser *all the better.*
um zwei Jahre älter *two years older.*
    2. *Adv. around.*
um und um *around.*
um herum *all around.*
    3. *Conj.* (um . . . zu), *in order to.*
Um den Frieden zu erhalten, dankt der Prinz ab. *The prince abdicates in order to preserve peace.*
    4. *Prefix.* 1) *inseparable* (*implies the meaning of around*).
Gärten umgeben das Schloss. *The castle is surrounded by gardens.*
    b) *separable* (*implies the meaning of to upset, to transform*).
Er warf den Stuhl um. *He overturned the chair.*
umändern *to change, alter.*
Umänderung f. *change, alteration.*
umarbeiten *to remodel.*
Umarbeitung f. *remodeling.*
umarmen *to embrace, hug.*
Umarmung f. *embrace, hug.*
Umbau m. *rebuilding, reconstruction.*
umbinden *to tie around, put on.*
umblättern *to turn over.*
umblicken *to look about.*
umdrehen *to turn, turn round.*
Umdrehung f. *turning round.*
umfahren *to drive around, make a detour.*
Umfahrt f. *circular tour.*
umfallen *to topple over.*
Umfang m. *circumference, extent, size.*
umfangreich *comprehensive, extensive.*
umfassen *to clasp, embrace, enclose.*
umfassend *comprehensive, extensive, complete, full.*
umformen *to transform, remodel.*
Umfrage f. *inquiry.*
Umgang m. *association, relations.*
umgänglich *sociable.*
Umgangssprache f. *colloquial speech.*
umgeben *to surround.*
Umgebung f. *surroundings, environs.*
Umgegend f. *neighborhood, vicinity.*
UMGEHEN *to go around, circulate, haunt, evade.*
umgehend antworten *to answer by return.*
umgekehrt *opposite, reverse, contrary.*
umgestalten *to alter, transform, reform.*

umgraben *to dig up.*
UMHER *around, about, here and there.*
umherblicken *to glance around, look around.*
umhin *about.*
Ich kann nicht umhin. *I can't help (refrain from).*
umhüllen *to wrap, cover, veil, envelope.*
Umkehr f. *return, change.*
UMKEHREN *to turn back, turn around, turn upside down, invert, reverse.*
Umkehrung f. *inversion, reversal.*
umkleiden *to change clothes.*
umkommen *to perish, die*
Umkreis m. *circle, circuit, periphery.*
umkreisen *to revolve, circle around.*
Umkreisung f. *encirclement.*
Umlauf m. *rotation, revolution, circulation.*
in Umlauf setzen *to circulate.*
umleiten *to divert* (*traffic*).
Umleitung f. *detour.*
Strassenbau! Umleitung! *Road under repair! Detour!*
umliegend *surrounding, neighboring.*
umpflanzen *to transplant.*
umreissen *to knock down, to pull, to blow down* (*trees*).
Umriss m. *sketch, outline, contour.*
Umsatz m. *sale, turnover.*
umschalten *to switch over.*
Umschalter m. *switch, commutator.*
UMSCHLAG m. *envelope, cover, wrapper, hem, compress, change.*
umschlagen *to fell, knock down, put on, change.*
umschliessen *to enclose.*
umschwärmen *to swarm around.*
Umschwung m. *change, revolution.*
umsehen *to look back, round.*
Sie sehen sich nach einer neuen Wohnung um. *They are looking for a new apartment.*
Umsicht f. *circumspection, prudence, caution.*
umsichtig *cautious, prudent.*
umsonst *gratis, for nothing; in vain.*
UMSTAND m. *circumstances, fact.*
ohne Umstände *without ceremony.*
mildernde Umstände *extenuating circumstances.*
sich Umstände machen *to put oneself out.*
Sie ist in anderen Umständen. *She is expecting a baby.*
Umstände machen *to make a fuss.*
unter allen Umständen *in any case, by all means.*
unter keinen Umständen *on no account.*
unter gewissen Umständen *in certain circumstances.*

in anderen Umständen sein   *to be pregnant, expecting a child.*

umständlich *laborious.*

Umsteigefahrschein *m. transfer-ticket.*

einen Umsteigefahrschein verlangen *to ask for a transfer (ticket).*

umsteigen *to change trains.*

umstritten *disputed, controversial.*

Umsturz *m. downfall, revolution.*

umstürzen *to throw down, overturn.*

Umtausch *m. exchange, conversion of money.*

umtauschen *to change for.*

umtun *to drape around.*

umwechseln *to exchange, change (money).*

Umweg *m. detour.*

Umwelt *f. surroundings, environment.*

umwenden *to turn, turn over.*

umwickeln *to wrap up.*

umziehen *to change clothes.*

Umzug *m. procession, change of residence, move.*

unabhängig *independent.*

Unabhängigkeit *f. independence.*

unabkömmlich *indispensable, essential.*

unablässig *incessant.*

unabsehbar *incalculable.*

unabsichtlich *unintentional.*

unabwendbar *inevitable.*

unachtsam *careless, negligent.*

unangebracht *out of place.*

unangemessen *inadequate, improper.*

unangenehm *unpleasant, disagreeable.*

unannehmbar *unacceptable.*

Unannehmlichkeit *f. inconvenience, trouble.*

Unansehnlichkeit *f. annoyance.*

unanständig *improper, indecent.*

unappetitlich *unappetizing, uninviting.*

Unart *f. bad behavior, rudeness.*

unartig *naughty, uncivil.*

unauffindbar *undiscoverable.*

unaufgefordert *unasked.*

unaufhaltsam *inevitable, impetuous.*

unaufhörlich *incessant, incessantly.*

unaufmerksam *inattentive.*

unaufrichtig *insincere.*

unausbleiblich *unfailing, certain.*

unausführbar *impracticable, not feasible.*

unaussprechlich *inexpressible.*

unausstehlich *intolerable, unbearable.*

unbarmherzig *unmerciful, pitiless, brutally.*

Unbarmherzigkeit *f. harshness, mercilessness.*

unbeabsichtigt *unintentional, inadvertent.*

unbeachtet *unnoticed.*

unbeanstandet *not objected to, unopposed.*

unbeantwortet *unanswered.*

unbedachtsam *inconsiderate, thoughtless.*

unbedenklich *harmless.*

unbedeutend *insignificant, trifling.*

unbedingt *unconditional, absolute.*

Sie müssen unbedingt dabei sein. *You must be there whatever may happen.*

unbeeinflusst *unprejudiced.*

unbefangen *impartial, unprejudiced.*

Unbefangenheit *f. impartiality; facility.*

unbefriedigend *unsatisfactory, unsatisfactorily.*

unbefriedigt *unsatisfied.*

unbefugt *unauthorized, incompetent.*

unbegabt *not gifted, not clever.*

unbegreiflich *inconceivable.*

unbegrenzt *unbounded, unlimited.*

unbegründet *unfounded, groundless.*

Unbehagen *n. discomfort.*

unbehaglich *uncomfortable.*

unbehilflich *helpless.*

unbehindert *unrestrained.*

unbeholfen *clumsy.*

UNBEKANNT *unknown.*

Er ist hier unbekannt. *He is a stranger here.*

unbekümmert *unconcerned.*

unbeliebt *unpopular.*

unbemerkt *unnoticed.*

UNBEQUEM *uncomfortable, inconvenient.*

Unbequemlichkeit *f. discomfort.*

unberechenbar *incalculable.*

unberechtigt *unauthorized, unjustified.*

unberührt *untouched, intact, innocent.*

unbeschädigt *undamaged, uninjured.*

unbescheiden *immodest, insolent.*

unbeschreiblich *indescribable.*

unbeschwert *unburdened.*

unbesehen *without inspection, hesitation.*

unbesiegbar *invincible.*

Unbesonnenheit *f. indiscretion, imprudence.*

unbesorgt *unconcerned.*

Seien Sie unbesorgt! *Don't worry.*

unbeständig *unstable, unsteady.*

unbestechlich *incorruptible.*

unbestimmt *undetermined, undefined, indefinite.*

unbestreitbar *indisputable.*

unbeträchtlich *trivial.*

unbeugsam *inflexible, stubborn.*

unbeweglich *immovable, fixed.*

unbewohnt *uninhabited.*

unbewusst *unconscious.*

unbezahlbar *priceless, invaluable.*

unbezwingbar *invincible.*

unbrauchbar *useless, of no use.*

UND *and*

und so weiter *and so forth.*

Undank *m. ingratitude.*

undankbar *ungrateful.*

Undankbarkeit *f. ingratitude.*

undenkbar *unconceivable.*

undeutlich *indistinct, vague.*
Unding *n. absurdity, monstrosity.*
unduldsam *intolerant.*
undurchdringlich *impenetrable.*
uneben *uneven, rough.*
unecht *not genuine, false, improper,*
    artificial.
unehelich *illegitimate.*
unehrbar *indecent, immodest.*
unehrenhaft *dishonorable, discreditable.*
unehrlich *dishonest.*
uneigennützig *unselfish, disinterested.*
uneinig *disunited.*
Uneinigkeit *f. discord, disagreement.*
unempfindlich *insensible.*
UNENDLICH *infinite, endless, infinitely.*
   unendlich klein *infinitesimal.*
unentbehrlich *indispensable.*
unentgeltlich *free of charge.*
unentschieden *undecided.*
unentschlossen *irresolute.*
unentschuldbar *inexcusable.*
unentwickelt *undeveloped.*
unerbittlich *inexorable.*
unerfahren *inexperienced.*
unerforschlich *impenetrable.*
unerfreulich *unpleasant, unsatisfactory.*
unerfüllbar *unrealizable.*
unerhört *unheard of, insolent.*
unerklärlich *inexplicable.*
unerlaubt *illicit, unlawful.*
unermesslich *boundless, infinite.*
unermüdlich *untiring.*
unerreichbar *inaccessible.*
unerreicht *unequaled.*
unerschrocken *fearless.*
unerschütterlich *imperturbable.*
unersetzlich *irreplaceable.*
unerträglich *unbearable, intolerable.*
unerwartet *unexpected.*
unerwünscht *undesired, unwelcome.*
unerzogen *uneducated, ill-bred.*
UNFÄHIG *incapable, unable.*
Unfähigkeit *f. inefficiency.*
Unfall *m. accident.*
Unfallversicherung *f. insurance against*
    accidents.
unfehlbar *certainly, unfailing.*
unfreiwillig *involuntary.*
unfreundlich *unfriendly, unpleasant.*
unfruchtbar *unproductive, sterile.*
Unfug *m. wrong, mischief, nonsense.*
ungeachtet *not esteemed; notwithstanding.*
ungebildet *uneducated.*
ungebührlich *excessive, undue.*
ungebunden *unbound, unrestrained.*
ungedeckt *uncovered (also for a check).*
ungeduldig *impatient, impatiently.*
ungeeignet *unsuitable, unfit.*

UNGEFÄHR *approximately, about, nearly.*
   von ungefähr *from about.*
ungefährlich *harmless.*
ungehalten *angry.*
Ungeheuer *monster.*
ungeheuer *huge, enormous, vast, monstrous.*
ungehorsam *disobedient.*
ungelegen *inconvenient.*
ungelernt *unskilled.*
ungemein *unusual, extremely.*
ungemütlich *uncomfortable.*
ungeniessbar *inedible, unpalatable.*
ungenügend *insufficient.*
ungepflegt *neglected, untidy.*
UNGERECHT *unjust.*
ungerechtfertigt *unjustified.*
Ungerechtigkeit *f. injustice.*
UNGERN *unwillingly, reluctant.*
ungeschehen *undone, remedied.*
Ungeschick *n. misfortune.*
Ungeschicklichkeit *f. awkwardness.*
ungeschickt *awkward, clumsy.*
ungesetzlich *illegal.*
ungestört *undisturbed.*
ungestüm *impetuous, vehement.*
ungesund *unhealthy.*
ungetreu *faithless.*
ungewiss *uncertain.*
Ungewissheit *f. uncertainty.*
ungewöhnlich *unusual, strange.*
ungewohnt *unaccustomed, unfamiliar.*
ungezogen *ill-bred, naughty.*
Unglaube *m. disbelief.*
ungläubig *incredulous, skeptical.*
unglaublich *incredible.*
ungleich *unequal, unlike.*
UNGLÜCK *n. misfortune, bad luck,*
    accident.
unglücklich *unfortunate, unlucky.*
unglücklickerweise *unfortunately.*
Unglücksvogel *m. unlucky person.*
Ungnade *f. disgrace, displeasure.*
   in Ungnade fallen bei *to displease*
      someone, to fall into disgrace.
ungültig *void, invalid.*
   für ungültig erkären *to annul.*
ungut
   Nichts für ungut. *No harm meant.*
Unheil *n. mischief, harm, disaster, calamity.*
unheilbar *incurable, irreparable.*
unheilvoll *disastrous.*
unheimlich *sinister.*
unhöflich *impolite, rude.*
Uniform *f. uniform.*
UNIVERSITÄT *f. university, college.*
unkenntlich *unrecognizable.*
Unkenntnis *f. ignorance, unawareness.*
unklar *not clear.*
unklug *imprudent, unwise.*

Unkosten *pl. expenses.*
Unkraut *n. weeds.*
unleserlich *illegible.*
unliebenswürdig *unamiable, unkind.*
unlogisch *illogical.*
unmässig *immoderate, inordinate.*
unmenschlich *inhuman.*
Unmenschlichkeit *f. inhumanity, cruelty.*
unmerklich *imperceptible.*
unmittelbar *immediate, direct.*
UNMÖBLIERT *unfurnished.*
unmodern *old-fashioned, antiquated.*
UNMÖGLICH *impossible.*
Unmöglichkeit *f. impossibility.*
unmoralisch *immoral.*
unmündig *under age, minor*
   unmündig sein *to be a minor.*
unnachgiebig *unyielding, inflexible.*
unnachsichtig *strict, severe.*
unnahbar *unapproachable, inaccessible.*
unnatürlich *unnatural, affected.*
UNNÖTIG *unnecessary, needless.*
unordentlich *disorderly, untidy.*
UNORDNUNG *f. disorder.*
   in Unordnung bringen *to mess up.*
unparteiisch *impartial.*
unpassend *inappropriate.*
unpersönlich *impersonal.*
unpraktisch *impractical.*
unpünktlich *unpunctual.*
Unrecht *n. injustice.*
   im Unrecht *in the wrong.*
   Unrecht haben *to be wrong.*
UNRECHT *wrong, unjust, unfair.*
unredlich *dishonest.*
unregelmässig *irregular.*
unreif *unripe.*
unrein *unclean.*
   ins Unreine schreiben *to make a rough copy.*
Unruhe *f. uneasiness.*
Unruhen *pl. riots.*
unruhig *restless, uneasy.*
Unruhstifter *m. agitator (pol.) troublemaker*
UNS *acc. and dat. of the pers. pron. wir; reflexive and reciprocal pron.: us, to us, ourselves, each other.*
unsachlich *subjective, personal.*
unsagbar *unspeakable.*
unsauber *dirty, filthy.*
Unsauberkeit *f. dirt, filth.*
unschädlich *harmless.*
   unschädlich machen *to render harmless, neutralize, disarm.*
unschätzbar *invaluable.*
unscheinbar *insignificant, plain, homely.*
unschlüssig *wavering, irresolute.*
UNSCHULDIG *innocent.*
unselbständig *helpless, dependent.*

UNSER *Poss. adj. our.*
UNSER (er, –e –es) *Poss. pron. ours.*
unsereins *people like us.*
unsererseits *as for us, for our part.*
unseresgleichen *people like us.*
unserethalben *for our sakes, on our behalf.*
unseretwegen *for our sake.*
unseretwillen *for our sake.*
UNSICHER *unsafe, uncertain, unsteady.*
Unsicherheit *f. insecurity, uncertainty.*
Unsinn *m. nonsense.*
Unsitte *f. bad habit, abuse.*
unsterblich *immortal.*
unstet *changeable, unsteady, variable.*
unsympathisch *unpleasant.*
untätig *inactive.*
UNTEN *below, beneath, underneath.*
   von oben bis unten *from top to bottom, from head to foot.*
   nach unten *downwards.*
   von unten auf *right from the bottom.*
UNTER 1. *Prep. (dat. when answering question, Wo?; acc. when answering question, Wohin?, and depending on the idiom): under, underneath, below, beneath, among, during, by.*
   Ich habe meine Schuhe unter das Bett gestellt. *I put my shoes under the bed.*
   Ich sass unter den Zuschauern. *I sat among the spectators.*
   Unter anderem hat sie mir gesagt ... *Among other things, she told me ...*
   unter freiem Himmel *in the open air.*
   unter uns gesagt *between us.*
   unter vier Augen *privately ("under four eyes").*
   unter Vorbehalt aller Rechte *all rights reserved.*
   jemandem etwas unter die Nase reiben *to rub one's nose in something.*
   unter diesen Umständen *under these circumstances.*
   2. *Prefix.* a) *separable (when meaning under).*
   Die Sonne geht im Westen unter. *The sun sets in the West.*
   b) *inseparable when not meaning under.*
   Wir unterhielten uns über die Ferien. *We talked about the holidays.*
unterbauen *to lay a foundation.*
unterbelichten *to underexpose (photo).*
Unterbewusstsein *n. subconsciousness.*
unterbieten *to undersell.*
UNTERBRECHEN *to interrupt, disconnect, cut off.*
   Fräulein, wir sind unterbrochen worden. *Operator, we have been cut off.*

Unterbrechung *f. interruption.*
unterbringen *to put up, accommodate, place.*
unterdessen *meanwhile, in the meantime.*
unterdrücken *to oppress, suppress.*
Unterdrückung *f. repression, oppression.*
untereinander *among ourselves, reciprocally.*
Unterernährung *f. malnutrition.*
Unterführung *f. underpass.*
Untergang *m. setting, going down,*
   destruction, fall; decline.
  der Sonnenuntergang *the sunset.*
UNTERGEHEN *to go down, set, sink.*
Untergrundbahn *f. subway.*
unterhalb *below.*
Unterhalt *m. maintenance, living.*
UNTERHALTEN *to support, maintain, keep*
  up.
  sich gut unterhalten *to have a good*
   time.
  sich unterhalten *to converse, talk.*
unterhandeln *to negotiate, to confer.*
Unterhemd *n. undershirt, vest.*
Unterhosen *pl. shorts, drawers.*
unterirdisch *underground.*
Unterkleidung *f. underwear.*
unterkommen *to find accommodation, find*
  employment.
Unterkunft *f. accommodation.*
Unterlage *f. foundation, support, base*
  (plate), evidence, pad.
Unterlass *m. stopping*
  ohne Unterlass *incessantly.*
unterlassen *to discontinue, neglect, fail to.*
unterlegen *to lay under, put under.*
unterliegen *to be defeated, to be subject to.*
Unterlippe *f. lower lip.*
Untermieter *m. subtenant.*
UNTERNEHMEN *to undertake, attempt.*
unternehmend *enterprising.*
Unternehmer *m. contractor.*
Unternehmung *f. enterprise, undertaking.*
unterordnen *to subordinate, submit.*
Unterordnung *f. subordination.*
unterreden *to converse, confer with.*
Unterredung *f. talk, conference (press).*
UNTERRICHT *m. instruction, teaching,*
  education, lesson.
unterrichten *to teach, instruct.*
Unterrock *m. slip, petticoat.*
unterschätzen *to underestimate, underrate.*
unterscheiden *to distinguish, differentiate,*
  discriminate.
  sich unterscheiden *to differ.*
Unterscheidung *f. distinction, discrimination.*
UNTERSCHIED *m. difference.*
  ohne Unterschied *alike.*
unterschiedlich *different, distinct.*
unterschiedslos *indiscriminately.*
unterschlagen *to embezzle, to suppress.*

Unterschlagung *f. embezzlement,*
  suppression.
unterschreiben *to sign.*
Unterschrift *f. signature.*
Unterseeboot *n. submarine.*
unterstehen *to stand under, be subordinate.*
  sich unterstehen *to dare.*
unterstützen *to support, aid, assist.*
Unterstützung *f. support, aid, relief.*
untersuchen *to examine, investigate.*
Untersuchung *f. examination, investigation.*
Untertasse *f. saucer.*
Untertitel *m. subtitle (movie).*
Unterwäsche *f. underwear.*
unterwegs *on the way.*
Unterweisung *f. instruction.*
Unterwelt *f. underworld.*
unterwerfen *to subjugate.*
unterwürfig *submissive.*
unterzeichnen *to sign, ratify.*
Unterzeichner *m. signatory.*
Unterzeichnung *f. signature, ratification.*
untragbar *not transferable, not negotiable;*
  unbearable.
untrennbar *inseparable.*
UNTREU *untrue, unfaithful.*
untröstlich *disconsolate.*
unübersehbar *immense, vast.*
unübertrefflich *unequaled.*
ununterbrochen *continuously.*
unverantwortlich *irresponsible.*
unverbesserlich *incorrigible.*
unverbindlich *not obligatory, without*
  obligation.
unverdient *undeserved.*
unverdorben *unspoiled, pure.*
unvergänglich *imperishable, immortal.*
unvergleichlich *incomparable.*
unverheiratet *unmarried.*
unverhofft *unexpected.*
unverkennbar *unmistakable.*
unverletzt *unhurt, uninjured.*
unvermeidlich *inevitable.*
Unvermögen *n. inability, incapacity,*
  powerlessness.
unvermutet *unexpected.*
unvernünftig *unreasonable.*
unverrichtet *unperformed, unaccomplished.*
  unverrichteter Sache *unsuccessfully.*
unverschämt *impudent, fresh.*
unversehens *unexpectedly.*
unversehrt *intact, safe, undamaged.*
unverständlich *unintelligible,*
  incomprehensible.
unverwandt *fixed, resolute, steadfast.*
unverwüstlich *indestructible, inexhaustible.*
unverzeihlich *unpardonable.*
unverzollt *duty unpaid.*
unverzüglich *immediate, instant, prompt.*

unvollkommen *imperfect.*

unvollständig *incomplete, defective.*

unvorhergesehen *unforeseen.*

UNVORSICHTIG *careless.*

unvorteilhaft *unprofitable, unbecoming.*

unweiblich *unwomanly.*

unweit *not far off, near.*

Unwesen *n. mischief, abuse.*

  sein Unwesen treiben   *to be up to mischief.*

unwesentlich *unessential, immaterial.*

  Das ist ganz unwesentlich.   *That does not matter.*

Unwetter *n. violent, stormy weather, storm.*

unwiderruflich *irrevocable.*

unwiderstehlich *irresistible.*

Unwille *m. indignation.*

unwillkommen *unwelcome.*

unwillkürlich *instinctively, involuntarily.*

unwirksam *ineffective, inefficient.*

unwirtlich *inhospitable, dreary.*

unwirtschaftlich *uneconomic.*

unwissend *ignorant, unaware.*

UNWOHL *not well, indisposed.*

Unwohlsein *n. indisposition.*

unwürdig *unworthy.*

Unzahl *f. endless number.*

unzählig *countless.*

unzeitgemäss *old-fashioned.*

unzerbrechlich *unbreakable.*

unzivilisiert *uncivilized, barbarian.*

unzufrieden *dissatisfied.*

unzulänglich *inaccessible.*

unzulässig *inadmissible.*

unzureichend *insufficient.*

unzuverlässig *unreliable.*

unzweideutig *unequivocal, explicit.*

unzweifelhaft *undoubted, indubitable.*

üppig *luxuriant, abundant, voluptuous.*

Üppigkeit *f. luxury.*

uralt *very old, ancient, primeval.*

Uraufführung *f. first performance, opening night.*

Ureinwohner *m. original inhabitant.*

Urgrosseltern *pl. great-grandparents.*

Urkunde *f. deed, document, record.*

Urkundenfälscher *m. forger of documents.*

urkundlich *documentary, authentic.*

Urlaub *m. leave, furlough, vacation.*

  der bezahlte Urlaub   *the paid vacation.*

Urquell *m. primary source.*

URSACHE *f. cause, reason.*

  Keine Ursache!   *Don't mention it!*

Ursprung *m. source, origin, beginning.*

ursprünglich *original.*

URTEIL *n. judgment, decision, sentence, opinion.*

  ein Urteil fällen über   *to sentence.*

urteilen *to judge, pass a sentence, give an opinion.*

urteilsfähig *competent to judge.*

urteilslos *without judgment.*

Urteilsspruch *m. sentence, verdict.*

Vagabund *m. vagabond.*

Vanille *f. vanilla.*

Variante *f. variant.*

Variation *f. variation.*

variieren *to vary.*

Vase *f. vase.*

VATER *m. father.*

Vaterhaus *n. home (of one's childhood).*

Vaterland *n. native land, fatherland.*

vaterländisch *national, patriotic.*

väterlicherseits *on the father's side.*

vaterlos *fatherless.*

Vaterstadt *f. native town.*

vegetarisch *vegetarian.*

Veilchen *n. violet.*

Vene *f. vein.*

Ventil *n. valve, air valve, vent.*

verabreden *to agree upon, make an agreement.*

  verabredet sein   *to have a date or appointment.*

Verabredung *f. agreement, engagement; appointment.*

verabscheuen *to detest.*

verabschieden *to dismiss, discharge.*

  sich verabschieden   *to say good-bye.*

verachten *to despise, scorn, disdain.*

verächtlich *contemptuous, disdainful.*

Verachtung *f. contempt, scorn, disdain.*

verallgemeinern *to generalize.*

veraltet *old, obsolete.*

veränderlich *variable, unstable.*

VERÄNDERN *to change, alter, vary.*

Veränderung *f. change, alteration, variation.*

verängstigt *intimidated.*

Veranlagung *f. talent.*

veranlassen *to cause.*

Veranlassung *f. reason, suggestion.*

veranschlagen *to estimate.*

  zu hoch veranschlagen   *to overrate.*

veranstalten *to arrange, organize, set up.*

Veranstaltung *f. arrangement, performance, event.*

verantworten *to answer for, account for.*

verantwortlich *responsible.*

VERANTWORTUNG *f. responsibility.*

  auf seine Verantwortung   *at his own risk.*

  zur Verantwortung ziehen   *to call to account.*

verantwortungslos *irresponsible.*

verarbeiten *to process, work up, manufacture, to treat.*

Verarbeitung *f. workmanship, manufacturing.*

Verband *m. bandage, association.*

verbannen *to banish, exile.*

Verbannung *f. banishment, exile.*

verbergen *to hide.*

VERBESSERN *to improve, correct.*

Verbesserung *f. improvement, correction.*

verbeugen *to bow.*

Verbeugung *f. bow, reverence.*

verbiegen *to bend, twist.*

verbieten *to forbid.*

  Rauchen verboten! *No smoking!*

  Strengstens verboten! *Strictly forbidden!*

verbinden *to tie, bind, bandage, connect, combine, join.*

  Fräulein, Sie haben mich falsch verbunden! *Operator, you gave me the wrong number!*

  sich verbinden *to unite.*

  sich zu Dank verbunden fühlen *to feel indebted to.*

verbindlich *obligatory, courteous.*

Verbindlichkeit *f. obligation.*

VERBINDUNG *f. union, combination.*

  sich in Verbindung setzen mit *to get in touch with.*

Verbindugsstrasse *f. connecting road, feeder road.*

verblüffen *to disconcert, perplex.*

verblüffend *amazing.*

Verblüffung *f. stupefaction, amazement.*

verbluten *to bleed to death.*

verborgen *hidden, concealed, secret.*

Verborgenheit *f. concealment, retirement, seclusion.*

Verbot *n. prohibition, ban.*

verboten *prohibited, forbidden.*

Verbrauch *m. consumption.*

verbrauchen *to consume, use.*

Verbraucher *m. consumer.*

Verbrechen *n. crime.*

Verbrecher *m. criminal.*

verbrecherisch *criminal.*

verbreiten *to spread, diffuse.*

verbrennen *to burn, cremate.*

  sich verbrennen *to burn oneself.*

Verbrennung *f. burning, combustion.*

verbringen *to spend, pass time.*

verbunden *connected.*

verbürgen *to guarantee, vouch for.*

Verdacht *m. suspicion.*

verdächtig *suspicious.*

verdächtigen *to distrust.*

verdammen *to condemn.*

verdammenswert *damnable.*

Verdammnis *f. damnation, perdition.*

Verdammung *f. condemnation.*

verdanken *to owe something.*

Verdauung *f. digestion*

Verdeck *n. covering, awning*

Verderb *m. ruin.*

Verderben *n. ruin, destruction.*

  jemanden ins Verderben stürzen *to ruin a person.*

VERDERBEN *to spoil, ruin.*

  Ich möchte es mir nicht mit ihm verderben. *I don't want to displease him.*

  sich den Magen verderben *to upset one's stomach.*

Verderber *m. corrupter.*

verderblich *perishable, pernicious.*

verdienen *to earn, gain, deserve, merit.*

Verdienst *m. gain, profit, earnings.*

Verdienst *n. merit.*

verdienstvoll *deserving.*

verdient *deserving.*

  sich verdient machen um *to deserve well of.*

Verdikt *n. verdict.*

verdolmetschen *to interpret, translate.*

verdoppeln *to double.*

verdorben *spoiled.*

verdrängen *to displace, push aside.*

verdrehen *to twist, sprain.*

  einem den Kopf verdrehen *to turn one's head, to drive someone crazy.*

verdriessen *to annoy, displease.*

verdummen *to grow stupid.*

verdünnen *to thin, dilute.*

Verdünnung *f. attenuation, rarefaction, dilution.*

verdunsten *to evaporate.*

Verdunstung *f. evaporation.*

verdursten *to die of thirst.*

veredeln *to ennoble, improve, refine, finish.*

verehren *to respect, worship, adore.*

Verehrer *m. worshipper.*

Verehrung *f. respect, veneration.*

vereidigen *to swear in, put on oath.*

Vereidigung *f. swearing in, taking of an oath.*

Verein *m. union, association.*

vereinbar *compatible, consistent.*

Vereinbarung *f. agreement, arrangement.*

vereinfachen *to simplify.*

vereinigen *to join, unite, reconcile.*

  die Vereinigten Staaten von Amerika. *The United States of America.*

vereisen *to turn to ice.*

vereiteln *to frustrate, thwart.*

verelenden *to sink into poverty.*

vererben *to bequeath, transmit, hand down.*

verewigen *to perpetuate, immortalize.*

verfahren *to act, behave.*

Verfall *m. decay, ruin.*

  im Verfall geraten *to go to ruin, decay.*

verfallen *to decline, go to ruin, grow weaker, expire.*
   verfallen lassen *to let go to waste.*
   verfallene Züge *sunken features.*
verfassen *to compose, write.*
Verfasser *m. author, writer.*
Verfassung *f. state, condition.*
verfaulen *to decay.*
verfliegen *to fly away, disappear, vanish.*
verfolgen *to follow, pursue, prosecute.*
   heimlich verfolgen *to shadow.*
   gerichtlich verfolgen *to prosecute.*
Verfolgung *f. pursuit, prosecution.*
verfügbar *available.*
verfügen *to arrange, decree, obtain.*
   verfügen über *to dispose of, have at one's disposal.*
   zur Verfügung stellen *to place at one's disposal.*
verführen *prevail upon, seduce, to lead astray.*
Verführer *m. tempter, seducer.*
verführerisch *tempting, seductive.*
Verführung *f. temptation.*
Vergangenheit *f. past; past tense (grammar).*
vergänglich *transitory, perishable.*
Vergaser *m. carburetor.*
vergeben *to give away, dispose of, confer, forgive.*
vergebens *in vain, vainly.*
Vergebung *f. pardon, forgiveness, bestowal.*
vergelten *to pay back, repay, retaliate.*
Vergeltung *f. recompense, reprisal.*
VERGESSEN *to forget, neglect.*
vergesslich *forgetful.*
Vergesslichkeit *f. forgetfulness.*
vergiften *to poison.*
Vergiftung *f. poisoning.*
Vergleich *m. comparison, agreement, arrangement.*
VERGLEICHEN *to compare, check, settle.*
VERGNÜGEN *n. pleasure, joy, fun.*
vergnügen (sich) *to amuse, enjoy oneself.*
VERGNÜGT *pleased, glad.*
   Ich komme mit Vergnügen. *I'll be delighted to come.*
   Viel Vergnügen! *Have a good time!*
   Vergnügungsreise *f. pleasure trip.*
vergnügungssüchtig *pleasure-seeking.*
vergraben *to bury, hide in the ground.*
vergriffen *out of print.*
vergrössern *to enlarge, magnify.*
Vergrösserung *f. enlargement.*
Vergünstigung *f. privilege, favor.*
Verhältnis *n. relation, ratio, love-affair.*
verhältnismässig *relative, proportional.*
verhasst *hated, hateful, odious.*
verheimlichen *to conceal, keep secret.*

verheiraten *to marry off.*
   sich verheiraten *to get married.*
verherrlichen *to glorify.*
Verherrlichung *f. glorification.*
verhindern *to hinder, prevent.*
Verhinderung *f. hindrance, draw-back.*
Verhör *n. examination, trial.*
verhören *to examine, interrogate.*
verhungern *to die of hunger.*
verirren *to lose one's way, go astray.*
VERKAUF *m. sale.*
VERKAUFEN *to sell.*
   billiger verkaufen *to undersell.*
   zu verkaufen *for sale.*
VERKÄUFER *m. (–in, f.) sales person, vendor.*
verkäuflich *saleable.*
VERKEHR *m. traffic, circulation, communication, trade.*
Verkehrschild *n. traffic sign, road sign.*
Verkehrsmittel *n. means of communication or transport, passenger vehicle.*
Verkehrsordnung *f. traffic regulations*
Verkehrsstauung *f. traffic jam, congestion.*
Verkehrszeichen *n. traffic sign, road sign.*
verkehren *to associate, transform, to reverse, convert, change, run (buses).*
   verkehren mit *to associate with, see a great deal of.*
Verkehrsampel *f. traffic light.*
Verkehrsschutzmann *m. traffic policeman.*
Verkehrsunfall *m. traffic-accident.*
verkehrt *wrong, backwards, upside down, absurd.*
   verkehrt gehen *to go the wrong way.*
verkennen *to fail to recognize, mistake, misunderstand, undervalue.*
verkleiden *to disguise, camouflage.*
Verkleidung *f. disguise, camouflage.*
verkommen *to be ruined, become bad, degenerate.*
Verkommenheit *f. depravity, degeneracy.*
verkörpern *to personify, incarnate, embody.*
Verlag *m. publication (Austria), publishing firm.*
verlangen *to demand, desire, require.*
   auf Verlangen *by request, on demand.*
   verlangen nach *to long for, to desire.*
verlängern *to extend, prolong.*
Verlängerung *f. extension, prolonging.*
Verlass *m. trustworthiness.*
   Auf ihn ist kein Verlass. *He cannot be relied on.*
VERLASSEN *to leave, abandon, desert.*
Verlauf *m. lapse, development*
verlaufen *to elapse, to take its course*
   sich verlaufen *to get lost*
verlegen *embarrassed, self-conscious, confused.*

um etwas verlegen sein   *to be at a loss for.*

um Geld verlegen sein   *to be short of money.*

Verlegenheit *f. embarrassment, difficulty.*

Verleger *m. publisher.*

verleihen *to lend out, confer, bestow, grant.*

verletzbar *vulnerable, susceptible.*

verletzen *to hurt, injure, offend.*

Verletzung *f. injury, offense, violation.*

verleugnen *to deny, injure, offend.*

Verleugnung *f. denial, denunciation.*

verleumden *to calumniate, slander.*

Verleumder *m. slanderer.*

verleumderisch *slanderous.*

Verleumdung *f. slander, defamation, libel.*

(sich) VERLIEBEN *to fall in love.*

verliebt *in love.*

Sie ist verliebt bis über die Ohren.   *She is head over heels in love.*

VERLIEREN *to lose, waste, disappear.*

An ihm ist nicht viel verloren.   *He's no great loss.*

Ich habe keinen einzigen Augenblick zu verlieren.   *I don't have a single moment to lose.*

(sich) verloben *to get engaged.*

Verlobte *m. & f. fiancé(e).*

Verlobung *f. engagement.*

Verlust *m. loss, waste, escape.*

vermehren *to increase.*

Vermehrung *f. increase.*

vermieten *to rent, let, hire out.*

Vermieter *m. landlord.*

vermissen *to miss.*

vermuten *to suppose, presume, suspect.*

vermutlich *presumable, probable.*

vernachlässigen *to neglect.*

Vernachlässigung *f. neglect.*

verneigen *to bow.*

Verneigung *f. bow.*

vernichten *to annihilate, destroy.*

Vernichtung *f. annihilation, destruction.*

VERNUNFT *f. reason, understanding, intelligence, good sense, judgment.*

Vernunft annehmen   *to listen to reason.*

zur Vernunft bringen   *to bring to one's senses.*

vernünftig *reasonable, sensible.*

veröffentlichen *to publish.*

Veröffentlichung *f. publication.*

verordnen *to order, decree.*

Verordnung *f. order, decree, prescription.*

verpacken *to pack up, wrap up.*

Verpackung *f. packing up, wrapping up.*

verpfänden *to pawn, mortgage.*

verpflegen *to board, to provide for.*

Verpflegung *f. feeding, board, food.*

Zimmer mit Verpflegung.   *Room and board.*

verpflichten *to oblige, bind, engage.*

sich verpflichten   *to commit (bind) oneself.*

verpflichtet sein   *to be under obligation.*

Verpflichtung *f. obligation, duty, engagement.*

Verrat *m. treason, betrayal.*

verraten *to betray, disclose, reveal.*

Verräter *m. traitor.*

verräterisch *treacherous.*

verrechnen *to reckon up, charge, account; miscalculate.*

Verrechnung *f. settling of an account, reckoning.*

verreisen *to go away.*

vereist sein   *to be away.*

verrichten *to execute, perform, accomplish.*

die Hausarbeit verrichten   *to do the housework.*

Verrichtung *f. execution, performance, function, work.*

VERRÜCKT *crazy, mad.*

Vers *m. verse, stanza.*

versagen *to deny, refuse; fail, miss.*

VERSAMMELN *to assemble, bring together, gather.*

sich versammeln   *to gather.*

Versammlung *f. gathering, assembly, meeting.*

versäumen *to neglect, omit, miss.*

verschaffen *to get, obtain, secure, procure*

verschenken *to give away.*

verschicken *to send away, dispatch, evacuate.*

Verschickung *f. dispatch, transportation, evacuation.*

VERSCHIEDEN *different from, distinct, various.*

verschlafen *to oversleep, sleepy.*

verschlimmern *to aggravate, to make worse.*

Verschlimmerung *f. deterioration.*

verschlucken *to swallow the wrong way.*

Verschluss *m. lock, fastener, clasp, seal, plug, zipper.*

verschmachten *to languish.*

verschonen *to spare, exempt from.*

verschönern *to beautify, embellish, adorn.*

Verschönerung *f. embellishment.*

verschreiben *to prescribe, order in writing, write for.*

sich verschreiben   *to make a mistake in writing.*

verschwenden *to waste, lavish.*

Verschwender *m. spendthrift, extravagant person.*

verschwenderisch *wasteful, extravagant.*

verschwiegen *discreet, close.*

Verschwiegenheit f. *secrecy, discretion.*

verschwistert *like brothers and sisters, closely united.*

Versehen n. *mistake, oversight.*

VERSEHEN *to provide, furnish, supply with; to overlook.*

   aus Versehen *by mistake.*

   ehe man sich's versieht *unexpectedly, suddenly.*

   den Dienst eines andern versehen *to stand in for someone*

   sich versehen *to make a mistake.*

VERSETZEN *to displace, transfer, pledge, pawn.*

   den Verstand verlieren *to go out of one's mind. Just put yourself in my place.*

Versetzung f. *transfer, moving up.*

VERSICHERN *to insure, affirm.*

Versicherung f. *insurance.*

versinnbildlichen *to symbolize, represent.*

versöhnen *to reconcile, conciliate.*

Versöhnung f. *reconciliation.*

versorgen *to provide, supply.*

Versorger m. *support, breadwinner.*

Versorgung f. *maintenance, providing (for)*

verspätet *late.*

Verspätung f. *delay, lateness.*

   Verspätung haben *to be late.*

verspielen *to lose, gamble away.*

VERSPRECHEN *to promise.*

   Ich habe mich nur versprochen. *It was only a slip of the tongue.*

   sich etwas versprechen von *to expect much of.*

Versprechung f. *promise.*

VERSTAND m. *mind, sense, brain, intellect.*

   den Verstand verlieren *to go out of one's mind.*

   zu Verstand kommen *to arrive at the age of discretion.*

verständig *intelligent, sensible, wise.*

verständigen *to inform, notify.*

   sich verständigen *to come to an understanding with.*

Verständigung f. *understanding.*

verständlich *understandable, clear, comprehensible.*

   sich verständlich machen *to make oneself understood.*

Verständlichkeit f. *intelligibility, clearness.*

Verständnis *comprehension, understanding.*

   Verständnis haben für *to appreciate.*

verständnislos *unappreciative, stupid.*

verständnisvoll *understanding, appreciative.*

Versteck n. *hiding place.*

verstecken *to hide, conceal.*

versteckt *hidden, concealed.*

   versteckte Absichten *ulterior motives.*

VERSTEHEN *to understand, comprehend, know.*

   falsch verstehen *to misunderstand.*

   Ich verstehe nicht! *I don't understand!*

   sich verstehen *to understand each other.*

   sich von selbst verstehen *to go without saying.*

   Was verstehen Sie darunter? *What do you understand by that?*

   zu verstehen geben *to give to understand.*

versteifen *to stiffen.*

versteigern *to sell at auction.*

Versteigerung f. *auction.*

verstellbar *adjustable.*

verstellen *to change order or position, shift, block, disguise.*

Verstellung f. *dissimulation, disguise, hypocrisy.*

versteuern *to pay duty on.*

verstimmen *to annoy, upset.*

Verstimmung f. *ill humor, bad temper.*

Versuch m. *experiment, trial, attempt.*

VERSUCHEN *to try, attempt, taste, endeavor.*

   es versuchen mit *to give a trial to, put to the test.*

Versuchung f. *temptation.*

vertagen *to adjourn.*

vertauschen *to exchange, substitute.*

verteidigen *to defend.*

Verteidiger m. *defender, advocate, attorney.*

Verteidigung f. *defense.*

verteilen *to distribute, dispense, assign.*

Verteiler m. *distributor, retailer.*

Verteilung f. *distribution.*

Vertrag m. *contract, treaty, agreement.*

VERTRAGEN *to carry away, bear, stand, endure, tolerate, digest.*

   ich kann diese Speise nicht vertragen. *This food does not agree with me.*

   sich vertragen *to get along.*

   sich wieder vertragen *to settle one's differences, to be reconciled.*

   einen Spass vertragen *to take a joke.*

Vertrauen n. *confidence.*

vertrauen *to trust.*

vertrauensvoll *trusting.*

vertrauenwürdig *trustworthy.*

vertraulich *confidential.*

Vertraulichkeit f. *confidence.*

vertraut *familiar.*

   im Vertrauen *in confidence, confidentially.*

   im Vertrauen auf *relying on, trusting to.*

   sich vertraut machen *to become familiar.*

Vertraute(r) m. f. *intimate friend.*

vertreiben *to drive away, expel, scatter.*

vertreten *to represent, substitute for; to sprain.*

Vertreter *m. representative, substitute.*

VERTRETUNG *f. representation, replacement.*

  eine Vertretung übernehmen *to take the place of, represent.*

vertrösten *to console, put off.*

verunglücken *to have an accident.*

verursachen *to cause.*

verurteilen *to sentence, condemn.*

Verurteilung *f. sentence, condemnation.*

vervielfältigen *to multiply, duplicate, reproduce.*

verwachsen *overgrown, deformed.*

verwahren *to keep, put away.*

verwaisen *to become an orphan.*

verwaist *orphaned, deserted.*

verwandeln *to transform.*

verwandt *related, similar, allied.*

Verwandte *m. f. relation, relative.*

Verwandtschaft *f. relationship, relations.*

verwechseln *to take for, mistake for.*

Verwechslung *f. mistake, confusion.*

verweigern *to deny, refuse.*

Verweigerung *f. denial, refusal.*

Verweis *m. reproof, reprimand, reference.*

Verweisung *f. exile, banishment.*

verwendbar *applicable.*

VERWENDEN *to use, utilize, employ, expend.*

  sich verwenden für *to put in a good word for.*

  verwenden auf *to put in on, spend on.*

  Zeit verwenden auf *to devote time to.*

Verwendung *f. use, utilization, application.*

verwirklichen *to realize, materialize.*

Verwirklichung *f. realization, materialization.*

Verwöhnung *f. spoiling, pampering.*

verwundern *to surprise.*

Verwunderung *f. surprise, astonishment.*

verzagen *to lose heart, despair.*

VERZEIHEN *to pardon, forgive, excuse.*

  Verzeihen Sie! *Excuse me!*

verzeihlich *excusable.*

VERZEIHUNG *f. pardon, excuse.*

  Ich bitte Sie um Verzeihung! *Please excuse me!*

Verzicht *m. resignation, renunciation.*

verzichten *to renounce, resign, forgo.*

verzinsen *to pay interest on.*

verzögern *to delay.*

verzollen *to pay duty on.*

  Haben Sie etwas zu verzollen? *Have you anything to declare?*

Verzollung *f. payment of duty, clearance.*

verzweifeln *to despair*

verzweifelt *desperate, despairing.*

Verzweiflung *f. despair, desperation.*

  zur Verzweiflung bringen *to drive one mad.*

Veto *n. veto.*

  Veto einlegen *to veto a thing.*

VETTER *m. cousin.*

Vieh *n. cattle.*

Viehhändler *m. cattle dealer.*

VIEL *much, a great deal, a lot of.*

  ein bisschen viel *a little too much.*

  sehr viel *a great many.*

  in vielem *in many respects.*

  noch einmal so viel *as much again.*

  viele *many.*

  zu viel *far too much.*

  Viel Glück! *Lots of luck!*

  Viel Vergnügen! *Have a good time!*

vielgerühmt *much-praised.*

VIELLEICHT *perhaps.*

vielmalig *frequent, repeated.*

vielseitig *versatile; many-sided.*

vielumstritten *widely discussed/disputed.*

VIER *four.*

  zu vieren, zu viert *four of us.*

Viereck *n. square.*

viereckig *square, quadrangular.*

VIERTE *fourth.*

VIERTEL *n. quarter, fourth.*

  Es ist Viertel vor zwei. *It is a quarter to two.*

vierteljährlich *quarterly.*

Viertelstunde *f. a quarter of an hour.*

viertelstündlich *every quarter of an hour.*

VIERZEHN *fourteen.*

  vierzehn Tage *two weeks.*

VIERZEHNTE *fourteenth.*

VIERZIG *forty.*

VIERZIGSTE *fortieth.*

Violine *f. violin.*

virtuos *masterly.*

Virtuose(-sin) *m. (f.) virtuoso.*

Virtuosität *f. virtuosity.*

Vision *f. vision.*

Visite *f. visit.*

Visitenkarte *f. visiting-card.*

Vitrine *f. showcase.*

VOGEL *m. bird.*

  den Vogel abschiessen *to carry off the prize, to steal the show.*

Vogelscheuche *f. scarecrow.*

Vokabel *f. word.*

Vokabelschatz *m. vocabulary (range).*

VOLK *n. people, nation, crowd.*

  das arbeitende Volk *the working classes.*

  der Mann aus dem Volk *the man in the street.*

Volksabstimmung *f. plebiscite.*

Volkslied *n. folk song.*

Volksschule *f. elementary or primary school.*

volkstümlich *national, popular.*

Volksversammlung *f. public meeting.*

VOLL 1. *adj. & adv. full, filled, complete, whole, entire; fully, completely.*

  aus vollem Herzen *from the bottom of the heart.*

  aus voller Kehle *at the top of one's voice.*

  den Mund voll nehmen *to boast.*

  Die Rechnung ist voll bezahlt. *The bill is paid in full.*

  in voller Fahrt *at full speed.*

    One cannot take him too seriously.

  2. *Prefix.* a) *separable* (*meaning to fill*)

  Sie giesst die Gläser voll. *She fills up the glasses.*

  b) *inseparable* (*meaning to accomplish, finish*).

  Er vollführte eine gute Leistung. *He executed a good performance.*

Vollbart *m. beard.*

vollblütig *full-blooded.*

vollbringen *to finish, accomplish, complete.*

Volldampf *m. full steam.*

vollenden *to complete, to bring to a close.*

Vollendung *f. completion, perfecting.*

volles Vertrauen *complete confidence.*

völlig *complete, entire, quite.*

volljährig *of age.*

Volljährigkeit *f. majority* (*of age*).

VOLLKOMMEN *perfect, complete.*

Vollkommenheit *f. perfection.*

Vollkraft *f. full vigor.*

Vollmacht *f. full power, power of attorney.*

Vollmilch *f. unskimmed milk.*

Vollmond *m. full moon.*

vollständig *complete.*

vollzählig *complete, full, completely, absolutely.*

VON 1. *pret.* (*dat.*). *from, by, with, of, on, upon, about.*

  Amerika wurde von Kolumbus entdeckt. *America was discovered by Columbus.*

  Der Platz war voll von Menschen. *The place was full of people.*

  ein Gedicht von Heine *a poem by Heine.*

  eine Feder von Gold *a gold pen.*

  von heute ab *from today on.*

  Von meinem Fenster sehe ich auf den Garten. *From my window I see the garden.*

  2. *adv.: apart, separate.*

  von einander *apart.*

  von klein auf *from childhood* (*on*).

  von mir aus *as far as I am concerned.*

  von selbst *by itself, automatically.*

  von Nutzen sein *to be needful, necessary.*

VOR 1. *prep.* (*dat. when answering question, Wo?; acc. when answering question, Wohin?, and depending on the idiom*), *before, in front of, ahead of, for, with, against, from.*

  Das Bild ist vor mir. *The picture is in front of me.*

  Es ist ein Viertel vor elf. *It is a quarter to eleven.*

  Ich werde sie vor ihm warnen. *I will warn her against him.*

  nach wie vor *as usual.*

  nicht vor *not until.*

  vor acht Tagen *a week ago.*

  vor allem *above all, first of all.*

  vor der Klasse *before class.*

  vor Hunger sterben *to die of hunger.*

  Vor ihm müssen Sie sich in Acht nehmen. *With him, you must be on your guard.*

  vorzeiten *formerly*

  vorab *above all.*

  2. *separable prefix* (*implies movement forward, presentation, demonstration*).

  Der Lehrer las ein Gedicht vor. *The teacher read a poem aloud.*

  Die Soldaten rückten vor. *The soldiers moved forward.*

  Wir bereiten uns auf die Prüfung vor. *We prepare ourselves for the examination.*

Vorabend *m. evening before.*

vorahnen *to have a presentiment.*

Vorahnung *f. presentiment.*

voran *ahead, before.*

vorangehen *to precede.*

  mit gutem Beispiel vorangehen *to set a good example.*

Voranschlag *m. estimate.*

Voranzeige *f. preliminary advertisement.*

Vorarbeit *f. preliminary work.*

Vorarbeiter *m. foreman.*

VORAUS *in front of, ahead of.*

  etwas voraus haben vor *to have an advantage over a person.*

  im Voraus *in advance.*

  weit voraus *way ahead.*

  vorausgehen *to lead the way, precede.*

Voraussage *f. prediction, prophecy.*

voraussetzen *to presuppose, assume.*

Voraussetzung *f. supposition, assumption.*

voraussichtlich *presumable, probable.*

Vorbehalt *m. reservation, proviso.*

  ohne Vorbehalt *unconditionally.*

  unter Vorbehalt aller Rechte *all rights reserved.*

vorbehalten *to keep in reserve, withhold.*

  sich vorbehalten *to reserve to oneself.*

vorbehaltlos *unconditional.*

vorbei *by, along, past, over, gone.*

vorbereiten *to prepare, make ready.*

Vorbereitung *f. preparation.*

Vorbeugungsmassregel *m. preventive measure.*

Vorbild *n. model, standard.*

vorbildlich *model, ideal.*

Vorbildung *f. preparatory training, education.*

vorder *fore, forward, anterior.*

Vordergrund *m. foreground.*

Vorderhaus *n. front part of the house.*

vordringlich *urgent.*

voreilig *hasty, rash.*

Voreiligkeit *f. precipitation, rashness.*

voreingenommen *prejudiced.*

Voreingenommenheit *f. prejudice.*

vorenthalten *to keep back, withhold.*

Vorfall *m. occurrence, event.*

vorfallen *to occur, happen, take place.*

Vorfreude *f. joy of anticipation.*

vorführen *to demonstrate, produce.*

Vorführung *f. demonstration.*

Vorgang *m. occurrence.*

Vorgänger *m. predecessor.*

VORGEHEN *to go on, go forward, go first, lead, take place, occur, act, be of special importance.*

Gehen Sie vor! *Go right ahead!*

Vorgeschichte *f. prehistory.*

Vorgeschmack *m. foretaste.*

Vorgesetzte *m. & f. chief, boss*

VORGESTERN *the day before yesterday.*

vorhaben *to have on, wear, to intend, plan.*

Haben Sie morgen etwas vor? *Do you have any plans for tomorrow?*

vorhalten *to hold up, to hold out.*

Vorhang *m. curtain.*

vorher *before, beforehand, in advance, previously.*

vorherrschen *to predominate, prevail.*

vorherrschend *predominant, prevailing.*

Vorkenntnis *f. previous knowledge.*

vorkommen *to come forward, occur, happen.*

Es kommt Ihnen nur so vor. *You are just imagining that.*

Vorkommnis *n. occurrence, event.*

Vorlage *f. presentation of documents.*

vorlassen *to give precedence to.*

vorläufig *preliminary.*

Vorleger *m. mat, rug.*

vorlesen *to read aloud.*

Vorlesung *f. lecture.*

vorletzt *one before the last.*

Vorliebe *f. predilection, preference.*

vormachen *to put, place before, impose on someone, fool.*

vormerken *to make a note of, put down.*

Vormittag *m. morning ("before noon").*

Vormund *m. guardian.*

Vormundschaft *f. guardianship.*

VORN *in front, in front of.*

nach vorn *forward.*

nach vorne heraus wohnen *to live in the front part of a house.*

von vorn *from the front.*

von vorn anfangen *to start afresh.*

vor vorn herein *from the first.*

Vorname *m. Christian name, first name.*

vornehm *of high rank, noble, distinguished.*

Vornehmheit *f. distinction, high rank.*

vornehmlich *principally, chiefly, especially.*

Vorort *m. suburb.*

Vorplatz *m. court, hall, vestibule.*

Vorrang *m. precedence, priority.*

Vorrat *m. store, stock, provision.*

vorrätig *in stock, on hand.*

nicht mehr vorrätig *out of stock.*

Vorratskammer *f. storeroom, pantry.*

Vorrede *f. words of introduction; opening speech.*

vorsagen *to dictate, say, prompt.*

Vorsatz *m. purpose.*

Vorschlag *m. proposal, proposition.*

vorschlagen *to propose, offer.*

vorschreiben *to set a copy.*

Vorschrift *f. copy, direction.*

vorschriftmässig *according to instructions.*

vorsehen *to provide for, consider, take care.*

Vorsehung *f. providence.*

VORSICHT *f. foresight, caution, prudence.*

Vorsicht! *Take care! Beware!*

Vorsicht Stufe! *Mind the step!*

vorsichtig *cautious, prudent.*

vorsichtshalber *as a precaution.*

Vorsichtsmassregel *f. precautionary measure.*

Vorsitz *m. presidency, chairman.*

den Vorsitz führen *to preside in the chair.*

Vorspeise *f. hors d'oeuvre.*

vorsprechen *to pronounce, recite.*

Vorsprung *m. projection, projecting part.*

Vorstadt *f. suburb.*

Vorstand *m. board of directors.*

vorstellen *to place before, put in front of, demonstrate, introduce, represent, act.*

sich etwas vorstellen *to imagine something.*

sich vorstellen *to introduce oneself.*

VORSTELLUNG *f. introduction, presentation, performance, picture.*

Wann fängt die Vorstellung an? *When does the performance start?*

Vorstellungsvermögen *n. imagination.*

Vorteil *m. advantage, profit.*

VORTEILHAFT *advantageous, favorable.*

vorteilhaft aussehen *to look one's best.*

Vortrag *m. reciting, delivery, execution, lecture.*

vortragen *to carry forward, recite, declaim, execute, perform.*

vortrefflich *excellent, admirable, splendid.*

Vortrefflichkeit *f. excellence.*

vorüber *past, over, by, along.*

vorübergehen *to go by, pass.*

Vorurteil *n. prejudice.*

vorurteilslos *unprejudiced.*

Vorverkauf *m. booking in advance* (theater); *advance sale.*

vorvorgestern *three days ago.*

Vorwahl *f. primary election.*

Vorwand *m. pretext, pretense, excuse.*

VORWÄRTS *forward, onward, on.*

     Vorwärts! *Go on! Go ahead!*

vorwärtsgehen *to go on, advance, progress.*

vorwärtskommen *to get on, advance, prosper.*

vorwärtskommend *predominant.*

Vorwurf *m. reproach.*

     Vorwürfe machen *to blame.*

vorwurfsvoll *reproachful.*

vorzeigen *to show, produce, exhibit, display.*

vorzeitig *premature, precocious.*

vorziehen *to draw forward, prefer.*

Vorzimmer *n. antechamber.*

Vorzug *m. preference, superiority.*

vorzüglich *excellent, superior, first-choice.*

Vorzüglichkeit *f. excellency, superiority.*

Vorzugspreis *m. special price.*

Vorzugsrecht *n. privilege.*

W

WAAGE *f. balance, scales.*

     einem die Waage halten *to be a match for.*

     sich die Waage halten *to counterbalance each other.*

     wagerecht *horizontal level.*

WACH *awake, alive, brisk.*

Wachdienst *m. guard duty.*

Wache *f. guard, watch, sentry.*

WACHEN *to be awake, remain awake.*

     wachen über *to watch over.*

Wachs *n. wax.*

wachsam *vigilant, watchful.*

Wachsamkeit *f. vigilance.*

WACHSEN *to grow, increase, extend.*

     ans Herz wachsen *to grow fond of.*

     einem gewachsen sein *to be a match for one.*

     einer Sache gewachsen sein *to be equal to a task.*

Wachstum *n. growth, increase.*

Wacht *f. guard, watch.*

Wächter *m. watchman, guard.*

wack(e)lig *shaky, unsteady.*

Waffe *f. weapon, arm.*

Waffel *f. wafer, waffle.*

Waffeleisen *n. waffle-iron.*

Waffenschein *m. gun-license.*

Waffenstillstand *m. armistice.*

WAGEN *m. car, automobile, railroad car, cab, wagon.*

Wagen *to venture, risk, dare.*

     gewagt *daring, risky, perilous.*

Wagnis *n. risk.*

WAHL *f. choice, selection, election.*

     seine Wahl treffen *to make one's choice.*

     vor die Wahl stellen *to let one choose.*

wahlberechtigt *entitled to vote.*

WÄHLEN *to choose, select, pick out, elect, dial.*

     Wählen abhalten *to hold elections.*

Wähler *m. elector, selector.*

wählerisch *particular, fastidious.*

Wahlkampf *m. election, contest.*

wahllos *indiscriminately.*

Wahlstimme *f. vote.*

Wahn *m. delusion, illusion.*

Wahnsinn *m. insanity, madness, craziness.*

wahnsinnig *insane, mad.*

WAHR *true, sincere, genuine, real, proper, veritable.*

     etwas nicht wahr haben wollen *not to admit a thing.*

     Nicht wahr? *Isn't it? Don't you think so?*

     so wahr ich lebe *as sure as I live.*

     wahr werden *to come true.*

WÄHREND 1. *prep.* (gen.): *during, for, in the course of.*

     Während des Winters verbringen wir unsere Ferien in den Bergen. *During the winter we spend our vacations in the mountains.*

     2. *conj. while.*

     Sie kam, während Sie weg waren. *She came while you were out.*

WAHRHEIT *f. truth.*

     Ich habe ihm gehörig die Wahrheit gesagt. *I really gave him a piece of my mind.*

wahrheitsgetreu *truthful, true.*

wahrnehmbar *perceptible, noticeable.*

wahrsagen *to foretell, to predict.*

Wahrsagerin *f. fortune teller.*

WAHRSCHEINLICH *probable, likely.*

Wahrscheinlichkeit *f. probability.*

Währung *f. standard, currency.*

Waise *f. & m. orphan.*

Waisenhaus *m. orphanage.*

Wal *m. whale.*

WALD *m. forest, woodland.*

waldig *wooded.*

Waldung *f. woodland, wood.*

Wall *m. rampart, dike.*

Walnuss f. walnut.

walzen to waltz.

Walzer m. waltz.

WAND f. wall, partition.

Wandel m. change, alteration.

    Handel und Wandel trade, commerce.

wandelbar perishable, changeable, fickle.

wandern to wander, to hike.

Wanderschaft f. trip, tour, travels.

Wanderung f. traveling, migration.

Wandgemälde n. mural painting, fresco.

Wandschrank m. cupboard.

Wandteppich m. tapestry, wall hanging.

Wankelmut m. inconsistency, fickleness.

WANN when

    wann immer whenever.

    dann und wann now and then.

Wanne f. tub, bath.

WARE f. article, goods, merchandise.

Warenhaus n. department store.

WARM warm.

    Ist es Ihnen warm genug? Are you warm enough?

    warm stellen to keep hot.

Wärme f. heat, warmth.

WÄRMEN to warm, heat.

Wärmflasche f. hot-water bottle

warnen to warn, caution.

Warnung f. warning.

Warnungssignal n. danger signal.

WARTEN to wait, attend to, nurse.

    warten auf to wait for.

    warten lassen to keep waiting.

Wärter m. attendant, caretaker.

Wartesaal m. waiting-room.

Wartezimmer n. doctor's waiting room.

WARUM why, for what reason.

WAS what, whatever, that which, which, that.

    Ach was! Nonsense!

    Nein so was! Well, I never!

    was . . . auch immer no matter what, whatever.

    was für ein what sort of, what a.

    was mich betrifft as for me.

    Ich will dir was sagen. I'll tell you something.

Waschbecken n. wash basin.

WÄSCHE f. wash; linen, underclothing.

    in die Wäsche geben to send to the laundry.

    schmutzige Wäsche soiled linen, dirty clothes.

Wäschegeschäft n. haberdashery, lingerie store.

Wäscheklammer f. clothespin.

Wäscheleine f. clothesline.

waschen to wash.

Wäscherei f. laundry.

Waschmaschine f. washing machine.

WASSER n. water.

    fliessendes Wasser running water.

    mit allen Wassern gewaschen sein to be cunning.

    sich über Wasser halten to keep one's head above water.

    zu Wasser und zu Lande by land and sea.

Wasserabbluss m. drain.

Wasserball m. water polo.

Wasserbehälter m. reservoir, tank.

wasserdicht waterproof.

Wasserfall m. waterfall.

Wasserfarbe f. water-color.

Wasserflugzeug n. sea plane.

Wasserglas n. glass, tumbler.

wasserhältig containing water.

wässerig watery.

    einem den Mund wässerig machen to make a person's mouth water.

Wasserkanne f. watering-can.

Wasserleitung f. water supply, water pipes, faucet.

Wasserspiegel m. water-surface.

Wasserstiefel pl. rubber boots.

Wasserstoffbombe f. hydrogen bomb (H-bomb).

Wasserstrasse f. waterway.

Watte f. wadding, cotton-wool.

weben to weave.

Weber m. weaver.

Wechsel m. change, alteration, succession, turn.

    gezogener Wechsel draft.

Wechselgeld n. change (money).

    Bitte, zahlen Sie ihr Wechselgeld nach. Please count your change.

Wechselkurs m. rate of exchange.

WECHSELN to change, exchange, alternate, shift.

    seinen Wohnort wechseln to move; to change one's residence.

    den Besitzer wechseln to change ownership.

wechselseitig reciprocal, mutual, alternate.

WECKEN to wake, awaken.

Wecker m. alarm-clock.

weder neither.

    weder . . . noch neither . . . nor.

WEG m. way, path, road, street, walk.

    am Weg by the roadside.

    auf halbem Weg halfway.

    aus dem Weg gehen to make way for, stand aside.

    in die Wege leiten to prepare for.

    seiner Wege gehen to go one's way.

    sich auf den Weg machen to set out.

    in den Weg kommen to get into the way.

    in Wege stehen to stand in the way.

auf dem Wege *on the way.*

WEG 1. *adv. away, off, gone, lost, disappeared.*

Hände weg! *Hands off!*

Ich muss weg. *I must go.*

2. *separable prefix (implies a motion away from the speaker).*

Er warf das alte Buch weg. *He threw the old book away.*

Geh weg! *Go away!*

wegbleiben *to stay away, be omitted.*

wegbringen *to take away, remove.*

WEGEN *prep. (gen.): because of, for the sake of, owing to.*

Wegen des Krieges konnte ich nicht von Europa zurückkommen. *Because of the war, I could not come back from Europe.*

wegfahren *to drive off, away.*

weggehen *to go away, depart, leave.*

weglegen *to put away.*

wegnehmen *to take away, carry off, confiscate, occupy.*

Wegweiser *m. signpost, roadsign.*

wegwerfen *to throw away.*

wegwerfend *disparaging, contemptuous.*

WEH *sore, aching, painful.*

weh tun *to ache, to hurt.*

wehleidig *plaintive.*

Wehmut *f. sadness, melancholy.*

wehmütig *sad, melancholy.*

Wehrdienst *m. military service.*

wehren *to hinder, forbid, arrest, defend.*

wehrfähig *able-bodied.*

wehrlos *unarmed, defenseless, weak.*

Wehrmacht *f. armed forces.*

Wehrpflicht *f. conscription.*

wehrpflichtig *liable to military service.*

Weib *n. woman.*

weiblich *female, feminine, womanly.*

Weiblichkeit *f. womanhood, feminine nature.*

WEICH *soft, mold, mellow, tender, smooth.*

weiches Ei *soft-boiled egg.*

weichen *to retreat, give in, yield; soften, soak.*

weichherzig *soft-hearted.*

weichlich *soft, flabby, weak.*

weigern *to refuse.*

Weigerung *f. refusal.*

Weihe *f. consecration, initiation, inauguration.*

weihen *to consecrate, dedicate, devote.*

WEIHNACHTEN *pl. Christmas.*

weihnachtlich *of Christmas.*

Weihnachtsabend *m. Christmas Eve.*

Weihnachtsbaum *m. Christmas tree.*

Weihnachtslied *n. Christmas carol.*

WEIL *because, since.*

Weile *f. while, space of time.*

Damit hat es gute Weile. *There is no hurry.*

Eile mit Weile. *Haste makes waste.*

WEIN *m. wine, vine.*

Weinberg *m. vineyard.*

WEINEN *to weep, cry.*

Weinessig *m. wine vinegar.*

Weinfass *n. wine cask.*

Weinkarte *f. winelist.*

Weinlese *f. vintage.*

Weinprobe *f. wine-tasting.*

Weinrebe *f. vine.*

Weinstock *m. vine.*

Weinstube *f. tavern.*

Weintraube *f. grape.*

WEISE *f. manner, way, tune.*

auf diese Weise *in this way.*

in der Weise, dass *in such a way that, so that.*

WEISEN *to show, refer, direct, point out, point at.*

Weisheit *f. wisdom, prudence.*

weismachen *to make one believe, hoax.*

WEISS *white, blank, clean.*

Weisser Sonntag *Sunday after Easter.*

weissagen *to predict, prophesy.*

Weissager *m. (–in, f.) prophet.*

WEIT *distant, far, vast, loose, wide, big.*

bei weitem *by far, by much.*

bei weitem nicht *by no means.*

es weit bringen *to get on well, be successful.*

nicht weither sein *not to be worth much.*

von weitem *from a distance.*

weit gefehlt *quite wrong.*

weit und breit *far and wide.*

weit voraus *way ahead.*

weit weg *far away.*

wenn alles so weit ist *when everything is ready.*

weitab *far away.*

weitaus *by far.*

Weite *f. width, size, extent, distance, length.*

WEITER *further, farther, more, else, additional.*

bis auf weiteres *until further notice.*

des weiteren *furthermore.*

nichts weiter *nothing more.*

niemand weiter *no one else.*

Nur weiter! *Go on!*

ohne weiteres *immediately.*

und so weiter *and so on.*

was weiter *what else.*

wenn's weiter nichts ist *if that's all there is to it.*

Weitere *n. rest, remaining part.*

weiterführen *to continue, carry on.*

weitergeben *to pass on to.*

weiterhin *furthermore, moreover.*

Weiterreise f. continuation of a trip.

weitgehend far-reaching, full, much.

weither from afar.

weitläufig distant, wide, extensive, roomy.

weitschweifig detailed, tedious.

weitsichtig far-sighted.

Weizen m. wheat, corn.

WELCH (ein) what (a)

　Welch ein Zufall! What a coincidence!

WELCH(-ER, -E, -ES) 1. inter. pron. &
　　adj. what, who, whom, which.
　2. rel. pron. what, which, that, who,
　　whom.

Welle f. wave, surge.

　Wellen schlagen to rise in waves.

Wellenlinie f. wavy line.

Wellenreiter m. surf-rider.

WELT f. world, universe, people.

　alle Welt everybody, everyone in the
　　world.

　auf der Welt on earth.

　auf die Welt kommen to come into the
　　world, be born.

　aus der Welt schaffen to put out of the
　　way.

　in der ganzen Welt on earth.

　in die Welt setzen (zur Welt bringen)
　　to give birth to.

Weltall n. universe.

Weltanschauung f. world outlook.

weltbekannt world-famous.

weltfremd secluded, solitary.

Weltmacht f. world power.

Weltmann m. man of the world.

Weltmeister m. world champion.

Weltraum m. space, universe.

Weltuntergang m. end of the world.

WEM dat. of wer. to whom.

WEN acc. of wer. whom.

Wende f. turn, turning point.

wenden to turn, turn around.

　Bitte wenden! Please turn over!

　sich wenden an to return to (someone).

Wendepunkt m. turning point.

WENIG little, few, a few.

　ein wenig a little, a bit.

WENIGER less, fewer, minus.

　immer weniger less and less.

　nichts weniger als anything but.

　vier weniger eins four minus one.

wenigst (er,-e,-es) least.

wenigstens at least.

WENN if, in case of, when.

　auch wenn even if.

　immer wenn whenever.

　Rufen Sie mich an, wenn Sie kommen
　　wollen! Call me when you want to
　　come.

　selbst wenn even if, supposing that.

　wenn auch (wenn gleich, wenn
　　schon) although.

　Wenn das nur wahr wäre! If it were only
　　true!

　wenn nur provided that.

　wenn schon! What of it!

　wenn Sie kommen könnten If you could
　　come.

WER inter. pron. who, what.

　wer anders who else.

　wer auch immer whoever.

　Wer (ist) da? Who is it?

werben to recruit, to win, to advertise.

Werbung f. advertising.

WERDEN 1. to become, turn out, prove,
　　happen.

　Was soll aus ihr werden? What's to
　　become of her?

　2. aux. verb to form future and passive,
　　shall, will, is, are.

werfen to throw, cast, toss.

WERK n. work, labor, production, doing,
　　performance, deed.

　ans Werk! Go to it! Begin!

　ins Werk setzen to set going.

　Das ist sein Werk. That's his doing.

Werkstatt f. workshop.

Werkstelle f. place of work.

Werktag m. working day.

werktags on weekdays.

werktätig active

　die werktätige Bevölkerung working
　　classes.

Werkzeug m. utensil.

WERT worth, valuable, worthy, honored,
　　esteemed.

　im Werte von at a price of.

　nichts wert sein to be no good.

Wertangabe f. declaration of value.

Wertgegenstand pl. valuables.

wertlos worthless.

Wertpapier n. security, bond.

Wertsachen pl. valuables.

Wertung f. evaluation, appraisal.

wertvoll valuable, precious.

Wesen n. creature, soul, personality.

wesentlich essential, substantial.

WESSEN gen. of wer. whose?

Weste f. waistcoat, vest.

Westen m. the West, Occident.

　nach Westen west (direction).

westlich western, occidental.

Wettbewerb n. contest.

Wette f. bet, wager.

　eine Wette machen to make a bet.

　um die Wette laufen to race someone.

wetteifern to emulate; to vie.

wetten to bet, wager.

WETTER n. weather.

Alle Wetter! *My word!*

Heute ist das Wetter wunderschön! *The weather is wonderful today!*

Wetterbericht *m. meteorological report.*

Wetterlage *f. weather conditions.*

Wettkampf *m. match, contest, prize fighting.*

Wettrennen *n. race, racing.*

WICHTIG *important.*

sich wichtig machen *to act important.*

WIDER 1. *prep. (acc.). against, contrary to, versus.*

Wider meinen Willen *against my will.*

2. *inseparable prefix. (con–, re–, anti–, contra–)*

widerhallen *to echo, resound.*

widerlegen *to refute.*

Widerlegung *f. refutation.*

widerlich *repulsive, disgusting.*

Widerrede *f. contradiction.*

widerrufen *to revoke, withdraw, retract, cancel.*

widersetzen (sich) *to oppose, resist.*

widerspiegeln *to reflect, mirror.*

Widersprechen *to contradict, to talk back to.*

Widerspruch *m. contradiction, disagreement.*

Widerstand *m. resistance, opposition.*

Widerwille *m. repugnance, disgust.*

widerwillig *reluctant, unwilling.*

widmen *to dedicate.*

Widmung *f. dedication.*

WIE *how, as, such, like.*

so . . . wie *as . . . as.*

wie auch immer *however.*

Wie bitte? *What did you say?*

wie dem auch sei *be that as it may.*

Wie geht es Ihnen? *How are you?*

wie gesagt *as has been said.*

WIEDER 1. *adv. again, anew, back, in return for.*

hin und wieder *now and then.*

immer wieder *again and again.*

2. *prefix.* a) *inseparable. In verb wiederholen (to repeat).* b) *separable (implies the idea of repetition or opposition).*

wiederbekommen *to get back, recover.*

wiederbeleben *to revive, reanimate.*

Wiederbelebungsversuch *m. attempt at resuscitation.*

wiederfinden *to find, recover.*

wiedererkennen *to recognize.*

wiedererlangen *to get back.*

wiedererobern *to reconquer.*

Wiedergabe *f. return; reproduction, recital (work of art).*

wiedergeben *to give back, return.*

wiedergewinnen *to recover, regain, reclaim.*

Wiedergutmachung *f. reparation.*

WIEDERHOLEN *to repeat, renew, reiterate, fetch, bring back.*

Wiederholung *f. repetition, reiteration.*

im Wiederholungsfalle *if it should happen again.*

wiederhören *to hear again.*

auf Wiederhören! *Good-bye! (radio, tel.).*

WIEDERSEHEN *to see again, meet again.*

auf Wiedersehen! *Good-bye! So long!*

Wiege *f. cradle.*

wiegen *to weigh, to rock, move to, shake, sway.*

Wiese *f. meadow.*

wieso *why.*

WIEVIEL *how much.*

Der wievielte ist heute? *What date is today?*

wieviele *how many.*

WILD *wild, rough, angry, furious, savage, untidy.*

Wild *n. game (hunting).*

Wildbraten *m. venison.*

Wilddieb *m. poacher.*

Wildente *f. wild duck.*

Wildleder *n. deerskin, suede.*

Wildnis *f. wilderness, desert.*

WILLE *m. will, say, determination, purpose.*

aus freiem Willen *voluntarily.*

guter Wille *kind intention.*

letzter Wille *last will.*

willenlos *lacking will power, irresolute.*

Willenlosigkeit *f. lack of will power.*

Willenskraft *f. will power.*

Willkommen *n. welcome, reception.*

Willkür *f. discretion, arbitrariness.*

willkürlich *arbitrary, despotic.*

WIND *m. wind, breeze.*

bei Wind und Wetter *in storm and rain (all types of bad weather).*

guter Wind *fair wind.*

in den Wind reden *to talk in vain.*

in den Wind schlagen *to disregard.*

vor dem Wind segeln *to run before the rain.*

Windel *f. baby's diaper.*

windeln *to swaddle.*

winden *to wind.*

windig *windy, breezy.*

Windstille *f. calm.*

Wink *m. sign, nod, wink.*

Winkel *m. corner, angle, secret spot.*

winken *to wave, nod, wink, wave.*

WINTER *m. winter.*

im Winter *in winter.*

Winterschlaf *m. hibernation.*

Wintersport *m. winter sports.*

Wintersportplatz *m. winter resort.*

winzig *tiny, diminutive.*

Winzigkeit *f. tininess.*

Wirbel *m. whirlpool, eddy.*

Wirbelknochen *m. vertebra.*

wirbeln *to whirl.*

Wirbelsäule *f. spine.*

Wirbelsturm *m. tornado, hurricane.*

wirken *to act, do, work, produce.*

WIRKLICH *real, actual, true, genuine.*

Wirklichkeit *f. reality, actuality.*

wirksam *active, effective.*

Wirkung *f. action, working, operation.*

wirkungslos *ineffectual, inefficient.*

wirkungsvoll *effective, striking.*

Wirt *m. host, proprietor, landlord.*

wirtlich *hospitable.*

Wirtschaft *f. housekeeping, economy, tavern, public house.*

   die Wirtschaft führen *to keep house, to manage things.*

wirtschaften *to manage, run the business.*

Wirtschaftsgeld *n. housekeeping money.*

Wirtschaftslage *f. economic situation.*

Wirtshaus *n. inn, public house.*

WISSEN *n. knowledge, learning.*

   meines Wissens *as far as I know.*

   wider besseres Wissen *against one's better judgment.*

WISSEN *to know, be aware of, understand, be acquainted with.*

   Ich weiss nicht. *I don't know.*

   nicht dass ich wüsste *not that I am aware of.*

   Bescheid wissen über *to be well informed about.*

   wissen um *to know of or about.*

   wissen von *to be informed or aware of.*

   Ihnen wissen lassen *to let you know.*

Wissenschaft *f. science, knowledge.*

Wissenschaftler (–in) *m. (f.) scientist, scholar.*

wissenswert *worth knowing, interesting.*

Witwe *f. widow.*

Witwer *m. widower.*

Witz *m. wittiness, witticism, wit, joke, pun.*

witzig *witty.*

WO *where, in which; when.*

   wo auch immer *wherever.*

woanders *elsewhere.*

wobei *in the course of which, whereby, in which, upon which.*

WOCHE *f. week.*

   diese Woche *this week.*

   heute in einer Woche *a week from today.*

Wochenende *n. weekend.*

wochenlang *for weeks.*

wochentags *on weekdays.*

Wochenschau *newsreel; weekly publication.*

wöchentlich *weekly.*

wodurch *by which, whereby, how.*

wofür *for which, for what.*

WOHER *from where, from what place?*

   Woher wissen Sie das? *How do you know that?*

WOHIN *to where, to what place?*

WOHL *n. welfare, prosperity, good health.*

   sich wohl fühlen *to feel well.*

WOHL *well, all right, probably, presumably, very likely, indeed.*

   Er wird wohl noch kommen. *He may yet come.*

   Ich verstehe wohl. *I can well understand.*

   Leben Sie wohl! *Good-bye!*

   wohl oder übel *willy nilly.*

   Zum Wohl! *To you! (a toast)*

Wohlbehagen *n. comfort, ease.*

wohlbekannt *well-known, familiar.*

Wohlfahrt *f. welfare.*

wohlgefällig *pleasant, agreeable.*

Wohlgefühl *f. pleasant feeling, sense of well-being.*

wohlhabend *well-to-do, wealthy.*

Wohlklang *m. harmony, melody.*

wohlschmeckend *tasty, palatable.*

Wohlstand *m. well-being, wealth, fortune.*

wohltuend *comforting, pleasant.*

wohlverdient *well-deserved, merited.*

WOHNEN *to live, dwell, reside, stay.*

   zur Miete wohnen *to live as a tenant, rent-payer.*

wohnhaft *living, dwelling.*

wohnlich *comfortable, cozy.*

WOHNUNG *f. house, dwelling, residence, flat.*

Wohnviertel *n. residential district.*

Wohnzimmer *n. living room*

Wolf *m. wolf.*

Wolke *f. cloud.*

   aus allen Wolken fallen *to be thunderstruck.*

Wolkenbruch *m. cloudburst.*

Wolkenkratzer *m. skyscraper.*

WOLLE *f. wool.*

WOLLEN *to want, wish, will, desire, like, mean.*

   Das will etwas heissen. *That means something.*

   Das will was heissen. *That's really something.*

   Er mag wollen oder nicht. *Whether he likes it or not.*

   Wie Sie wollen. *As you like.*

WOMIT *with what, by which, with which.*

   Womit kann ich dienen? *What can I do for you?*

womöglich *if possible.*

WORAN *whereon, by what.*

   woran liegt es? *how is it that? what is the reason for it?*

WORAUF *on what, upon which.*

WORAUS *of what, out of which.*

WORIN *in which, in what.*

WORT *n. word, expression, saying, promise.*

aufs Wort gehorchen   *to obey implicitly.*

das grosse Wort führen   *to brag.*

das Wort ergreifen   *to begin to speak.*

das Wort führen   *to be spokesman.*

einen beim Wort nehmen   *to take one at one's word.*

Er hat sein Wort gebrochen.   *He broke his promise.*

Ich habe kein Wort davon gewusst.   *I did not know a thing about it.*

ins Wort fallen   *to interrupt, cut short.*

mit anderen Worten   *in other words.*

Sie macht viele Worte.   *She talks too much.*

ums Wort bitten   *to ask for the floor.*

zu Wort kommen lassen   *to let one speak.*

geflügelte Worte   *familiar quotations.*

Wörterbuch *n. dictionary.*

Wortschatz *m. vocabulary.*

wortwörtlich *word for word.*

WORÜBER *of what, about which, whereof.*

WORUNTER *among what, which.*

WOVON *about what, which.*

WOVOR *of what, for what, before what, which.*

WOZU *to which end, of what, for what, which.*

wund *sore, wounded.*

Wunde *f. wound.*

Wunder *n. wonder, miracle.*

sein blaues Wunder erleben   *to be amazed.*

Wunder verrichten   *to perform miracles.*

WUNDERBAR *wonderful, marvelous.*

Wunderbar!   *Wonderful! Splendid!*

wunderbarerweise *strange to say.*

Wunderkind *n. child prodigy.*

wunderlich *strange, odd.*

WUNDERN *to astonish, surprise.*

sich wundern   *to be surprised, wonder.*

wunderschön *beautiful, lovely, exquisite.*

WUNSCH *m. wish, desire, request.*

auf Wunsch   *by request, if desired.*

Hätten Sie noch einen Wunsch?   *Is there anything else you'd like?*

nach Wunsch   *as one desires.*

WÜNSCHEN *to wish, desire, long for.*

Glück wünschen   *to congratulate (wish luck).*

Was wünschen Sie?   *May I help you?*

Ich wünsche Ihnen alles Gute.   *I wish you all the best.*

Würde *f. dignity, honor, title, rank.*

in Amt und Würden   *holding a high office.*

würdelos *undignified.*

würdevoll *dignified.*

würdig *worthy, deserving of, respectable.*

würdigen *to value, appreciate.*

jemanden keines Blickes würdigen   *to ignore someone completely.*

Würfel *m. die, cube.*

Der Würfel ist gefallen.   *The die is cast.*

würfeln *to play dice.*

Würfelspiel *n. dice game.*

Würfelzucker *m. lump of sugar.*

würgen *to choke, strangle.*

Wurm *m. worm.*

Wurst *f. sausage.*

Würze *f. seasoning, spice, condiment.*

Wurzel *f. root.*

würzen *to season.*

würzig *spicy.*

wüst *waste, deserted, desolate, wild, dissolute.*

Wüste *f. desert.*

WUT *f. rage, fury.*

in Wut geraten   *to fly into a rage.*

vor Wut kochen,   *to boil, fume with rage.*

wüten *to rage, be furious.*

wütend *enranged, furious.*

x-beliebig *at random.*

x-mal *every so often, any number of times.*

Y *the twenty-fifth letter of the alphabet.*

Y-Achse *f. (math) y-axis.*

Yacht (or Jacht) *f. yacht.*

Yard *n. yard.*

Yen *m. yen.*

Z

zagen *to be afraid, hesitate.*

zähe *tough, tenacious, stubborn, stingy.*

ZAHL *f. figure, number, numeral.*

zahlbar *payable, due.*

zahlen *to pay.*

ZÄHLEN *to count, number, calculate.*

gezahlt   *numbered.*

Zahlkarte *f. money-order form.*

zahllos *countless, innumerable.*

zahlreich *numerous.*

Zahltag *m. pay-day.*

Zahlung *f. payment.*

Zahlungsanweisung *f. postal or money order.*

zahlungsfähig *solvent (financially).*
zahm *tame, domestic.*
zähmen *to tame, break in.*
ZAHN *m. tooth.*
  ein schlechter Zahn *a bad tooth.*
  sich die Zähne putzen *to brush one's teeth.*
  einem auf den Zahn fühlen *to sound out a person.*
  falsche Zähne *artificial teeth.*
Zahnarzt (–in) *m. (f.) dentist.*
Zahnbürste *f. toothbrush.*
Zahnfleisch *n. gum(s).*
Zahnfüllung *f. filling.*
zahnlos *toothless.*
Zahnpasta *f. toothpaste.*
Zahnschmerzen *pl. toothache.*
Zahnstein *m. tartar.*
Zahnstocher *m. toothpick.*
Zahnweh *n. toothache.*
Zange *f. pincers, tongs, pliers.*
Zank *m. quarrel.*
zanken *to quarrel.*
zanksüchtig *quarrelsome.*
ZART *tender, soft, delicate, fragile, frail.*
zartfühlend *tactful, sensitive.*
Zartgefühl *n. delicacy of feeling.*
Zartheit *f. tenderness, delicacy.*
Zauber *m. magic, charm, spell.*
Zauberei *f. magic, witchcraft.*
Zauberflöte *f. magic flute.*
zauberhaft *magical, enchanting.*
zauberkünstler *m. illusionist.*
zaubern *to practice magic, conjure.*
zaudern *to hesitate, delay.*
Zaun *m. hedge, fence.*
  Streit von Zaune brechen *to pick a quarrel.*
Zebra *n. zebra.*
Zehe *f. toe.*
Zehenspitze *f. point of the toe.*
  auf Zehenspitzen gehen *to tiptoe.*
ZEHN *ten.*
zehnfach *tenfold.*
ZEHNT *tenth.*
Zeichen *n. sign, signal, token, brand.*
  zum Zeichen dass *as a proof that.*
Zeichensetzung *f. punctuation.*
Zeichensprache *f. sign language.*
ZEICHNEN *to draw, design, mark.*
ZEICHNUNG *f. drawing, sketch, design.*
Zeigefinger *m. forefinger, index.*
ZEIGEN *to show, point at, point out, exhibit, display.*
Zeiger *m. hand of the clock, pointer.*
ZEIT *f. time, duration, period, epoch, season.*
  Damit hat es Zeit. *There is no hurry.*
  die freie Zeit *leisure, spare time.*

Es ist an der Zeit. *It is high time.*
höchste Zeit *high time.*
in der letzten Zeit *lately.*
in jüngster Zeit *quite recently.*
Lassen Sie sich Zeit! *Take your time!*
mit der Zeit *gradually, in the course of time.*
Zeit seines Lebens *during life.*
zu gleicher Zeit *at the same time.*
zur rechten Zeit *in the nick of time.*
zur Zeit *at present.*
Zeitablauf *m. lapse of time.*
Zeitalter *n. age, generation.*
zeitgemäss *timely, seasonable.*
Zeitgenosse *m. contemporary.*
zeitgenössisch *contemporary.*
ZEITIG *early, timely, mature, ripe.*
Zeitmangel *m. lack of time.*
Zeitrechnung *f. chronology.*
Zeitpunkt *m. time, moment.*
Zeitschrift *f. journal, periodical, magazine.*
ZEITUNG *f. newspaper, paper.*
Zeitungsausschnitt *m. press cutting.*
Zeitungskiosk *m. newsstand.*
Zeitungsnotiz *f. notice, item, paragraph.*
Zeitungsstand *m. newsstand.*
Zeitungsinserat *n. newspaper advertisement, notice.*
Zeitungsverkäufer *m. news vendor.*
Zeitverschwendung *f. loss of time.*
Zeitvertreib *m. pastime, amusement.*
Zeitwort *n. verb.*
Zelle *f. cell, booth.*
Zelt *n. tent, canopy.*
Zement *m. cement.*
Zentimeter *m. & n. centimeter (.3937 inch).*
Zentrale *f. central office, station, telephone exchange.*
Zentralheizung *f. central heating.*
ZENTRUM *n. center.*
zerbrechen *to break, smash.*
  sich den Kopf zerbrechen *to rack one's brains.*
zerbrechlich *fragile.*
Zerbrechlichkeit *f. fragility, brittleness.*
Zeremonie *f. ceremony.*
zerreissbar *tearable.*
zerreissen *to tear, rip up.*
zerren *to drag, pull.*
  eine Muskel zerren *to strain a muscle.*
zerschmettern *to crush, destroy.*
zerstören *to destroy, demolish, devastate, ruin.*
Zerstörer *m. destroyer, devastator.*
Zerstörung *f. devastation, demolition, destruction.*
zerstreuen *to disperse, scatter, dissipate, divert.*
zerstreut *absent-minded.*

Zerstreuung f. dispersion, distraction.

Zerwürfnis n. disagreement, quarrel, strife.

Zettel m. slip, note, label, ticket, poster, bill.

Zeug n. stuff, material, cloth, fabric, utensils, things.

Zeuge m. witness.

zeugen to testify, bear witness, give evidence.

Zeugenaussage f. evidence, deposition.

Zeugenvernehmung f. hearing of witnesses.

Ziege f. goat.

Ziegel m. brick, tile.

Ziegelstein m. brick.

ZIEHEN to pull, draw, haul, tug, tow, extract, move, migrate, weigh.
   den Kürzeren ziehen   to get the worst of it.
   nach sich ziehen   to have consequences.
   Er zieht den Hut.   He tips his hat.
   zur Rechenschaft ziehen   to call to account.
   ein Gesicht ziehen   to make faces.
   in Betracht ziehen   to take into consideration.

Ziehung f. drawing of lottery.

Ziel n. goal.
   sich ein Ziel setzen   to aim at.

zielbewusst systematic, methodical.

zielen to aim.

ziellos aimless.

Zielscheibe f. target.
   Zielscheibe des Spottes sein   to be a laughing stock.

ziemen to become, be suitable.

ZIEMLICH rather, pretty, fairly, quite, considerable.
   so ziemlich   about, pretty much.
   ziemlich viele   quite a few.

Zierde f. ornament, decoration.

zieren to decorate, adorn, embellish.

zierlich elegant, graceful, delicate.

Ziffer f. figure, cipher.

Zifferblatt n. dial, face.

ZIGARETTE f. cigarette.

Zigarettenetui n. cigarette-case.

Zigarettenspitze f. cigarette-holder.

Zigarre f. cigar.

Zigarrenkiste f. cigar-box.

Zigeuner m. gypsy.

ZIMMER n. room, apartment, chamber.

Zimmerdecke f. ceiling.

Zimmermädchen n. chambermaid.

Zimmermann m. carpenter.

zimperlich supersensitive, prudish, affected.

Zimt m. cinnamon.

Zinn n. tin, pewter.

Zins m. tax, duty, rent; interest.
   auf Zinsen ausleihen   to lend money at interest.

   mit Zins und Zinseszins   in full measure.

Zinseszins m. compound interest.

Zinsfuss m. rate of interest.

Zirkel m. compasses.

Zirkus m. circus.

Zitat n. quotation.

Zitrone f. lemon.

Zitronenlimonade f. lemonade.

Zitronensaft m. lemon juice.

zittern to tremble, shake, quiver, shiver.

zivil civil, reasonable, moderate.
   in Zivil   in plain clothes.

Zivilbevölkerung f. civilian population.

Zivilisation f. civilization.

zivilisieren to civilize.

zögern to hesitate, delay, linger.

ZOLL m. duty, toll, tariff, customs.

Zoll m. inch.

Zollabfertigung f. customs inspection, clearance.

ZOLLAMT n. customhouse.

Zollbeamte m. customhouse officer.

zollfrei free of duty.

Zollgebühr f. duty.

Zöllner m. customs collector.

zollpflichtig subject to customs.

Zollstock m. yardstick.

Zone f. zone.

Zopf m. braid, pigtail.

Zorn m. anger, rage, wrath.

Zornig angry.

ZU 1. prep. (dat.). to, at, by, near, beside, for, with, in front of, on.
   Die Deutschen essen gern Kartoffeln zum Fleisch.   Germans like to eat potatoes with meat.
   Et war nicht zu Hause.   He was not at home.
   Ich gehe zu meiner Tante.   I am going to my aunt's house.
   Setzen Sie sich zu mir!   Sit down by me.
   Wenn es friert, wird das Wasser zu Eis.   When it freezes, water turns to ice.
   Wit essen Eier zum Frühstück.   We eat eggs for breakfast.
   zu Fuss/zu Pferd   on foot, on horseback.
   zu meinem Erstaunen   to my surprise.
   zum König gekrönt werden   to become a king.
   zum Teil   partly.
   zum "Weisses Rössi"   at the "White Horse" (inn).
2. adv. too (more than enough), toward.
   zu viel   too much.
3. before infinitive to.
   Sie wussten nicht was tun.   They did not know what to do.
4. Separable prefix (implies direction

118

toward the speaker, increase,
continuation, closing, confession).

Sie liefen dem Walde zu. They ran toward
the forest.

Der Verbrecher gab es zu. *The criminal
confessed.*

Ich darf nicht mehr zunehmen. *I must not
gain more weight.*

Mach die Tür zu! *Close the door!*

Zubehör m. & n. accessories, trimmings,
belongings.

zubereiten to prepare, cook, mix.

Zubereitung f. preparation.

Zucht f. breeding, training, education; breed,
race, stock.

züchten to breed, grow, cultivate, train.

züchtig chaste, modest.

züchtigen to punish, correct, chastise.

zucken to jerk, twitch.

mit den Achseln zucken *to shrug one's
shoulders.*

ZUCKER m. sugar.

Zuckerguss m. icing.

zuckerhältig containing sugar.

zuckerkrank diabetic.

zuckern to sugar, sweeten.

Zuckerwerk n. confectionery, sweets.

zudem besides, moreover.

zudrücken to shut, close.

ein Auge zudrücken *to turn a blind eye,
to overlook.*

zuerst at first, in the first place.

Zufahrt f. driveway, approach.

Zufall m. chance, accident, occurrence.

durch Zufall *by accident.*

zufällig casual, by accident, by chance.

zufällig tun to happen to do.

zufälligerweise by chance.

Zuflucht f. refuge, shelter.

sine Zuflucht nehmen zu *to take refuge
with.*

ZUFRIEDEN satisfied, content.

sich zufrieden geben *to rest content with.*

zufrieden lassen *to let alone, leave in
peace.*

Zufriedenheit f. contentment, satisfaction.

zufriedenstellen to content, satisfy.

zufriedenstellend satisfactory.

ZUG m. train; drawing, draft; procession,
march, impulse; feature,
characteristic.

Er liegt in den letzten Zügen. *He is
breathing his last.*

Zug um Zug *without delay,
uninterruptedly.*

Wann kommt der Schnellzug aus Berlin
an? *When does the express train
from Berlin arrive?*

Das ist ein Zug seines Charakters. *This is*

a feature of his character.

Zugabe f. extra, addition, encore, confession.

Zugang m. entrance, door, access.

zugänglich accessible, open to.

zugeben to add, allow, permit, admit.

Zügel m. bridle, rein.

zügellos unbridled, unrestrained.

Zugeständnis n. concession, admission.

Zugluft f. draught, current of air.

zugunsten in favor of, for the benefit of.

zugute (halten) to allow for, take into
consideration, give credit for.

zugute kommen *to come in handy, be an
advantage to.*

Zuhilfenahme f. (unter Zuhilfenahme von)
with the help of.

zuhören to listen to.

Zuhörer m. hearer, listener.

Zuhörerschaft f. audience.

ZUKUNFT f. future.

zukünftig future.

zulächeln to smile at.

Zulage f. addition, raise.

zulangen to hand, give.

zulässig admissible, permissible.

Zulassung f. admission, permission.

zulegen to add something to.

ZULETZT finally, ultimately,

zuletzt kommen *to arrive last.*

zuliebe (tun) to do for someone's sake.

einem zuliebe tun *to please someone.*

zumachen to close, shut, fasten; to hurry.

zumal especially, particularly.

zumindest at least.

zumuten to expect of.

sich zu viel zumuten *to attempt too much.*

Zumutung f. unreasonable demand.

zunächst first, first of all, above all.

zünden to catch fire, inflame, arouse
enthusiasm.

zunehmen to grow, increase, get fuller.

zuneigen to lean forward, incline.

Zuneigung f. liking, affection, sympathy,
inclination.

ZUNGE f. tongue.

Das Wort liegt mir auf der Zunge. *I have
the word on the tip of my tongue.*

eine belegte Zunge *a coated tongue.*

eine feine Zunge haben *to be a gourmet.*

zurechnungsfähig responsible, of sound
mind.

Zurechnungsfähigkeit f. accountability,
responsibility before the law.

zurecht right, in order, in time.

zurechtfinden to find one's way about.

**zurechtsetzen (einem den Kopf
zurechtsetzen)** to bring one to
reason.

ZURÜCK 1. adv. back, backwards, late,

behind. 2. separable prefix (implies the idea of a return motion; back).

Wir kamen erst um elf Uhr zurück. *We only came back at eleven.*

zurückbeben *to start back, recoil.*

zurückbehalten *to keep back, retain.*

zurückbekommen *to get back, recover.*

zurückbleiben *to stay behind.*

zurückbringen *to bring back.*

zurückfahren *to drive back, return.*

zurückfordern *to demand back.*

zurückgehen *to go back, return, retreat, decrease, decline.*

zurückgezogen *retired, secluded, lonely.*

Zurückgezogenheit *f. retirement, seclusion.*

zurückhalten *to hold back, delay, detain.*

zurückhaltend *reserved.*

zurückkehren *to return, go back, come back.*

zurücklassen *to leave behind.*

zurücknehmen *to take back.*

zurücksetzen *to put back, replace, reduce, neglect.*

Zurücksetzung *f. reduction (in price).*

zurückstellen *to put back, replace, reserve, put aside.*

zurücktreten *to step back, withdraw, resign.*

zurückversetzen *to put back, restore.*

sich in eine Zeit zurückversetzen *to go back (in imagination) to a time.*

zurückweisen *to send away, to turn back, send back, repulse.*

zurückzahlen *to pay back, repay.*

Zurückzahlung *f. repayment.*

zurückziehen *to draw back, take back.*

Zuruf *m. acclamation, shout, call.*

zurufen *to call to, shout to.*

Zusage *f. acceptance, promise.*

ZUSAGEN *to promise, please, appeal.*

einem etwas auf den Kopf zusagen *to tell a person plainly.*

ZUSAMMEN *together, altogether.*

zusammenfassen *to sum up, summarize.*

zusammenfassend *comprehensive.*

zusammengehören *to belong together, match, be correlated.*

Zusammenhalt *m. holding together, cohesion, solidarity.*

Zusammenhang *m. connection, relationship.*

zusammenhangslos *disconnected.*

Zusammenkunft *f. meeting, reunion, assembly.*

Zusammenstoss *m. collision, clash, crash.*

zusammenstossen *to smash, collide.*

zusammentreffen *to meet each other, coincide.*

zusammenzählen *to count up, add up.*

Zusatz *m. addition.*

zusätzlich *additional.*

ZUSCHAUER *m. spectator.*

Zuschauerraum *m. theater auditorium.*

Zuschlag *m. addition, increase in price.*

zuschlagpflichtig *liable to additional payment.*

zuschliessen *to lock, lock up.*

Zuschrift *f. letter, communication.*

zuschulden *adv. guilty.*

sich etwas zuschulden kommen lassen *to be guilty of doing something.*

zusehen *to look on, watch for, wait.*

zusichern *to assure of, promise.*

Zusicherung *f. insurance.*

zusprechen *to encourage.*

Trost zusprechen *to comfort, console.*

Zuspruch *m. consolation, exhortation, encouragement, pep talk.*

ZUSTAND *m. state, condition, position, situation.*

zustande bringen *to do, get done, achieve.*

zuständig *belonging to, responsible, authorized, competent.*

Zuständigkeit *f. competence, power, jurisdiction.*

zustimmen *to consent, agree.*

Zustimmung *f. consent.*

Zustrom *m. influx, crowd, multitude.*

zutrauen *to believe (one) capable of.*

zutraulich *confiding, trusting.*

zutreffend *correct, right, applicable.*

ZUTRITT *m. admission, entrance.*

Zutritt verboten! *No admittance!*

zuverlässig *reliable, trustworthy.*

Zuversicht *f. confidence, trust.*

zuversichtlich *confident.*

ZUVIEL *too much.*

zuvor *before, previously, formerly.*

zuvorkommen *to come first.*

zuvorkommend *obliging.*

Zuvorkommenheit *f. politeness, kindness.*

ZUWEILEN *sometimes, now and then, occasionally.*

zuwider (sein) *to be repugnant.*

Das ist mir zuwider. *I hate it.*

zuzahlen *to pay extra.*

zuziehen *to draw together, call, invite, consult.*

Zwang *m. compulsion, constraint, force, pressure.*

Zwang antun *to do violence to*

sich keinen Zwang antun *not to stand on ceremony.*

zwanglos *free and easy.*

Zwanglosigkeit *f. freedom, ease.*

Zwangslage *f. condition of constraint, quandary, "jam."*

sich in einer Zwangslage befinden *to be under compulsion.*

zwangsläufig *necessarily, inevitably.*

ZWANZIG *twenty.*

Zwanziger *m. figure 20, a 20-year old.*

in den Zwanzigern sein   *to be in one's twenties.*

ZWANZIGSTE *twentieth.*

ZWAR *indeed, although.*

und zwar   *in fact, namely.*

ZWECK *m. purpose, design, aim, object, end, goal.*

keinen Zweck haben   *to be of no use.*

Zu welchem Zweck?   *Why? For what purpose?*

zwecklos *useless, purposeless.*

Zwecklosigkeit *f. uselessness, aimlessness.*

zweckmässig *expedient.*

ZWEI *two.* zwo *two* (coll.)

zu zweien   *by pairs, two by two.*

zweideutig *ambiguous.*

zweifach *twofold, double.*

ZWEIFEL *m. doubt, suspicion.*

zweifelhaft *doubtful.*

zweifellos *indubitable.*

zweifeln *to doubt, question, suspect.*

Zweifelsfall *m.*

im Zweifelsfall   *in case of a doubt.*

Zweig *m. branch.*

Zweiggeschäft *n. branch (office).*

Zweikampf *m. duel.*

zweimal *twice.*

zweireihig *having two rows, columns; double-breasted.*

Zweisitzer *two-seater.*

ZWEITE *second, next.*

zu zweit   *two by two.*

zweitens *secondly, in the second place.*

Zwerg *m. dwarf.*

Zwieback *m. rusk, biscuit.*

Zwiebel *f. onion, bulb (plant).*

Zwielicht *n. twilight, dusk.*

Zwilling *m. twin.*

zwingen *to compel, force, get through, finish.*

zwingend *forcible.*

zwinkern *to blink, wink.*

Zwirn *m. thread, sewing-cotton.*

ZWISCHEN *prep. (dat. when answering question, Wo?; acc. when answering question, Wohin?, and depending on the idiom). among, between.*

Zwischen den Städten Duisburg und Köln liegt Düsseldorf.   *Between the cities of Duisburg and Cologne lies Düsseldorf.*

zwischen drei und vier   *between three and four.*

Er läuft zwischen die Wagen.   *He walks between the cars.*

Zwischenbemerkung *f. incidental remark, verbal aside.*

Zwischendeck *n. lower deck.*

zwischendurch *through, in the midst of.*

Zwischenfall *m. incident, episode.*

Zwischenlandung *f. intermediate landing or stop (flight).*

Zwischenpause *f. interval, break.*

Zwischenraum *m. space, gap, interval.*

Zwischenzeit *f. interval.*

in der Zwischenzeit   *in the meantime.*

zwitschern *to twitter, chirp.*

ZWÖLF *twelve.*

ZWÖLFTE *twelfth.*

Zyklus *m. cycle, course, series.*

Zylinder *m. cylinder.*

Zyniker *m. cynic.*

zynisch *cynical.*

Zynismus *m. cynicism.*

GLOSSARY OF
PROPER NAMES

Albrecht *Albert.*
Alfred *Alfred.*
Andress *Andrew.*
Anne *Ann.*
Anton *Anthony.*
August *August.*
Barbara *Barbara.*
Bernhard *Bernard.*
Bertha *Bertha.*
Eduard *Edward.*
Elisabeth (Else) *Elizabeth.*
Emilie *Emily.*
Emma *Emma.*
Erich *Eric.*
Ernst *Ernest.*
Eugen *Eugene.*
Franz *Frank.*
Franziska *Frances.*
Friederich *Frederick.*
Fritz *Fred.*
Genoveva *Genevieve.*
Georg *George.*
Gertrud (Trudchen) *Gertrude.*
Gretchen *Margaret.*
Gustav *Gustave.*
Heinrich *Henry.*
Helene *Helen.*
Ilse *Elsie.*
Jakob *James, Jacob.*
Johann *John.*
Johanna *Jane, Joan.*
Josef *Joseph.*
Karl *Charles.*
Katharina (Kätchen) (Käthe)
       Katherine (Kate).
Klaus *Nicholas.*
Lotte *Charlotte.*
Ludwig *Lewis.*
Luise *Louise.*
Maria *Mary.*
Mark *Mark.*
Martha *Martha.*
Michael *Michael.*
Minna *Wilhelmina.*
Moritz *Maurice.*
Otto *Otto.*
Paul *Paul.*
Paula *Paula.*
Peter *Peter.*
Richard *Richard.*
Robert *Robert.*
Rosa *Rose.*
Rüdiger *Roger.*
Rudolph *Ralph.*

Susanne *Susan.*
Theodor *Theodore.*
Therese *Theresa.*
Thomas *Thomas.*
Walter *Walter.*
Wilhelme *William.*

GLOSSARY OF
GEOGRAPHICAL NAMES

Aachen *n. Aix-la-Chapelle.*
Afrika *n. Africa.*
Ägypten *n. Egypt.*
die Alpen *pl. Alps.*
Amerika *n. America*
  die Vereinigten Staaten *pl. the United*
         States (of America).
  Nord-Amerika *n. North America.*
  Süd-Amerika *n. South America.*
  Mittel-Amerika *n. Central America.*
Antwerpen *n. Antwerp.*
Asien *n. Asia.*
Atlantik *m. (der Atlantische Ozean)*
         Atlantic (the Atlantic Ocean).
Australien *n. Australia.*
Belgien *n. Belgium.*
Berlin *n. Berlin.*
Bonn *n. Bonn.*
Bosnien *n. Bosnia*
Brasilien *n. Brazil.*
Brüssel *n. Brussels.*
Dänemark *n. Denmark.*
Deutschland *n. Germany.*
England *n. England.*
Europa *n. Europe.*
Frankfurt a.M. *n. Frankfurt on the Main.*
Frankreich *n. France.*
Gemeiuschaft Unabhängiger Staaten
         f. Commonwealth of Independent
         States (formerly the U.S.S.R.)
Griechenland *n. Greece.*
Haag (den) *The Hague.*
Hamburg *n. Hamburg.*
Herzegowina *n. Herzegovina*
Holland *n. Holland.*
Indien *n. India.*
Irland *n. Ireland.*
Israel *n. Israel.*
Italien *n. Italy.*
Japan *n. Japan.*
Jugoslawien *n. Yugoslavia*
Kanada *n. Canada.*
Köln *n. Cologne.*
Kroatien *n. Croatia*
London *n. London.*

Madrid   *n. Madrid.*
Mexiko   *n. Mexico.*
Moskau   *n. Moscow.*
München   *n. Munich.*
Norwegen   *n. Norway.*
Nürnberg   *n. Nuremberg.*
Österreich   *n. Austria.*
Paris   *n. Paris.*
Polen   *n. Poland.*
Portugal   *n. Portugal.*
Preussen   *n. Prussia.*
Rhein   *m. Rhine.*
Rheinland   *n. Rhineland.*
Rom   *n. Rome.*
Rumänien   *n. Rumania.*

Russland   *n. Russia.*
Saar   *f. Saar*
Sachsen   *n. Saxony.*
Schlesien   *n. Silesia.*
Schottland   *n. Scotland.*
Schweden   *n. Sweden.*
Schweiz   *f. Switzerland.*
Serbien   *n. Serbia*
Slowakei   *f. Slovakia*
Spanien   *n. Spain.*
Stille Ozean (der)   *Pacific Ocean.*
Tschechische Republik   *f. Czech Republic*
Türkei   *f. Turkey.*
Ungarn   *n. Hungary.*
Wien   *n. Vienna.*

English-German

A

a (an) *ein, eine.*
abandon (to) *verlassen.*
abbreviate (to) *abkürzen.*
abbreviation *Abkürzung, f.*
ability *Fähigkeit, f.*
able *fähig.*
able (to be) *können.*
abolish (to) *abschaffen.*
about *ungefähr, um* (acc.) (around).
above *über, oberhalb.*
abroad *im Ausland.*
absence *Abwesenheit, f.*
absent *abwesend.*
absolute *unbedingt, völlig.*
absorb (to) *aufsaugen.*
abstain (to) *sich enthalten.*
abstract *abstrakt.*
absurd *unvernünftig, sinnlos.*
abundant *reichlich.*
abuse *Missbrauch, m.*
academy *Akademie, f.*
accent *Akzent, m.*
accent (to) *betonen.*
accept (to) *annehmen.*
acceptance *Annahme, f.*
accident *Unfall, m.; Zufall, m.* (chance).
accidental *zufällig.*
accidentally *nebenbei.*
accommodate (to) *unterbringen, sich an*
    passen.
accommodation *Unterkunft, f.*
accompany (to) *begleiten.*
accomplish (to) *vollführen.*
accord *Übereinstimmung, f.*
according to *zu* (dat.); *zufolge dem.*
account *Rechnung, f.; Konto, n.* (balance).
  on no account   *auf keinen Fall.*
  to pay the account   *die Rechnung bezahlen.*
accuracy *Genauigkeit, f.*
accurate *genau, richtig, akkurat.*
accuse (to) *anklagen, beschuldigen.*
accustom (to) *gewöhnen.*
ace *Ass, n.*
ache *Schmerz, m.*
ache (to) *schmerzen.*
achieve (to) *vollbringen, leisten.*
achievement *Vollbringung, f.; Leistung*
    (result).
acid *sauer* (adj.), *Säure* (noun), *f.*
acknowledge (to) *anerkennen.*
acknowledgment *Anerkennung, f.*
acquaintance *Bekannte, m. & f.*
acquire (to) *erwerben.*
across *gegenüber.*
act *Handlung, f.; Akt, m.* (of a play); *Gesetz,*
    n. (law).

active *tätig.*
activity *Tätigkeit, f.*
actor *Schauspieler, m.*
actress *Schauspielerin, f.*
actual *wirklich.*
acute *akut.*
adopt (to) *anpassen.*
add (to) *zufügen.*
addition *Zusatz, m.; Addition, f.* (math).
  in addition to *zusätzlich zu* (dat.).
address *Adresse, f.; Anschrift, f.; Ansprache,*
    f.; Anrede, f. (speech).
address (to) *adressieren; anreden,*
    ansprechen, sich wenden an (speech).
adequate *ausreichend, genügend.*
adjective *Eigenschaftswort, Adjektiv, n.*
adjoining *angrenzend, anstossend.*
administer (to) *verwalten.*
admiral *Admiral, m.*
admiration *Bewunderung, f.*
admire (to) *bewundern.*
admission *Eintritt, m.*
admit (to) *einlassen; zugeben* (concede).
admittance *Zutritt, m.*
  no admittance   *Zutritt verboten.*
adopt (to) *adoptieren* (child); *annehmen*
    (idea).
adult *Erwachsene(r)* (noun), *m. & f.;*
    erwachsen (adj.).
advance (to) *vorangehen* (lead); *steigen*
    (price).
  in advance   *im Voraus.*
advantage *Vorteil, m.*
adventure *Abenteuer, n.*
adverb *Adverb, n.*
advertise (to) *anzeigen; Reklame machen.*
advertisement *Anzeige, f.; Reklame, f.*
advice *Rat, m.*
advise (to) *raten.*
affair *Sache, f.* (thing); *Angelegenheit, f.;*
    Veranstaltung (party, meeting) *f.*
affect (to) *betreffen.*
affected *geziert, affektiert* (pretentious);
    gerührt (moved).
affection *Zuneigung, f.*
affectionate *herzlich, zärtlich, liebevoll.*
affirm (to) *bestätigen, bekräftigen.*
affirmation *Bestätigung, f.; Bekräftigung, f.*
afloat *schwimmend, auf dem Meere.*
afraid *ängstlich.*
after *nach* (dat.).
afternoon *Nachmittag, m.*
afterward *nachher.*
again *wieder.*
against *gegen* (acc.); *wider* (acc.).
age *Alter, n.* (also old age); *Epoche, f.*
    (history).
agency *Vertretung, f.*
agent *Agent, m.*

aggravate (to) *verschlimmern; ärgern* (annoy), *reizen*.
ago *vor* (dat.).
   three days ago *vor drei Tagen*.
agree (to) *übereinstimmen*.
agreeable *angenehm*.
agreed *abgemacht*.
agreement *Übereinstimmung, f.; Vertrag, m.* (contract).
   to be in agreement with *einverstanden sein*
agricultural *landwirtschaftlich*.
agriculture *Landwirtschaft, f.*
ahead *voran, voraus*.
aid *Hilfe, f.*
   first aid *Erste Hilfe*.
aid (to) *helfen*.
aim *Ziel, n.; Zweck, m.*
aim (to) *erreichen; zielen* (shooting)
   to aim at *richten gegen*
air *Luft, f.*
air force *Luftwaffe, f.*
air mail *Luftpost, f.*
airfield *Flugplatz, m*
airplane *Flugzeug, n.*
airport *Flughafen, m.*
aisle *Seitenschiff, n.* (church); *gang, m.* (hall).
alarm *Alarm, m.*
alarm clock *Wecker, m.*
alcohol *Alkohol, m.*
alike *gleich, ähnlich*.
all *ganz, alles*.
   all right *in Ordnung, bestimmt*.
   not at all *keineswegs überhaupt micht*.
alliance *Verbindung f.; Allianz, f.* (pact).
allow (to) *erlauben, gestatten*.
allowed *gestattet*
ally *Verbündete, m.*
almost *fast, beinahe*.
alone *allein*.
along *entlang*.
already *schon, bereits*.
also *auch*.
altar *Altar, m.*
alter (to) *ändern, verwandeln*.
alternate *abwechselnd*.
alternate (to) *abwechseln*.
although *obwohl, obgleich*.
altitude *Höhe, f.*
altogether *zusammen; gänzlich* (wholly).
always *immer*
amaze (to) *erstaunen*.
amazement *Verwunderung, f.*
ambassador *Botschafter, m.*
ambassadress *Botschafterin, f.*
ambitious *ehrgeizig*.
amend (to) *berichtigen, (ab)ändern, verbessern*.

American *Amerikaner* (noun, *m.*); *amerikanisch* (adj.); *Amerikanerin* (f.).
among *mitten; unter* (dat. or acc.).
amount *Betrag, m.*
ample *geräumig, umfassend*.
amuse (to) *amüsieren*.
amusement *Unterhaltung, f.*
amusing *amüsant*.
analyze (to) *analysieren*.
ancestors *Vorfahren, pl.*
anchor *Anker, m.*
ancient, *uralt, alt, aus alten Zeiten*.
and *und*.
anecdote *Anekdote, f.*
angel *Engel, m.*
anger *Ärger, m.*
angry *ärgerlich, bös*.
animal *Tier, n.*
animate (to) *beleben*.
annex *Nebengebäude, n.*
annihilate (to) *vernichten*.
anniversary *Hochzeitstag, m.*
announce (to) *ansagen*.
announcement *Anzeige, f.*
annoy (to) *ärgern, belästigen*.
annual *jährlich*.
annul (to) *annullieren; ungültig machen*.
anonymous *anonym*.
another *ein anderer*.
answer *Antwort, f.*
answer (to) *antworten*.
answering machine *Anrufbeanworter, m.*
anterior *vorhergehend*.
anticipate (to) *vorhersehen* (foresee). *erwarten* (expect).
antique *altertümlich, antik*.
anxiety *Unruhe, f.; Ängstlichkeit f.*
anxious *unruhig, ängstlich, bekümmert*.
any *etwas* (some); *irgend ein; irgend welche* (whatever).
anybody *irgendjemand*.
anyhow *sowieso*.
   anyway *sowieso*.
anything *irgendetwas*.
anywhere *irgendwo*.
apart *abseits, getrennt*.
apartment *Wohnung, f.*
apiece *pro Stück*.
apologize (to) *sich entschuldigen*.
apparent *scheinbar, anscheinend*.
appeal (to) *gefallen*.
appear (to) *erscheinen*.
appearance *Erscheinung, f.*
appease (to) *besänftigen*.
appendix *Anhang, m.*
appetite *Appetit, m.*
applaud (to) *applaudieren; klatschen*.
applause *Applaus, m.*

apple *Apfel, m.*
application *Antrag, m.* (request);
    Gewissenhaftigkeit, f. (diligence).
    application form *Anmeldungs–*
    Antragsformular.
apply (to) *sich bewerben um* (for a job);
    auftragen (use).
appoint (to) *ernennen.*
appointment *Verbredung, f.*
appreciate (to) *schätzen.*
appreciation *Anerkennung, f.*
appropriate *angemessen.*
approve (to) *genehmigen.*
April *April, m.*
apron *Schürze, f.*
arbitrary *eigenwillig, beliebig.*
arcade *Arkade, f.*
architect *Architekt, m.; Baumeister, m.*
architecture *Architektur, f.*
ardent *feurig, glühend.*
area *Gebiet, n.*
argue (to) *verhandeln, diskutieren.*
argument *Wortwechsel, m.*
arise (to) *aufsteigen; auftauchen* (emerge);
    aufstehen (get up).
arm *Arm, m.*
    firearms *Waffen, pl.*
arm (to) *bewaffnen.*
arms control *Abrüstung, f.*
army *Heer, n.; Armee, f.*
around *herum, um* (acc.).
arouse (to) *erregen* (revolt); *erwecken*
    (suspicion); *aufwecken* (wake up).
arrange (to) *ordnen, arrangieren.*
arrangement *Ordnung, f.* (order);
    Anordnung, f. (preparation).
arrest *Verhaftung, f.*
arrest (to) *verhaften.*
arrival *Ankunft, f.*
arrive (to) *ankommen.*
art *Kunst, f.*
article *Artikel, m.*
artificial *künstlich.*
artificial intelligence *kunstliche Intelligenz*
    (computer), *f.*
artist *Künstler, m.*
artistic *künstlerisch, kunstvoll.*
as *als* (when); *so* (as much); *da* (because).
    as . . . as *so . . . wie.*
    as long as *so lange wie.*
    as soon as *sobald.*
    as to *mit Bezug auf* (business); *was . . .*
    anbetrifft.
    as well *sowohl, auch.*
    as yet *bis jetzt.*
ascertain (to) *feststellen.*
ash *Asche, f.*
ashamed *beschämt, verschämt* (shy).
aside *beiseite, abseits.*

ask (to) *fragen, bitten* (um).
asleep *schlafend.*
aspire (to) *streben nach.*
aspirin *Aspirin, n.*
assault *Angriff, m.*
assemble (to) *sich versammeln.*
assembly *Versammlung, f.* (congress);
    Gesellschaft, f.
assign (to) *zuteilen, aufgeben.*
assist (to) *beistehen,* (aus) *helfen.*
assistant *Gehilfe, m., Gehilfin, f.;*
    Assistent(in) m. (f.).
associate (to) *anschliessen, verbinden.*
assume (to) *annehmen.*
assurance *Versicherung, f.*
assure (to) *versichern.*
astonish (to) *erstaunen.*
astound (to) *verblüffen.*
astronaut *astronaut(in, f.) m.*
asylum *Asyl, n.*
at *in* (dat. or acc.); *beim, zu* (dat.).
    at home *zu Hause* (heim)
    at first *zuerst.*
    at last *endlich.*
    at once *sofort.*
    at times *zuweillen, manchmal*
    (sometimes).
athlete *Athlet, m.*
athletics *Gymnastik, f.*
atmosphere *Atmosphäre, f.*
attach (to) *anhängen.*
attain (to) *erreichen.*
attempt (to) *versuchen.*
attend (to) *beiwohnen, besuchen* (school).
attendant *Gehilfe, m.*
attention *Aufmerksamkeit, f.*
attic *Dachkammer, f., Dachstube f.*
attitude *Haltung, f.; Einstellung, f.*
    (mental).
attorney *Anwalt, m.*
attract (to) *anziehen.*
attraction *Anziehung, f.*
attractive *schön, anziehend, reizend.*
audience *Zuhörer, pl, Zuhörerschaft f.;*
    Audienz, f.; Publikum n.
August *August, m.*
aunt *Tante, f.*
author *Autor, m.*
authority *Autorität, f.*
authorize (to) *ermächtigen.*
automatic *automatisch.*
automobile *Auto, n.*
autumn *Herbst, m.*
available *vorhanden, verfügbar, erhältlich.*
average *Durchschnitt, m.*
avoid (to) *vermeiden.*
awake *wach.*
awake (to) *wecken; erwachen* (oneself).
award *Belohnung, f.*

award (to) *zuerkennen, zusprechen, verleihen.*

aware *gewahr, bewusst.*

  I'm fully aware that ...   *Es ist mir völlig bewusst (klar), dass ...*

away *fort, weg.*

  to go away *weggehen.*

awful *furchtbar.*

awkward *ungeschickt.*

baby *Kind, n.*

back *Rücken* (noun, *m.*) (body); *zurück* (adv.).

background *Hintergrund, m.*

backwards *rückwärts.*

bacon *Speck, m.*

bad *schlecht.*

badge *Marke, f., Abzeichen, n.* (Verdienst); *Medaille f.* (military).

bag *Beutel, m., Tüte, f.* (paper bag).

baggage *Gepäck, n.*

baker *Bäcker, m.*

bakery *Bäckerei, f.*

balance *Gleichgewicht, n.*

balcony *Balkon, m.*

ball *Ball, m.*

balloon *Ballon, m.*

banana *Banane, f.*

band *Band, n.; Musikkapelle, f.*

bandage *Verband, m.*

banister *Treppengeländer, n.*

bank *Bank, f., Ufer, n.* (of a river).

bank note *Banknote, f.*

bankruptcy *Bankrott, m.; Konkurs, m.*

banquet *Bankett, n.; Festessen, n.*

bar *Bar, f.* (for drinks).

barber *Frisör, m.*

bare *bloss, bar, unbekleidet.*

barefoot *barfuss.*

barge *Barke, f. Lastschiff, n.*

barn *Scheune, f.*

barrel *Fass, n.*

barren *unfruchtbar.*

basin *Becken, n.*

basis *Grundlage, f.*

basket *Korb, n.*

bath *Bad, n.*

bathroom *Badezimmer, n.*

bathe (to) *baden.*

battle *Schlacht, f.; Kampf, m.*

bay *Bucht, f.*

be (to) *sein.*

  to be hungry *hungrig sein, Hunger haben.*

  to be right *Recht haben.*

  to be thirsty *Durst haben, durstig sein.*

  to be tired *müde sein.*

  to be wrong *Unrecht haben, im Unrecht sein.*

beach *Strand, m.*

bean *Bohne, f.*

bear (to) *aushalten.*

beard *Bart, m.*

beat (to) *schlagen.*

beautiful *schön, wunderschön.*

beauty *Schönheit, f.*

beauty parlor *Schönheitssalon, m.*

because *weil, denn* (for).

become (to) *werden.*

becoming *passend, vorteilhaft.*

bed *Bett, n.*

beef *Rindfleisch, n.*

beer *Bier, n.*

beet *Rübe, f.*

before *vor* (dat. or acc.); *bevor* (conj.).

beg (to) *betteln.*

beggar *Bettler, m.*

begin (to) *beginnen, anfangen.*

beginning *Anfang, f.*

behave (to) *sich betragen, sich benehmen.*

behavior *Verhalten, m.; Behnehmen, n.*

behind *hinter* (dat. or acc.).

belief *Glaube, m.*

believe (to) *glauben.*

bell *Glocke, f.*

belong (to) *gehören.*

below *unter* (dat. or acc.).

belt *Gürtel, m.*

bench *Bank, f.*

bend (to) *biegen.*

beneath *unten; unter* (dat. or acc.).

benefit *Vorteil, m.*

beside *neben* (dat. or acc.).

besides *ausserdem.*

best *beste (der, die, das)* (adj.); *am besten* (adv.).

bet *Wette, f.*

bet (to) *wetten.*

betray (to) *verraten.*

better *besser.*

between *zwischen* (dat. or acc.).

beware (to) *sich hüten.*

  Beware! *Achtung!*

beyond *jenseits* (gen.).

bicycle *Fahrrad, n.*

bid (to) *bieten; befehlen* (order).

big *gross.*

bill *Rechnung, f.*

  bill of fare *Speisekarte, f.*

billion *Milliarde f.* (Am.), *Billion.*

bind (to) *binden.*

bird *Vogel, m.*

birth *Geburt, f.*

birthday *Geburtstag, m.*

biscuit *Zwieback, m., Keks, m.*

bishop *Bischof, m.*

bit *Stück, n. Gibiss, n.* (horse).
bite *Biss, m.*
bite (to) *beissen.*
bitter *bitter.*
bitterness *Bitterkeit, f.*
black *schwarz. Schwarz* (person) *m. & f.*
blade *Klinge, f.* (razor); *Blatt, n.* (grass).
blame *Schuld, f.; Tadel, m.*
blame (to) *tadeln, rügen.*
blank *unbeschrieben* (page); *verwundert*
     (expression).
blanket *Decke, f.*
bleed (to) *bluten.*
bless (to) *segnen.*
blessing *Segnung, f.; Segen, m.*
blind *blind.*
block *Block, m.*
block (to) *versperren.*
blood *Blut, n.*
blotter *Löschpapier, n.*
blouse *Bluse, f.*
blow *Schlag, m.*
blow (to) *blasen; putzen* (nose).
blue *blau.*
blush (to) *erröten.*
board *Brett, n.* (plank); *Verpflegung, f.*
     (food).
boarding house *Pension, f.*
boarding pass *Bordkarte, f., Einsteigarte, f.*
boast (to) *prahlen.*
boat *Boot, n.*
body *Körper, m.*
boil (to) *kochen, sieden.*
boiler *Kessel, m., Heisswasserspeicher, m.*
bold *kühn.*
bomb *Bombe, f.*
     atom bomb. *Atombombe, f.*
bond *Aktie, f.* (stock).
bone *Knochen, m.*
book *Buch, n.*
bookseller *Buchhändler, m.*
bookstore *Buchhandlung, f.*
border *Grenze, f.*
boring *langweilig.*
born *geboren.*
borrow (to) *borgen, leihen.*
boss *Boss, m., Chef, m.*
both *beide.*
bother (to) *ärgern, plagen, bemühen.*
     Don't bother! `` *Bemühen Sie sich nicht!*
bottle *Flasche, f.*
bottle opener *Flaschenöffner, m.*
bottom *Boden, m.*
bounce (to) *aufspringen.*
bowl *Schale, f.*
box *Schachtel, f.*
boy *Junge, m.*
bracelet *Armband, n.*
braid *Borte, f.; Zopf, m.* (hair), *Haarflechte, f.*

brain *Gehirn, n.*
brake *Bremse, f.*
branch *Ast, m.* (tree); *Filiale, f.* (business).
brave *tapfer.*
brassiere *Büstenhalter, m.*
bread *Brot, n.*
break (to) *brechen; lösen* (engagement).
breakfast *Frühstück, n.*
     have breakfast   *frühstücken.*
breath *Atem, m.*
breathe (to) *atmen.*
breeze *Wind, m.; Brise, f.*
bribe (to) *bestechen.*
brick *Backstein, m.*
bride *Braut, f.*
     bridegroom   *Bräutigam, m.*
bridge *Brücke, f.*
brief *kurz.*
bright *hell, klar.*
brighten (to) *erheitern; sich aufklären*
     (weather).
brilliant *glänzend.*
bring (to) *bringen.*
bring up (to) *erziehen* (a person).
British *britisch.*
broad *weit, breit.*
broil (to) *braten.*
broken *zerbrochen.*
brook *Bach, m.*
broom *Besen, m.*
brother *Bruder, m.*
brother-in-law *Schwager, m.*
brown *braun.*
bruise (to) *quetschen, zerstossen.*
brush *Bürste, f.*
bubble *Blase, f.*
bucket *Eimer m.*
buckle *Schnalle, f.*
bud *Knospe, f.*
budget *Budget, n; Wirtschaft, f.* (house).
build (to) *bauen.*
building *Gebäude, n.*
bulletin *Bulletin, n., Bekanntmachung, f.;*
     Ansage, f.
bundle *Bündel, n.*
burn (to) *(ver)brennen.*
burst (to) *bersten; platzen.*
bus *Autobus, m. Omnibus, m.*
bush *Busch, m.*
business *Geschäft, n.*
businessman *Geschäftsmann, m.; Kaufmann,*
     m.; **businesswoman** *Geschäftsfrau, f.*
busy *beschäftigt.*
but *aber; sondern* (neg.).
butcher *Metzger, m.; Fleischer, m.*
butcher shop *Metzgerei, f.; Fleischerei, f.*
butter *Butter, f.*
button *Knopf, m.*
buy (to) *kaufen.*

buyer *Käufer, m.*

by *von* (dat.); *durch* (acc.); *neben* (dat. & acc.) (close to); *um* (acc.) (time).

byte *Byte, m.*

C

cab *Taxi, n.*

cabbage *Kohl, m.; Kraut, n.*

cable *Kabel, n.*

cage *Käfig, m.*

cake *Kuchen, m.*

calendar *Kalender, m.*

calf *Kalb, n.*

call *Ruf, m.; Anruf* (telephone) *m.*

call (to) *rufen; anrufen; telefonieren* (telephone); *heissen* (name).

calm *ruhig.*

camera *Kamera, f.; Fotoapparat m.*

camp *Lager, n.*

camp (to) *lagern, zelten.*

can *Büchse, f.; Dose, f.*

can (to be able) *können.*

can opener *Büchsenöffner, m.*

cancel (to) *rückgängig machen, absagen, annulieren* (annul), *durchstreichen.*

candidate *Kandidat, m.*

candle *Kerze, f.*

candy *Bonbons, pl.*

cap *Mütze, f.*

capital *Haupstadt, f.* (city); *Kapital, n.* (finance).

capital punishment *Toddesstrafe* (death penalty), *f.*

capricious *launisch; eigensinning* (temperamental).

captain *Hauptmann, n.* (army); *Kapitän, m.* (navy).

captive *Gefangene, m.*

capture (to) *fangen; einnehmen.*

car *Wagen, m., Auto, n.*

carbon paper *Durchschlagpapier, n.*

card *Karte, f.; Ausweis* (I.D.) *m.*

care *Sorge, f.* (anxiety); *Sorgfalt, f.* (caution).

  care of   *per Adresse*

  take care of   *pflegen*

care (to) *sich sorgen.*

  care about   *sich kümmern um*

  care for (to like)   *gern haben.*

  I don't care.   *Das ist mir gleich.*

career *Laufbahn, f.; Karriere, f.*

careful *vorsichtig, sorgfältig.*

careless *nachlässig, sorglos.*

caress *Liebkosung, f.*

carpenter *Zimmermann, m.*

carpet *Teppich, m.*

carry (to) *tragen.*

carve (to) *schnitzen.*

case *Fall, m.; Aktentasche, f.*

  in case   *im Falle, falls*

cash *Bargeld, n.*

  to pay cash   *bar zahlen.*

cash (to) *einlösen, kassieren.*

cashier *Kassierer, m.*

cassette *Kassette, f.*

  cassette tape deck   *Kassettendeck, n.*

castle *Schloss, n.*

cat *Katze, f.*

catch (to) *fangen.*

category *Kategorie, f.*

cathedral *Dom, m.*

Catholic *katholisch.*

cattle *Vieh, n.*

cause *Grund, m.; Ursache, f.*

cause (to) *verursachen.*

cease (to) *aufhören.*

ceiling *Decke, f.*

celebrate (to) *feiern.*

cellar *Keller, m.*

cement *Zement, m.*

cemetery *Friedhof, m.*

censorship *Zensur, f.*

center *Zentrum, n.; Mittelpunkt, m.*

central *zentral.*

central heating *Zentralheizung, f.*

century *Jahrhundert, n.*

cereal *Getreide, n.* (grain); *Mehlspeise, f.* (prepared).

ceremony *Zeremonie, f.*

certain *gewiss, sicher.*

certainty *Gewissheit, f.; Sicherheit, f.*

certificate *Zeugnis, n.; Zertifikat, n.*

chain *Kette, f.*

chair *Stuhl, m.*

chairman (-woman) *Vorsitzende, m.* (f) *Präsident, m.*

chalk *Kreide, f.*

challenge *Herausforderung, f.; Aufforderung, f.*

challenge (to) *herausfordern.*

champion *Meister, m.*

  world champion   *Weltmeister, m.*

chance *Zufall, m.*

change *Veränderung, f.; Kleingeld, n.* (money).

change (to) *ändern; wechseln* (money).

chapel *Kapelle, f.*

chapter *Kapitel, n.*

character *Charakter, m.*

characteristic *charakteristisch.*

charge (to) *beladen; berechnen* (price); *anklagen* (law).

charitable *wohltätig.*

charity *Wohltätigkeit, f. Nächstenliebe, f.*

charming *reizend.*

chase (to) *jagen.*

chat (to) *plaudern.*
cheap *billig.*
cheat (to) *betrügen.*
check *Scheck, m.; Rechnung, f.* (in a restaurant).
check (to) *knotrolliern; aufgeben, nachprüfen* (baggage).
cheek *Wange, f.*
cheer (to) *aufheitern.*
cheerful *heiter, freudig, fröhlich.*
cheese *Käse, m.*
chemical *chemisch.*
cherish (to) *schätzen.*
cherry *Kirsche, f.*
chest *Brust, f.; Kiste, f.* (box).
    chest of drawers *Kommode, f.*
chestnut *Kastanie, f.*
chew (to) *kauen.*
chicken *Huhn, n.; Hühnchen, n., Huhn, n.*
chief *Leiter, m., Vorgesetzte(r) m.; chef, m.*
chief (adj.) *haupt-.*
chime *Glockenspiel,n.*
chimney *Schornstein, m.*
chin *Kinn, n.*
china *Porzellan, n.*
chip *Span, m.; Splitter, m.*
chocolate *Schokolade, f.*
choice *Wahl, f.*
choir *Chor, m.*
choke (to) *ersticken.*
choose (to) *auswählen.*
chop *Kotelett, n.*
Christian *Christ* (noun) *m.; christlich* (adj.).
Christmas *Weihnachten, f. pl.*
church *Kirche, f.*
cigar *Zigarre, f.*
cigarette *Zigarette, f.*
circle *Kreis, m.*
circular *rund.*
circulate (to) *kreisen, umlaufen.*
circumstances *Umstände, pl.*
citizen *Bürger, m.*
city *Stadt, f.*
city hall *Rathaus, m.*
civil *zivil, bürgerlich.*
civilization *Zivilisation, f.*
civilize (to) *zivilisieren.*
claim *Forderung, f; Rechtsanspruch, m.*
claim (to) *fordern.*
clamor *Geschrei, n.*
clap (to) *klatschen.*
class *Klasse, f.; Kategorie, f.*
classify (to) *klassifizieren.*
clause *Klausel, f.; Satzglied, m.*
clean *rein, sauber.*
clean (to) *reinigen.*
cleaners *Reinigungsanstalt, f.*
cleanliness *Reinlichkeit, f.; Sauberkeit, f.*
clear *klar.*

clerk *Angestellte, m.*
clever *klug, schlau.*
climate *Klima, n.*
climb (to) *steigen* (stairway)*; besteigen* (mountain).
clip *Klammer, f.*
clip (to) *beschneiden* (cut)*; scheren zusammenfügen* (attach)*; festhalten.*
clock *Uhr, f.*
close *nahe.*
close (to) *zumachen, schliessen.*
closed *geschlossen.*
closet *Schrank, m.*
cloth *Tuch, n.*
clothes *Kleider, pl.*
cloud *Wolke, f.*
cloudy *bewölkt.*
clover *Klee, m.*
club *Klub, m.; Kreuz* (cards).
coal *Kohle, f.*
coarse *roh.*
coast *Küste, f.*
coat *Mantel, m.* (overcoat)*; Anzug, m.* (suit).
code *Gesetzbuch, n.* (law)*; Kodex, m.*
coffee *Kaffee, m.*
coffin *Sarg, m.*
coin *Münze, f.*
cold *kalt.*
coldness *Kälte, f.*
collaborate (to) *zusammenarbeiten.*
collar *Kragen, m.; Halsband, n.* (dog).
collect (to) *sammeln.*
collection *Sammlung, f.*
collective *gesamt.*
college *Universität, f.*
colonial *kolonial.*
colony *Kolonie, f.*
color *Farbe, f.*
color (to) *färben.*
column *Spalte, fl., Kollonne, f.* (military)*; Säule, f.* (arch).
comb *Kamm, m.*
comb (to) *kämmen.*
combination *Verbindung, f.; Zusammenstellung, f.; Verknüpfung, f.*
combine (to) *verbinden, zusammenstellen.*
come (to) *kommen.*
    come back *zurückkommen.*
comedy *Komödie, f.*
comet *Komet, m., Schweifstern, m.*
comfort *Behaglichkeit, f.; Trost, m.* (moral).
comfort (to) *trösten.*
comfortable *bequem.*
comma *Komma, n.*
command *Befehl, m.*
command (to) *befehlen.*
commander *Befehlshaber, m.*
commercial *geschäftsmässig, handelsüblich; Fernsehwerbung, f.* (TV commercial).

commission *Kommission, f.*
commit (to) *begehen.*
common *gemein, gewöhnlich.*
Commonwealth of Independent States *das Commonwealth Unabhängiger Nationen, n.*
communicate (to) *mitteilen.*
communication *Mitteilung, f.*
community *Gemeinde, f.*
compact disc (CD) *Compact Disc, f.; Kompaktplatte, f.*
companion *Genosse, m.*
company *Gesellschaft, f.* (social); *Kompanie, f.* (military).
compare (to) *vergleichen.*
comparison *Vergleich, m.*
compel *zwingen, nötigen.*
compete (to) *konkurrieren.*
competition *Konkurrenz, f.; Tournier, n.* (sports), *Wettbewerb, n.* (sports).
complain (to) *sich beklagen.*
complaint *Klage, f.*
complete *vollenden.*
complex *Komplex,* (noun) *m.; verwickelt* (adj.); *kompliziert* (adj.).
complexion *Gesichtsfarbe, f.*
complicate (to) *verwickeln, komplizieren.*
complicated *verwickelt, kompliziert.*
compliment *Kompliment, n.*
compose (to) *komponieren.*
composer *Komponist, m.*
composition *Komposition, f.*
compromise *Kompromiss, m.; Vergleich, m.*
compromise (to) *einen Kompromiss machen, kompromittieren.*
computer *Computer, m.*
conceit *Einbildung, f.*
conceited *eingebildet.*
conceive (to) *ersinnen, ausdenken, schwanger werden* (med.).
concentrate (to) *konzentrieren.*
concern *Angelegenheit, f.* (matter); *Sorge, f.* (anxiety); *Geschäft, n.* (business).
concern (to) *betreffen.*
concert *Konzert, n.*
concrete *konkret, wesenhaft.*
condemn (to) *verurteilen, verdammen.*
condense (to) *kondensieren.*
condition *Zustand, m.*
conduct *Benehmen, n.*
conduct (to) *führen; dirigieren* (music).
conductor *Führer, m.* (guide); *Schaffner, m.* (vehicle); *Dirigent, m.* (music).
confess (to) *gestehen; beichten* (church).
confession *Geständnis, n.; Beichte, f.* (church).
confidence *Vertrauen, n.*
confident *vertrauend, vertrauensvoll.*
confidential *vertraulich, geheim.*
confirm (to) *bestätigen.*

confirmation *Bestätigung, f.*
congratulate (to) *gratulieren.*
congratulations *Glückwunsch, m.*
connect (to) *verbinden.*
connection *Verbindung, f.*
conquer (to) *erobern, besiegen.*
conquest *Eroberung, f.; Sieg, m.*
conscience *Gewissen, n.*
conscientious *gewissenhaft.*
conscious *bewusst.*
consent *Einwilligung, f.; Genehmigung, f.*
conservative *konservativ.*
consider (to) *betrachten* (look); *bedenken* (think).
considerable *beträchtlich, bedeutend.*
consideration *Betrachtung, f.*
consist of (to) *bestehen aus* (dat.).
consistent *übereinstimmend, fest, dicht.*
constant *beständig.*
constitution *Verfassung, f.; Gesundheit, f.* (health).
constitutional *verfassungsmässig.*
consul *Konsul, m.*
contagious *ansteckend.*
contain (to) *enthalten.*
container *Behälter, m.*
contemporary *Zeitgenosse* (noun) *m.; zeitgenössisch* (adj.).
content *zufrieden.*
content (to) *befriedigen.*
contents *Inhalt, m.; Gehalt, m.*
continent *Kontinent, m.*
continual *fortwährend.*
continue (to) *fortfahren.*
contract *Vertrag, m.*
contractor *Unternehmer, m.*
contradict (to) *widersprechen.*
contradiction *Widerspruch, m.*
contradictory *widersprechend.*
contrary *Gegenteil* (noun) *n.; entgegengesetzt* (adj.).
on the contrary *im Gegenteil.*
contrast *Gegensatz, m.*
contrast (to) *vergleichen, gegenüberstellen.*
contribute (to) *beitragen.*
contribution *Beitrag, m.*
control *Kontrolle, f.*
control (to) *kontrollieren.*
controversy *Meinungsverschiedenheit, f.; Kontroverse, f.; Angemessenheit, f.*
convenience *Bequemlichkeit, f.*
convenient *passend; bequem* (practical).
convent *Kloster, n.*
convention *Versammlung, f.*
conversation *Gespräch, n.; Unterhaltung, f.*
converse (to) *sich unterhalten.*
convert (to) *umwandeln einlösen* (bonds).
convict (to) *verurteilen.*
conviction *Verurteilung, f.*

convince (to) *überzeugen.*
cook *Koch, m.; Köchin, f.*
cook (to) *kochen.*
cool *kühl.*
cool (to) *kühlen.*
copy *Kopie, f.*
cork *Kork(en) m.; Stöpsel, m.*
corkscrew *Korkenzieher, m.*
corn *Mais, m.*
corner *Ecke, f.*
corporation *Körperschaft, f., Korporation, f.*
correct *richtig.*
correct (to) *berichtigen, korrigieren.*
correction *Verbesserung, f., Berichtigung, f.*
correspond (to) *korrespondieren.*
correspondence *Briefwechsel, m.*
correspondent *Korrespondent, m.*
corresponding *entsprechend.*
corrupt (to) *verderben.*
corruption *Verdorbenheit, f.*
cost *Kosten, f.*
costume *Kostüm, n.*
cottage *Häuschen, n.*
cotton *Baumwolle, f.; Watte, f. (pharmacy).*
couch *Sofa, n., Couch, f.*
cough *Husten, m.*
count *Graf, m. (nobility); Zählung, f.*
count (to) *zählen.*
counter *Ladentisch, m.*
countess *Gräfin, f.*
countless *zahllos.*
country *Land, n.; Vaterland, n. (fatherland).*
countryman *Landsmann, m.*
couple *Paar, n.*
coupon *Coupon, Kupon, m.*
courage *Mut, m.*
course *Lauf, m. (direction); Kursus, m.*
  (studies), *Verlauf, m. (illness).*
court *Gericht, n.*
courteous *zuvorkommend.*
courtesy *Höflichkeit, f.*
courtyard *Hof, m., Spielplatz, m.*
cousin *Vetter, m.; Cousine, f.*
cover *Decke, f.*
cow *Kuh, f.*
crack *Riss, m.*
crack (to) *knacken.*
cradle *Wiege, f.*
crash *Zusammenbruch, m., Absturz, m.*
  (plane); *Zusammenstoss, m. (auto).*
crazy *verrückt.*
cream *Sahne, f., Rahm, m.*
create (to) *schaffen*
creature *Geschöpf, n.; Wesen, n.*
credit *Kredit, m.*
creditor *Gläubiger, m.*
crime *Verbrechen, n.*
crisis *Krise, f.*
crisp *knusperig.*

critic *Kritiker, m.*
critical *kritisch.*
criticize (to) *kritisieren.*
crooked *krumm.*
crop *Ernte, f.*
cross *Kreuz, n.*
crossing *Übergang, m.*
crossroad *Strassenkreuzung, f., Kreuzweg, m.*
crouch (to) *hocken.*
crow *Krähe, f.*
crowd *Menge, f.; Gedränge, n.*
crowd (to) *überfüllen, zusammendrängen.*
crowded *überfüllt, wimmelnd.*
crown *Krone, f.*
crown (to) *krönen.*
cruel *grausam, unmenschlich.*
cruelty *Grausamkeit, f.*
crumb *Krume, f., Krümchen, m. Krümel, m.*
crumble (to) *zerbröckeln.*
crust *Kruste, f.*
crutch *Krücke, f.*
cry *Ruf, m.; Geschrei, n.*
cry (to) *weinen (weep); schreien (shout).*
cuff *Manschette, f.*
cunning *listig, verschmitzt, verschlagen.*
cup *Tasse, f.*
cure *Heilung, f.*
curiosity *Neugier, f.*
curious *neugierig.*
curl *Locke, f.*
current *Strom (noun) m.; laufend (adj.),*
  jetzig (adj.), gegenwärtig.
curtain *Vorhang, m., Gardine, f.*
curve *Kurve, f.*
cushion *Kissen, n.*
custom *Sitte, f.*
customary *gebräuchlich.*
customer *Kunde, m. (-in), f.*
customshouse *Zollamt, n.*
customs official *Zollbeamte, m.*
cut *Schnitt, m.*
cut (to) *schneiden.*

D

dagger *Dolch, m.*
daily *täglich.*
dainty *zierlich.*
dairy *Milchgeschäft, n.*
dam *Damm, m., Deich, m.*
damage *Schaden, m.*
damage (to) *beschädigen.*
damp *feucht.*
dance *Tanz, m.*
dance (to) *tanzen.*
danger *Gefahr, f.*
dangerous *gefährlich.*
dark *dunkel.*

darkness *Dunkelheit, f.*

dash (to) *sich beeilen, bespritzen* (water),
    losstürzen (auf).

data processing *Datenverarbeitung f.*

date *Datum, n.; Verabredung, f.* (meeting).

daughter *Tochter, f.*

dawn *Morgendämmerung, f.*

day *Tag, m.*

  day after tomorrow *übermorgen.*

  day before yesterday *vorgestern.*

  yesterday *gestern.*

dazzle (to) *blenden, verblüffen.*

dead *tot.*

deaf *taub.*

deal *Teil, m.; Geschäft, n.* (business).

  a great deal of *sehr viel*

  to strike up a deal with

      someone *jemandem ein Geschäft*

      machen

  it's a deal (coll.) *abgemacht!*

  big deal! *gross Wichtigkeit!* (coll.)

deal (to) *ausgeben* (cards), *verteilen,*
    zuteilen, handeln (mit).

dealer *Händler, m.; Geber, m.* (cards).

dear *lieb; teuer* (also expensive).

death *Tod, m.*

debate *Debatte, f., Verhandlung, f.*

debt *Schuld, f.*

debtor *Schuldner, m.*

decanter *Karaffe, f.*

decay *Verfall, m.* (ruin); *Fäulnis, f.* (rot).

decay (to) *verfallen, verfaulen.*

deceased *verstorben.*

deceit *Falschheit, f.*

deceive (to) *betrügen.*

December *Dezember, m.*

decent *anständig.*

decide (to) *entscheiden.*

decided *entschieden.*

decision *Entscheidung, f.; Entschluss, m.*

decisive *entscheidend.*

deck *Deck, n.*

declare (to) *erklären.*

decline *Untergang, m. Fall, m.*

decline (to) *verfallen, abweisen; deklinieren*
  (grammar); *untergehen.*

decrease *Abnahme, f.; Verminderung, f.*

decrease (to) *abnehmen, vermindern.*

decree *Verordnung, f.*

dedicate (to) *widmen.*

deed *Tat, f.*

deep *tief.*

deer *Hirsch, m.*

defeat *Niederlage, f.*

defeat (to) *besiegen.*

defect *Fehler, m.*

defend (to) *verteidigen.*

defense *Verteidigung, f.*

defiance *Trotz, m.*

define (to) *definieren.*

definite *bestimmt.*

defy (to) *trotzen.*

degree *Grad, m.*

delay *Verzögerung, f.*

delay (to) *aufhalten.*

delegate *Delegierte(r), m.,*
      Bevollmächtigte(r), m.

delegate (to) *delegieren.*

deliberate (to) *erwägen.*

deliberately *absichtlich.*

delicacy *Delikatesse, f.; Leckerbissen, m.*

delicate *zart.*

delicious *köstlich.*

delight *Freude, f.; Vergnügen, n.*

delighted *erfreut.*

deliver (to) *liefern.*

deliverance *Befreiung, f.*

delivery *Ablieferung, f.; Abgabe, f.*

demand *Forderung, f.; Nachfrage, f.*
    (business); *Verlangen, n.*

demand (to) *fordern.*

democracy *Demokratie, f.*

demonstrate (to) *demonstrieren.*

demonstration *Darlegung, f.; Demonstration,*
    f. (political).

denial *Verleugnung, f.*

denounce (to) *denunzieren, offentlich*
    anklagen.

dense *dicht.*

density *Dichte, f.*

dentist *Zahnarzt, m.*

deny (to) *ableugnen, verleugnen.*

departure *Abreise, f.*

department *Abteilung, f.*

depend (to) *abhängen.*

dependent *abhängig.*

deplore (to) *bedauern, beweinen.*

deposit *Anzahlung, f.*

depreciation *Wertminderung, f.*

depress (to) *niederdrücken.*

depression *Depression, f.*

deprive (to) *berauben, entziehen.*

depth *Tiefe, f.*

deride (to) *verlachen, verhöhnen.*

derive (to) *ableiten.*

descend (to) *abstammen.*

descendant *Nachkomme, m; Abkömmling, m.*

descent *Abstieg, m.; Abstammung, f.* (family).

describe (to) *beschreiben.*

description *Beschreibung, f.*

desert *Wüste, f.*

desert (to) *verlassen.*

deserve (to) *verdienen.*

design *Zeichnung, f.* (drawing); *Absicht, f.*
    (intention).

designer *Zeichner, m.*

desirable *wünschenswert.*

desire (to) *wünschen.*

desire *Wunsch, m.*
desirous *begierig.*
desk *Pult, n.*
desolate *trostlos.*
despair *Verzweiflung, f.*
despair (to) *verzweifeln.*
desperate *verzweifelt.*
despise (to) *verachten.*
despite *trotz* (gen.).
dessert *Nachtisch, m.*
destiny *Schicksal, n.*
destroy (to) *zerstören.*
destruction *Zerstörung, f.*
detach (to) *ablösen, freimachen*
detail *Einzelheit, f.*
detain (to) *aufhalten.*
detect (to) *entdecken, aufdecken* (crime).
detective *Detektiv, m.*
detective story *Kriminalgeschichte, f.;*
    Detektivroman, m.
determination *Entschlossenheit, f.*
determine (to) *bestimmen.*
detest (to) *verabscheuen.*
detour *Umweg, m.*
detract (to) *abziehen, entziehen, vermindern.*
detrimental *schädlich.*
develop (to) *entwickeln.*
development *Entwicklung, f.*
device *Kunstgriff, m; Gerät, n.*
devil *Teufel, m.*
devise (to) *ersinnen, ausdenken.*
devoid *ohne* (acc.), *bar* (gen.).
devote (to) *widmen*
devour (to) *verschlingen, verzehren.*
dew *Tau, m.*
dial *Zifferblatt, n.* (clock); *Wähler, m.*
    (phone).
dial (to) *wählen.*
dialect *Dialekt, m.*
dialogue *Dialog, m.*
diameter *Durchmesser, m.*
diamond *Diamant, m.*
diary *Tagebuch, n.*
dictate (to) *diktieren.*
dictation *Diktat, n.*
dictionary *Wörterbuch, n.; Lexikon, n.*
die (to) *sterben.*
diet *Diät, f.*
differ (to) *sich unterscheiden.*
difference *Unterschied, m.*
different *verschieden.*
difficult *schwierig.*
difficulty *Schwierigkeit, f.*
dig (to) *graben.*
digest (to) *verdauen.*
dignity *Würde, f.*
dim *trübe.*
dimension *Dimension, f.; Mass, n.;*
    Ausmass, n.

diminish (to) *vermindern.*
dining room *Speisesaal, m.*
dinner *Abendessen, n.*
dine (to) *essen, speisen.*
dip (to) *senken, (ein)tauchen.*
diplomacy *Diplomatie, f.*
diplomat *Diplomat, m.*
direct *direkt.*
direct (to) *den Weg zeigen* (show the way).
direction *Richtung, f.*
director *Direktor, m.*
directory *Adressbuch, n.; Telefonbuch*
    (phone), *n.*
dirt *Schmutz, m.*
dirty *schmutzig.*
disability *Unfähigkeit, f.;*
    Körperbehinderung, f.
disabled *unfähig, behindert.*
disadvantage *Nachteil, m.*
disagree (to) *uneinig sein, nicht zustimmen.*
disagreeable *unangenehm.*
disagreement *Meinungsverschiedenheit, f.*
disappear (to) *verschwinden.*
disappearance *Verschwinden, n.*
disappoint (to) *enttäuschen.*
disapprove (to) *missbilligen, ablehnen.*
disaster *Unglück, n.; Katastrophe, f.*
disastrous *unheilvoll, schrecklich.*
discharge *Entlassung, f.* (dismissal);
    Abfeuern, n. (gun).
discharge (to) *entlassen* (person); *abfeuern*
    (firearm), *abschiessen* (firearm).
discipline *Zucht, f., Disziplin, f.*
disclaim (to) *bestreiten.*
disclose (to) *enthüllen, offenbaren.*
disclosure *Enthüllung, f. Mitteilung f.,*
    Offenbarung, f.
discomfort *Unbehaglichkeit, f.*
disconnect (to) *trennen, abschalten.*
discontent *unzufrieden.*
discontinue (to) *aufhören.*
discord *Zwietracht, f.*
discount *Diskonto, m.* (financial); *Rabatt, m.*
discourage (to) *entmutigen.*
discouragement *Entmutigung, f.*
discover (to) *entdecken.*
discovery *Entdeckung, f.*
discreet *diskret, vorsichtig.*
discretion *Besonnenheit, f.; Urteil, n.*
discuss (to) *besprechen, sich unterhalten*
    (*über*)
discussion *Besprechung, f.; Diskussion, f.*
disdain *Verachtung, f.*
disdain (to) *verschmähen, verachten.*
disease *Krankheit, f.*
disgrace *Schande, f.* (shame); *Ungnade, f.*
disguise *Verkleidung, f.*
disguise (to) *verkleiden.*
disgust *Ekel, m., Abscheu, m.*

disgust (to) (*an*)*ekeln.*
disgusted *ekelhaft, angeekelt.*
dish *Speise, f.* (food); *Teller, m.* (plate).
dishonest *unehrlich.*
disk *Scheibe, f.*
diskette *Diskette, f.*
dislike *Widerwille, m., Abneigung, f., der Widerwille, m.*
dislike (to) *nicht mögen, nicht lieben.*
dismiss (to) *entlassen.*
   dismissal   *Entlassung, f.*
disobey (to) *nicht gehorchen.*
disorder *Unordung, f.*
dispense (to) *verteilen.*
displace *verschieben, verrücken, verdrängen.*
display *Entfaltung f.* (unfold); *Schau, f.* (exposition).
displease (to) *missfallen, missachten.*
displeasure *Missfallen, n.*
disposal *Verfügung, f.*
dispose (to) *anordnen, verfügen.*
dispute *Streit, m.*
dispute (to) *streiten.*
dissolve (to) *auflösen.*
distance *Entfernung, f.*
distant *entfernt.*
distinct *deutlich.*
distinction *Auszeichnung, f.; Unterschied, m.* (difference).
distinguish (to) *unterscheiden.*
distort (to) *verdrehen.*
distract (to) *verwirren, ablenken.*
distress *Not, f.*
distress (to) *betrüben, beunruhigen.*
distribute (to) *verteilen.*
district *Distrikt, m.*
distrust *Misstrauen, n.*
distrust (to) *misstrauen.*
disturb (to) *stören.*
disturbance *Störung, f.*
ditch *Graben, m.*
dive (to) *tauchen.*
divide (to) *verteilen.*
divine *göttlich.*
division *Teilung, f.; Trennung, f.*
divorce (to) *scheiden.*
divorced *geschieden.*
dizziness *Schwindel, m.*
dizzy *schwindlig.*
do (to) *tun, machen.*
dock *Dock, n.; Anlegeplatz, m.*
doctor *Arzt, m.*
doctrine *Lehre, f.*
document *Urkunde, f. Dokument, n.*
dog *Hund, m.*
doll *Puppe, f.*
dome *Kuppel, f.*
domestic *häuslich; einheimisch* (native).
domestic animal *Haustier, n.*

dominate (to) *beherrschen.*
door *Tür, f.*
dose *Dosis, f.*
dot *Punkt, m.*
double *doppelt.*
doubt *Zweifel, m.*
doubt (to) *zweifeln.*
doubtful *zweifelhaft.*
doubtless *ohne Zweifel.*
dough *Teig, m.*
down *unter* (dat. or acc.); *hinunter, herunter.*
dozen *Dutzend, n.*
draft *Weichsel, m.* (money); *Zeichnung, f.* (drawing); *draft Zug, m.* (air); *ziehen, n.* (milit.); *Bier vom Fass* (beer), *n.*
drag (to) *schleppen.*
drain (to) *entwässern abfliessen lassen.*
drama *Drama, n.*
draw (to) *zeichen.*
draw back (to) *schleppen.*
drawer *Schublade, f.*
drawing-room *Gesellschaftszimmer, n.; Salon, m.; Wohnzimmer, n.*
dread *Furcht, f.*
dread (to) *fürchten.*
dreadful *furchtbar, schrecklich.*
dream *Traum, m.*
dream (to) *träumen.*
dreamer *Träumer, m.*
dress *Kleid, n.*
dress (to) *sich anziehen.*
dressmaker *Schneiderin, f.*
drink *Getränk, n.*
drink (to) *trinken.*
drip (to) *tropfen, tröpfeln.*
drive (to) *fahren.*
drive (computer) *Laufwerk, n.*
driver *Chauffeur, m.*
drop *Fall, m.; Tropfen, m.* (liquid).
drown (to) *ertrinken.*
drug *Droge, f.*
drug addiction *Rauschgiftsucht, f.*
drug dealer *Drogenhändler, m.; Pusher, m.* (coll.).
drugstore *Apotheke, f.; Drogerie, f.*
drum *Trommel, f.*
drunk *betrunken.*
dry *trocken.*
dry (to) *trocknen.*
dryness *Trockenheit, f.*
duchess *Herzogin, f.*
duck *Ente, f.*
due *Verfallszeit, f.; Fälligkeitstermin* (due date), *fallig sein* (to be due).
duke *Herzog, m.*
dull *trüble* (weather); *matt* (color); *dumpf* (sound), *fad(e)* (book).
dumb *stumm; dumm* (stupid).

deaf and dumb *taubstumm.*
during *während* (gen.).
dust *Staub, m.*
dust (to) *abstauben; ausbürsten* (clothes).
dusty *staubig.*
Dutch *holländisch.*
duty *Pflicht, f.; Dienst, m.* (service); *Zoll, m.* (customs).
dwarf *Zwerg, m.*
dwell (to) *wohnen.*
dye *Farbe, f.*
dye (to) *färben.*

E

each *jeder.*
  each other *einander.*
  each time *jedesmal.*
eager *eifrig.*
eagle *Adler, m.*
ear *Ohr, n.*
early *früh.*
earn (to) *verdienen.*
earnest *ernst.*
earth *Erde, f.*
ease *Bequemlichkeit, f.* (comfort); *Ruhe, f.* (calm); *Linderung, f.* (relief); *Leichtigkeit, f.* (facility).
ease (to) *lindern, erleichtern.*
easily *leicht.*
east *Osten, m.*
Easter *Ostern, pl.*
eastern *östlich.*
easy *leicht.*
eat (to) *essen.*
echo *Echo, n.; Widerhall, m.*
echo (to) *widerhallen.*
economical *wirtschaftlich; sparsam.*
economize (to) *sparen.*
economy *Sparsamkeit, f.; Wirtschaft, f.* (of a country).
economy class *Touristenklasse, f.*
edge *Schneide, f.* (blade); *Rand, m.* (rim); *Kante, f.; Vorteil* (advantage), *f.*
edition *Ausgabe, f.; Auflage, f.*
editor *Redakteur, m.*
editorial *Leitartikel* (noun) *m.; redaktionell* (adj.).
education *Bildung, f.; Erziehung, f.*
effect *Wirkung, f.*
effective *wirkungsvoll.*
efficiency *Leistungsfähigkeit, f.*
effort *Anstrengung, f.; Bestreben, n.* (endeavor).
egg *Ei, n.* (*Eier,* pl.).
egoism *Egoismus, m.; Selbstsucht, f.*
eight *acht.*
eighteen *achtzehn.*

eighteenth *achtzehnt.*
eighth *achte, m. f.*
eightieth *achtzigste, m.f.*
eighty *achtzig.*
either *oder.*
  either ... or *entweder ... oder.*
elastic *elastisch.*
elbow *Ellbogen, m.*
elder *älter.*
elderly *älterer, ältlich.*
eldest *Älteste, m. & f.*
elect (to) *erwählen.*
election *Wahl, f.*
elector *Wähler, m.*
electrical *elektrisch.*
electricity *Elektrizität, f.*
elegant *elegant.*
element *Element, n.*
elementary *elementar.*
elephant *Elefant, m.*
elevator *Aufzug, m.; Fahrstuhl, m.*
eleven *elf.*
eleventh *elfte.*
eliminate (to) *ausscheiden, beseitigen.*
eloquence *Beredsamkeit, f.; Redegabe, f.*
eloquent *beredt, redegewandt.*
else *ander, anders; sonst* (otherwise).
  anyone else *irgend ein anderer.*
  elsewhere *anderswo.*
  everybody else *jeder andere.*
  nobody else *sonst niemand.*
  someone else *ein anderer.*
elude (to) *ausweichen, entgehen.*
embark (to) *(sich) einschiffen.*
embarrass (to) *in Verlegenheit bringen.*
embarrassing *unangenehm, beschämend.*
embarrassment *Verlegenheit, f.*
embassy *Botschaft, f.*
embody *verkörpern.*
embrace (to) *umarmen.*
embroidery *Stickerei, f.*
emerge (to) *herauskommen, hervortreten.*
emergency *Notfall, m.*
eminent *hervorragend.*
emotion *Erregung, f.; Rührung, f.*
emperor *Kaiser, m.*
emphasis *Betonung, f.*
emphasize (to) *betonen.*
emphatic *nachdrücklich.*
empire *Reich, n.*
employee *Angestellte, m. or f.*
employer *Arbeitgeber, m.*
employment *Arbeit, f.; Beschäftigung, f.; Tätigkeit, f.*
empty *leer.*
enable (to) *befähigen.*
enamel *Email, n.; Emaille, f.*
enclose (to) *einschliessen.*

enclosure *Anlage, f.* (letter); *Einzäunung, f.* (fence).

encourage (to) *ermutigen.*

encouragement *Ermutigung, f.*

end *Ende, n.*

end (to) *enden, aufhören.*

endeavor *Bestreben, n.; Bemühung, f.*

endeavor (to) *such bemühen.*

endorse (to) *unterzeichnen* (a check), *gutheissen.*

endure (to) *ertragen, aushalten.*

enemy *Feind, m.*

energy *Energie, f.*

energy crisis *Energiekrise, f.*

enforce (to) *durchsetzen.*

engage (to) *anstellen.*

engaged *beschäftigt* (busy); *verlobt.*

engagement *Verpflichtung, f.* (appointment); *Beschäftigung, f.* (business); *Verlobung, f.* (marriage).

engine *Maschine, f.; Lokomotive, f.* (train).

engineer *Ingenieur, m.*

English *englisch.*

engrave (to) *eingravieren.*

enjoy (to) *geniessen, amüsieren.*

   enjoy oneself *sich amüsieren.*

enjoyment *Vergnügen, n.*

enlarge (to) *vergrössern.*

enlist (to) *sich freiwillig melden* (military); *anwerben* (soldiers); *Dienste in Anspruch nehmen* (one's services).

enormous *ungeheuer.*

enough *genug.*

enter (to) *hineingehen.*

   Enter! *Herein!*

entertain (to) *unterhalten.*

entertainment *Unterhaltung, f., Schau, f.* (show).

enthusiasm *Begeisterung, f.*

enthusiastic *begeistert.*

entire *ganz.*

entitle (to) *berechtigen.*

entrance *Eingang, m.*

entrust (to) *anvertrauen.*

enumerate (to) *aufzählen.*

envelope *Umschlag, m.; Kuvert, n.*

envious *neidisch.*

envy *Neid, m.*

envy (to) *beneiden.*

episode *Episode, f.; Nebenhandlung, f.*

equal *gleich.*

equal (to) *gleichen.*

equality *Gleichheit, f.; Gleichberechtigung, f.* (pol.).

equator *Äquator, m.*

equilibrium *Gleichgewicht, n.*

equip (to) *ausrüsten.*

equipmeat *Ausrüstung, f.*

era *Zeitalter, n.*

erase (to) *ausstreichen, ausradieren.*

eraser *Gummi, m.*

erect (to) *errichten.*

err (to) *sich irren.*

errand *Auftrag, m.*

error *Irrtum, m.*

escalator *Rolltreppe, f.*

escape *Flucht, f.*

escape (to) *entlaufen.*

escort (to) *begleiten, eskortieren.*

especially *besonders.*

essay *Aufsatz, m.*

essence *Essenz, f.* (extract); *Wesen, n.*

essential *wesentlich.*

establish (to) *errichten, gründen.*

establishment *Gründung, f.*

estate *Vermögen, n.* (wealth); *Gut, n.* (land).

esteem *Achtung, f.*

esteem (to) *(hoch) schätzen, (hoch) achten.*

estimate *Kostenanschlag, m.* (cost); *Schätzung, f.* (appraisal); *Meinung* (opinion).

estimate (to) *veranschlagen, schätzen.*

eternal *ewig.*

eternity *Ewigkeit, f.*

European *Europäer* (noun) *m.; europäisch.* (adj.)

evade (to) *entfliehen.*

evasion *Ausflucht, f.*

eve *Vorabend, m.*

even *eben* (adj.); *sogar* (adv.).

evening *Abend, m.*

   Good evening! *Guten Abend!*

evening clothes *Gesellschaftsanzug, m.*

evening dress *Abendkleid, n.* (woman's).

event *Ereignis, n.*

ever *je, jemals.*

every *jeder*

   everybody *jedermann.*

   everything *alles.*

   everywhere *überall.*

evidence *Beweis, m.; Zeugnis, n.*

evident *offenbar, klar.*

evil *Übel* (noun) *n.; schlecht* (adj.).

evoke (to) *hervorrufen.*

evolve (to) *herausarbeiten, sich entwickeln.*

exact *genau.*

exaggerate (to) *übertreiben.*

exaggeration *Übertreibung, f.*

exalt (to) *erheben, veredeln.*

exaltation *Erhebung, f.*

examination *Prüfung, f.*

examine (to) *prüfen.*

example *Beispiel, n.*

exceed (to) *überschreiten.*

excel (to) *übertreffen.*

excellence *Vortrefflichkeit, f.*

excellent *vortrefflich, ausgezeichnet.*

except *ausgenommen; ausser* (dat.).

except (to) *ausnehmen, ausschliessen.*
exception *Ausnahme, f.*
exceptional *aussergewöhnlich.*
exceptionally *ausnahmsweise.*
excess *Übermass, n.*
excessive *übermässig.*
exchange *Tausch, m.*
exchange (to) *wechseln.*
excite (to) *aufregen.*
excitement *Aufregung, f.*
exclaim (to) *ausrufen.*
exclamation *Ausruf, m.*
exclude (to) *ausschliessen.*
exclusive *auschliesslich.*
excursion *Ausflug, m.*
excuse *Verzeihung, f.; Entschuldigung, f.*
excuse (to) *verzeihen, entschuldigen.*
   Excuse me *Verzeihung!*
   (Entschuldigung!)
execute (to) *ausführen* (carry out);
   hinrichten (put to death).
execution *Ausführung, f.* (of plan or idea);
   Hinrichtung, f. (of person).
exempt (to) *befreien.*
exercise *Übung, f.*
exercise (to) *üben.*
exert (to) *sich anstrengen.*
exertion *Anstrengung, f.*
exhaust (to) *erschöpfen.*
exhaustion *Erschöpfung, f.*
exhibit (to) *ausstellen.*
exhibition *Ausstellung, f.*
exile *Verbannung, f.*
exile (to) *verbannen.*
exist (to) *existieren.*
existence *Existenz, f.*
exit *Ausgang, m.*
expand (to) *(sich) ausdehnen.*
expansion *Ausdehnung, f.*
expensive *teuer.*
experience *Erfahrung, f.*
experience (to) *erfahren.*
experiment (to) *experimentieren.*
expert *Fachmann, m.*
expire (to) *verscheiden, ablaufen.*
explain (to) *erklären.*
explanation *Erklärung, f.*
explanatory *erklärend.*
explode (to) *explodieren.*
exploit *Heldentat, f.*
exploit (to) *ausnützen.*
explore (to) *erforschen.*
explosion *Explosion, f.*
export (to) *ausführen, exportieren.*
export *Ausfuhr, f.; Export, m.*
expose (to) *aussetzen.*
express *Schnellzug, m.*
express (to) *ausdrücken.*
expression *Ausdruck, m.*

expressive *ausdrucksvoll.*
expulsion *Ausstossung, f.; Vertreibung, f.*
exquisite *vorzüglich, köstlich.*
extend (to) *verlängern, ausdehnen.*
extensive *ausgedehnt.*
extent *Weite, f.* (distance); *Umfang, m.;*
   Verlängerung, f. (time).
exterior *Äussere* (noun *n.*); *äusserlich* (adj.).
exterminate (to) *ausrotten.*
external *äusserlich, auswärtig.*
extinction *Erlöschen, n.*
extinguish (to) *erlöschen.*
extra *extra.*
extraordinary *aussergewöhnlich.*
extravagant *verschwenderisch, überspannt.*
extreme *äusserst.*
eye *Auge, n.*
eyebrow *Augenbraue, f.*
eyeglasses *Brille, f.*
eyelash *Wimper, f.*
eyelid *Augenlid, n.*
eyesight *Sehkraft, f.*

fable *Fabel, f.*
face *Gesicht, n.*
face (to) *unter die Augen treten,*
   gegenüberstehen.
facilitate (to) *erleichtern.*
facility *Leichtigkeit, f.; Erleichterungen, f.*
facsimile *Telefax, n; Telebrief, m.; Fax, n.*
fact *Tatsache, f.*
   in fact *in der Tat.*
   as a matter of fact *im übrigen.*
factory *Fabrik, f.*
factual *tatsächlich.*
faculty *Fähigkeit, f.* (ability); *Fakultät, f.*
   (school).
fade (to) *welken.*
faded *verschossen, verblichen* (color).
fail (to) *fehlen; unterlassen* (neglect);
   durchfallen (exam).
   without fail *ganz gewiss, unfehlbar.*
failure *Misserfolg, m.*
faint (to) *ohnmächtig werden.*
fainting spell *Ohnmacht, f.*
fair *schön* (weather); *hell* (complexion);
   ehrlich (just), *gerecht, fair.*
   fair play *ehrliches Spiel.*
faith *Glaube, m.* (religion); *Treue, f.*
faithful *treu.*
fall *Fall, m.; Sturz, m.; Herbst, m.* (autumn).
fall (to) *fallen, stürzen.*
false *falsch.*
fame *Ruhm, m.*
familiar *vertraut, bekannt.*
family *Familie, f.*

famine *Hungersnot, f.*
famous *berühmt.*
fan *Ventilator, m.* (ventilator); *Windfahre, f.*
  (of a windmill); *Lüfter, m.* (electric).
fancy *Neigung* (noun) *f.; bunt* (adj.).
fantastic *fantastisch.*
far *weit, fern.*
farce *Posse, f.*
fare *Fahrpreis, m.*
farewell *Abschied, m.*
  Farewell!   *Lebe wohl!*
farm *Bauernhof, m.*
farmer *Landwirt, m.*
farming *Landwirtschaft, f.*
farther *weiter, ferner.*
fashion *Mode, f.*
fashionable *elegant, modisch, modern.*
fast *schnell.*
fasten (to) *befestigen.*
fat *Fett* (noun) *n.; fett, dick* (adj.).
fatal *tödlich, fatal.*
fate *Schicksal, n.*
father *Vater, m.*
father-in-law *Schwiegervater, m.*
faucet *Wasserhahn, m.*
fault *Fehler, m.*
favor *Gunst, f.*
  Do me a favor.   *Tun Sie mir einen*
    Gefallen!
favor (to) *vorziehen, bevorzugen,*
    begünstigen.
favorable *günstig, vorteilhaft.*
favorite *Günstling, m.; Liebling, m.;*
    Lieblings-, (adj.)
fax *Telefax, m; fax, m.*
fear *Furcht, f.*
fear (to) *fürchten.*
fearless *furchtlos.*
feather *Feder, f.*
feature (*Gesichts)zug, m.;* (facial) *Merkmal,*
    n.; Film, m. (movie).
February *Februar, m.*
federal *Bundes-, föderativ* (adj.).
federation *Staatenbund, -e, m.; Bundesstaat,*
    -en, m.
fee *Gebühr, f.*
feeble *schwach.*
feed (to) *füttern.*
feel (to) *fühlen.*
feeling *Gefühl, n.*
fellow *Kamerad, m.*
fellowship *Kameradschaft, f.;*
    Gemeinschaft, f.
female *weiblich.*
feminine *fraulich.*
fence *Zaun, m.*
fencing *Fechten, n.*
fender *Kotflügel, m.*
ferocious *wild.*

ferry *Fähre, f.*
fertile *fruchtbar.*
fertilize (to) *befruchten.*
fertilizer *Düngemittel, n.; Dünger, m.*
fervent *inbrünstig, feurig.*
fervor *Inbrunst, f.*
festival *Fest, n.*
fetch (to) *holen.*
fever *Fieber, n.*
few *wenige.*
  a few   *ein paar.*
fiction *Dichtung, f.*
field *Acker, m.; Feld, n.*
fierce *wild.*
fiery *feurig*
fifteen *fünfzehn.*
fifteenth *fünfzehnte.*
fifth *fünfte.*
fiftieth *fünfzigste.*
fifty *fünfzig.*
fig *Feige, f.*
fight *Kampf, m.*
fight (to) *kämpfen.*
figure *Figur, f.; Ziffer* (number).
file *Feile, f.* (tool); *Registratur, f.;*
    Briefordner, m.
fill (to) *füllen.*
filling (tooth) *Füllung, f.*
film *Film, m.*
filthy *schmutzig.*
final *endgültig.*
finance *Finanz, f.*
finance (to) *finanzieren.*
financial *finanziell.*
find (to) *finden.*
fine *Geldstrafe* (noun) *f.; fein* (adj.) (opp. of
    coarse); schön (adj.) (elegant).
finger *Finger, m.*
finish (to) *beenden.*
fire *Feuer, n.*
fireman *Feuerwehrmann, m.*
fireplace *Kamin, m.*
firm *Firma,* (noun) *f.; fest, stark* (adj.).
first *erster.*
  at first   *zuerst.*
fish *Fisch, m.*
fish (to) *fischen.*
fisherman *Fischer, m.*
fishing *Fischen, n.; Angeln, n.*
fist *Faust, f.*
fit *Anfall,* (noun) *m.; passend* (adj.)
    (becoming); *tauglich* (adj.) (capable).
fitness *Angemessenheit, f.; Eignung, f.*
five *fünf.*
fix (to) *reparieren.*
flag *Fahne, f.*
flame *Flamme, f.*
flank *Seite, f.*
flash *Blitz, m.* (lightning); *Aufflammen, n.*

flashlight *Taschenlampe, f.; Blitzlicht, n.,* (camera flash).

flat *flach.*

flatter (to) *schmeicheln.*

flatterer *Schmeichler, m.*

flattery *Schmeichelei, f.*

flavor *Aroma, n.; Geschmack, m.*

fleet *Flotte, f.*

flesh *Fleisch, n.*

flexibility *Biegsamkeit, f.*

flexible *biegsam.*

flight *Flug, m.*

fling (to) *werfen, Schleudern.*

flint *Kieselstein, m.; Feuerstein, n.*

float (to) *treiben.*

flood *Überschwemmung, f.; Flut, f.*

flood (to) *überschwemmen.*

floor *Boden, m.; Stock, m.* (story).

floppy disc *Floppy-disk, f.; Diskette, f.*

flourish (to) *blühen.*

flourishing *blühend.*

flow (to) *fliessen, strömen.*

flower *Blume, f.*

fluid *flüssig.*

fly *Fliege, f.*

fly (to) *fliegen.*

foam *Schaum, m.*

fog *Nebel, m.*

fold *Falte, f.*

fold (to) *falten.*

foliage *Laubwerk, n.*

follow (to) *folgen.*

following *folgend.*

fond *zärtlich, liebevoll.*

fondness *Zärtlichkeit, f.*

food *Essen, n.*

fool *Narr, m.*

foolish *töricht, lächerlich.*

foot *Fuss, m.*

football *Fussball, m.; Fussballspiel, m.*

footstep *Schritt, m.*

for *für* (acc.)*; zu* (dat.)*; wegen* (gen.) (on account of)*; denn* (because).
    as for me   *was mich betrifft.*
    for a year   *während eines Jahres.*
    for example   *zum Beispiel.*
    word for word   *Wort für Wort.*

forbid (to) *verbieten.*

force *Kraft, f.; Gewalt, f.*

force (to) *zwingen.*

foreground *Vordergrund, m.*

forehead *Stirn, f.*

foreign *fremd, ausländisch.*

foreigner *Fremder, m.; Ausländer, m.*

forest *Wald, m.*

forget (to) *vergessen.*

forgetfulness *Vergesslichkeit, f.*

forget-me-not *Vergissmeinnicht, n.*

forgive (to) *vergeben, verzeihen.*

forgiveness *Vergebung, f.*

fork *Gabel, f.*

form *Form, f.*

formal *offiziell, formell.*

formation *Bildung, f.*

former *früher; erster* (as opposed to latter)*, vorherig, ehemalig.*

formerly *vormals.*

formula *Formel, f.*

forsake (to) *verlassen.*

fort *Festung, f.*

fortieth *vierzigste.*

fortunate *glücklich.*

fortunately *glücklicherweise.*

fortune *Vermögen, n.; Glück, n.* (luck).

forty *vierzig.*

forward *vorwärts.*

forward (to) *absenden, nachscheicken.*

foster (to) *pflegen.*

foul *faul.*

found (to) *gründen.*

foundation *Gründung, f.; Grundlage, f.*

founder *Gründer, m.*

fountain *Brunnen, m.*

fountain pen *Füllfeder, f.*

four *vier.*

fourteen *vierzehn.*

fourteenth *vierzehnte.*

fourth *vierte.*

fowl *Geflügel, n.*

fox *Fuchs, m.*

fragile *zerbrechlich.*

fragment *Bruchstück, n.*

fragrance *Duft, m.*

fragrant *duftig.*

frail *zart, gebrechlich.*

frame *Rahmen, m.*

frame (to) *rahmen.*

frank *aufrichtig, freimütig.*

frankness *Offenheit, f.*

free *frei.*

freedom *Freiheit, f.*

freeze (to) *frieren.*

freight *Fracht, f.*

French *französisch.*

frequent *häufig.*

frequently *oft, öfters*

fresh *frisch.*

friction *Reibung, f.; Friktion, f.*

Friday *Freitag, m.*

fried *gebraten.*

friend *Freund, m.*

friendly *freundlich.*

friendship *Freundschaft, f.*

frighten (to) *erschrecken.*

frightening *schrecklich, erschreckend.*

fringe *Rand, m.*

frivolity *Leichtsinn, f.*

frog *Frosch, m.*

from *von, aus* (dat.); *nach* (dat.) (according to).
    from morning till night   *von früh bis spät.*
    from time to time   *von Zeit zu Zeit.*
    from top to bottom   *von oben bis unten.*
front *Vorderseite, f.; Front, f.* (military).
frozen *gefroren.*
fruit *Frucht, sing. f.; Obst, coll., n.*
fry (to) *braten*
    fried eggs   *Spiegeleier, pl.*
    fried potatoes   *Bratkartoffeln, pl.*
frying pan *Bratpfanne, f.*
fuel *Brennstoff, m.; Treibstoff, m.*
fulfill (to) *erfüllen.*
full *voll.*
fully *voll.*
fun *Scherz, m.; Spass, m.*
    to have fun   *sich amüsieren.*
    to make fun   *sich lustig machen.*
function *Funktion,* (math) *f.; Tätigkeit, f.; amtliche Pflicht, f.*
function (to) *funktionieren.*
fund *Fonds, m.; Kapital, m.*
fundamental *grundlegend; wesentlich.*
funeral *Begräbnis, n.*
funny *komisch.*
fur *Pelz, m.*
furious *wütend, rasend.*
furnace *Ofen, m.*
furnish (to) *möblieren.*
furniture *Möbel, f.*
furrow *Furche,* (agric.) *f.; Runzel* (on skin), *f.*
further *weiter.*
fury *Wut, f.*
future *Zukunft* (noun) *f.; zukünftig* (adj.).

G

gaiety *Fröhlichkeit, f.; Heiterkeit, f.*
gain *Gewinn, m.*
gain (to) *gewinnen; zunehmen* (weight).
gallant *tapfer, ritterlich.*
gallery *Galerie, f.*
gallop *Galopp, m.*
gamble (to) *spielen.*
game *Spiel, n.*
garage *Garage, f.*
garbage *Abfall, m.; Müll, m.*
garden *Garten, m.*
gardener *Gärtner, m.*
garlic *Knoblauch, n.*
gas *Gas, n.*
gasoline *Benzin, n.*
gate *Tor, n.; Sperre, f.* (railroad).
gather (to) *sammeln, sich versammeln*
gay *lustig.*
gear *Getriebe, n.; Gang, m.* (motor).

gem *Edelstein, m.*
general *General, m.* (military); *allgemein* (adj.).
generality *Allgemeinheit, f.*
generalize (to) *verallgemeinern.*
generation *Generation, f.*
generosity *Freigebigkeit, f.; Grossmut, f.* (magnanimity).
generous *grosszügig.*
genius *Genie, n.*
genteel *fein, vornehm.*
gentle *artig, vornehm, sanft.*
gentleman *Herr, m.*
gentleness *Sanftheit, f.*
genuine *echt.*
geographical *geographisch.*
geography *Geographie, f.*
germ *Keim, m.; Bakterien* (us. pl.); *Bazillus, m.*
German *Deutsche(r)* (noun) *m.; deutsch* (adj.).
gesture *Gebärde, f.*
get (to) *bekommen, erwerben, holen* (fetch); *werden* (become).
    get down   *hinunterkommen.*
    get off   *absteigen.*
    get up   *aufstehen.*
ghastly *grässlich.*
ghost *geist, m.*
giant *Riese, m.*
gift *Geschenk, n.*
gifted *begabt.*
girl *Mädchen, n.*
give (to) *geben.*
    to give back   *zurückgeben*
glad *froh.*
gladly *gern.*
glance *Blick, m.*
glass *Glas, n.*
glasses *Brille, f.*
gleam *Schein, m.; Schimmer, m.*
gleam (to) *scheinen, glänzen*
glitter *Glanz, m.; Glitzen, n.*
globe *Kugel, f.; Globus, m.*
gloomy *düster.*
glorious *glorreich.*
glory *Ruhm, m.*
glove *Handschuh, m.*
glow *Glut, f.; Glühen, n.*
glue *Leim, m.*
go (to) *gehen.*
    to go away   *weggehen, fortgehen.*
    to go back   *zurückgehen.*
    to go in   *hineingehen.*
    to go out   *herausgehen, ausgehen.*
    to go to bed   *zu Bett gehen.*
God *Gott, m.*
godchild *Patenkind, n.*
godfather *Pate, m.*

godmother *Patin, f.*

gold *Gold, n.*

golden *golden.*

golf *Golf (spiel), n.*

good *gut.*
  Good afternoon! *Guten Tag!*
  Good evening! *Guten Abend!*
  Good morning! *Guten Morgen!*
  Good night! *Gute Nacht!*

good-bye *Auf Wiedersehen!*

good-looking *gut aussehend.*

goodness *Güte, f.*

goods *Waren, pl.*

goodwill *guter Wille, m.*

goose *Gans, f.*

gossip *Klatsch, m.; Geschwätz, n.*

gossip (to) *klatschen.*

govern (to) *regieren.*

grace *Gnade, f.; Anmut, f. (charm).*

graceful *anmutig, hold, graziös.*

grade *Grad, m.*

grain *Korn, n, Getreide, n.; Körnchen, n. (sand).*

grammar *Grammatik, f.*

grand *grossartig.*

grandchild *Enkelkind, n.*

granddaughter *Enkelin, f.*

grandfather *Grossvater, m.*

grandmother *Grossmutter, f.*

grandson *Enkel, m.*

grant *Bewilligung, f.; Schenkung, f.*

grant (to) *bewilligen, gestatten.*

grape *Weintraube, f.*

grapefruit *Pompelmuse, f.*

grasp *Griff, m.*

grasp (to) *greifen, fassen.*

grass *Gras, n.*

grateful *dankbar.*

gratitude *Dankbarkeit, f.*

grave *Grab, (noun) n.; ernst (adj.).*

gravy *Sauce, f.; (Braten) sosse, f.*

gray *grau.*

grease *Fett, n.*

great *gross, herrlich (coll.); wunderbar (coll.).*

greatness *Grösse, f.*

greedy *gierig, gefrässig.*

green *grün.*

greet (to) *grüssen.*

greeting *Gruss, m.*

grief *Kummer, m.*

grieve (to) *sich grämen.*

grin (to) *grinsen.*

grind (to) *mahlen.*

groan *Stöhnen, n.*

groan (to) *stöhnen.*

grocer *Kolonialwarenhändler, m.*

grocery store *Kolonialwarenladen, m.*

gross *grob.*

ground *Boden, m.*

group *Gruppe, f.*

group (to) *gruppieren.*

grow (to) *wachsen; an (bauen) (crops); züchten (animals).*

growth *Gewächs, n.*

grudge *Groll, m.*

guaranteed *garantiert.*

guess *Vermutung, f.*

guess (to) *raten.*

guide *Führer, m.*

gum *Zahnfleisch, n. (teeth).*
  chewing gum *Kaugummi, n.*

gun *Gewehr, n.*

gush *Guss, m.*

gush (to) *hervorströmen.*

H

habit *Gewohnheit, f.*

habitual *gewöhnlich.*

hail *Hagel, m.*

hair *Haar, n.*

hairdo *Frisur, f.*

hairdresser *Frisör, m.; Friseuse, f.*

hairpin *Haarnadel, f.*

half *halb.*

hall *Halle, f.; Saal, m., Diele, f.*

ham *Schinken, n.*

hammer *Hammer, m.*

hand *Hand, f.*

hand (to) *(über) reichen.*

handbag *Handtasche, f.*

handful *Handvoll, f.*

handkerchief *Taschentuch, n.*

handle *Griff, m.*

handle (to) *anfassen, behandeln*

handsome *stattlich, hübsch, schön.*

handy *handlich.*

hang (to) *hängen.*

happen (to) *geschehen.*

happiness *Glück, n.*

happy *glücklich.*

harbor *Hafen, m.*

hard *hart.*

hard disk *Hartplatte, f.; Magnetplatte, f.*

harden (to) *härten.*

hardly *kaum.*

hardness *Härte, f.*

hardware *Eisenwaren, pl.*

hardware store *Eisenwarengeschäft, n.*

hardy *abgehärtet, robust, kräftig.*

hare *Hase, m.*

harm *Schaden, m.*

harm (to) *schädigen.*

harmful *schädlich*

harmless *harmlos.*

harmonious *harmonisch.*

harmony *Harmonie, f.*
harsh *rauh, hart* (touch); *sauer* (taste); *grell* (sound/color); *schroff.*
harvest *Ernte, f.*
haste *Eile, f.*
hasten (to) *eilen.*
hat *Hut, m.*
hate *Hass, m.*
hate (to) *hassen.*
hateful *gehässig.*
hatred *Hass, m.*
haughty *hochmutig, arrogant.*
have (to) *haben.*
haven *Hafen, m.; Zufluchtsort, m.; Asyl, n.*
hay *Heu, n.*
he *er.*
head *Kopf, m.* (of a person); *Chef, m.* (of a firm); *Haupt, n.* (of a government).
headache *Kopfschmerzen, pl.*
headphones *Kopfhörer (pl.).*
heal (to) *heilen.*
health *Gesundheit, f.*
healthy *gesund.*
heap *Haufen, m.*
heap (to) *(auf)häufen.*
hear (to) *hören.*
hearing *Gehör, n.*
heart *Herz, n.*
heaven *Himmel, m.*
heavy *schwer.*
hedge *Hecke, f.*
heel *Ferse, f.* (of the foot); *Absatz, m.* (of a shoe).
height *Höhe, f.*
heir *Erbe, m.*
hell *Hölle, f.*
helm *Ruder, n.*
help *Hilfe, f.*
help (to) *helfen.*
helpful *behilflich.*
hem *Saum, m.*
hen *Huhn, n.; Henne, f.*
her *ihr* (pers. pr., dat.; poss. adj.); *sie* (pers. pr., acc.).
herb *Kraut, n.; Gewürzkraut, n.* (culinary).
herd *Herde, f.*
here *hier.*
herewith *hiermit.*
hero *Held, m.*
heroic *heldenhaft, heroisch.*
heroine *Heldin, f.*
herring *Hering, m.*
hers *ihr (er, -e, -es).*
herself *sie (ihr) selbst; sich.*
hesitate (to) *zögern.*
hide (to) *verstecken.*
hideous *scheusslich.*
high *hoch.*
higher *höher.*

hill *Hügel, m.*
him *ihn* (acc.); *ihm* (dat.).
himself *er (ihm, ihn) selbst; sich.*
hinder (to) *hindern.*
hint *Wink, m.*
hint (to) *andeuten.*
hip *Hüfte, f.*
hire (to) *mieten.*
his *sein* (poss. adj.); *sein(er, -e, -es)* (pron.).
hiss (to) *zischen.*
historian *Geschichtsschreiber, m.*
historical *historisch.*
history *Geschichte, f.*
hoarse *heiser.*
hoe *Hacke, f.*
hold *Halt, m.*
hold (to) *halten.*
hole *Loch, n.*
holiday *Feiertag, m.*
holidays *Ferien, pl.* (vacation).
holy *heilig.*
homage *Huldigung, f.*
home *Heim, n.*
homosexual *homosexuell* (adj.), *Homosexuelle(r), m./f.*
honest *ehrlich.*
honesty *Ehrlichkeit, f.*
honey *Honig, m.*
honeymoon *Flitterwochen, pl.; Hochzeitsreise, f.* (honeymoon trip)
honor *Ehre, f.*
honor (to) *ehren.*
honorable *ehrenvoll.*
hood *Kapuze, f.; Haube n.* (car), *Verdeck, n.*
hoof *Huf, m.*
hook *Haken, m.*
hope *Hoffnung, f.*
hope (to) *hoffen.*
hopeful *hoffnungsvoll.*
hopeless *hoffnungslos.*
horizon *Horizont, m.*
horizontal *horizontal.*
horn (auto) *Hupe, f.*
horrible *schrecklich.*
horse *Pferd, n.*
horseback (on) *zu Pferde.*
hosiery *Strümpfe, f.; Strumpfwaren, pl.*
hospitable *gastfreundlich.*
hospital *Krankenhaus, n.; Hospital, n.*
host *Gastgeber, m.; Wirt, m.*
hostess *Gastgeberin, f.; Wirtin, f.*
hostile *feindlich.*
hot *heiss.*
hotel *Hotel, n.; Gasthof, m.*
hour *Stunde, f.*
house *Haus, n.*
household *Haushalt, m.*
housekeeper *Haushälterin, f.*
housemaid *Hausmädchen, n.*

how *wie*
  How are you? *Wie geht's?*
however *dennoch, wie ... auch immer.*
howl *Heulen, n.*
howl (to) *heulen.*
human *menschlich.*
humane *human.*
humanity *Menschlichkeit, f.*
humble *demütig.*
humid *feucht.*
humiliate *erniedrigen, demütigen.*
humility *Demut, f.*
humor *Humor, m.*
hundred *hundert.*
hundredth *hundertste.*
hunger *Hunger, m.*
hungry *hungrig.*
hunt *Jagd, f.*
hunter *Jäger, m.*
hurricane *Orkan, m.*
hurry *Eile, f.*
  Hurry up! *Beeilen Sie sich!*
hurt (to) *verwunden; verletzen.*
husband *Mann, m.; Gatte, m.*
hush (to) *schweigen.*
hyphen *Bindestrich, m.*
hypocrite *Heuchler, m.*

I

I *ich.*
ice *Eis, n.*
ice cream *Eis, n.; Speiseeis, n.*
icy *eisig.*
idea *Idee, f.; Einfall, m.*
ideal *Ideal,* (noun) *n.; ideal* (adj.).
idealism *Idealismus, m.*
idealist *Idealist, m.*
identical *identisch.*
identity *Identität, f.*
idiot *Idiot, m.*
idle *müssig, träge, unbeschäftigt.*
idleness *Müssigkeit, f.; Faulheit, f.;*
    Trägheit, f.
if *wenn, ob.*
ignoble *unedel.*
ignorance *Unwissenheit, f.*
ignorant *unwissend.*
ignore (to) *ignorieren, nich beachten.*
ill *krank*
illegal *gesetzwidrig, ungesetzlich, illegal.*
illness *Krankheit, f.*
illusion *Täuschung, f.*
illustrate (to) *illustrieren.*
illustration *Abbildung, f.*
image *Einbildungskraft, f.; Ebenbild, n.;*
    Bild, n.
imagination *Fantasie, f.*

imagine (to) *sich einbilden.*
imitate (to) *nachahmen.*
imitation *Nachahmung, f.*
immediate *unmittelbar.*
immediately *sogleich, sofort.*
immigrant *Immigrant, m.*
imminent *bevorstehend, unmittelbar.*
immobility *Unbeweglichkeit, f.*
immoral *unmoralisch.*
immorality *Unsittlichkeit, f.*
immortal *unsterblich.*
immortality *Unsterblichkeit, f.*
impartial *unparteiisch.*
impassible *gefühllos.*
impatience *Ungeduld, f.*
imperfect *Vergangenheit* (noun) *f.* (in
    grammar); *unvollkommen* (adj.).
impertinence *Unverschämtheit, f.*
impetuosity *Ungestüm, n.*
import *Einfuhr, f.; Import, m.*
import (to) *einführen, importieren.*
important *wichtig.*
imported *importiert.*
importer *Importeur, m.*
impossible *unmöglich.*
impress (to) *Eindruck machen, beeindrucken.*
impression *Eindruck, m.*
imprison (to) *einsperren.*
improve (to) *verbessern.*
improvement *Verbesserung, f.*
improvise (to) *improvisieren.*
imprudence *Unvorsichtigkeit, f.;*
    Unklugheit, f.
imprudent *unklug.*
impulse *Antrieb, m. Anregung, f.*
impure *unrein.*
in *in* (dat.).
inadequate *unzulänglich, ungenügend.*
inaugurate (to) *eröffnen.*
incapable *unfähig.*
incapacity *Unfähigkeit, f.*
inch *Zoll, m.*
incident *Vorfall, m.*
include (to) *einschliessen.*
included *eingeschlossen.*
income *Einkommen, n.*
income tax *Einkommensteuer, f.*
incomparable *unvergleichlich, nicht*
    vergleichbar.
incompatible *unvereinbar.*
incompetent *unfähig, unzulänglich.*
incomplete *unvollständig.*
inconvenient *lästig, unbequem, beschwerlich.*
incorrect *unrichtig.*
increase *Erhöhung, f.*
increase (to) *sich vermehren, erhöhen.*
incredible *unglaublich.*
indebted *verschuldet; verpflichtet.*
indecision *Unentschlossenheit, f.*

indeed *tatsächlich.*
independence *Unabhängigkeit, f.*
independent *unabhängig.*
index *Inhaltsverzeichnis, n.*
index *Register* (in a book).
index card *Karteikarte, f.*
index finger *Zeigefinger, m.*
indicate (to) *hinweisen, andeuten,*
    bezeichnen.
indicative *Indikativ* (noun) *m.* (in grammar);
    anzeigend (adj.); *hinweisend* (adj.).
indifference *Gleichgültigkeit, f.*
indifferent *gleichgültig.*
indigestion *Verdauungsstörung, f.*
indignant *empört.*
indignation *Entrüstung, f; Empörung, f.*
indirect *indirekt.*
indiscreet *indiskret.*
indiscretion *Unbedachtsamkeit, f.;*
    Indiskretion, f. (polit.).
indispensable *unentbehrlich.*
individual *einzeln, persönlich.*
indolent *träge.*
indoors *im Hause, zu Hause.*
induce (to) *veranlassen, verursachen.*
indulge (to) *sich hingeben.*
indulgence *Verwöhnung, f.*
indulgent *nachsichtig.*
industrial *industriell.*
industrious *fleissig.*
industry *Industrie, f.*
inefficient *unfähig.*
infancy *Kindheit, f.*
infant *kleines Kind, n.; Baby, n.;*
    Säugling, m.
infantry *Infanterie, f.*
infection *Infektion, f.*
inferior *minderwertig.*
infernal *höllisch.*
infinite *unendlich.*
infinity *Unendlichkeit, f.*
influence *Einfluss, m.*
influence (to) *beeinflussen.*
inform (to) *benachrichtigen.*
information *Auskunft, f.; Nachricht, f.*
    (news).
ingenious *geistig.*
ingenuity *Scharfsinn, m.*
inhabit (to) *bewohnen.*
inhabitant *Einwohner, m.*
inherit (to) *erben.*
inheritance *Erbgut, n.*
inhuman *unmenschlich.*
initial *Anfangsbuchstabe, m.*
initial (adj.) *anfänglich, ursprünglich*
initiate (to) *anfangen, einleiten, einführen.*
initiative *Initiative, f.*
injection *Einspritzung, f.; Spritze, f.*
injury *Verletzung, f.*

injustice *Ungerechtigkeit, f.*
ink *Tinte, f.*
inkwell *Tintenfass, n.*
inland *Binnenland, n.; innenländisch,*
    (adj.).
inn *Gasthof, m.; Gasthaus, n.*
innkeeper *Gastwirt, m.*
innocent *unschuldig.*
innocence *Unschuld, f.*
inquire (to) *sich erkundigen, nachfragen.*
inquiry *Erkundigung, f.; Anfrage, f.;*
    Nachfrage, f.
insane *geisteskrank.*
inscription *Inschrift, f.*
insect *Insekt, n.*
insensible *unempfindlich.*
inseparable *unzertrennlich.*
inside *drinnen.*
insight *Einsicht, f.*
insignificant *unbedeutend.*
insincere *unaufrichtig, heuchlerisch.*
insinuate (to) *andeuten.*
insist (to) *bestehen auf.*
insistence *Beharren, n.; Bestehen, n.*
inspect (to) *besichtigen, untersuchen.*
inspection *Besichtigung, f.; Untersuchung, f.*
inspiration *Inspiration, f., Begeisterung, f.*
inspire *begeistern, erwecken.*
install (to) *einstellen, installieren.*
installment *Rate, f.; Teilzahlung, f.*
instance *Beispiel, n.; Fall, m.*
instant *Augenblick, m.*
instantly *sofort.*
instead of *anstatt* (gen.).
institute (to) *einführen, gründen.*
institution *Anstalt, f.*
instruct (to) *unterrichten.*
instructor *Lehrer, m.; Erzieher, n.*
instruction *Anweisung, f.; Unterricht, m.*
    (teaching).
instrument *Instrument, n.*
insufficient *ungenügend.*
insult *Beleidigung, f.*
insult (to) *beleidigen.*
insurance *Versicherung, f.*
insure (to) *versichern.*
intact *unversehrt, unberührt.*
intellectual *intellektuell.*
intelligence *Intelligenz, f.*
intelligent *intelligent.*
intend (to) *beabsichtigen.*
intense *intensiv.*
intensity *Heftigkeit, f.*
intent *Absicht, m.; Plan, m.*
intent (adj.) *eifrig, beschäftigt (mit),*
    gerichtet, gespannt.
intention *Absicht, f.*
interest *Interesse, n.*
interesting *interessant.*

interfere (to) *sich einmischen,*
    dazwischentreten.

interior *Innere, n.*

intermediate *mittel.*

intermission *Pause, f.*

international *international.*

interpret (to) *interpretieren, übersetzen;*
    deuten (emotion), *dolmetschen.*

interpreter *Dolmetscher, m.*

interrupt (to) *unterbrechen.*

interval *Pause, f.; Zwischenzeit, f.*

interview *Interview, n.; Besprechung, f.*

intimacy *Vertrautheit, f.*

intimate *vertraut, zu verstehen geben.*

into *in* (dat. or acc.).

intolerant *unduldsam, intolerant.*

intonation *Tonfall, m.* (phonetics).

introduce (to) *vorstellen.*

introduction *Vorstellung, f.*

intuition *unmittelbare Erkenntnis, f.;*
    Anschauungsvermögen, n. (intuitive
    faculty).

invade (to) *einfallen, eindringen* (in),
    angreifen.

invent (to) *erfinden.*

invention *Erfindung, f.*

inventor *Erfinder, m.*

invert (to) *umkehren, umdrehen.*

invest (to) *investieren; anlegen* (money).

investment *Kapitalanlage, f.*

invisible *unsichtbar.*

invitation *Einladung, f.*

invite (to) *einladen.*

invoice *Faktura, f.; Warenrechnung, f.*

invoke (to) *anflehen, beschwören.*

involve (to) *verwickeln.*

iodine *Jod, n.*

Irish *irländisch.*

iron *Eisen, n.* (metal); *Bügeleisen, n.* (for
    ironing).

iron (to) *bügeln, plätten.*

irony *Ironie, f.*

irrefutable *unwiderlegbar.*

irregular *unregelmässig.*

irresistible *unwiderstehlich.*

irritate (to) *reizen, ärgern.*

island *Insel, f.*

isolate (to) *absondern, isolieren.*

Israel *Israel, n.*

Israeli *israeli* (adj.), *Israeli, m./f., Israelit(in),*
    m./f.

issue *Ausgabe, f.*

it *es.*

Italian *Italiener* (noun) *m.; italienisch* (adj.).

itch (to) *jucken.*

its *sein* (poss. adj.); *sein(er, -e, -es),* (poss.
    pron.), *ihr, dessen, deren.*

itself *selbst,* (emphatic), *sich* (refl.), *für sich*
    (by itself), *an sich* (in itself).

ivory *Elfenbein, n.*

ivy *Efeu, n.*

J

jacket *Jacke, f., Jackett, m.*

jail *Gefängnis, n.*

jam *Marmelade, f.*

January *Januar, m.*

Japanese *Japaner* (noun) *m.; japanisch*
    (adj.).

jar *Krug, m.*

jaw *Kiefer, m.*

jealous *eifersüchtig.*

jealousy *Eifersucht, f.*

jelly *Gelee, n.*

jewel *Juwel, n.*

jeweler *Juwelier, m.*

Jewish *jüdisch.*

job *Arbeit, f., Stellung, f. Posten, m., Job, m.*

join (to) *sich auschliessen an, verbinden,*
    zusammenfügen (mit).

joint *Gelenk, n.*

joke *Witz, m.; Scherz, m.; Spass, m.*

joke (to) *scherzen.*

jolly *lustig.*

journalist *Journalist, m.*

journey *Reise, f.*

joy *Freude, f.*

joyous *freudig.*

judge *Richter, m, Schiedsrichter, m.* (sports).

judge (to) *urteilen.*

judgment *Urteil, n.; gerichtliche*
    Entscheidung, f.

judicial *gerichtlich.*

juice *Saft, m.*

July *Juli, m.*

jump *Sprung, m.; Satz, m.*

jump (to) *springen.*

June *Juni, m.*

junior *jünger.*

jungle *Dschungel, m.*

just *recht* (fair); *gerecht* (justice); *gerade*
    (recent).

justice *Gerechtigkeit, f.*

justify (to) *rechtfertigen.*

K

keen *scharf.*

keep (to) *behalten* (retain); *hindern;*
    (hinder), *aufbewahren.*

keep off *abhalten.*

keep on *fortfahren.*

keep up *aufrechterhalten.*

kernel *Kern, m.*

kettle *Kessel, m.*
key *Schlüssel, m.*
keyboard (computer) *Tastatur, f.*
kick *Fusstritt, m.*
kick (to) *ausschlagen, treten, einen Fusstritt geben.*
kidneys *Nieren, pl.*
kill (to) *töten.*
kin *Blutsverwandtschaft, f.*
kind *Art* (noun) *f.; gütig* (adj.).
kindly *freundlich.*
kindness *Güte, f.; Freundlichkeit, f.*
king *König, m.*
kingdom *Königreich, n.*
kiosk *kiosk, m.; Verkaufsstand, m.*
kiss *Kuss, m.*
kiss (to) *küssen.*
kitchen *Küche, f.*
kit *Werkzeugtasche, f.*
kite *Drache, m.*
knee *Knie, n.*
kneel (to) *knieen.*
knife *Messer, n.*
knight *Ritter, m.*
knit (to) *stricken.*
knock *Schlag, m.; Hieb, m.* (beating); *Klopf, m.; Griff, m.* (door).
knock (to) *klopfen, schlagen, hauen, stossen; anklopfen* (door).
knot *Knoten, m.*
know (to) *wissen* (have knowledge of); *kennen* (be acquainted with).
knowledge *Kenntnis, f.*

L

label *Etikett, n.; Marke* (brand), *f.*
labor *Arbeit, f.*
laboratory *Laboratorium, n.*
laborer *Arbeiter, m.*
lace *Spitze, f.* (ornamental); *Senkel, m.* (of a shoe).
lack *Mangel, m.*
lack (to) *mangeln.*
lady *Dame, f.*
lake *See, m.*
lamb *Lamm, n.*
lame *lahm.*
lamp *Lampe, f.*
land *Land, n.*
land (to) *landen.*
landscape *Landschaft, f.*
language *Sprache, f.*
languish (to) *schmachten.*
languor *Schlaffheit, f.*
lantern *Laterne, f.*
large *gross.*
laser *Laser, m.*

laser beam *Laserstrahl, m.*
laser printer *Laserdrucker, m.*
last *letzt.*
  last year *voriges Jahr.*
last (to) *dauern.*
lasting *dauernd.*
latch *Klinke, f.* (knob); *Drücker.*
late *spät.*
lately *kürzlich.*
latter *letzter.*
laugh (to) *lachen.*
laughter *Gelächter, n.*
lavish *freigebig.*
lavish (to) *überhäufen.*
law *Gesetz, n.; Recht, n.* (code).
lawful *rechtmässig.*
lawn *Rasen, m.*
lawyer *Rechtsanwalt, m.*
lay (to) *legen.*
layer *Schicht, f.*
lazy *faul.*
lead *Blei, n.*
lead (to) *führen.*
leader *Führer, m.*
leadership *Führung, f.*
leaf *Blatt, n.*
leak *Leck, n.*
leak (to) *durchsickern.*
lean (adj.) *mager.*
lean (to) *lehnen.*
leap (to) *springen, hupfen.*
leap *Sprung, m.*
learn (to) *lernen.*
learned *gelehrt.*
learning *Gelehrsamkeit, f.*
least *wenigste.*
  at least *mindestens, wenigstens.*
leather *Leder, n.*
leave (to) *verlassen* (abandon); *weggehen* (on foot); *wegfahren* (by vehicle).
lecture *Vortrag, m.*
left *link, links.*
  to the left *links.*
leg *Bein, n.*
  leg of lamb *Hammelkeule, f.*
legal *gesetzmässig, gesetzlich.*
legend *Sage, f.*
legislation *Gesetzgebung, f.*
legislator *Gesetzgeber, m.*
legitimate *legitim.*
leisure *Freizeit, f.*
lemon *Zitrone, f.*
lemonade *Limonade, f.*
lend (to) *(aus) leihen, verleihen.*
length *Länge, f.*
lengthen (to) *verlängern.*
lesbian *lesbich* (adj.), *Lesbierin, f.*
less *weniger.*
lesson *Stunde, f.; Lektion, f.* (in book).

let (to) *lassen; gestatten* (allow); *vermieten* (rent).

letter *Buchstabe, m.* (alphabet); *Brief, m.* (correspondence).

level *Niveau, n.*

liable *haftbar.*

liar *Lügner, m.; Lügnerin, f.*

liberal *liberal.*

liberty *Freiheit, f.*

library *Bibliothek, f.*

license *Erlaubnis, f.; Führerschein, m.* (driver's license).

lick (to) *lecken.*

lie *Lüge, f.*

lie (to) *lügen* (falsify); *liegen* (rest).

lieutenant *Leutnant, m.*

life *Leben, n.*

lift (to) *heben, hochheben, aufheben.*

light *Licht* (noun) *n.; leicht* (adj.).

light (to) *anzünden* (match, fire).

to light up   *erleuchten.*

lighten (to) *erhellen* (brightness); *erleichtern* (weight).

lighter *Feuerzeug, n.*

lighthouse *Leuchtturm, m.*

lighting *Beleuchtung, f.*

lightning *Blitz, m.*

like *wie* (as); *ähnlich* (similar).

like (to) *gern haben, mögen, gefallen.*

I'd like to   *ich möchte.*

likely *wahrscheinlich.*

likeness *Ähnlichkeit, f.*

likewise *gleichfalls.*

liking *Vorliebe, f.*

limb *Glied, n.*

limit *Grenze, f.; Beschränkung, f.* (limitation).

limit (to) *begrenzen, beschränken.*

limp (to) *hinken, humpeln.*

line *Linie, f.*

line up (to) *sich anstellen.*

linen *Wäsche, f.* (household); *Leinwand, f.* (fabric).

linger (to) (*ver*) *weilen, sich lange aufhalten.*

lingerie *Damenwäsche, f.*

lining *Futter, n.*

link *Glied, n.*

link (to) *verbinden, verknüpfen.*

lion *Löwe, m.*

lip *Lippe, f.*

lipstick *Lippenstift, m.*

liquid *Flüssigkeit* (noun) *f.; flüssig* (adj.).

liquor *Alkohol, m.; Likör, m.* (liqueur).

list *Liste, f.*

literary *literarisch.*

literature *Literatur, f.*

little *klein.*

a little   *ein wenig.*

live *lebend.*

live (to) *leben.*

lively *lebhaft, lebendig, munter.*

liver *Leber, f.*

load *Last, f.* (burden); *Ladung, f.* (cargo).

load (to) *laden.*

loan (*ver*)*leihen.*

lobby *Vorhalle, f., Foyer, n.*

local *lokal, örtlich.*

locate (to) *orientieren, finden, festlegen.*

location *Platz, m.; Lage, f.*

lock *Schloss, n.*

lock (to) *zuschliessen, verschliessen, abschliessen.*

locomotive *Lokomotive, f.*

log (*Holz*) *Klotz, m.*

logic *Logik, f.*

logical *logisch.*

loneliness *Einsamkeit, f.*

lonely *einsam.*

long *lang.*

long ago   *vor langer Zeit; längst.*

for a long time   *seit langer Zeit; seit langem.*

long (to) *sehnen.*

long for   (to) (*sich*) *sehen* (*nach*)

longer *länger.*

longing *Sehnsucht, f.*

look *Blick, m.*

look (to) *schauen; aussehen* (appear).

Look!   *Sehen Sie her!*

Look out!   *Passen Sie auf!*

to look forward   *sich freuen auf* (rejoice); *entgegensehen.*

loose *lose.*

loosen (to) *losmachen, loslassen.*

lose (to) *verlieren.*

loss *Verlust, m.; Schaden, m.*

lost *verloren, verschwunden.*

lot (a) *viel* (much).

a lot of   *eine Menge.*

loud *laut.*

love *Liebe, f.*

love (to) *lieben.*

lovely *schön, reizend.*

low *niedrig.*

lower (to) *niederlassen, herunterlassen, vermindern* (decrease).

loyal *treu.*

loyalty *Treue, f.*

luck *Glück, n.*

lucky *glücklich.*

luggage *Gepäck, n.*

luminous *leuchtend.*

lump *Klumpen, m.*

lunacy *Wahnsinn, m.*

lunch *Mittagessen, n.*

lung *Lunge, f.*

luxurious *prächtig, luxuriös.*

luxury *Luxus, m.; Aufwand, m.*

M

machine *Maschine, f.*
mad *verrückt.*
madam *gnädige Frau.*
made *gemacht.*
madness *Wahnsinn, m.*
magazine *Zeitschrift, f.*
magistrate *Magistrat, m.*
magnificent *prachtvoll, glänzend, herrlich.*
maid *Dienstmädchen, n.* (servant).
mail *Post, f.*
main *haupt-*
  the main thing   *die Hauptsache.*
mainly *hauptsächlich.*
maintain (to) *erhalten; unterhalten*
  (support).
maintenance *Unterhalt, m.*
majesty *Majestät, f.*
major *Major, m.*
majority *Mehrheit, f.*
make (to) *machen.*
man *Mann, m.; Mensch, m.* (human being).
manage (to) *führen, verwalten, wissen*
  umzugehen mit (coll.).
management *Leitung, f.*
manager *Leiter, m.; Regisseur, m.* (theater);
  Manager, m.
manicure *Maniküre, f.*
mankind *Menschheit, f.*
manner *Art, f.; Weise, f.*
manners *Benehmen, n.*
manufacture *Fabrikation, f.; Herstellung, f.*
manufactured *hergestellt.*
many *viele.*
map *Landkarte, f.*
marble *Marmor, m.*
March *März, m.*
march *Marsch, m.*
march (to) *marschieren.*
margin *Rand, m.*
marine *Marine, f.*
mark *Kennzeichen, n.*
mark (to) *markieren* (score); *notieren,*
  aufschreiben.
market *Markt, m.*
marketplace *Marktplatz, m.*
marriage *Heirat, f.*
married *verheiratet.*
marry (to) *heiraten, sich verheiraten; trauen*
  (perform the ceremony).
  to marry off   *verheiraten.*
marvel *Wunder, n.*
marvel (to) *sich wundern.*
marvelous *wunderbar.*
masculine *männlich.*
mask *Maske, f.*
mask (to) *maskieren.*

mason *Maurer, m.*
mass *Masse, f.; Messe, f.* (church).
massage *Massage, f.*
master *Meister, m.*
master (to) *meistern.*
masterpiece *Meisterwerk, n.; Meisterstück, n.*
match *Streichholz, n.* (incendiary); *Gleiche,*
  n. (comparative).
match (to) *zusammenpassen; gewachsen sein*
  (to be a match for).
material *Material, n.*
maternal *mütterlich.*
mathematics *Mathematik, f.*
matter *Angelegenheit, f.* (affair); *Stoff, m.*
  (substance).
  What's the matter?   *Was ist los?*
mattress *Matratze, f.*
mature *erwachsen, reif.*
May *Mai, m.*
may *dürfen* (to be allowed); *mögen* (to be
  likely).
mayor *Bürgermeister, m.*
me *mich* (acc.); *mir* (dat.).
meadow *Wiese, f.*
meal *Mahl, n.*
mean *übel* (unkind), *Mittel* (Math).
mean (to) *meinen* (to be of the opinion);
  bedeuten (to signify).
  What does it mean?   *Was bedeutet das?*
meaning *Bedeutung, f.* (significance).
means *Mittel, n.*
meanwhile *inzwischen.*
measure *Mass, n.*
measure (to) *messen.*
meat *Fleisch, n.*
mechanic *Mechaniker, m.*
mechanical *mechanisch.*
medal *Medaille, f.* (jewel).
medical *ärztlich.*
medicine *Medizin, f.* (science); *Arznei, f.*
  (medication).
mediocre *mittelmässig.*
mediocrity *Mittelmässigkeit, f.*
meditate (to) *grübeln, sinnen, nachdenken.*
meditation *Nachdenken, n.*
medium *mittel.*
meet (to) *treffen.*
  Pleased to meet you.   *Sehr erfreut, Sie*
  kennenzulernen.
meeting *Versammlung, f.*
melon *Melone, f.*
melt (to) *schmelzen.*
member *Mitglied, n.*
memorize (to) *auswendig lernen.*
memory *Gedächtnis, n.*
mend (to) *reparieren.*
mental *geistig.*
mention (to) *erwähnen.*
menu *Speisekarte, f.*

merchandise *Ware, f.*
merchant *Kaufmann, m.*
merciful *barmherzig, mitleidvoll.*
merciless *unbarmherzig.*
mercury *Quecksilber, n.*
mercy *Barmherzigkeit, f., Gnade, f.*
merit *Verdienst, n.*
merit (to) *verdienen.*
merry *fröhlich, heiter, lustig.*
message *Nachricht, f.*
messenger *Bote, m.*
metal *Metall, n.*
metallic *metallisch.*
method *Methode, f.*
Mexican *Mexikaner* (noun) *m.; mexikanisch* (adj.)
microphone *Mikrofon, n.*
microwave oven *Mikrowellengerät, n., Mikrowellenherd, m.*
middle *Mitte, f.*
middle aged *von mittlerem Alter*
Middle Ages *Mittelalter, n.*
midnight *Mitternacht, f.*
midway *halbwegs.*
might *Macht, f.*
mighty *mächtig.*
mild *leicht, mild, sanft.*
mildness *Milde, f.*
mile *Meile, f.*
military *militärisch.*
milk *Milch, f.*
milkman *Milchhändler, m., Milchmann, m.*
milky way *Milchstrasse, f.*
mill *Mühle, f.*
miller *Müller, m.; Müllerin, f.*
milliner *Modistin, f.*
million *Million, f.*
millionaire *Millionär, m.*
mind *Verstand, m.; Sinn, m.*
mind (to) *beachten* (to pay heed); *aufpassen* (also to watch over).
mine *Grube, f.* (coal).
mine (poss. pr.) *mein* (er, -e, -es).
miner *Bergmann, m.*
mineral *mineralisch.*
mineral *Mineral, n.*
minister *Minister* (state), *m.; Geistliche, m.* (church).
ministry *Ministerium n.* (state); *Amt, n.* (church).
mink *Nerz, m.*
minor *Minderjährige(r), m.*
minority *Minderheit, f.*
minute *Minute, f.*
     Just a minute!   *Einen Augenblick!*
     Wait a minute!   *Warten Sie einen Augenblick!*
     Any minute now!   *Jeden Augenblick!*
miracle *Wunder, n.*

mirror *Spiegel, m.*
miscellaneous *gemischt, verschieden.*
mischief *Unfug, m.*
mischievous *boshaft.*
miser *Geizhals, m.*
miserly *geizig.*
misfortune *Unglück, n.*
Miss *Fräulein, n.*
miss (to) *versäumen, fehlen.*
mission *Mission, f., Aufgabe, f.* (someone).
mist *Nebel, m.*
mistake *Fehler, m.*
mistaken *irrtümlich.*
     You are mistaken.   *Sie sind im Irrtum.*
Mister *Herr.*
mistrust (to) *misstrauen.*
misunderstand (to) *missverstehen.*
misunderstanding *Missverständnis, n.*
misuse (to) *missbrauchen.*
mix (to) *mischen.*
mixture *Mischung, f.*
mob *Pöbel, m.*
mobile *beweglich.*
mobilization *Mobilmachung, f.* (mil.), *Mobilisierung, f.*
mobilize (to) *mobilisieren.*
mock (to) *verspotten.*
mockery *Spott, m.; Spotterei, f.*
mode *Mode, f.*
model *Modell, n.*
moderate *mässigen.*
moderation *Mässigkeit, f.*
modern *modern.*
modest *bescheiden.*
modesty *Bescheidenheit, f.*
modification *Veränderung, f.*
modify (to) *verändern.*
moist *feucht.*
moisten *anfeuchten.*
moment *Augenblick, m.; Moment, m.*
     Just a moment.   *Einen Augenblick.*
monarchy *Monarchie, f.*
monastery *Kloster, n.*
Monday *Montag, m.*
money *Geld, n.*
monitor *Bildschirm, m.; Monitor, m.; Fenster, n.*
monk *Mönch, m.*
monkey *Affe, m.*
monologue *Monolog, m.*
monorail *Einschienbahn, f.*
monotonous *eintönig.*
monotony *Eintönigkeit, f.*
monster *Ungeheuer, n.*
monstrous *ungeheuer.*
month *Monat, m.*
monthly *monatlich.*
monument *Denkmal, n.*
monumental *monumental, kolossal.*

mood *Stimmung, f.; Laune, f.* (temper).
moody *launisch.*
moon *Mond, m.*
moonlight *Mondschein, m.*
mop *Mop, m.*
moral *Moral, f.*
morality *Sittlichkeit, f.*
more *mehr.*
moreover *darüber hinaus.*
morning *Morgen, m.*
morsel *Bissen, m.; Brocken, m.*
mortal *sterblich.*
morality *Sterblichkeit, f.*
mortgage *Hypothek, f.*
mortgage (to) *verpfänden.*
mosquito *Mücke, f.*
most *am meisten.*
    most of *die meisten.*
mostly *meistens.*
moth *Motte, f.*
mother *Mutter, f.*
mother-in-law *Schwiegermutter, f.*
motion *Bewegung, f.*
motionless *bewegungslos.*
motivate (to) *anregen, begründen,*
       motivieren.
motor *Motor, m.*
mount (to) *montieren; aufkleben* (paste);
       besteigen (horse).
mountain *Berg, m.*
mountainous *bergig.*
mourn (to) *trauern.*
mournful *traurig.*
mourning *Trauer, f.*
mouse *Maus, f.*
mouth *Mund, m.*
move (to) *bewegen.*
movement *Bewegung, f.*
movies *Kino, n.*
moving *rührend.*
much *viel*
    How much? *Wieviel?*
mud *Schlamm, m.*
muddy *schlammig.*
mule *Maultier, n.; Maulesel, m.*
multiply (to) *multiplizieren.*
multitude *Menge, f.*
mumble (to) *murmeln.*
municipal *städtisch.*
munition *Munition, f.*
murder *Mord, m.*
murder (to) *ermorden.*
murderer *Mörder, m.*
murmur (to) *murmeln, rauschen.*
muscle *Muskel, m.*
museum *Museum, n.*
mushroom *Pilz, m.*
music *Musik, f.*
musical *musikalisch.*

musician *Musiker, m.*
must *müssen.*
mustache *Schnurrbart, m.*
mustard *Senf, m.; Mostrich, m.*
mute *stumm.*
mutton *Hammelfleisch, n.*
my *mein.*
myself *ich* (*mich, mir*) *selbst.*
mysterious *geheimnisvoll.*
mystery *Geheimnis, n.*

N

nail *Nagel, m.*
nail (to) *nageln.*
naive *harmlos, naïv.*
naked *nackt.*
name *Name, m.*
    first name *Vorname, m.*
    last name *Zuname, m.; Familienname*
       (family name).
    What is your name? *Wie heissen Sie?*
namely *nämlich.*
nap *Schläfchen, n.*
napkin *Serviette, f.*
narrow *eng.*
nasty *garstig, ekelhaft.*
nation *Nation, f.*
national *national.*
nationality *Nationalität, f.*
native *Eingeborene, m., f., n.*
    native country *Heimat, f.*
natural *natürlich.*
naturally *natürlich.*
nature *Natur, f.*
naughty *unartig.*
naval *See-.*
navy *Flotte, f.; Kriegsmarine, f.*
near *nah.*
nearly *beinahe.*
neat *nett, ordentlich.*
neatness *Niedlichkeit, f.; Sauberkeit, f.*
necessary *notwendig.*
necessity *Notwendigkeit, f.*
neck *Hals, m.*
necklace *Halsband, n.*
necktie *Krawatte, f.; Schlips, m.* (colloquial).
need *Not, f.; Bedürfnis, f.*
need (to) *brauchen.*
needle *Nadel, f.*
needless *unnötig.*
needy *dürftig, bedürftig.*
negative *Negative, m.*
neglect *Vernachlässigung, f.*
neglect (to) *vernachlässigen.*
negotiate (to) *verhandeln, abschliessen*
       (treaty); *nehmen* (a curve in road).

negotiation *Unterhandlung, f.;*
    Verhandlung, f.
neighbor *Nachbar, m.*
neighborhood *Nachbarschaft, f.*
neither *kein(er, -e, -es).*
    neither . . . nor *weder . . . noch.*
nephew *Neffe, m.*
nerve *Nerv, m.*
    What a nerve! *So eine Frechheit!*
nervous *nervös.*
nest *Nest, n.*
net *Netz, n.*
neuter *Neutrum, n.*
neutral *neutral.*
never *niemals, nie*
    Never mind! *Das macht nichts!*
nevertheless *trotzdem; auf alle Fälle.*
new *neu.*
news *Nachrichten, pl.*
newspaper *Zeitung, f.*
next *nächst.*
nice *nett.*
nickname *Spritzname, m.*
niece *Nichte, f.*
night *Nacht, f.*
nightgown *Nachthemd, n.*
nightmare *Alpdrücken, n.; Alptraum, m.*
nine *neun.*
nineteen *neunzehn.*
ninety *neunzig.*
ninth *neunte.*
no *nein; kein* (adj.).
    no longer *nicht mehr.*
    no matter *ungeachtet* (gen.)
nobility *Adel, m.*
noble *adlig, eder* (fig).
nobody *niemand.*
noise *Geräusch, n.*
noisy *geräuschvoll.*
nominate (to) *ernennen.*
nomination *Ernennung, f.*
none *kein(e, -er, -es).*
nonsense *Unsinn, m .*
noon *Mittag, m.*
nor *noch, auch nicht* (nor I).
normal *normal.*
north *Norden, m.*
northern *nordisch, nördlich.*
northeast *Nordosten, m.*
northwest *Nordwesten, m.*
nose *Nase, f.*
nostril *Nasenloch, n.*
not *nicht.*
note *Note, f.*
note (to) *notieren.*
notebook *Notizbuch, n.*
nothing *nichts.*
notice (to) *bemerken.*
notification *Benachrichtung, f.*

notify (to) *benachrichtigen.*
notion *Idee, f.; Begriff, m.*
noun *Name, m.*
nourish (to) *nähren.*
nourishment *Nahrung, f.*
novel *Roman, m.*
novelty *Neuheit, f.*
November *November, m.*
now *jetzt*
    now and then. *dann und wann;*
        manchmal.
nowadays *heutzurage.*
nowhere *nirgendwo.*
nuclear *Kern-, Atom-,*
    weapon *Kernwaffe, f.; Atomwaffe, f.*
    fission *Kernspaltung, f.*
    physics *Kernphysik, f.*
nude *nackt, bloss.*
nuisance *Unfug, m.*
null *null*
    null and void *null und nichtig.*
numb *gefühllos.*
number *Nummer, f.*
numerous *zahlreich.*
nun *Nonne, f.*
nurse *Krankenschwester, f.* (for the sick);
    Kindermädchen (for children).
nursery *Kinderstube, f.* (children); *Gärtnerei,*
    f. (trees).
nursery rhyme *Kinderlied, n.*
nut *Nuss, f.*
nutcracker *Nussknacker, m.*

O

oak *Eiche, f.*
oar *Ruder, n.*
oat *Hafer, m.*
oath *Eid, m.*
obedience *Gehorsam, m.*
obedient *gehorsam.*
obey (to) *gehorchen.*
object (to) *einwenden, dagegen sein.*
objection *Einwand, m.*
objective *objektiv.*
objectively *sachlich.*
obligation *Verpflichtung, f.*
oblige (to) *verpflichten.*
obliging *gefällig.*
obscure *unklar, verborgen, unbekannt.*
obscurity *Dunkelheit, f.*
observation *Beobachtung, f.*
observatory *Sternwarte, f.*
observe (to) *beobachten.*
obstacle *Hindernis, n.*
obstinacy *Eigensinn, m.*
obstinate *eigensinnig.*
obvious *klar.*

obviously *offenbar, deutlich.*

occasion *Gelegenheit, f.*

occasional *gelegentlich.*

occasionally *zuweilen, dann und wann.*

occupation *Beschäftigung, f.*

occupy (to) *besitzen; besetzen* (military); *bewohnen* (house).

occur (to) *vorkommen* (an event); *einfallen* (a thought), *vorfallen.*

occurrence *Vorfall, m.*

ocean *Ozean, m.*

October *Oktober, m.*

odd *ungerade* (uneven); *sonderbar* (unusual); *seltsam.*

odor *Geruch, m.*

of *von* (dat.); *aus* (dat.) (made of).

of course   *natürlich.*

off *fort, weg.*

off and on *ab und zu.*

offend (to) *beleidigen.*

offense *Beleidigung, f.*

offensive *beleidigend.*

offer (to) *anbieten,* (dar) *bieten.*

offering *Angebot, n.*

office *Büro, n.*

official *offiziell.*

often *oft, oftmals, öfters, häufig.*

oil *Öl, n.*

old *alt.*

olive *Olive, f.*

olive oil *Olivenöl, n.*

on *auf* (dat. or acc.); *an* (dat. or acc.) (date).

at once   *sofort.*

once and for all   *ein für allemal.*

once in a while   *manchmal.*

once more   *noch einmal.*

one *eins* (number), *ein(er, -e).*

one (pr.) *man.*

oneself *sich, sich selbst.*

onion *Zwiebel, f.*

only *nur.*

open *offen.*

open (to) *öffnen.*

opener *Öffner, m.*

opening *Öffnung, f.*

opera *Oper, f.*

operate (to) *operieren* (med.); *betätigen; funktionieren, wirken.*

operation *Operation, f.*

opinion *Meinung, f.*

opponent *Gegner, m.*

opportune *gelegen, günstig.*

opportunity *Gelegenheit, f.*

oppose (to) *sich widersetzen gegen, gegenüberstehen.*

opposite *gegenüber.*

opposition *Widerstand, m.*

oppress (to) *unterdrücken.*

oppression *Unterdrückung, f.*

optician *Optiker, m.*

optimism *Optimismus, m.*

optimistic *optimistisch.*

or *oder.*

orange *Apfelsine, f. Orange, f.*

orange juice *Apfelsinensaft, m.*

orator *Redner, m.*

orchard *Obstgarten, m.*

orchestra *Orchester, n.*

ordeal *Prüfung, f.; Qual, f.* (fig.).

order *Ordnung, f.* (neatness); *Bestellung, f.* (commercial); *Befehl, m.* (command); *Orden, m.* (decoration).

out of order   *kaputt.*

to put in order   *in Ordnung bringen.*

order (to) *ordnen* (regulate); *bestellen* (commercial); *befehlen* (command).

ordinary *gewöhnlich.*

organ *Orgel, f.* (music); *Organ, n.* (anatomy).

organization *Organisation, f.*

organize (to) *organisieren.*

Orient *Orient, m.*

oriental *orientalisch.*

origin *Ursprung, m.* (source); *Herkunft, f.* (descent).

original *original, ursprünglich.*

originality *Originalität, f.*

ornament *Ornament, n.*

orphan *Waisenkind, n.*

orthodox *orthodox.*

other *ander*

other than *anders als, verschieden* (von).

ought (to) *sollen.*

ounce *Unze, f.*

our *unser.*

ours *unser(er, -e, -es).*

out *aus* (dat.); *hinaus, heraus.*

out of   *ausser* (dat.)

outcome *Folge, f.; Ergebnis, n.*

outdo (to) *übertreffen.*

outdoors *im Freien.*

outer *äusser.*

outlast *überdauern.*

outlaw *Geächtete(r), m.*

outlaw (to) *achten, verbieten.*

outlay *Auslage, f., Ausgabe, f.*

outlet *Auslass, m.; Absatz, m.* (market).

outline *Umriss, m.*

outlook *Aussicht, f.*

output *Produktion, f.; Leistung, f.* (machine).

outrage *Unverschämtheit, f.; Schandtat, f.; Frevel, m .*

outrageous *frevelhaft, empörend, schändlich.*

outside *Aussenseite* (noun) *f.; draussen* (outdoors); *ausserhalb* (besides).

oval *oval.*

oven *Ofen, m.*

over *über* (acc.); *vorbei* (finished).
    over and over   *wieder und wieder.*
overboard *über Bord.*
overcoat *Mantel, m.*
overcome (to) *überwinden.*
overflow (to) *überfliessen.*
overlook (to) *übersehen.*
overrun *überrennen, überlaufen.*
overseas *nach Übersee.*
overthrow *umstürzen, stürzen* (govt.).
overwhelm (to) *überwältigen.*
owe (to) *schulden.*
owl *Eule, f.*
own *eigen.*
own (to) *besitzen* (possess); *bekennen*
       zugeben (admit).
owner *Besitzer, m.*
ox *Ochse, m.*
oxygen *Sauerstoff, m.*
oyster *Auster, f.*
ozone *ozon, n.*

P

pace *Schritt, m; Tempo, n.*
pace (to) *schreiten.*
pacific *friedlich.*
pack *Kartenspiel, n.* (cards).
pack (to) *(ein)packen, verpacken, Packung,*
       f. (cigarettes); *Rucksack, m.;*
       Tornister, m.
package *Paket, n.*
page *Seite, f.*
pager *Pager, m.; Beeper, m.*
pain *Schmerz, m.*
pain (to) *schmerzen.*
painful *schmerzhaft.*
painless *schmerzlos.*
paint *Farbe, f.*
paint (to) *malen* (art); *(an)streichen* (a
       wall), *spritzen lassen* (car).
painter *Maler, m.*
painting *Gemälde, n.*
pair *Paar, n.*
pajamas *Pyjama, m.*
palace *Palast, m.*
pale *blass.*
palm *Palme, f.*
pamphlet *Broschüre, f.*
pan *Pfanne, f.*
pancake *Pfannkuchen, m.*
pane *Scheibe, f.*
panic *Panik, f.*
panorama *Panorama, n.*
panties *Schlüpfer, m.*
pants *Hose, f.*
paper *Papier, n.*
parachute *Fallschirm, m.*

parade *Parade, f.*
paragraph *Paragraph, m; Absatz, m.*
parallel *parallel.*
paralysis *Lähmung, f.*
paralyzed *gelähmt.*
parcel *Paket, n., Päckchen, n.*
pardon *Verzeihung, f; Entschuldigung, f.*
pardon (to) *vergeben, entschuldigen.*
parenthesis *Klammern, f.*
parents *Eltern, pl.*
Parisian *Pariser, m.*
park *Park, m.*
park (to) *parken.*
parliament *Parlament, n.*
parrot *Papagei, m.*
parsley *Petersilie, f.*
part *Teil, n.* (share); *Ersatzteil*
       (replacement).
part (to) *teilen, sich trennen* (separate);
       auseinander gehen.
partial *teilweise.*
partiality *Vorliebe, f.*
particular *besonder(er, -e, -es).*
particularly *besonders.*
partner *Partner, m.; Sozius, m.*
party (political) *Partei, f.; Gesellschaft, f.*
       (society); *Party; f.* (social).
pass *Ausweis, m.*
pass (to) *durchgehen, vorbeigehen; bestehen*
       (exam); *überholen* (overtake a car).
passage *Durchgang, m.; Überfahrt, f.*
       (travel).
passenger *Passagier, m.*
passion *Leidenschaft, f.*
passionately *leidenschaftlich.*
passive *Passiv, n.*
passport *Pass, m.*
past *Vergangenheit* (noun) *f.; vorbei, vorig*
       (time); *nach* (on the clock).
    ten past six   *zehn nach sechs.*
    last month   *vorigen Monat*
    last week   *vorige Woche*
    last year   *voriges Jahr*
paste *Kleister, m. Teig* (cul.).
paste (to) *kleistern, kleben.*
pastry *Gebäck, n.*
pastry shop *Konditorei, f.*
patch *Flicken, m.*
patch (to) *flicken.*
patent *Patent, n.*
paternal *väterlich.*
path *Weg, m; pfad, m.; Bahn, f.* (elec.).
pathetic *pathetisch.*
patience *Geduld, f.*
patient *Patient* (noun) *m.; geduldig* (adj.).
patriot *Patriot, m.*
patriotic *patriotisch.*
patron *Gönner, m.; Patron, m.; Förd-*
       erer, m.

patronage *Begünstigung, f.; Schutz, m.*

patronize (to) *unterstützen.*

pattern *Muster, n.*

pause *Pause, f.*

pave (to) *pflastern.*

pavement *Pflaster, n.*

paw *Pfote, f.*

pay *Lohn, m.; Bezahlung, f., Gehalt, n.*

pay (to) *zahlen, bezahlen.*

payment *Bezahlung, f.*

pea *Erbse, f.*

peace *Frieden, m.*

peaceful *friedlich.*

peach *Pfirsich, m.*

peak *Gipfel, n.*

peanut *Erdnuss, f.*

pear *Birne, f.*

pearl *Perle, f.*

peasant *Bauer, m.*

pebble *Kiesel(stein), m.*

peculiar *sonderbar.*

pedal *Pedal, n.*

pedantic *pedantisch.*

pedestrian *Fussgänger, m.*

peel *Rinde, f.; Schale, f.*

peel (to) *schälen.*

pen *Feder, f.*

    fountain pen   *Füllfeder, f.*

penalty *Strafe, f., Todesstrafe (death).*

pencil *Bleistift, m.*

penetrate (to) *durchdringen.*

peninsula *Halbinsel, f.*

penitence *Reue, f.*

pension *Pension, f.*

people *Leute, pl.*

pepper *Pfeffer, m.*

peppermint *Pfefferminz, m.*

per *pro.*

perceive (to) *wahrnehmen.*

percentage *Prozentsatz, m.*

perfect *vollkommen.*

perfection *Vollkommenheit, f.*

perfectly *gänzlich; völlig.*

perform (to) *verrichten; aufführen;*
    vortragen (theater); durchführen.

performance *Vorstellung, f.; Aufführung, f.*

perfume *Parfüm, f.*

perfume (to) *parfümieren.*

perhaps *vielleicht.*

period *Periode, f.; Punkt, m. (typ.).*

periodical *periodisch; Zeitschrift, f.*

permanent *ständig.*

permission *Erlaubnis, f.*

permit *Erlaubnisschein, m.*

permit (to) *erlauben.*

peroxide *Hyperoxyd, n., Superoxyd, n.*

perpetual *immerwährend, andauernd,*
    fortwährend.

perplex *verwirren.*

persecute (to) *verfolgen.*

persecution *Verfolgung, f.*

perseverance *Ausdauer, f.*

persist (to) *beharren.*

person *Person, f.*

personal *persönlich.*

personality *Persönlichkeit, f.*

perspective *Perspektive, f.*

perspiration *Schweiss, m.*

persuade (to) *überzeugen, überreden.*

pertaining *betreffend.*

petrol *Benzin, n.*

petticoat *Unterrock, m.*

petty *kleinlich.*

pharmacist *Apotheker, m.*

pharmacy *Apotheke, f.*

phenomenon *Phänomen, n.*

philosopher *Philosoph, m.*

philosophical *philosophisch.*

philosophy *Philosophie, f.*

phonograph *Plattenspieler, m.*

photograph *Fotografie, f., Aufnahme, f.*

photograph (to) *aufnehmen.*

photographer *Fotograf, m.*

photostat *Photokopie, f.; Fotokopie.*

phrase *Frase, f.*

physical *körperlich.*

physician *Arzt, m; Doktor, m.*

piano *Klavier, n.*

pick (to) *pflücken.*

pick up (td) *aufheben, abholen.*

picnic *Picknick, n.*

picture *Bild, n.*

picturesque *malerisch.*

pie *Torte, f.*

piece *Stück, n.*

pier *kai, m.; Landungssteg, m.*

pig *Schwein, n.*

pigeon *Taube, f.*

pile *Haufen, m., Stapel, m.*

pile (to) *aufhäufen, (auf) stapeln.*

pilgrim *Pilger, m.*

pill *Pille, f.*

pillar *Säule, f.*

pillow *Kissen, n.*

pilot *Pilot, m.*

    automatic pilot   *Steuergerät, n.*

pin *Stechnadel, f.*

pinch (to) *kneifen.*

pink *rosa.*

pious *fromm.*

pipe *Pfeife, f. (tobacco); Rohr, n.*
    (plumbing).

pirate *Seeräuber, m.; Pirat, m.*

pistol *Pistole, f.*

pitiful *mitleidig.*

pity *Mitleid, n.*

place *Platz, m.; Stelle, f. (spot, situation);*
    Ort, m. (locality).

take place *stattfinden.*
place (to) *stellen, legen, setzen.*
plain *Ebene* (noun) *f.; einfach* (adj.).
plan *Plan, m.* (project); *Entwurf, m.*
plan (to) *ausdenken.*
plane *Flugzeug, n.*
planet *Planet, m.*
plant *Pflanze, f.*
plant (to) *pflanzen.*
plaster *Verputz, m.; Pflaster, n.* (med.).
plastic *Kunststoff* (noun) *m.; plastisch* (adj.).
plate *Teller, m.*
platform *Bahnsteig, m.* (station).
platter *Platte, f.*
play *Spiel, n.; Stück, n.* (theater).
play (to) *spielen.*
plea *Gesuch, n.; Einrede, f.*
plead (to) *plädieren* (law); *inständig bitten; anflehen.*
pleasant *angenehm.*
please *bitte.*
please (to) *gefallen.*
pleasure *Vergnügen, n.*
pledge *Pfand, n. Verspechen, n.*
plenty *genug* (enough); *reichlich* (abundance).
plot *Verschwörung, f.* (conspiracy); *Handlung, f.* (of a story).
plot (to) *anstiften, heimlich planen.*
plow *Pflug, m.*
plow (to) *pflügen.*
plum *Pflaume, f.*
plumber *Klempner, m.*
pneumonia *Lungenentzündung, f.*
pocket *Tasche, f.*
poem *Gedicht, n.*
poet *Poet, m.; Dichter, m.*
poetic *poetisch.*
poetry *Dichtung, f.*
point *Punkt, m.; Spitze, f.*
point (to) *spitzen, hinweisen, richten auf.*
pointed *spitz(ig).*
poise *Gleichgewicht, n. (Körper) haltung, f.*
poison *Gift, n.*
poison (to) *vergiften.*
poisonous *giftig.*
polar *polar.*
pole *Pol, m.*
police *Polizei, f.*
policeman *Schutzmann, m.; Polizist, m.*
policy *Politik, f.; Police, f.* (insurance).
Polish *polnisch.*
polish *Glanz, m., Politur, f.*
polish (to) *glänzend machen, polieren.*
polite *höflich.*
politeness *Höflichkeit, f.*
political *politisch.*
pollution *Verschmutzung, f.*
pond *Teich, m.*

pool *Schwimmbad, n.*
poor *arm.*
Pope *Papst, m.*
popular *volkstümlich; beliebt* (liked).
population *Bevölkerung, f.*
pork *Schweinefleisch, n.*
port *Hafen, m.*
porter *Träger, m.*
portrait *Bild, n.; Porträt, n.*
Portuguese *Portugiese* (noun) *m.; portugiesisch* (adj.).
position *Stellung, f.* (job), *Lage, f.* (site).
positive *bestimmt, positiv.*
possibility *Möglichkeit, f.*
possible *möglich.*
post *Post, f.; Stelle, f.* (job).
postage *Porto, n.*
postcard *Postkarte, f.*
poster *Plakat, n.*
posterity *Nachkommenschaft, f.*
post office *Postamt, n.*
pot *Topf, m.*
potato *Kartoffel, f.*
pound *Pfund, n.*
pour (to) *giessen.*
poverty *Armut, f.*
powder *Pulver, n.* (gun); *Puder, m.* (cosmetic).
powder (to) *pudern.*
power *Macht, f., Gewalt, f.*
powerful *mächtig.*
practical *praktisch.*
practice (to) *üben.*
praise *Lob, n.*
praise (to) *loben, rühmen.*
prank *Streich, m.*
pray (to) *beten.*
prayer *Gebet, n.*
preach (to) *predigen.*
preacher *Prediger, m.*
precaution *Vorsicht, f.*
precede (to) *vorangehen.*
preceding *vorangehend.*
precept *Vorschrift, f.; Beispiel, n.* (example).
precious *kostbar, unschätzbar.*
precise *genau; steif* (formal).
precision *Genauigkeit, f.*
predecessor *Vorgänger, m.*
predict *voraussagen, vorhersagen.*
preface *Vorwort, n.*
prefer (to) *vorziehen.*
preference *Vorzug, m.*
pregnant *schwanger.*
prejudice *Vorurteil, n.*
preliminary *einleitend, vorbereitend.*
preparation *Vorbereitung, f.*
prepare (to) *vorbereiten, zubereiten.*
prepay (to) *vorauszahlen.*
prescribe (to) *verschreiben.*

prescription *Rezept, n.*
presence *Gegenwart, f.; Anwesenheit, f.*
present *Gegenwart, f.* (grammar), *Geschenk, n.* (gift), *anwesend* (adj.).
preserve (to) *erhalten; konservieren* (food); *bewahren.*
preserves *Konserven, f.; Eingemachte, n.; Konfitüren, f.* (jellies, jams).
preside (to) *präsidieren.*
president *Präsident, m.*
press *Presse, f.*
press (to) *drücken; bügeln* (clothes).
pressing *dringend.*
pressure *Druck, m.; Blutdruck* (blood-); *Drücken, n.*
prestige *Prestige, n.; Ansehen, n.*
presume (to) *vermuten.*
pretend (to) *vorgeben, vortäuschen.*
pretext *Vorwand, m.*
pretty *hübsch, nett.*
prevail (to) *vorherrschen, siegen.*
prevent (to) *verhindern.*
prevention *Verhinderung, f.*
previous *frühere.*
prey *Raub, m.*
price *Preis, m.*
price-cutting *Preissenkung, f.*
price tag *Preisschild, n.*
price war *Preiskrieg, m.*
pride *Stolz, m.*
priest *Priester, m.*
prince *Prinz, m.*
principal *haupt-* (adj.); *Haupt-, n.*
principle *Grundsatz, m.; Prinzip, n.*
print (to) *drucken.*
printer *Drucker, m.*
prison *Gefängnis, n.*
prisoner *Gefangene, m.*
private *privat.*
privilege *Vorrecht, n.*
prize *Preis, m.*
prize (to) *schätzen.*
probable *wahrscheinlich.*
problem *Problem, n.; Schwierigkeit, f.*
procedure *Verfahren, n.*
proceed (to) *fortschreiten.*
process *Verfahren, n.; Prozess, m.; Verlauf, m.*
procession *Prozession, f.*
proclaim (to) *bekanntmachen.*
produce (to) *erzeugen, hervorbringen, herstellen.*
production *Erzeugung, f.; Produktion, f.; Herstellung, f.; Fabrikation, f.*
productive *fruchtbar, schöpferisch, erzeugend.*
profession *Beruf, m.*
professional *beruflich, berufsmässig.*

professor *Professor, m. Lehrer, m.* (school).
profile *Profil, n.*
profit *Gewinn, m; Profit, m.*
profit (to) *gewinnen, profitieren.*
program *Programm, n.*
progress *Fortschritt, m.*
progress (to) *vorwärtskommen, weiterkommen.*
progressive *fortschrittlich.*
prohibit (to) *verbieten.*
prohibition *Verbot, n. Untersagung, f.*
project *Projekt, n.; Unternehmen, n.*
project (to) *hervorstehen, entwerfen.*
promise (to) *versprechen.*
prompt *schnell, sofortig.*
pronoun *Fürwort, n.*
pronounce (to) *aussprechen.*
pronunciation *Aussprache, f.*
proof *Beweis, m.*
propaganda *Propaganda, f.*
proper *passend, anständig* (decent).
property *Eigentum, n.*
proportion *Verhältnis, n.; Mass, n.*
proposal *Vorschlag, m.*
propose (to) *vorschlagen.*
prose *Prosa, f.*
prospect (to) *Aussicht, f.*
prosper (to) *gedeihen.*
prosperity *Wohlstand, m.*
prosperous *gedeihlich, blühend.*
protect (to) *schützen.*
protection *Schutz, m.*
protector *Beschützer, m.*
protest *Einspruch, m.; protest, m.*
protest (to) *protestieren, sich auflehnen (gegen).*
Protestant *Protestant, m.*
proud *stolz.*
prove (to) *beweisen, bestätigen.*
proverb *Sprichwort, n.*
provide (to) *versorgen.*
provided that *vorausgesetzt dass.*
province *Provinz, f.*
provincial *provinziell.*
provision *Lebensmittelvorrat, m.; Beschaffung, f., Besorgung, f.*
provoke (to) *herausfordern, reizen.*
prowl *herumschleichen, herumstreichen.*
proximity *Nähe, f.*
prudence *Vorsicht, f.*
prudent *klug, vorsichtig, umsichtig.*
prune *Backpflaume, f.*
psychological *psychologisch.*
psychology *Psychologie, f.*
public *Publikum* (noun) *n.; öffentlich* (adj.).
publication *Herausgabe, f.* (literary); *Veröffentlichung, f.* (notification).
publish (to) *herausgeben* (book); *veröffentlichen* (announcement).

publishing house *Verlag, m.*
publisher *Verleger, m.*
pull (to) *ziehen.*
pump *Pumpe, f.*
punish (to) *bestrafen.*
punishment *Strafe, f.*
pupil *Schüler, m.; Schülerin, f.*
purchase (to) *kaufen.*
purchase *Einkauf, m.*
pure *rein.*
purity *Reinheit, f.*
purple *Purpur, m.*
purpose *Absicht, f., Zweck, m.*
purse *Geldtasche, f., Portemonnaie, n.; Handtasche, f.*
pursue (to) *verfolgen, nachgehen.*
push (to) *stossen.*
put (to) *legen* (lay); *setzen,* (set); *stellen* (place).
    put down *aufschreiben.*
    put off *aufschieben.*
    put on *anziehen.*
    put up *aufstellen.*
    put into practice *einsetzen.*
    put a question to someone *eine Frage richten an.*
puzzle *Rätsel, n.*
puzzle (to) *verwirren.*

Q

quaint *seltsam.*
qualify *befähigen, qualifizieren.*
quality *Qualität, f.*
quantity *Quantität, f.*
quarrel *Streit, m.*
quarter *Viertel, n.*
queen *Königin, f.*
queer *seltsam, eigenartig.*
quench (to) *löschen* (thirst); *auslöschen* (fire).
question *Frage, f.*
question (to) *fragen.*
quick *schnell, geschwind, rasch.*
quiet *ruhig.*
quit (to) *verlassen, aufgeben.*
quite *ganz.*
quote (to) *anführen* (a fact); *zitieren* (a passage).

R

rabbi *Rabbiner, m.*
rabbit *Kaninchen, n.; Hase, m.* (hare).
race *Rennen, n.* (contest); *Rasse, f.* (species).
radiate (to) *strahlen.*

radiator *Heizkörper, m.; Kühler* (motor).
radio *Radio, n; Rundfunk, m.*
rag *Lappen, m.*
rage *Wut, f.*
ragged *zerlumpt, zerfetzt.*
rail *Schiene, f.*
railroad *Eisenbahn, f.*
railroad car *Eisenbahnwagen, m.*
rain *Regen, m.*
rain (to) *regnen.*
rainbow *Regenbogen, m.*
raincoat *Regenmantel, m.*
rainy *regnerisch.*
raise (to) *erhöhen.*
raisin *Rosine, f.*
rake *Rechen, m.; Harke, f.*
rank *Rang, m.; Glied, n.* (mil.).
rapid *schnell.*
rapidly *schnell, geschwind, rasch.*
rapture *Entzücken, n.*
rash *Hautausschlag* (noun) *m.* (skin); *hastig* (adj.).
rat *Ratte, f.*
rate *Kurs, m.* (exchange); *Preis, m.*
rate (to) *(ab)schätzen.*
rather *ziemlich, lieber, eher.*
ration *Ration, f.*
rational *vernünftig.*
rave (to) *schwärmen.*
raw *roh.*
ray *Strahl, m.*
razor *Rasiermesser, n.*
razor blade *Rasierklinge, f.*
reach (to) *erreichen, greifen* (nach).
reach *Reichweite, f.*
react (to) *reagieren, entgegenwirken.*
read (to) *lesen.*
reading *Lesen, n.; Lektüre, f.*
ready *fertig.*
real *wirklich.*
realization *Verwirklichung, f.*
realize (to) *verwirklichen.*
really *wirklich.*
rear *Hintergrund* (noun) *m.; hinter* (adj.).
rear (to) *grossziehen, aufziehen* (children); *züchten* (animals).
reason *Grund, m.* (cause); *Vernunft, f.* (intelligence).
    it stands to reason *es versteht sich.*
reason (to) *logisch denken, vernüftig urteilen.*
reasonable *vernünftig.*
reasoning *Schlussfolgerung, f.; Urteilen, n.*
reassure (to) *beruhigen.*
rebel *Rebell, m.*
rebel (to) *sich auflehnen, rebellieren.*
rebellion *Empörung, f.; Aufstand, m.*
recall (to) *sich erinnern* (memory); *zurückrufen* (to summon back).*

receipt *Quittung, f.*
receive (to) *empfangen, erhalten, bekommen.*
receiver *Empfäger, m.*
recent *neu.*
recently *neulich.*
reception *Empfang, m.*
recess *Ferien f.* (school)*; Pause, f.*
reciprocal *gegenseitig.*
recite (to) *aufsagen; rezitieren* (drama).
recognize (to) *erkennen.*
recollect (to) *sich erinnern an.*
recollection *Erinnerung, f.*
recommend (to) *empfehlen.*
recommendation *Empfehlung, f.*
reconcile (to) *versöhnen.*
record *Rekord, m.* (sports).
    phonograph record *(Schall)platte, f.*
recover (to) *sich erholen* (illness).
    zurückerhalten (to get back)*; neu*
    uberziehen (quilt, sofa).
recruit *Rekrut, m.* (mil.).
recruit (to) *rekrutieren, (an)werben.*
red *rot.*
Red Cross *Das Rote Kreuz, n.*
redeem (to) *erlösen.*
reduce (to) *herabsetzen; abnehmen* (weight).
reduction *Nachlass, m.; Verminderung, f.*
reed *Schilf, n.*
reef *Riff, n.*
refer (to) *sich beziehen.*
reference *Bezugnahme, f.*
referring (to) *mit Bezugnahme auf.*
    in reference to (corresp.) *Betreff/Betrifft.*
refine (to) *verfeinern.*
refinement *Verfeinerung, f.*
reflect (to) *zurückstrahlen; widerspiegeln.*
reflection *Widerschein, m.* (image);
    Überlegung, f. (thoughts).
reform *Besserung, f.*
reform (to) *sich bessern, reformieren.*
refrain (to) *sich enthalten.*
refresh (to) *erfrischen.*
refreshment *Erfrischung, f.*
refrigerator *Kühlschrank, m.*
refuge *Zufluchtsort, m.*
    take refuge *flüchten.*
refugee *Flüchtling, m.*
refund *Rückzahlung, f.*
refund (to) *zurückzahlen.*
refusal *Verweigerung, f., Ablehnung, f.*
refuse (to) *ablehnen, verweigern.*
refute (to) *widerlegen.*
regard *Ansehen, n.*
regardless *ungeachtet, ohne Rücksicht auf.*
regime *Regime, n.*
regiment *Regiment, n.*
register (to) *eintragen* (membership)*;*
    einschreiben (letter)*; sich*
    immatrikulieren (university).

regret *Bedauern, n., Reue, f.*
regret (to) *bedauern.*
regular *regelmässig.*
regulate *regulieren.*
regulation *Vorschrift, f.*
rehearsal *Probe, f.*
rehearse (to) *Probe halten.*
reign *Herrschaft, f.*
reign (to) *herrschen.*
reinforce (to) *verstärken.*
reject (to) *ablehnen.*
rejoice (to) *sich freuen.*
relapse *Rückfall, m.*
relate (to) *erzählen.*
relation *Verwandtschaft, f.*
relationship *verwandtschaftliche Beziehung,*
    f.; Verhältnis, n.
relative *Verwandte, m./f.*
relax (to) *entspannen.*
relaxation *Entspannung, f.*
release *Befreiung, f.*
release (to) *freilassen.*
reliable *zuverlässig.*
relic *Überbleibsel, n.; Relique, f.;* (religious).
relief *Erleichterung, f.; Linderung, f.* (of
    pain).
relieve (to) *erleichtern, lindern.*
religion *Religion, f.*
religious *religiös.*
relinquish (to) *aufgeben.*
relish (to) *mit Appetit geniessen.*
relish *Geschmack, m.; Genuss (an), m.*
reluctance *Widerwille, n.*
reluctant *widerwillig.*
rely (to) *sich verlassen (auf).*
remain (to) *bleiben.*
remainder *Rest, m.*
remark *Bemerkung, f.*
remark (to) *bemerken.*
remarkable *bemerkenswert.*
remedy *Arznei, f.* (medicine)*; Hilfsmittel, n.*
    (cure).
remember (to) *sich erinnern (an).*
remembrance *Erinnerung, f.*
remind (about) (to) *mahnen.*
remorse *Reue, f.*
remote *entfernt* (distance)*; rückständig;*
    abgelegen (distance).
removal *Beseitigung, f.*
remove (to) *entfernen.*
renew (to) *erneuern.*
renewal *Erneuerung, f.*
rent *Miete, f.*
rent (to) *mieten.*
repair *Reparatur, f.*
repay (to) *zurückzahlen.*
repeat (to) *wiederholen.*
repent (to) *bereuen.*
repetition *Wiederholung, f.*

replace *zurückerstatten* (things taken); *ersetzen.*

reply *Antwort, f.*

reply (to) *antworten.*

report *Bericht, m.; Zeugnis, n.* (report card).

report (to) *berichten.*

reporter *Reporter, m.*

represent (to) *vertreten.*

representation *Vertretung, f.*

representative *Vertreter, m.*

repress (to) *unterdrücken.*

represson *Unterdrückung, f..*

reprimand *Verweis, m; Tadel, m.*

reprimand (to) *tadeln.*

reprisal *Vergeltungsmassnahme, f.*

reproach *Vorwurf, m.*

reproach (to) *vorwerfen.*

reproduce (to) *reproduzieren.*

reproduction *Reproduktion, f.; Vervielfältigung, f.*

republic *Republik, f.*

repulse *zurücktreiben, zurückschlagen.*

reputation *Ruf, m.; Ansehen, n.*

request *Bitte, f.; Ersuchen, n.*

request (to) *bitten.*

require (to) *benötigen.*

requirement *Bedarf, m.*

rescue (to) *retten.*

research *Forschung, f.*

resent (to) *verübeln.*

resentful *aufgebracht, ärgerlich.*

resentment *Verdruss, m.*

reservation *Reservation, f.*

reserve (to) *reservieren.*

reservoir *Behälter, m.*

residence *Wohnstätte, f.*

resident *Bewohner, m.*

resign (to) *aufgeben, austreten* (Aus.).

resignation *Rücktritt, m.*

resist (to) *widerstehen.*

resistance *Widerstand, m.*

resolute *entschlossen.*

resolution *Beschluss, m.*

resolve (to) *sich entschliessen* (decide); *lösen; aufklären* (problem).

resort *Kurort, m.* (health); *Luftkurort, m.; Erholungsort, m.; Zuflucht, f.* (recourse); *als letzter Ausweg* (as a last resort).

resource *Hilfsmittel, n.*

respect *Achtung, f.*

respectful *ehrfürchtig, achtungsvoll.*

responsibility *Verantwortlichkeit, f.*

responsible *verantwortlich.*

rest *Ruhe, f.*

rest (to) *ruhen; sich ausruhen.*

restaurant *Restaurant, n.*

restless *unruhig.*

restoration *Wiederherstellung, f.*

restore (to) *wiederherstellen, restaurieren.*

restrain (to) *zurückhalten.*

restraint *Zurückhaltung, f.*

restrict (to) *beschränken.*

restriction *Einschränkung, f.; Beschränkung, f.*

result *Resultat, n.; Ergebnis, n.; Folge, f.*

result (to) *folgen; sich ergeben.*

resume (to) *wiederaufnehmen, wieder anfangen.*

retail *Einzelverkauf, m.; Kleinhandel, m.*

retail (to) *im Kleinhandel verkaufen.*

retain (to) *behalten.*

retaliate (to) *vergelten.*

retaliation *Vergeltung, f.*

retire (to) *sich zurückziehen, in den Ruhestand treten.*

retirement *Zurückgezogenheit, f.; Pensionierung, f.*

retract *widerrufen; zurückziehen.*

retreat *Rückzug, m.*

retreat (to) *sich zurückziehen.*

return *Rückkehr, f.*

return (to) *zurückkehren.*

reveal (to) *offenbaren, enthüllen.*

revelation *Offenbarung, f.*

revenge *Rache, f.*

revenge (to) *rächen.*

revenue *Einkommen, n.*

reverence *Ehrerbietung, f.*

reverend *ehrwürdig.*

reverse *Rückseite, f.; Kehrseite* (side of a coin).

reverse (to) *umkehren.*

review (to) *überprüfen; rezensieren* (critical); *wiederholen.*

review *Überblick, m. Parade, f.* (army); *Revue, f.* (theater), *Rezension, f.* (book).

revise (to) *revidieren* (critique); *überarbeiten.*

revive *auffrischen, wieder zu Bewusstsein bringen.*

revival *Wiederbelebung, f.*

revoke (to) *widerrufen.*

revolt *Aufstand, m.*

revolt (to) *sich empören.*

revolution *Revolution, f.*

revolve (to) *sich drehen.*

reward *Belohnung, f.*

reward (to) *belohnen.*

rhyme *Reim, m.*

rhyme (to) *reimen.*

rib *Rippe, f.*

ribbon *Band, n.*

rice *Reis, m.*

rich *reich.*

richness *Reichtum, m.*

rid (to get) *loswerden.*
riddle *Rätsel, n.,*
ride *Fahrt, f.*
ridiculous *lächerlich.*
rifle *Gewehr, n.*
right (noun) *Recht, n.*
right *richtig* (correct); *rechts* (position).
   all right   *ganz gut.*
righteous *gerecht.*
rigid *steif, fest, starr.*
rigor *Strenge, f.*
rigorous *streng, scharf, hart.*
ring *Ring, m.*
   wedding ring   *Trauring, m.*
ring (to) *ringen, läuten; schellen* (bell).
rinse (to) *spülen, ausspülen.*
riot (to) *Aufruhr, f.*
ripe *reif.*
ripen (to) *reifen.*
rise *Steigung, f.*
rise (to) *aufstehen* (get up); *steigen*
   (increase, mount), *aufgehen* (sun).
risk *Gefahr, f.*
risk (to) *riskieren, wagen.*
rite *Ritus, m.*
ritual *rituell.*
rival *Rivale, m.; Konkurrent, m.*
rivalry *Mitbewerbung, f., Konkurrenz, f.*
river *Fluss, m.*
roach *Schabe, f.; Schwabe, f.*
road *Weg, m.*
roar (to) *brüllen.*
roast *Braten, m.*
roast (to) *braten.*
rob (to) *rauben.*
robber *Räuber, m.*
robbery *Diebstahl, m.*
robe *Morgenrock, m.*
robot *Roboter, n.*
robust *stark, kräftig.*
rock *Felsen, m.*
rock (to) *wiegen, schaukeln.*
rocky *felsig.*
rocket *Rakete, f.*
rod *Rute, f.; Stab, m.*
roll *Rolle, f.* (cylinder); *Brötchen, n.* (bread);
   Semmel, f. (Aust.).
roll (to) *rollen.*
Roman *Römer* (noun) *m.; römisch* (adj).
romantic *romantisch.*
roof *Dach, n.*
room *Zimmer, n.* (of a house); *Weltraum, m.*
   (space).
   There is no room.   *Da ist kein Platz.*
roomy *geräumig.*
root *Wurzel, f.*
rope *Seil, n.; Strick, m.*
rose *Rose, f.*
rot (to) *faulen; vermodern.*

rough *rauh* (coarse); *roh* (crude); *stürmisch*
   (stormy).
round *Runde* (noun) *f.; rund* (adj.).
round *um* (acc.); *herum.*
round-trip *Rundreise, f.*
rouse (to) *aufwecken; erregun* (to stir up).
routine *Routine, f.*
row *Reihe, f.*
row (to) *rudern.*
royal *königlich.*
rub (to) *reiben.*
rubber *Gummi, m.*
ruby *Rubin, m.*
rude *grob, unhöflich.*
ruffle (to) *ausser Fassung bringen* (to
   upset); *kräuseln.*
ruin *Ruine, f.*
ruin (to) *ruinieren.*
rule *Regel, f.*
rule (to) *regieren, herrschen.*
ruler *Lineal, n.*
rum *Rum, m.*
rumor *Gerücht, n.*
run (to) *rennen, laufen.*
   run away   *weglaufen.*
rural *ländlich.*
rush (to) *Sturz, m.; Andrang, m.* (crowd).
Russian *Russe* (noun) *m.; russisch* (adj.).
rust (to) *rosten.*
rusty *rostig.*
rye *Roggen, m.*

S

sacred *heilig.*
sacrifice *Opfer, n.*
sacrifice (to) *opfern.*
sacrilege *Entweihung, f.*
sad *traurig.*
sadden (to) *betrüben.*
saddle *Sattel, m.*
sadness *Traurigkeit, f.*
safe *Schliessfach* (noun) *m.* (of a bank);
   wohlbehalten (adj.) (in safekeeping);
   sicher (adj.) (secure).
safety *Sicherheit, f.*
sail (to) *segeln.*
sail *Segel, n.*
sailor *Matrose, m.*
saint *Heilige, m. & f.*
   patron saint   *Schutzheilige, m. & f.*
sake (for the . . . of) *um . . . willen.*
salad *Salat, m.*
salami *Salami, f.*
salary *Gehalt, n.*
sale *Verkauf, m.; Ausverkauf, m.* (bargain).
saleslady *Verkäuferin,f.*
salesman *Verkäufer, m.*

salmon *Lachs, m.*
salt *Salz, n.*
salute *Gruss, m.*
salute (to) *grüssen.*
salvation *Rettung, f.*
Salvation Army *Heilsarmee, f.*
same *der- (die-, das-) selbe*
   the same as *der-, die-, dasselbe wie.*
   all the same *es spielt keine Rolle.*
sample *Muster,n.*
sanctuary *Zufluchtsort, m.*
sand *Sand, m.*
sandal *Sandale, f.*
sandwich *belegtes Butterbrot, n.*
sandy *sandig.*
sanitary *hygienisch.*
sap *Saft, m.*
sapphire *Saphir, m.*
sarcasm *Sarkasmus, m.*
sarcastic *sarkastisch.*
sardine *Sardine, f.*
satiate (to) *sättigen.*
satin *Seiden, m.*
satisfaction *Befriedigung, f.*
satisfactory *zufriedenstellend.*
satisfy (to) *befriedigen.*
saturate (to) *durchtränken, imprägnieren,*
   (chem.).
Saturday *Samstag, m.; Sonnabend, m.*
sauce *Sauce, f.; Sosse, f.*
saucer *Untertasse, f.*
sausage *Wurst, f.*
savage (adj.) *wild, ungezähmt.*
save (to) *sparen (hoard), retten (rescue).*
saving *Ersparnis, f.*
savior *Erretter, m.*
say (to) *sagen.*
scale *Schuppe, f.; Tonleiter, f. (music).*
scales *Waage, f.*
scalp *Skalp, m.; Kopfhaut, f.*
scan (to) *flüchtig überblicken.*
scandal *Skandal, m.*
scanty *knapp, dürftig.*
scar *Narbe, f.*
scarce *knapp.*
scarcely *kaum.*
scare (to) *erschrecken.*
scarf *Schal, m.*
scarlet *scharlachrot.*
scattered *verstreut.*
schedule *Stundenplan, m. (time); Fahrplan*
   (train, bus).
scheme *Schema, n.; Entwurf, m.*
scholar *Gelehrte, m. & f.*
school *Schule, f.*
schoolteacher *Lehrer, m.; Lehrerin, f.*
science *Wissenschaft, f.*
scientific *wissenschaftlich.*
scientist *Wissenschafter, m.*

scissors *Schere, f.*
scold (to) *schelten.*
scorn *Verachtung, f.*
scorn (to) *verachten.*
scornful *verächtlich, höhnisch.*
Scottish *schottisch.*
scrape (to) *kratzen; schaben (vegetables).*
scraper *Schaber, m.*
scratch *Schramme, f.; Kratzwunde,f.*
scratch (to) *kratzen.*
scream *Schrei, m.*
scream (to) *schreien.*
screen *Schirm, m.*
   movie screen *Leinwand, f.*
screw *Schraube, f.*
scribble (to) *kritzeln.*
scruple *Skrupel, m.*
scrupulous *gewissenhaft.*
scrutinize (to) *genau prüfen.*
scuba diving (*Sport*)*tauchen, n.*
sculptor *Bildhauer, m.*
sculpture *Bildhauerei, f.*
sea *Meer, n.*
seal *Siegel, n.; Seehund, m. (animal).*
seal (to) *siegeln.*
seam *Naht, f.*
search *Suche, f.; Untersuchung, f. (customs).*
search (to) *suchen, untersuchen.*
seashore *Seeküste, f.*
seasickness *Seekrankheit, f.*
season *Jahreszeit, f.; Saison, f. (events).*
seat *Sitz, m.*
seat (to) *setzen; Platz verschaffen.*
seat belt *Sicherheitsgurt, m.*
second *zweit(er, -e, -es).*
secret *Geheimnis (noun) n.; geheim, (adj.).*
secretary *Sekretär, m.; Sekretärin, f.*
sect *Sekte, f.*
section *Teil, m.*
secure *sicher.*
secure (to) *sichern.*
security *Sicherheit, f.*
see (to) *sehen.*
seed *Samen, m.*
seek (to) *suchen.*
seem (to) *scheinen.*
seize (to) *ergreifen, fassen.*
seldom *selten, rar.*
select (to) *(aus)wählen.*
selection *Auswahl, f.*
selfish *selbstsüchtig; egoistisch.*
selfishness *Selbstsucht, f.*
self-service *Selbstbedienung.*
sell (to) *verkaufen.*
semicolon *Semikolon, n.*
senate *Senat, m.*
senator *Senator, m.*
send (to) *senden.*
senior *Ältere(r).*

sensation *Gefühl, n.* (feeling); *Sensation, f.* (excitement); *Sinnesempfindung, f.*
sense *Sinn, m.*
senseless *sinnlos.*
sensibility *Vernünftigkeit, f.*
sensible *vernünftig.*
sensitive *empfindlich.*
sensitivity *Empfindlichkeit, f.*
sensual *sinnlich.*
sensuality *Wollust, f., Sinnlichkeit, f.*
sentence *Urteil, n.* (legal); *Satz, m.* (grammar).
sentiment *Gefühl, n.*
sentimental *sentimental.*
sentimality *Sentimentalität, f.*
separate *einzeln, getrennt.*
separate (to) *trennen.*
separately *besonders, getrennt.*
separation *Trennung, f.*
September *September, m.*
serene *heiter, friedlich.*
sergeant *Sergeant, m.; Unteroffizier, m.*
series *Serie, f.*
serious *ernst.*
seriousness *Ernsthaftigkeit, f.*
servant *Diener, m.*
serve (to) *dienen.*
service *Dienst, m.; Gottesdienst, m.* (church service).
session *Sitzung, f.*
set (adj.) *festgelegt.*
set *Sammlung, f.* (collection); *Untergang, m.;* (sun); *Satz, m.* (series); *Service, n.* (dishes).
set (to) *setzen; stellen* (clock).
  to set the table *decken.*
settle (to) *abrechnen* (accounts); *erledigen* (conclude); *festsezen.*
  . . . in a territory *sich niederlassen.*
  . . . in a place *ansässig werden.*
settlement *Begleichung, f.; Erledigung, f.; Siedlung, f.* (houses).
seven *sieben.*
seventeen *siebzehn.*
seventeenth *siebzehnte.*
seventh *siebte.*
seventieth *siebzigste.*
seventy *siebzig.*
several *mehrere.*
  several times *mehrmals.*
severe *streng* (stern, rigorous); *heftig* (pain).
severity *Strenge, f.*
sew (to) *nähen.*
sewage *Kloakenwasser, n.*
sewer *Abwasserkanal, m.*
sex *Geschlecht, n.*
shabby *schäbig.*
shade *Schatten, m.*
shadow *Shatten, m.*

shady *schattig.*
shake (to) *schütteln; zittern* (tremble).
  handshake *Händedruck, m.*
shallow *seicht, oberflächlich* (fig.).
shame *Schande, f.* (disgrace); *Scham, f.* (modesty).
shameful *schändlich.*
shameless *schamlos.*
shampoo *Shampoo, n.; Haarwaschmittel, m.*
shape *Form, f.*
share *Teil, m.; Anteil, m. Aktie, f.* (stock).
share (to) *teilen, (sich) beteiligen.*
shareholder *Aktionär, m.*
sharp *scharf.*
sharpen *schärfen.*
shave (to) *sich rasieren.*
she *sie.*
shed *Hütte, f.*
shed (to) *vergiessen* (spill); *abwerfen* (discard).
sheep *Schaf, n.*
sheer *rein, lauter.*
sheet *(Bett)laken, n.; Blatt, n.* (paper).
shelf *Brett, n.*
shell *Muschel, f.; Geschoss, n.* (artillery).
shelter *Unterkunft, f.; Luftschutzraum, m.* (air raids).
shelter *unterstellen* (from exposure); *schützen* (from danger); *beherbergen.*
shepherd *Schäfer, m.*
shield *Schild, n.*
shield (to) *schützen.*
shift *Schicht, f.* (workers).
shift (to) *schieben, versetzen, umstellen.*
shine (to) *scheinen; putzen* (shoes).
ship *Schiff, n.*
ship (to) *senden, verschiffen, verfrachten.*
shipment *Verladung, f.; Verschiffung, f.; Beförderung, f.* (conveyance of goods).
shirt *Hemd, n.*
shiver *Schauer, m., Zittern, n.*
shiver (to) *(er)schauern.*
shock *Schlag, m.* (blow); *Stoss, m.*
shock (to) *anstossen* (scandalize); *erschüttern, schockieren.*
shoe *Schuh, m.*
shoemaker *Schuhmacher, m.*
shoot (to) *schiessen.*
shop *Laden, m.; Geschäft, n.*
shopping center *Einkaufszentrum, n.*
short *kurz.*
shorten (to) *kürzen.*
shorthand *Kurzschrift, f.; Stenographie, f.*
shorts *Unterhosen, pl.* (men's underwear); *kurze Hosen* (short pants).
shot *Schuss, m.*
shoulder *Schulter, f.*
shout *Schrei, m.*

shout (to) *schreien.*

shovel *Schaufel, f.*

show *Vorstellung, f.* (play); *Ausstellung, f.* (exhibition).

show (to) *zeigen, aufführen, ausstellen.*

showcase *Vitrine, f.; Schaukasten, m.*

shower *Schauer, m.* (rain); *Dusche, f.* (shower-bath).

shrill *schrill, gellend.*

shrimp *Garnele, f.*

shrink (to) *einlaufen.*

shrub *Strauch, m.; Busch, m.*

shrubbery *Gebüsch, n.*

shun (to) *meiden, sich fern halten* (*von*).

shut *geschlossen.*

shut (to) *schliessen.*

shy *schüchtern.*

sick *krank.*

sickness *Krankheit, f.*

side *Seite, f.*

sidewalk *Bürgersteig, m.*

siege *Belagerung, f.*

sigh *Seufzer, m.*

sight *Aussicht, f.; Anblick, m.*

sign (to) *seufzen, unterschreiben, unterzeichnen.*

sign *Zeichen, n.*

signal *Signal, n.*

signal (to) *signalisieren.*

signature *Unterschrift, f.*

significance *Bedeutung, f.*

significant *bezeichnend.*

signify (to) *bezeichnen* (indicate); *bedeuten* (mean).

silence *Schweigen, n.*

silent *still, schweigend, schweigsam.*

silk *Seide, f.*

silken *seiden.*

silly *dumm, albern, lächerlich.*

silver *Silber, n.*

silvery *silbern.*

similar *ähnlich.*

similarity *Ähnlichkeit, f.*

simple *einfach.*

simplicity *Einfachheit, f.*

simply *einfach, nur* (only).

simulate (to) *simulieren, vortäuschen.*

simultaneous *gleichzeitig.*

sin *Sünde, f.*

sin (to) *sündigen.*

since *seit* (dat.); *da, weil* (because).

sincere *aufrichtig, im Ernst.*

sincerity *Aufrichtigkeit, f.*

sing (to) *singen.*

singer *Sänger, m.; Sängerin, f.*

single *einzeln; ledig* (unmarried).

singular *einzigartig; seltsam* (strange).

sinister *unheilvoll, böse.*

sink *Gussstein, m.; Ausguss, m.*

sink (to) *sinken.*

sinner *Sünder, m.; Sünderin, f.*

sip (to) *nippen.*

sip *Schluck, m.; Schlückchen, n.*

sir *Herr, m.*

sister *Schwester, f.*

sister-in-law *Schwägerin, f.*

sit (to) *sitzen* (be seated); *sich setzen* (sit down).

   to sit for an exam *sich einer Prüfung unterziehen.*

   to sit for a portrait *sich malen lassen.*

site *Lage, f.; Bauplatz, m.* (of a building); *Stelle, f.*

situation *Lage, f.; Umstände, pl.*

six *sechs.*

sixteen *sechzehnte.*

sixteenth *sechzehnte.*

sixth *sechste.*

sixtieth *sechzigste.*

sixty *sechzig.*

size *Grösse, f.*

skate *Schlittschuh, m.*

skate (to) *Schlittschuh laufen.*

skeleton *Gerippe, n.; Skelett, n.*

sketch *Skizze, f.*

sketch (to) *skizzieren.*

skill *Geschicklichkeit, f.*

skillful *geschickt, kundig.*

skin *Haut, f.*

skirt *Rock, m.*

skull *Schädel, m.*

sky *Himmel, m.*

skyscraper *Wolkenkratzer, m.*

slam (to) *zuchlagen.*

slander (to) *verleumden.*

slap *Klaps, m.; Ohrfeige, f.* (in the face).

slate *Schiefer, m.; Dachschiefer.*

slaughter (to) *schlachten.*

slave *Sklave, m.; Sklavin, f.*

slavery *Sklaverei, f.*

sleep *Schlaf, m.*

sleep (to) *schlafen.*

sleeve *Ärmel, m.*

sleigh *Schlitten, m.*

slender *schlank.*

slice *Schnitte, f.; Scheibe* (bread).

slice (to) *in Scheiben schneiden.*

slide (to) *gleiten, rutschen.*

slight *gering, leichte Erkältung.*

slip (to) (*aus*)*rutschen, gleiten.*

   to slip on *anziehen* (clothes).

   to slip away *entschlüpfen.*

   to slip in *hineinschieben in.*

   to slip up *sich irren, im Irrtum sein.*

slip *Fehler, m.* (mistake); *Unterrock, m.* (lingerie).

slope *Abhang, m.*

slot *Einwurf, m. Schlitz, m.* (mail).

slow *langsam.*
slumber *Schlummer, m.*
slumber (to) *schlummern.*
sly *schlau.*
small *klein.*
smart *elegant* (clothes); *gescheit* (clever).
smash (to) *zerschmettern.*
smear (to) *beschmieren, einreiben.*
smell *Geruch, m.*
smell (to) *riechen.*
smile *Lächeln, n.*
smile (to) *lächeln.*
smoke *Rauch, m.*
smoke (to) *rauchen.*
smooth *glatt.*
smother (to) *ersticken.*
smuggle (to) *schmuggeln.*
snail *Schnecke, f.*
snake *Schlange, f.*
snapshot *Aufnahme, f.*
snatch (to) *ergreifen.*
sneer (to) *verhöhnen.*
sneeze (to) *niessen.*
snore (to) *schnarchen.*
snow *Schnee, m.*
snowstorm *Schneesturm, m.*
so *so.*
   and so on   *und so weiter.*
soak (to) *einweichen, durchnässen* (drench).
soap *Seife, f.*
sob *Schluchzen, n.*
sob (to) *schluchzen.*
sober *nüchtern.*
social *gesellschaftlich.*
society *Gesellschaft, f.*
sock *Sock, f.; kurzer Strumpf, m.*
soda *Sodawasser, n.; Sprudel, n.*
soft *weich.*
soften (to) *erweichen, aufweichen.*
software *Software f.*
soil (to) *beschmutzen.*
soil *Erde, f.; Boden, m.*
soiled *schmutzig, beschmutzt.*
solar energy *Sonnenenergie, f.,
            Solarenergie, f.*
soldier *Soldat, m.*
sole *Sohle, f.*
solemn *feierlich.*
solemnity *Feierlichkeit, f.*
solicit (to) *bitten, ersuchen.*
solid *fest, solide.*
solitary *einsam* (lonely); *einzeln* (one).
solitude *Einsamkeit, f.*
solution *Lösung, f.*
solve *lösen.*
some *einige* (a few); *etwas* (partial).
somebody *jemand.*
somehow *irgendwie.*
something *etwas.*

sometimes *zuweilen, manchmal.*
somewhat *etwas, einigermassen.*
somewhere *irgendwo.*
son *Sohn, m.*
song *Lied, n.*
son-in-law *Schwiegersohn, m.*
soon *bald.*
soot *Russ, m.*
soothe (to) *besänftigen; lindern* (pain).
sore *Geschwür* (noun) *n.; wund, schmerzhaft*
         (adj.); *empfindlich, verärgert*
         (annoyed).
   sore throat   *Halsschmerzen, pl.*
sorrow *Kummer, m.*
sorry *bekümmert.*
   I am sorry.   *Es tut mir leid.*
sort *Sorte, f.; Art, f.*
sort (to) *sortieren, einordnen.*
sound *Laut, m.; Geräusch, n.*
sound (to) *lauten, läuten* (telephone).
soup *Suppe, f.*
sour *sauer.*
source *Quelle, f.* (spring); *Ursprung, m.*
         (origin).
south *Süden, m.*
southeast *südöstlich* (adj.); *Südosten, m.*
southern *Süd-; südlich.*
southwest *südwestlich; Südwesten, m.*
sovereign *Herrscher, m.; Herrscherin, f.;
            Soverän, m.*
sow (to) *säen.*
space *Raum, m.; Zwischenraum, m.* (space
         between).
spacious *(ge)räumig.*
spade *Spaten, m.; Pik, n.* (cards).
Spanish *spanisch.*
spare *spärlich.*
spare (to) *entbehren, schonen.*
spark *Funke, m.*
sparkle (to) *funkeln, glänzen.*
sparrow *Sperling, Spatz, m.*
speak (to) *sprechen.*
special *besonders, extra.*
specialty *Spezialität, f.*
specific *eigen, spezifisch, genau.*
specify (to) *spezifizieren, anführen.*
spectacle *Schauspiel, n.; Schaustück, n.*
spectator *Zuschauer, m.*
speculate (to) *spekulieren.*
speech *Sprache, f.; Rede, f.*
speed *Geschwindigkeit, f.*
speedy *schnell, geschwind.*
spell *Zauber, m.* (charm).
spell (to) *buchstabieren, schreiben.*
spelling *Buchstabieren, n.*
spend (to) *ausgeben.*
sphere *Sphäre, f.*
spice *Gewürz, n.*
spice (to) *würzen.*

spicy *würzig.*
spider *Spinne, f.*
spill (to) *verschütten, vergiessen.*
spin (to) *spinnen.*
spine *Rückgrat, n.; Wirbelsäude, f.*
spirit *Geist, m.*
spiritual *geistig.*
spit (to) *spucken.*
spite *Bösartigkeit, f.*
   in spite of *trotz* (gen.), *trotzdem* (gen. or
     dat.).
splash (to) *(be)spritzen.*
splendid *prachtvoll.*
   Splendid! *Wunderbar!*
splendor *Pracht, f.; Glanz, m.*
split *Spalt, m.; Trennung, f.; Spaltung, f.*
split (to) *spalten.*
spoil (to) *verderben; verwöhnen* (child).
sponge *Schwamm, m.*
spontaneous *spontan.*
spoon *Löffel, m.*
spoonful *Löffelvoll, m.*
sport *Sport, m.*
spot *Fleck, m.* (stain); *Stelle, f.* (place).
spread (to) *verbreiten; bestreichen* (on
     bread).
spring *Frühling, m.* (season); *Sprung, m.*
     (jump); *Quelle, f.* (source).
spring (to) *springen.*
sprinkle *sprenkeln, bestreuen, sprengen.*
sprout *Sprössling, m.; Spross, m.*
spur *Sporn, m.*
spur (to) *anspornen.*
   on the spur of the moment *spontan.*
spurn (to) *verschmähen* (an offer);
     zurückstossen (a person).
spy *Spion, m.*
spy (to) *spionieren.*
squadron *Schwadron, f.; Eskadron, f.* (mil.);
     Batallion (tanks).
square *Quadrat, n.*
squeeze (to) *(aus)drücken.*
squirrel *Eichhörnchen, n.*
stabilize (to) *stabilisieren.*
stable *fest* (adj.); *stabil.*
stack *Stoss, m.* (wood).
stack (to) *aufstapeln, aufhäufen.*
stadium *Stadion, n.*
staff *Stab* (military), *m.; Personal, n.*
     (business).
stage *Bühne, f.* (theater); *Stadium, n.*
stain *Fleck, m.; Färbemittel* (dye), *n.*
stain (to) *(be)flecken, färben.*
stairs *Treppe, f.*
stammer (to) *stottern.*
stamp *Briefmarke, f.* (postage); *Stempel, m.*
stance *Haltung, f.; Stellung, f.*
stand *Stand, m.*
   Stand still *Stillstehen.*

to stand pain *den Schmerz aushalten.*
to stand on ceremony *Umstände machen.*
to stand back *zurücktreten.*
star *Stern, m.*
starch *Stärke, f.*
stare (to) *(an)starren.*
start *Anfang, m.*
start (to) *beginnen, anfangen.*
starve (to) *(ver)hungern.*
state *Staat, m.* (country); *Zustand, m.*
     (condition).
state (to) *angeben, vorbringen, erklären.*
stately *stattlich.*
statement *Erklärung, f.; Aufstellung, f.*
     (account).
stateroom *Kabine, f.; Prunksaal, m.*
station *Bahnhof, m.* (railroad); *Stellung, f.*
     (position).
statistics *Statistik, f.*
statue *Statue, f.*
stay *Aufenthalt, m.*
stay (to) *bleiben.*
steady *fest.*
steak *Beefsteak, n.*
steal (to) *stehlen.*
steam *Dampf, m.*
steamer *Dampfer, m.*
steel *Stahl, m.*
steep *steil.*
steer (to) *steuern.*
stem *Stengel, m.* (plant).
stenographer *Stenotypistin, f.*
stenography *Kurzschrift, f.;*
     Stenographie, f.
step *Schritt, m.; Stufe, f.* (stairs).
step (to) *schreiten.*
sterilized *sterilisiert.*
stern *ernst.*
stew *Ragout, n.; Eintopfgericht, n.*
stew (to) *schmoren, dünsten.*
steward *Steward, m.*
stick *Stock, m.*
stick (to) *stecken; ankleben* (paste).
stiff *steif.*
stiffen (to) *(ver)steifen; verstärken.*
stiffness *Steifheit, f.*
still *still, ruhig* (adj.); *jedoch, noch* (adv.).
still (to) *stillen, beruhigen.*
stimulant *Anregungsmittel, n.*
stimulate (to) *anregen.*
sting *Stich, m.*
sting (to) *stechen.*
stinginess *Geiz, m.*
stingy *geizig.*
stir (to) *rühren, bewegen.*
stirrup *Steigbügel, m.*
stitch *Stich, m.* (surgery); *Masche, f.* (sew).
stitch (to) *heften; nähen,* (sew).
stock *Warenbestand, m.; Vorrat, m.*

stocks and shares *Aktien und Wertpapiere (pl.).*

stock exchange *Borse, f.*

stocking *Strumpf, m.*

stomach *Magen, m.*

stone *Stein, m.*

stool *Schemel, m.*

stop *Haltestelle, f.*

stop (to) *halten, aufhören, haltmachen.* Stop! *Halt!*

store *Laden, m.; Warenhaus, n.; Geschäft, n.*

store (to) *lagern, aufbewahren; speichern* (on computer disk).

stork *Storch, m.*

storm *Sturm, m.*

story *Geschichte, f.; Erzählung, f.; Stockwerk, n.*

stove *Ofen, m.*

straight *gerade.* straight on *geradeaus.*

straighten *gerade machen, aufrichten.*

strain *Anstrengung, f.*

strange *seltsam, sonderbar.*

stranger *Ausländer, m.; Fremde, m.*

strap *Riemen, m.*

straw *Stroh, n.; Strohhalm, m.* (for drinking).

strawberry *Erdbeere, f.*

stream *Strom, m.*

street *Strasse, f.*

streetcar *Strassenbahn, f.*

strength *Kraft, f.*

strengthen *verstärken; kräftigen.*

strenuous *angestrengt.*

stress *Druck, m.; Betonung, f.* (accentuation).

stretch *Strecke, f.*

stretch (to) *strecken.*

strict *streng.*

stride *Schritt, m.*

string *Bindfaden, m.; Schnur* (cord), *f.* no strings attached *ohne Bedingungen.*

strip (to) *abstreifen, abziehen; entkleiden* (of clothes).

stripe *Streifen, m.*

strive (to) *streben.*

stroke *Strich, m.* (of a brush, pen); *Schlaganfall, m.* (med.).

stroll *Spaziergang, m.*

stroll (to) *spazierengehen.*

strong *stark.*

structure *Bau, m.*

struggle *Kampf, m.*

struggle (to) *kämpfen.*

stubborn *hartnäckig.*

student *Schüler, m.; Schülerin, f.; Student, m.; Studentin, f.* (college, univ.).

studio *Studio, n. Atelier, n.* (artist).

studious *lernbegierig, fleissig, arbeitsam.*

study *Studium, n.*

study (to) *studieren.*

stuff *Stoff, m.; Material, n.*

stuff (to) *stopfen, verstopfen.*

stumble (to) *stolpern.*

stump *Stumpf, m.*

stun (to) *betäuben.*

stunt *Sensation, f.; Kunststück, n.*

stupendous *fantastisch.*

stupid *dumm.*

stupidity *Dummheit, f.*

stupor *Betäubung, f.*

sturdy *kräftig.*

stutter (to) *stottern.*

style *Stil, m.*

subdue (to) *unterwerfen.*

subject *Angelegenheit, f.;* (matter); *Fach, n.* (school); *Fachgebiet, n.*

subjugate (to) *unterwerfen.*

subjunctive *Konjunktiv, m.*

sublime *erhaben.*

submission *Unterwerfung, f.*

submissive *unterwürfig.*

submit (to) *unterwerfen.*

subordinate *untergeordnet.*

subordination *Unterordnung, f.*

subscribe (to) *abonnieren.*

subscription *Abonnement, n.*

subsist (to) *bestehen, sich ernähren von, weiterbestehen.*

substance *Substanz, f.*

substantial *beträchtlich, wesentlich.*

substitute (to) *ersetzen.*

substitution *Ersatz, m.*

subtle *fein, raffiniert.*

subtract *abziehen.*

subtraction *Subtraktion, f.*

suburb *Vorstadt, f.*

subway *Untergrundbahn, f.*

succeed (to) *gelingen* (achieve).

success *Erfolg, m.*

successful *erfolgreich.*

succession *Nachfolge, f.*

successor *Nachfolger, m.*

such *Solch-.* Such a scandal! *Solch ein Skandal!*

sudden *plötzlich.*

sue (to) *verklagen.*

suffer (to) *leiden.*

suffering *Leiden, n.*

sufficient *genügend.*

sugar *Zucker, m.*

suggest (to) *andeuten, vorschlagen.*

suggestion *Vorschlag, m.*

suicide *Selbstmord, m.*

suit *Anzug, m.; Kostüm, n.* (lady's).

suitable *passend.*

sulk (to) *schmollen, trotzen.*

sullen *mürrisch, düster.*

sum *Summe, f.*

summary *Zusammenfassung, f.*

summer *Sommer, m.*

summit *Gipfel, m.*

summon (to) *vorladen, einberufen.*

sumptuous *prächtig, kostbar.*

sum up *zusammenfassen.*

sun *Sonne, f.*

sunbeam *Sonnenstrahl, m.*

Sunday *Sonntag, m.*

sunny *sonnig.*

sunrise *Sonnenaufgang, m.*

sunset *Sonnenuntergang, m.*

sunshine *Sonnenschein, m.*

superb *herrlich, vorzüglich.*

superficial *oberflächlich.*

superfluous *übeflüssig.*

superintendent *Inspektor, m.; Direktor, m.;*
    Verwalter, m.

superior *Vorgesetzte, m. & f.*

superiority *Überlegenheit, f.*

superstition *Aberglaube, m.*

supervise (to) *beaufsichtigen.*

supper *Abendessen, n.*

supplement *Nachtrag, m.; Anhang, m.;*
    Beilage, f. (of a newspaper).

supplementary *ergänzend.*

supply (to) *versorgen, beschaffen.*

support *Stutze, f.; Unterstützung, f.*

support (to) *(unter)stützen.*

suppose (to) *vermuten, annehmen.*

suppress (to) *unterdrücken.*

supreme *höchst, oberst.*

sure *gewiss, sicher.*

surety *Sicherheit, f.*

surface *Oberfläche, f.*

surgeon *Chirurg, m.*

surgery *Chirurgie, f.*

surname *Zuname, m.; Nachname, m.*

surpass *übertreffen.*

surprise *Überraschung, f.*

surprise (to) *überraschen.*

surrender *Übergabe, f.; Kapitulation, f.*

surrender (to) *aufgeben, übergeben.*

surroundings *Umgebung, f.*

survey *Übersicht, f.; Vermessung, f.*

survey (to) *besichtigen, vermessen.*

survive (to) *überleben.*

susceptibility *Empfänglichkeit, f.*

susceptible *empfänglich, empfindlich.*

suspect (to) *verdächtigen.*

suspense *Ungewissheit, f.; Spannung, f.*

suspicion *Verdacht, m.*

suspicious *verdächtig.*

sustain (to) *ernähren.*

swallow *Schluck, m. (gulp); Schwalbe, f.*
    (bird).

swallow (to) *verschlucken.*

swamp *Sumpf, m.*

swan *Schwan, m.*

swear (to) *schwören.*

sweat *Schweiss, m.*

sweat (to) *schwitzen.*

sweep (to) *kehren; fegen.*

sweet *süss.*

sweetness *Süsse, f.*

swell (to) *(an)schwellen.*

swift *schnell, rasch.*

swim (to) *schwimmen.*

swindle (to) *schwindeln.*

swindler *Schwindler, m.*

swing (to) *schwingen, schaukeln.*

Swiss *Schweizer (noun) m.; schweizerisch*
    (adj.).

switch *Schalter, m.*

sword *Schwert, n.*

syllable *Silbe, f.*

symbol *Symbol, n.*

symbolic *symbolisch.*

symbolize *symbolisieren.*

symmetrical *symmetrisch.*

sympathetic *mitfühlend.*

sympathize (to) *mitfühlen.*

sympathy *Sympathie, f.; Verständnis, n.*

symptom *Symptom, n.*

syrup *Sirup, m.*

system *System, n.*

systematic *systematisch, methodisch,*
    planmässig.

T

table *Tisch, m.*

tablecloth *Tischtuch, n.*

tacit *stillschweigend.*

taciturn *schweigsam.*

tact *Takt, m.*

tactful *taktvoll.*

tactless *taktlos.*

tail *Schwanz, m.*

tailor *Schneider, m.*

take (to) *nehmen.*

  to take an exam   *eine Prüfung ablegen.*

  to take heart   *Mut fassen.*

  to take a vacation   *Ferien machen; Urlaub*
    nehmen.

  to take time   *dauern.*

  to take an oath   *einen Eid ablegen.*

  to take part   *teilnehmen (an).*

  to take place   *stattfinden.*

  to take pleasure in   *Vergnügen finden an.*

  to take one's temperature   *Fieber messen.*

  to take a walk   *einen Spaziergang*
    machen.

  to take over   *übernehmen.*

tale *Erzählung, f.*

talent *Talent, n.; Begabung, f.*

talk *Rede, f.; Vortrag, m.*

talk (to) *reden, plaudern, sprechen.*

talkative *gesprächig.*

tall *hoch; gross* (people).

tame *zahm.*

tame (to) *zähmen.*

tangle (to) *verwickeln.*

tank *Tank, m.*

tapestry *Wandteppich, m.*

tar *Teer, m.*

tardy *spät.*

target *(Ziel)scheibe, f.*

tarnish (to) *trüben, anlaufen* (metal).

task *Aufgabe, f.*

taste *Geschmack, m.*

taste (to) *schmecken.*

tax *Steuer, f.*

taxi *Taxi, n.*

tea *Tee, m.*

teach (to) *unterrichten.*

teacher *Lehrer, m.; Lehrerin, f.*

team *Gruppe, f.; Mannschaft, f.* (sports).

tear *Träne, f.* (teardrop); *Riss, m.* (rip).

tear (to) *(zer)reissen.*

tease (to) *necken, ärgern.*

teaspoon *Teelöffel, m.*

technical *technisch.*

technique *Technik, f.*

technology *Technik, f.*

tedious *langweilig, ermüdend.*

telecommunications *Fernmeldewesen, n.*

telefax *Telefax, n.*

telegram *Telegramm, n.*

telegraph (to) *telegrafieren.*

telephone *Telefon, n.*

  telephone operator   *Telefonistin, f.*

telephone (to) *telefonieren, anrufen.*

tell (to) *sagen, erzählen.*

temper *Laune, f.*

temperate *gemässig, mässig.*

temperature *Temperatur, f.*

tempest *Sturm, m.; Gewitter, n.*

temple *Tempel, m.; Schläfe, f.* (head).

temporary *vorübergehend, vorläufig.*

tempt (to) *versuchen, verlocken.*

temptation *Versuchung, f.*

ten *zehn.*

tenacious *zäh, hartnäckig.*

tenacity *Zähigkeit, f.; Hartnäckigkeit, f.*

tenant *Mieter, m.*

tend (to) *sich neigen zu.*

tendency *Neigung, f.*

tender *zart, empfindlich.*

tennis *Tennis, n.*

tense *gespannt.*

tense *Zeitform, f.* (grammar).

tension *Spannung, f.*

tent *Zelt, n.*

tenth *Zehntel* (noun) *n.* (fraction); *zehnt-* (adj.).

tepid *lauwarm.*

term *Ausdruck* (expression), *m.; First* (time), *f.*

  to be on good terms   *auf gutem Fusse stehen.*

  not to be on speaking terms   *nicht miteinander sprechen.*

terrace *Terrasse, f.*

terrible *schrecklich.*

terrify (to) *(er)schrecken.*

territory *Gebiet, n.*

terror *Schrecken, m.*

test *Prüfung, f.*

test (to) *prüfen.*

testify (to) *bezeugen.*

testimony *Zeugnis, n.*

text *Text, m.*

textbook *Lehrbuch, n.*

than *als.*

thank (to) *danken.*

  Thank you! *Danke schön!*

thankful *dankbar.*

that *das* (demonstrative); *der, die, das, welch (er, -e, -es)* (relative); *dass, damit* (conjunction).

thaw *Tauwetter, n.*

thaw (to) *tauen.*

the *der, die, das.* (nom.).

theater *Theater, n.*

their *ihr.*

theirs *ihr(er, -e, -es).*

them *sie* (acc.); *ihnen* (dat.).

theme *Thema, n.*

themselves *sie (ihnen) selbst, sich.*

then *dann, damals.*

theory *Theorie, f.*

there *dort, da.*

  there is, there are   *es gibt.*

thereafter *danach.*

thereby *dadurch.*

therefore *deshalb, daher.*

thereupon *darauf.*

thermometer *Thermometer, n.*

these *diese.*

thesis *These, f., Doktorarbeit* (university).

they *sie.*

thick *dick.*

thief *Dieb, m.*

thigh *Schenkel, m.*

thimble *Fingerhut, m.*

thin *dünn.*

thing *Sache, f.; Ding, n.*

think (to) *denken.*

third *dritte.*

Third World *Dritte Welt, f.*

thirst *Durst, m.*

thirteen *dreizehn.*

thirteenth *dreizehnte.*

thirtieth *dreissigste.*

thirty *dreissig.*

this *dieser (-e, -es).*
thorn *Dorn, m.*
thorough *gründlich.*
though *zwar, obwohl, obgleich.*
thought *Gedanke, m.*
thoughtful *nachdenklich.*
thoughtless *rücksichtslos.*
thousand *tausend.*
thrash (to) *dreschen.*
thread *Faden, m.*
threat *Drohung, f.*
threaten (to) *drohen.*
three *drei.*
threshold *Schwelle, f.*
thrift *Sparsamkeit, f.*
thrifty *sparsam.*
thrill *spannendes Erregnis, m.*
thrill (to) *begeistern, packen.*
thrilling *ergreifend, begeisternd.*
thrive (to) *gedeihen.*
thriving *gedeihend, blühend.*
throat *Kehle, f.; Hals, m.*
throb (to) *klopfen.*
throne *Tron, m.*
throng *Menge, f.*
through *durch* (acc.)*; hindurch.*
throughout *durchaus.*
throw (to) *werfen.*
thumb *Daumen, m.*
thunder *Donner, m.*
thunder (to) *donnern.*
Thursday *Donnerstag, m.*
thus *so, auf diese Weise.*
thwart (to) *vereiteln.*
ticket *Karte, f.; Fahrkarte, f.* (train).
ticket window *Schalter, m.*
tickle (to) *kitzeln.*
ticklish *kitzlig.*
tide *Flut, f.* (high); *Ebbe, f.* (low).
tidiness *Ordentlichkeit, f.*
tidy *ordentlich.*
tie *Band, n.* (bond); *Krawatte, f.* (necktie).
tie (to) *binden.*
tiger *Tiger, m.*
tight *eng.*
tile *Ziegel, m.* (roof); *Kachel, f.* (wall);
    Fliese, f. (kitchen).
till *bis.*
    till now *bisher, bis jetzt.*
tilt (to) *kippen.*
timber *Bauholz, n.*
time *Zeit, f.*
    in the nick of time *zur rechten Zeit.*
    time of arrival *Ankunftszeit, f.*
    time of departure *Abfahrtszeit, f.*
    at the present time *gegenwärtig.*
    time is up *Die Zeit ist abgelaufen.*
    Once upon a time . . . *Es war*
      einmal . . .

to waste time (*die*) *Zeit verschwenden*
    (*vertreiben*)*.*
for the last time *zum letzten Mal.*
behind the times *rückständig.*
from time to time *von Zeit zu Zeit.*
on time *pünktlich.*
to have a good time *sich vergnügen, sich*
    amüsieren.
what time is it? *Wie spät ist es?*
timid *furchtsam, ängstlich.*
timidity *Furchtsamkeit, f.*
tin *Zinn, n.*
tiny *winzig.*
tip *Spitze, f.* (end); *Trinkgeld, n.* (money).
tip (to) *Trinkgeld geben.*
tire *Reifen, m.*
tire (to) *ermüden.*
tired *müde.*
tireless *unermüdlich.*
tiresome *langweilig, ermüdend.*
title *Titel, m.*
to *zu* (with infinitive); *nach, zu* (dat.); *an*
    (dat. or acc.).
toad *Kröte, f.*
toast *Toast, m.*
tobacco *Tabak, m.*
today *heute.*
toe *Zehe, f.*
together *zusammen.*
toil (to) *schwer arbeiten.*
toilet *Toilette, f.*
token *Andenken, n.; Münze, f.* (coin).
tolerable *erträglich.*
tolerance *Toleranz, f.; Duldung, f.*
tolerant *duldsam, tolerant, geduldig*
    (patient).
tolerate (to) *dulden.*
toll (to) *läuten, schlagen* (hours).
tomato *Tomate, f.*
tomb *Grab, n.*
tomorrow *morgen.*
ton *Tonne, f.*
tone *Ton, m.*
tongs *Zange, f.*
tongue *Zunge, f.*
tonight *heute abend.*
too *auch* (also); *zu* (excessive).
tool *Werkzeug, n.*
tooth *Zahn, m.*
toothbrush *Zahnbürste, f.*
toothpaste *Zahnpasta, f.*
toothpick *Zahnstocher, m.*
toothpowder *Zahnpulver, n.*
top *Gipfel, m.; Oberst, n.; Spitze, f.*
topic *Gesprächsstoff, m.; Thema, n.*
torch *Fackel, f.*
torment *Qual, f.*
torment (to) *quälen.*
torture *Folter, f.*

torture (to) *foltern*

toss (to) *werfen*

toss *Wurf, m.*

total *Gesamtsumme, f.; gesamt* (adj.)*; völlig* (adj.).

totally *gänzlich.*

touch (to) *berühren.*

touching *rührend.*

touchy *überempfindlich.*

tough *hart, zäh.*

tour *Rise, f.; Rundreise, f., Tour, f.*

tour (to) *herumreisen, durchreisen.*

tourist *Tourist, m.*

tournament *Turnier, n.*

toward *zu, nach* (dat.)*; gegen* (acc.).

towel *Handtuch, n.*

tower *Turm, m.*

town *Stadt, f.*

toy *Spielzeug, n.*

trace *Spur, f.*

trace (to) *durchzeichnen* (drawing)*, (nach) zeichnen.*

track *Spur, f.*

trade *Handel, m.*

tradition *Tradition, f.; alter Brauch, m.*

traditional *traditionell, üblich.*

traffic *Verkehr, m.*

tragedy *Tragödie, f.*

tragic *tragisch.*

trail *Pfad, m.; Weg, m.; Fährte, f.* (hunting).

train *Zug, m.*

train (to) *erziehen, schulen* (children)*; trainieren* (athletes).

training *Erziehung, f.*

traitor *Verräter, m.*

trample (to) *niedertreten.*

tranquil *ruhig.*

tranquility *Ruhe, f.*

transaction *Verhandlung, f.; Transaktion, f.*

transfer (to) *übertragen*

transit *Durchgang, m.*

transition *Übergang, m.*

transitory *vergänglich.*

translate (to) *übersetzun, f.*

translation *Übersetzung, f.*

translator *Übersetzer, m.*

transmission *Übersendung, f.*

transmit (to) *übersenden, übertragen.*

transparent *durchsichtig.*

transport *Transport, m.*

transport (to) *transportieren.*

transportation *Beförderung, f.; Überführung, f.; Transport, m.*

trap *Falle, f.*

trap (to) *fangen, ertappen.*

trash *Abfall, m.; Auswurf, m.*

travel *Reisen, n.*

travel (to) *reisen.*

traveler *Reisende, m. & f.*

tray *Tablett, n.*

treacherous *treulos, verräterisch.*

treachery *Treulosigkeit, f.*

treason *Verrat, m.*

treasure *Schatz, m.*

treasurer *Schatzmeister, m.*

treasury *Schatzamt, n.*

treat *Hochgenuss, m.*

treat (to) *behandeln, bearbeiten, spendieren.*

treatment *Behandlung, f.*

treaty *Vertrag, m.*

tree *Baum, m.*

tremble (to) *zittern.*

trembling *Zittern, n.*

tremendous *ungeheuer.*

trench *Graben, m.; Schützengraben, m.* (military).

trend *Neigung, f.*

trial *Probe, f.; Prozess, m.* (law).

triangle *Dreieck, n.*

tribe *Stamm, m.*

tribunal *Tribunal, n.*

tribune *Tribüne, f.*

tribute *Ehrung, f.; Hochachtung, f.*

trick *Kniff, m.; Trick, m.*

trifle *Kleinigkeit, f.*

trifling *kleinlich* (petty)*; gering* (minor).

trim (to) *stutzen* (hedges)*; kürzen* (hair).

trimming *Verzierung, f.; Garnierung, f.*

trip *Fahrt, f.*

trip (to) *stolpern.*

triple *dreifach.*

triumph *Triumph, m.; Sieg, m.*

triumph (to) *siegen.*

trivial *geringfügig.*

trolley car *Strassenbahnwagen, m.*

troop *Truppe, f.*

trot *Trab, m.*

trot (to) *traben.*

trouble *Unannehmlichkeit, f.; Schwierigkeit, f.*

   to go to the trouble   *sich Umstände machen.*

   to save oneself the trouble   *sich die Mühe ersparen.*

trousers *Hose, f.*

truck *Lastwagen, m.*

true *wahr.*

truly *wahrhaftig; aufrichtig.*

   yours truly   *hochachtungsvoll.*

trump *Trumpf, m.*

trump (to) *trumpfen.*

trumpet *Trompete, f.*

trunk *Koffer, m.*

trust *Vertrauen, n.*

trust (to) *trauen.*

trustworthy *zuverlässig.*

truth *Wahrheit, f.*

truthful *wahrhaft, genau.*

truthfully *aufrichtig, ehrlich gesagt,*
    wahrhaftig.
truthfulness *Ehrlichkeit, f., Wahrheit, f.*
try (to) *versuchen, probieren.*
tube *Rohr, n.*
tumble (to) *stürzen, stolpern.*
tumult *Getümmel, n.*
tune *Melodie, f.*
tune (to) *stimmen.*
tunnel *Tunnel, m.*
turf *Rasen, m.*
turkey *Truthahn, m.*
turmoil *Aufruhr, f.; Unruhe, f.*
turn (to) *drehen.*
  turn back *zurückkehren.*
  Turn left *Biegen Sie links ein!*
  to turn around *sich undrehen.*
  to turn pages *umblättern.*
  to turn upside down *auf den Kopf stellen.*
  It's your turn *Sie sind dran.*
  to turn against *sich wenden gegen.*
turnip *weisse Rübe, f.*
twelfth *zwölfte.*
twelve *zwölf.*
twentieth *zwanzigste.*
twenty *zwanzig.*
twice *zweimal.*
twilight *Zwielicht, n.*
twin *Zwilling* (noun) *m.; doppelt* (adj.).
twist (to) *drehen, wickeln.*
two *zwei.*
type *Modell, n.; Typ, m.*
type (to) *mit der Schreibmaschine schreiben.*
typewriter *Schreibmaschine, f.*
tyranny *Tyrannei, f.*
tyrant *Tyrann, m.*

U

ugliness *Hässlichkeit, f.*
ugly *hässlich.*
ultimate *(aller) letzt.*
umbrella *(Regen)schirm, m.*
umpire *Schiedsrichter, m.*
unable to *unfähig.*
unanimity *Einmütigkeit, f.; Einstimmigkeit, f.*
unanimous *einstimmig.*
unawares *unversehens.*
unbearable *unerträglich.*
unbelievable *unglaublich.*
unbutton (to) *aufknöpfen.*
uncertain *unsicher.*
uncertainty *Unsicherheit, f.*
unchangeable *unveränderlich.*
uncle *Onkel, m.*
uncomfortable *unbequem.*
uncommon *ungewöhnlich.*
unconscious *bewusstlos.*

unconsciousness *Ohnmacht, f.*
uncouth *ungebildet.*
uncover (to) *aufdecken; offenbaren*
    (feelings).
undecided *unentschieden.*
undefinable *unerklärbar, unerklärlich.*
undeniable *unleugbar, unbestreitbar.*
under *unter* (dat. or acc.).
undergo (to) *durchmachen, erleiden* (suffer).
underground *Untergrund* (noun) *n.;*
    unterirdisch (adj.).*; Untergrundbahn,*
    f. (subway).
underline (to) *unterstreichen.*
underneath *unten, unterhalb.*
understand (to) *verstehen.*
understanding *Verständnis, n.*
undertake (to) *unternehmen.*
undertaker *Leichenbestatter, m.*
undertaking *Unternehmen, n.*
underwear *Unterwäsche, f.*
undesirable *unerwünscht.*
undignified *würdelos.*
undo (to) *aufmachen; auflösen* (untie).
undress (to) *sich ausziehen.*
uneasy *beunruhigt.*
uneasiness *Beunruhigung, f.*
unemployed *arbeitslos.*
unequal *ungleich.*
unequaled *unvergleichlich.*
uneven *uneben.*
uneventful *ereignislos.*
unexpected *unerwartet.*
unfair *ungerecht.*
unfaithful *untreu.*
unfavorable *ungünstig.*
unforgettable *unvergesslich.*
unfortunate *unglücklich.*
unfortunately *unglücklicherweise, leider.*
ungrateful *undankbar.*
unhappily *leider.*
unhappy *unglücklich.*
unharmed *unverletzt.*
unhealthy *ungesund.*
unheard (of) *unerhört.*
uniform *Uniform* (noun) *f.; gleichförmig*
    (adj.).
uniformity *Gleichförmigkeit, f.*
uniformly *gleichförmig.*
unify (to) *vereinigen.*
unimportant *unwichtig.*
unintentional *unabsichtlich.*
union *Vereinigung, f.; Verband, m.;*
    Gewerkschaft, f. (trade union).
unit cost *Stückkosten* (pl.).
universal *universal.*
universe *Weltall, n.*
university *Universität, f.*
unjust *ungerecht.*
unkind *unfreundlich.*

unknown *unbekannt.*
unlawful *ungesetzlich.*
unless *es sei denn dass; ausgenommen wenn.*
unlike *unähnlich, anders als.*
unlikely *unwahrscheinlich.*
unlimited *unbeschränkt.*
unload (to) *abladen, ausladen.*
unluckily *unglücklicherweise.*
unnecessary *unnötig.*
unoccupied *unbesetzt; unbeschäftigt.*
unpack (to) *auspacken.*
unpleasant *unangehehm.*
unpublished *unveröffentlicht.*
unquestionably *fraglos.*
unravel (to) *enträtseln, auflösen.*
unreal *unwirklich.*
unreasonable *unvernünftig.*
unreliable *unzuverlässig.*
unrestrained *ungezwungen.*
unroll (to) *abwickeln, entrollen.*
unsafe *unsicher.*
unsatisfactory *unbefriedigend.*
unsatisfied *unbefriedigt.*
unscrupulous *bedenkenlos, skrupellos.*
unselfish *selbstlos.*
unsteady *unsicher, wackelig.*
unsuccessful *erfolglos.*
unsuitable *unpassend.*
untidy *unordentlich.*
untie (to) *aufbinden, losbinden.*
until *bis, an, zu* (dat.).
  until now *bisher.*
untrue *unwahr; untreu* (faithless).
unusual *ungewöhnlich.*
unwell *unwohl.*
unwholesome *ungesund.*
unwilling *widerwillig, unwillig.*
unwise *unklug.*
unworthy *unwürdig.*
up *auf* (dat. or acc.); *aufwärts; oben.*
uphold (to) *stützen, aufrechterhalten* (fig.).
upkeep *Instandhaltung, f.*
upon *auf, über* (dat. or acc.).
upper *ober.*
upright *aufrecht.*
uprising *Aufstand, m.*
upset *beunruhigt, aufgeregt.*
upset (to) *umkehren; aufregen* (distress).
upside down *drunter and drüber.*
upstairs *oben.*
upward *steigend, aufwärts.*
urge (to) *dringen, drängen, auffördern.*
urgent *dringend.*
us *uns.*
use *Gebrauch, m.; Verwendung, f.* (utility).
use (to) *gebrauchen; verwenden.*
used to (to be) *gewöhnt sein.*
useful *nützlich.*
useless *nutzlos.*

usual *gewöhnlich.*
utensil *Werkzeug, n.; Gerät, n.*
utility *Nützlichkeit, f.*
utilize (to) *nutzbar machen.*
utmost *äussert.*
  to the utmost *aufs Äusserste.*
utter (to) *äussern, aussprechen.*
utterly *durchaus.*

vacant *frei, leer, unbesetzt.*
vacation *Ferien, pl.; Urlaub* (from job).
vaccination *Impfung, f.*
vaccination certificate *Impfschein, m.*
vacuum (all purpose) *Allzwecksauger, m.,*
            Staubsauger (vacuum cleaner), *m.*
vaguely *unbestimmt.*
vain *eitel.*
  in vain *vergebens, umsonst.*
valiant *tapfer.*
valid *gültig.*
validity *Gültigkeit, f.*
valley *Tal, n.*
valuable *wertvoll.*
value *Wert, m.*
value (to) *schätzen.*
valued *geschätzt.*
valve *Ventil, n.*
vanilla *Vanille, f.*
vanish (to) *verschwinden.*
vanity *Eitelkeit, f.*
vanquish (to) *besiegen.*
vapor *Dampf, m.*
variable *veränderlich, wechselnd.*
variation *Abweichung, f.* (deviation),
            Variation, f.
varied *verschieden.*
variety *Abwechslung, f.; Mannigfaltigkeit, f.*
various *verschieden(e), mehrere.*
varnish (to) *lackieren.*
vary (to) *verschieden.*
vase *Vase, f.*
vast *ungeheuer* (gross); *weit.*
vault *Gewölbe, n.; Schatzkummer* (bank), *f.*
veal *Kalbfleisch, n.*
vegetable *Gemüse, n.*
vehicle *Fahrzeug, n.*
veil *Schleier, m.*
veil (to) *verschleiern.*
vein *Ader, f.* (body and mineral); *vene, f.*
velvet *Samt, m.*
venerable *ehrwürdig.*
venerate (to) *verehren.*
veneration *Verehrung, f.*
vengeance *Rache, f.*
ventilation *Lüftung, f.*
ventilator *Ventilator, m.; Lüftungsanlage, f.*

venture (to) *versuchen.*
verb *Zeitwort, n.*
verdict *Urteil, n.*
verge *Rand, m.*
   on the verge of   *am Rand* (gen).
verification *Bestätigung, f.*
verify (to) *bestätigen.*
verse *Vers, m.; Dichtung, f.* (poetry).
version *Version, f.;* (translation);
   Darstellung, f. (account).
very *sehr.*
vest *Weste, f.*
veterinarian *Tierarzt, m.*
VHS recorder *VHS Recorder, m.*
vice *Untugend, f.*
vice-president *Vizepräsident, m.*
vice versa *umgekehrt.*
vicinity *Nähe, f.; Nachbarschaft, f.*
victim *Opfer, n.*
victor *Sieger, m.*
victorious *siegreich.*
victory *Sieg, m.*
view *Aussicht, f.; Ansicht, f.* (opinion).
vigorous *kräftig.*
vile *abscheulich.*
village *Dorf, n.*
vine *Weinstock, m.; Rebe, f.*
vinegar *Essig, m.*
vineyard *Weingarten, m.*
violence *Gewalttätigkeit, f.; Heftigkeit, f.*
violent *gewaltig, heftig.*
violet *Veilchen, n.*
violet *violett.*
violin *Geige, f.*
violinist *Geiger, m.*
virtue *Tugend, f.*
virtuous *tugendhaft.*
visible *sichtbar.*
vision *Sehen, n.; Erscheinung, f.* (ghost).
visit *Besuch, m.*
visit (to) *besuchen.*
visitor *Besucher, m.*
visualize (to) *sich vorstellen.*
vital *lebens-; vital.*
vitality *Lebenskraft, f.*
vivacious *lebhaft.*
vivacity *Lebhaftigkeit, f.*
vivid *lebendig; leuchtend* (color).
vocabulary *Wortschatz, m.*
vocal *stimmlich.*
vocation *Beruf, m.*
vogue *Mode, f.*
voice *Stimme, f.*
void *Leere* (noun) *f.; leer* (empty); *ungültig*
   (invalid).
volcano *Vulkan, m.*
volume *Umfang, m.*
voluntary *freiwillig.*
vote (to) *wählen.*

vote *Stimme, f.*
vow *Gelübde, n.*
vow (to) *geloben.*
vowel *Vokal, m.*
vulgar *gemein, niedrig.*
vulnerable *verwundbar, verletzbar.*

W

wager *Wette, f.*
wager (to) *wetten.*
wages *Gehalt, n.*
waist *Taille, f.*
wait (to) *warten.*
   waiting room *Wartezimmer, n.*
waiter *Kellner, m.; Kellnerin, f.*
wake (to) *aufwecken.*
wake up (to) *aufwachen.*
walk *Spaziergang, m.*
walk (to) *gehen.*
   take a walk   *spazierengehen, einen*
     Spaziergang machen.
wall *Wand, f.*
wallet *Brieftasche, f.*
walnut *Walnuss, f.*
wander (to) *wandern.*
wanderer *Wanderer, m.*
want *Mangel, m.; Not, f.* (poverty).
want (to) *wollen.*
war *Krieg, m.*
ward *Station, f.* (hospital); *Mündel (m./f.)*
    (law).
ward off (to) *abwehren.*
wardrobe *Kleiderschrank, m.; Garderobe, f.*
ware *Ware, f.*
warehouse *Warenhaus, n.*
warm *warm.*
warm (to) *wärmen.*
warmth *Wärme, f.*
warn (to) *warnen.*
warning *Warnung, f.*
warrior *Krieger, m.*
wash (to) *waschen.*
washroom *Waschraum, m.*
waste *Verschwendung, f.*
waste (to) *verschwenden.*
watch *Uhr, f.*
watch (to) *wachen, achtgeben, aufpassen;*
    zusehen (to watch someone do work).
watchful *wachsam.*
water *Wasser, n.*
waterfall *Wasserfall, m.*
waterproof *wasserdicht.*
wave *Welle, f.*
wave (to) *schwenken; winken, wellen* (hair).
wax *Wachs, n.*
way *Weg, m.* (road); *Weise, f.* (manner).
we *wir.*

weak *schwach.*
weaken (to) *schwächen.*
weakness *Schwachheit, f.; Schwäche, f.*
wealth *Reichtum, m.*
wealthy *reich.*
weapon *Waffe, f.*
wear (to) *tragen, anhaben.*
weariness *Müdigkeit, f.; Langweile, f.*
weary *müde.*
weather *Wetter, n.*
weave (to) *weben.*
wedding *Hochzeit, f.*
Wednesday *Mittwoch, m.*
weed *Unkraut, n.*
week *Woche, f.*
weekend *Wochenende, n.*
weekly *wöchentlich.*
weep (to) *weinen.*
weigh (to) *wiegen.*
weight *Gewicht, n.*
welcome *Empfang, m.* (reception);
    freundliche Aufnahme, f.
welfare *Wohlfahrt, f.*
well *gut, wohl.*
well *Brunnen, m.*
  oil well   *Ölquelle, f.*
west *west, Westen, m.*
westwards *westwärts.*
wet *nass, feucht.*
whale *Walfisch, m.*
what *was; welch(er, -e, -es)* (which)
  what kind of   *was für ein.*
whatever *was auch.*
wheat *Weizen, m.*
wheel *Rad, n.*
when *wenn, als; wann* (interrogative).
whenever *so oft wie.*
where *wo; wohin* (whereto).
whereas *da, nun.*
wherever *überall wo.*
whether *ob.*
which *der (die, das); welch(-er, -e, -es).*
  which one   *welch(-er, -e, -es).*
while *Weile* (noun) *f.; indern, während*
    (conj.).
whim *Laune, f.; Einfall, m.*
whip *Peitsche, f.*
whisper (to) *flüstern.*
whistle *Pfeife, f.*
whistle *pfeifen.*
white *weiss.*
who *der (die, das), welch(er, -e, -es)*
    (pron.); *wer* (inter. pron.).
whoever *wer auch immer.*
whole *Ganze* (noun) *n.; ganz* (adj.).
wholesale *Grosshandel, m.*
wholesome *heilsam, gesund; Engrosgeschäft*
    (wholesale business), *n.*
whose *dessen (deren); wessen* (inter.)

why *warum.*
wicked *böse.*
wide *breit.*
widen (to) *breiten, erweitern.*
widow *Witwe, f.*
widower *Witwer, m.*
width *Weite, f. Breite, f.*
wife *Frau, f.*
wig *Perücke, f.*
wild *wild.*
wilderness *Wildnis, f.*
will *Wille, m.; Testament, n.* (legal).
will (to) *wollen.*
willing *gewillt.*
willingly *gern; mit Vergnügen.*
win (to) *gewinnen.*
wind *Wind, m.*
wind (to) *winden, aufwickeln.*
windbreaker *Anorak, m.*
window *Fenster, n.*
windy *windig.*
wine *Wein, m.*
wing *Flügel, m.*
wink *Blinzeln, n.; Augenzwinkern, n.*
wink (to) *blinzeln, zwinkern.*
winner *Sieger, m.*
winter *Winter, m.*
wipe (to) *wischen; ausrotten* (wipe out).
wire *Draht, m.*
wire (to) *kabeln, telegraphieren.*
wisdom *Weisheit, f.*
wise *weise.*
wish *Wunsch, m.*
wish (to) *wünschen.*
wit *Witz, m.; Geist, m.*
witch *Hexe, f.*
with *mit* (dat.)
withdraw (to) *zurückziehen; zurücknehmen*
    (statement); *abheben* (money).
wither (to) *verwelken.*
within *drinnen.*
without *ohne* (acc.).
witness *Zeuge, m.*
witness (to) *bezeugen.*
witticism *witzige Bemerkung, f.*
witty *witzig, geistreich.*
woe *Weh, n.*
wolf *Wolf, m.*
woman *Frau, f.*
wonder *Wunder, n.*
wonder (to) *sich wundern, sich fragen.*
wonderful *wunderbar, herrlich.*
wood *Holz, n.*
woods *Wald, m.*
woodwork *Holzwerk, n.*
wool *Wolle, f.*
word *Wort, n.*
  word by word   *Wort für Wort.*
word processor *Textverarbeiter, m.*

work *Arbeit, f.*
  work of art   *Kunstgegenstand, m.*
work (to) *arbeiten; sich beschäftigen.*
worker *Arbeiter, m.*
workshop *Werkstatt, f.*
world *Welt, f.*
worldly *weltlich.*
worried *besorgt.*
worry *Sorge, f.; Plage, f.*
worry (to) *besorgen; plagen.*
  Don't worry *Sorgen Sie sich nicht!*
    (*Machen Sie sich keine Sorgen!*)
worse *schlechter.*
worship *Gottesdienst, m.*
worship (to) *anbeten, verehren.*
worst *schlechtest.*
worth *Wert, m.*
worthless *wertlos.*
worthy *würdig.*
wound *Wunde, f.*
wound (to) *verwunden.*
wounded *verwundet.*
wrap (to) *einpacken,* (*ein*)*wickeln.*
wrath *Zorn, m.*
wreath *Kranz, m.*
wreck *Wrack, n. Schiffbruch, m.*
wreck (to) *zertrümmern, scheitern.*
wrestle (to) *wringen; sich quälen* (with a
  problem).
wrestler *Ringkämpfer, m.*
wrestling *Ringkampf, m.*
wretched *elend, unglückselig.*
wring (to) *ringen.*
wrist *Handgelenk, n.*
write (to) *schreiben.*
writer *Schreiber, m.; Schriftsteller, m.*
writing *Schreiben, n.; Schrift, f.* (work).
  in writing *schriftlich.*
wrong *unrecht, falsch.*
  You are wrong. *Sie haben Unrecht.*

X

X-ray *Röntgenstrahlen* (*pl.*).

Y

yacht *Yacht, f.*
yard *Hof, m.* (courtyard).
yarn *Garn, n.*
yawn *Gähnen, n.*
yawn (to) *gähnen.*
year *Jahr, n.;*
yearly *jährlich.*
yearn (to) *sich sehnen.*
yearning *Sehnen, n.; Sehnsucht, f.*

yeast *Hefe, f.*
yell (to) *schreien.*
yellow *gelb.*
yes *ja, doch.*
yesterday *gestern.*
yet *noch* (also besides)*; doch, dennoch*
  (however).
yield (to) *aufgeben* (give up)*; erzeugen*
  (produce).
yoke *Joch, n.*
yolk (*Ei*) *Dotter, n.* (of an egg)*; Eigelb, n.*
you *Sie, du* (familiar sing.)*; ihr* (familiar
  pl.)*; Sie, dich, euch* (acc.)*; ihnen, dir,*
  euch (dat.).
young *jung.*
  young lady *junge Dame, f.; Fräulein, n.*
your *ihr, dein, ihr.*
yours *ihr* (-*er, -e, -es*)*; dein*(-*er, -e, -es*).
yourself *Sie* (*ihnen*) *selbst; du* (*dich, dir*)
  selbst; ihr (*euch*).
youth *Jungend, f.*
yuletide *Weihnachtszeit, f.; Weihnachten, n.*

Z

zeal *Eifer, m.*
zealous *eifrig.*
zebra *Zebra, n.*
zero *Null, f.*
zipper *Reissverschluss, m.*
zone *Zone, f.*
zoo *Tierpark, m.; Zoo, m.*
Zoology *Zoologie, f.*

GLOSSARY OF PROPER NAMES

Albert *Albrecht.*
Alfred *Alfred.*
Andrew *Andreas.*
Ann *Anna.*
Anthony *Anton.*
August *August.*
Barbara *Barbara.*
Bernard *Bernhard.*
Bertha *Bertha.*
Charles *Karl.*
Charlotte *Lotte.*
Edward *Eduard.*
Elisabeth *Elisabeth, Else.*
Elsie *Ilse.*
Emily *Emilie.*
Eric *Erich.*
Ernest *Ernst.*
Eugene *Eugen.*
Frances *Franziska.*

Frank *Franz.*
Frederick *Friedrich.*
Fred *Fritz.*
George *Georg.*
Gertrude *Gertrud.*
Gustave *Gustav.*
Helen *Helene.*
Henry *Heinrich.*
Jane *Johanna.*
John *Johann, Hans.*
Joseph *Josef.*
Katherine *Katharina, Kätchen, Käthe.*
Lewis *Ludwig.*
Louise *Luise.*
Margaret *Gretchen, Margareta.*
Martha *Martha.*
Mary *Maria.*
Maurice *Mortiz.*
Michael *Michael.*
Nicolas *Nikolaus, Klaus.*
Otto *Otto.*
Paul *Paul.*
Peter *Peter.*
Ralph *Rudolf, Rolf.*
Roger *Rüdiger.*
Susan *Susanne.*
Theodore *Theodor.*
Theresa *Therese.*
Thomas *Thomas.*
Walter *Walter.*
William *Wilhelm.*

GLOSSARY OF
GEOGRAPHICAL NAMES

Africa *Afrika, n.*
Aix-la-Chapelle *Aachen, n.*
Alps *die Alpen, pl.*
America *Amerika, n.*
   North America *Nord-Amerika, n.*
   Central America *Zentral-Amerika, n.,*
      Mittel-Amerika, n.
   South America *Süd-Amerika, n.*
Antwerp *Antwerpen, n.*
Arabia *Arabien, n.*
Asia *Asien, n.*
Atlantic *Atlantik, m.*
Australia *Australien, n.*
Austria *Österreich, n.*
Belgium *Belgien, n.*
Berlin *Berlin, n.*
Bonn *Bonn, n.*
Bosnia *Bosnien n.*
Brazil *Brasilien, n.*
Brussels *Brüssel, n.*

Canada *Kanada, n.*
China *China, n.*
Cologne *Köln, m.*
Commonwealth of Independent States
   Gemeiuschaft Unabhängiger Staaten f.
Croatia *Kroatien n.*
Czech Republic *Tschechische Republik f.*
Denmark *Dänemark, n.*
Egypt *Ägypten, n.*
England *England, n.*
Europe *Europa, n.*
France *Frankreich, n.*
Frankfurt on the Main *Frankfurt a.M., n.*
Germany *Deutschland, n.*
Greece *Griechenland, n.*
Hague *Haag, m.*
Hamburg *Hamburg, n.*
Herzegovina *Herzegowina n.*
Holland *Holland, n.*
Hungary *Ungarn, n.*
India *Indien, n.*
Ireland *Irland, n.*
Israel *Israel, n.*
Italy *Italien, n.*
Japan *Japan, n.*
London *London, n.*
Madrid *Madrid, n.*
Mexico *Mexiko, n.*
Moscow *Moskau, n.*
Munich *München, n.*
Norway *Norwegen, n.*
Nuremberg *Nüremberg, Nürnberg, n.*
Pacific Ocean *Stille Ozean, m.*
Paris *Paris, n.*
Poland *Polen, n.*
Portugal *Portugal, n.*
Prussia *Preussen, n.*
Rhine *Rhein, m.*
Rhineland *Rheinland, n.*
Rome *Rom, n.*
Russia *Russland, n.*
Saar *Saar, f.*
Saxony *Sachsen, n.*
Scotland *Schottland, n.*
Serbia *Serbien n.*
Silesia *Schlesien, n.*
Slovakia *Slowakei f.*
Spain *Spanien, n.*
Sweden *Schweden, n.*
Switzerland *Schweiz, f.*
Turkey *Türkei, f.*
United States (of America) *die*
   Vereinigten Staaten, pl.
Vienna *Wien, n.*
Yugoslavia *Jugoslawien n.*